# THE CHRIST IN THE BIBLE COMMENTARY
## Volume One

# THE
# CHRIST IN THE BIBLE
# COMMENTARY

## Volume One

Genesis
Exodus
Leviticus
Numbers
Deuteronomy

# Dr. Albert B. Simpson

CHRISTIAN PUBLICATIONS
CAMP HILL, PENNSYLVANIA

Christian Publications
3825 Hartzdale Drive, Camp Hill, PA 17011

The mark of  vibrant faith

ISBN: 0-87509-490-2
LOC Catalog Card Number: 92-70937
© 1992 by Christian Publications
All rights reserved
Printed in the United States of America

92 93 94 95 96  5  4  3  2  1

Cover Design: Step One Design

# PUBLISHER'S INTRODUCTION

W hen Dr. Simpson first produced this series back in 1888, he stated that his intent was "to unfold the spiritual teachings of the Scriptures, especially with reference to the Person and work of Christ." (Preface, *Genesis, Exodus,* 1888 edition, p. vii.)

He also stated that two causes led to the publication of *The Christ in the Bible Series:*

1. The desire of friends "to obtain, in permanent form, the substance of the Bible teaching given at the Missionary Training College where most of these lectures were originally delivered."

2. "The call that comes to help the increasing number of consecrated Christians who are hungering for a deeper spiritual life and for a more profound acquaintance with the Word of God as it unfolds the fullness of Christ as Saviour, Sanctifier, Healer, and Coming Lord." (ibid., p. viii.)

Simpson's original intent was to include (1) an analysis of the spiritual teaching of the biblical book; (2) original and selected homiletic helps and illustrative materials; and (3) historical and geographical papers illustrative of the various books and subjects (ibid., p. viii). However, his involvement with the fledgling Christian and Missionary Alliance, The Missionary Training Institute, editing *The Word, the Work and the World,* pastoring the Gospel Tabernacle in New York and his heavy conference speaking schedule kept Simpson from completing the series as he originally planned. Instead, after completing seven volumes, Simpson began revising material from his expository preaching schedule. By 1910 he had volumes for all but Thessalonians through Jude. Christian Publications completed the set after Dr. Simpson's death by adding expository sermons on the missing books.

This new edition is based on the completed set. Instead of the 24 volumes of the last edition, we are combining the books into six hardcover volumes.

In contemplating the revision of this valuable commentary series, we felt it important to remain as true to the original Simpson as possible, yet we wanted to introduce Simpson to a brand new contemporary audience. In order to do that we first decided to do only a light editing: change archaic spellings; words that perhaps have obscure meanings to people today; and change sentence structure on some of the longer, drawn out sentences that were the norm at the turn of the century. We also decided to change the Scripture references to the New International Version.

Also to help modern readers, we added Scripture references. Simpson, like other writers of his day, would often quote Scripture, but would rarely provide the reference. Since this series is so strongly based on paralleling Old and New Testament references and symbols of Christ and redemption, we felt the text references would certainly strengthen the series.

We are excited at bringing back this valuable commentary set. In an age when North America Christians are begging for a deeper relationship with the Lord, these volumes will help both pastor and lay person alike in their pursuit of biblical understanding.

Finally, we at Christian Publications apologize to the evangelical community for ever allowing this landmark work to go out of print. Enjoy and learn as Simpson's depth once more is made available to the church.

Jonathan Graf
Editorial Director
Christian Publications

# CONTENTS

## Genesis

Introduction.................................................................1
General Plan and Scope of the Book .................................9
1.  The Beginning of the Universe..............................11
2.  The Beginning of the Human Race.........................23
3.  The Beginning of Sin ........................................33
4.  The Beginning of Redemption ..............................39
5.  The Beginning of the Nations ..............................55
6.  The Beginning of the Hebrew Race........................63
7.  The Beginning of the Life of Faith .......................71

## Exodus

Introduction.................................................................89
General Plan and Scope of the Book .................................93
1.  Israel's Bondage..............................................95
2.  Redemption ..................................................103
3.  Christian Pilgrimage as Prefigured in the Book
    of Exodus ...................................................119
4.  The Dispensation of the Law ..............................129
5.  The Revelation of Grace in Exodus .......................135

## Leviticus

General Plan and Scope of the Book .................................159
1.  The Four Offerings .........................................161
2.  The Priesthood...............................................175
3.  The Ordinances of Cleansing ..............................183
4.  The Day of Atonement or Complete Reconciliation ...191
5.  Holiness ......................................................199
6.  Fellowship as Illustrated in the Ancient Feasts ...........207
7.  The Divine Covenant, or Faithfulness to God...........215

# Numbers

General Plan and Scope of the Book .................................227
1. The Army .................................................................229
2. The Advance ............................................................239
3. The Failure and Retreat............................................245
4. God's Provision for Their Wilderness Life,
   Notwithstanding Their Failure .................................261
5. The Trials of the Wilderness.....................................275
6. The New Departure ..................................................285

# Deuteronomy

Introduction................................................................295
General Plan and Scope of the Book .................................299
1. Moses' First Address on the Plains of Moab..................301
2. Moses' Second Address on the Plains of Moab ............319
3. Moses' Third Address on the Plains of Moab...............357
4. Conclusion of the Book of Deuteronomy....................365

# GENESIS

# INTRODUCTION

## SECTION I—*Mosaic Authorship of the Pentateuch*

Until within the last century there was little dispute among Hebrew and Christian authorities about the Mosaic authorship of the five books which bear the name of the great law-giver. A few of the early Gnostics and several of the heretics of the second century questioned it, but the first serious attacks upon the genuineness and authenticity of these books, making any pretensions to Christian scholarship, are a little more than a hundred years old.

A Paris physician named Astruc is the modern author of the Higher Criticism in relation to the Mosaic books. He has been followed by a vast array of scholarship, including Knobel, Hupfield, DeWette, Bohlen, Bleek, Ewald, Kuenen, Wellhausen and even Delitzsch, who with great learning and eloquence have endeavored to establish hypotheses almost as varied as the various names that support them, and who agree only in the one particular, that they all ascribe the date of these books to a later period than Moses, but differ as widely with respect to the exact period of their authorship as the interval from Saul to Ezra. The majority of them regard the Pentateuch as the production of the time of Josiah, and their favorite theory is that this was the *Book of the Law*, said to be discovered by Hilkiah the priest, in that monarch's reign, and that he palmed it off on the credulity of the king. They admit that certain portions of the book were undoubtedly written by Moses, and that other portions, by different authors, were in existence as fragments long before this date, but they were then gathered together and put in their present form by some unknown author.

The first ground of this theory is the marked difference in the early chapters of Genesis between the different sections, especially with regard to the various names of God. In one entire section, He is called by the name Elohim, in another, Jehovah, and it has been inferred that these are independent narratives written by different authors and were called respectively the Elohist and Jehovist documents.

Their next argument is drawn from the unhistorical character of the book and its contradiction of many alleged facts, both in science, geography and history. The third ground of their theory is the resemblance of the style of the Pentateuch to the later books, especially Jeremiah. The fourth and last argument is based upon allusions in the books themselves, which require a later date than Moses. For example, sometimes the land is spoken of as being already occupied by the Hebrews and as if the writer were speaking from a Palestinian standpoint. Again they quote the expression "Unto this day" as implying a later authorship. They refer also to citations from ancient documents such as "the book of the wars of the Lord" and many other allusions to antiquity which imply a recent origin.

All these arguments have been met by competent scholarship. Any one who wishes to follow this subject more fully will find it ably discussed by Canon Spence in his introduction to the "Pulpit Commentary," and in the learned works of Canon Cook, Lange, Kurtz, Hegstenberg and others. The various names of God used in different sections are easily explained because of the different relations which God sustains in these various passages. In describing the work of creation, He is spoken of as Elohim, but when He comes to deal with men in covenant relations, He is Jehovah. With regard to alleged errors of statement and historical blunders, it has been shown that the references to ancient events and countries in these books are confirmed by all the most recent researches, and that the more fully the facts of science are corrected and established, the more wonderful is the harmony which they show with all the allusions of the Mosaic writings.

The third objection, with reference to the resemblance of the language to the style of later books, is easily explained by the fact that Jeremiah was a diligent student of the writings of Moses, which had just been discovered in the temple after being lost for years, and which no doubt gave the profoundest impulse to his religious life, and would naturally reappear in his own writings. The fourth objection, namely, allusions to the land as already occupied, might very naturally arise from the fact that Moses wrote from the standpoint of those who were to read his writings, and on the assumption that they were immediately to occupy the land, and hence he recognized it as already in their possession. It is exceedingly doubtful, however, whether any such allusions can be shown as are not capable of the simplest explanation. Without entering more fully into details on these arguments, it is sufficient to say on the other side:

First, that there was no reason in the nature of things why Moses should not write such a book, as we know from undoubted authority that literature was already in existence, and we have Chaldean records as early as the time of Abraham, closely resembling the writings of Moses, and containing the legendary accounts of the creation, the deluge and other events of antiquity.

Second, it is certain that Moses was commanded to prepare a book of some sort (Exodus 17:14). In several places within the Pentateuch itself, he is recognized as the author at least of certain portions.

Third, the Pentateuch can be traced back to the time of Moses. That it existed in the days of Ezra and Nehemiah is not disputed. In the days of Josiah it was recovered from the wreck of the temple by the high priest. The Hebrew prophets, in the closing days, both of Israel and Judah, refer again and again to it, and the Psalms of David are based upon its teachings, and continually refer to the law of the Lord. The teaching of Samuel was founded upon the Mosaic law, and the book of Joshua refers explicitly to it as the very ground of their faith and obedience, and the covenant on whose faithful observance their national prosperity depended.

Fourth, the Lord Jesus Christ and His apostles are unequivocal witnesses to these books as the writings of Moses (Matthew 19:7; Mark 12:19; Luke 16:31; John 1:45, 5:46–47; Acts 15:21; Romans 10:5).

The only answer to this irresistible argument which the advocates of the Higher Criticism can give is that Christ Himself must have been mistaken and imposed upon. It is fortunate that the true spirit and possibilities of this school have been permitted thus to appear, and a system which needs to descend to such an assumption of superior wisdom, even to the Lord Jesus Himself, will be considered with due caution by every devout believer.

Other reasons might be added, if necessary; such as the testimony of the Samaritan Pentateuch, of the Pharisees, Sadducees, and all other Jewish parties, and finally of the Mosaic institutions, and the Jewish people themselves whose existence cannot be explained unless we assume as their foundation such records and revelations as these books contain. The Higher Criticism has not succeeded any better in informing us who was the transcendent genius who gave us these writings than skeptics have in discovering the author of that most stupendous of all supposed inventions, namely the story of Jesus. An immortality and glory beyond that of Homer or Shakespeare awaits the happy genius who can be proved to have given to us such wondrous documents as the five books of Moses or the five evangelical histories of the New Testament. Until this is shown, intelligent faith may be content to rest, as has been well said, in the "ancient faith of both the Jewish and Christian churches, that the Pentateuch proceeded from the pen of Moses, the man of God."

## SECTION II—*Contents and Divisions of Genesis*

The book of Genesis is called in Hebrew, *Bereshith*, ordinarily translated, "beginning," or more literally meaning, "evolutions, or developments."

Taking it in both senses, it might be thus divided: *First, as a book of origins*, it describes the beginning of the universe (1:1 to 2:2); *Secondly, as a book of developments*, it divides itself into 10 sections by the recurring phrases "The generations of" (KJV). These are as follows:

1. The generations of the heaven and the earth. (2:4 to 4:26)
2. The generations of Adam. (5:1 to 6:8)
3. The generations of Noah. (6:9 to 9:29)
4. The generations of the sons of Noah. (10:1 to 11:9)
5. The generations of Shem. (11:10 to 11:26)
6. The generations of Terah. (11:27 to 25:11)
7. The generations of Ishmael. (25:12 to 25:18)
8. The generations of Isaac. (25:19 to 35:29)
9. The generations of Esau. (36:1 to 37:1)
10. The generations of Jacob. (37:2 to 50:26)

## SECTION III—*The Development of the Gospel in the Writings of Moses*

"*He wrote about me*" (John 5:46), said the Lord Jesus concerning Moses. The Gospel according to Moses is as real as the Gospel according to John. There are four gospels in the beginning of the Old Testament as well as in the commencement of the New.

The story of the Creation is full of Christ. He was the *Word* which God spoke when He *said*, "Let there be light" (Genesis 1:3). And it was His "Spirit" that "was hovering over the waters" (1:2). The creation of man in the image of God was a foreshadowing of the Incarnation, and the breathing of God's life into the breathless clay was a type of regeneration. The formation of woman out of the substance of the man while he slept symbolized the birth of the Church out of the bosom of her crucified Lord. The Garden of Eden and the Tree of Life all have their counterpart in the finished Redemption and Paradise restored. But the true Star of Hope rose in the midnight of the Fall. The glory of God's grace only appears in the hour of man's ruin and despair. How marvelous that grace as it comes seeking the guilty sinner and crying like the wail of a mother after a lost child, "Adam, where are you?" (3:9), as it almost overlooks the dreadful sin of the human pair in the greater wickedness of the real author of the evil, the serpent, and passes its judgment on him rather than on man. And then, as in the very words of judgment it proclaims the first glorious promise of redemption by the Seed of the woman, who should regain the lost inheritance and crush the tempter's head. Adam's faith quickly catches the gleam of hope and calls her name Eve, the mother of life, for the race her sin doomed to death. Then, in the coats of skins and the cherubim at Eden's gate, God gives the token of their justification and erects the Throne of Grace through which, henceforth, "the way to the tree of life" (3:24) must lie.

How delightful it is to find that the very name of God is significant of His grace! While He is being revealed simply as the Creator of the material universe, He is spoken of as "God" absolutely. But when He comes to deal directly with man, and especially fallen man, we find a new name, "Jehovah God," the God of Covenant Love.

That first word of judgment and promise is really the keynote of all that follows, not only in the writings of Moses but in the whole plan of redemption and revelation of the gospel. It describes three conflicts.

First, between the woman and the serpent. She had begun an unholy alliance with him. But it was not to continue. She was to understand and resist him. And woman has ever been the devil's truest foe.

Secondly, between the woman's seed and the serpent's seed. He was to have a seed on earth. The wicked are "the sons of the evil one" (Matthew 13:38) and of their "father, the devil" (John 8:44). The true seed of the woman is the children of God. These two races of men were to be opposed. They always have been and ever will be to the end. And whenever they have mingled, the result has been the death of true religion.

Thirdly, between the Divine Seed—Jesus Himself—and the serpent. This was to be the final and victorious stage of the conflict. By the bruising of His heel on Calvary He was to crush finally the serpent's head and terminate the terrible struggle forever.

The books of Moses simply develop this great conflict.

## THE ANTEDILUVIAN AGE

1. The serpent's seed is not hard to trace. The record of the race of Cain begins and ends in blood. The first step is self-righteous unbelief. Cain was the first Unitarian. He was willing to worship, and his worship was beautiful and aesthetic, but he was not willing to come as a sinner through the way of the cherubim and the atoning blood. And his rejection of this, the ancient gospel, led soon to every form of sin. The steps were envy, murder, separation from God and finally, utter worldliness. With no other God he gave himself up wholly to Mammon. Cain's race built the first city, invented the first musical instruments, perfected the first mechanical arts, instituted the first harem, and first prostituted beauty, culture, wealth and art to self and godless pleasure. There could be no other end than that which soon came, the judgment of the Flood.

2. The seed of the woman, begun in lowly and believing Abel, renewed in

Seth and his godly descendants, had its brightest example in Enoch, the type of perfect humanity. It finally reached its culmination under that dispensation in faithful Noah, who became the transition link to the next age.

These few noble witnesses maintained the conflict with evil while they lived. But already the line of separation had begun to disappear, the old enmity between the seeds became modified and at length obliterated, and in the days of Noah the two races had become merged in one promiscuous mass of wickedness, and nothing less than extermination could cure the fearful disease of sin. Man had grown physically more perfect by the union, but, alas! morally and spiritually so degenerate that he who had once been the image of his God was now but a splendid brute, and a savage one at that. Mercy was mingled with the judgment. One hundred and twenty years of respite were given, but at length the stroke of judgment fell, and only Noah's family was found to have accepted the gracious promise of escape.

3. And what was there in all this age to point to Christ? The sacrifice of Abel pointed to His cross, and Abel's own lowly spirit, shepherd life and innocent death were vivid types of the greater Seed. The ark of Noah foreshadowed His salvation. The life of Enoch was the type of His holy example. Enoch's prophecy was the first prophetic note of His glorious coming. And when we add the striving of the Spirit with the antediluvian race for 120 years, and the symbol of the dove amid the waters of the subsiding flood, we have a fair outline of the gospel before the deluge.

## THE POSTDILUVIAN AGE

The story of grace begins anew in the family of Noah.

Again the holy seed stands out in the line of Shem in the words of Noah's prophetic blessing. Jehovah is to be the God of Shem, and Japheth is at last to share his blessing. True, for a time the line can only be traced in fragments, such as Melchizedek, and perhaps Job, but it reaches its next distinct point in Abraham, through whose family it henceforth is to flow in covenant blessing.

The evil seed is more marked in this age than the good. Ham and Canaan are the first names of evil promise, and their descendants, Nimrod and the Babel builders, abundantly fulfill the expectation. The spirit of Cain reaches higher ambitions of worldly power and pride in the great empires of Assyria and Babylon and the tower which was to lead to heaven, but the hand of judgment strikes once more and scatters the presuming race to the four quarters of the globe.

And where is Christ in these dark times? In the sacrifice of Noah, in the rainbow covenant, in the priestly and kingly offices of Melchizedek, and in the Redeemer of Job, we see again the foreshadowing of the Cross of Calvary and the King of Peace.

## THE PATRIARCHAL AGE

1. The links become more regular now in the chain of blessing and the people of God. Abraham is the first and stands before us as the type of faith and separation. His faith is that of a brave and daring pioneer, and although many have since sailed over the same great trackless seas, yet he has been truly called the "Columbus of Faith." The two features of his faith are boldness and obedience. The steps were clearly marked—the stepping out with sealed orders and promises; the promise of the land, believed and vindicated by his victory over the invaders of Canaan; the promise of a seed, claimed and proved by his taking the name of Abraham, the father of a multitude; the testing of his faith and obedience even in the seeming loss of this promise in Isaac's offering up; and then the peaceful close of his great and lofty life. His faith led to separation. Well did he fulfill the promise respecting the woman's seed at enmity with the serpent's seed. He separated from Ur and its idolatry, from his old father, from Lot, from Ishmael, from Isaac even, from all but God.

Isaac is the next link, and represents the quiet and commonplace aspect of the godly life, and the passive side of faith. His was a patient and gentle life, but he was more distinctively than any of the patriarchs the very seed of promise.

Jacob stands out in vivid distinctness as the example of faith overcoming all the obstacles of a nature originally mean, selfish and unworthy. He is the seed "chosen not for good in him," but through the exceeding grace of God, and brought through the discipline of that grace to be the prince of faith and power, and the head of Israel's tribes. His life rises by four marked stages: first, the choice of the blessing; second, the revelation of God at Bethel; third, the trials that followed, culminating in the victory at Peniel; fourth, the discipline of his later years and sufferings, ending in the closing triumph of faith and patience when he could say, "delivered me from all harm" (Genesis 48:16), "I look for your deliverance, O LORD" (49:18). The supreme lesson of his life is the discipline of faith.

Joseph comes next with another lesson, namely, the triumph of faith, not now over our own sin, but over our innocent sufferings. The seed of the woman is in conflict with the serpent, first in his own family, and next in the great world empire. But he triumphs over both, and his victory leaves no wounds upon them, but brings to all the blessings of magnanimity and love.

Judah is the last link in this age, and his connection is through the prophetic words of the dying Jacob, pointing him out as the royal tribe through whom at length the King is to come and reign, not only over the tribes of Israel but the world.

Such was the seed of faith in this patriarchal age, and so we see them separated from the serpent's brood. They are separated at first from Chaldea, afterwards the seat of the world's great empire; and then separated next in Egypt, Satan's other seat; and in the next age to be separated from Egypt more signally still.

2. Now, where was the serpent's seed in these generations? We don't have to seek very far. Chaldea and Canaan, Egypt and Sodom, Ishmael and Esau, and even Job's wife and Joseph's brethren, in the very household of faith, represented but too well their ancient master, and manifested the old enmity of all his race to the people of God.

What traces have we of the Divine Seed? In the sacrifice of Isaac, in the wooing of Rebekah, in the dream of Jacob, and in the sovereignty of Judah, faith can see with no dim light the grace and glory of her Lord, and a form like unto the Son of God in the Gospel of Abraham and Moses.

# GENERAL PLAN AND SCOPE OF THE BOOK

$G$enesis is the book of beginnings. The Greek word *Genesis* means beginning, and it is the translation of the Hebrew word *Bereshith*, which also means beginning.

This is the first word in the book of Genesis in Hebrew, and so, as with the other books of Moses, it gives the title to the whole book. In the present instance this is the most proper title, for Genesis is literally a book of beginnings. It leads us to the springs from which all the streams of life and being have flowed during the ages that have followed.

Seven great beginnings are recorded in this book. They comprise the sum of the things more fully unfolded in the subsequent books of the Bible.

1. The beginning of the universe, the heavens and the earth.
2. The beginning of the human race.
3. The beginning of sin—at least of human sin and divine judgment concerning it.
4. The beginning of redemption, of which the whole Bible is the progressive unfolding.
5. The beginning of nations and the branching out of the great tree of humanity into the families and races which have subsequently peopled the whole earth and developed into all the tribes and tongues of the world today.
6. The beginning of the Hebrew race, which is selected out of the nations and becomes henceforth the special instrument of divine providence and grace in the working out of God's plan for the world.
7. The beginning of the life of faith on the part of God's own

chosen children, as He calls them and separates them to Himself from the wreck of sin, and the mass of the human family and educates them one by one for His great purposes of grace and glory.

# CHAPTER 1

## THE BEGINNING OF THE UNIVERSE

### Genesis 1:1–2:3

The 11th chapter of Hebrews tells us, "By faith we understand that the universe was formed at God's command, so that what is seen was not made out of what was visible."

### A QUESTION OF FAITH

The facts of creation, therefore, are not open questions for human speculation, but are the subjects of special divine revelation; and the very first province of faith has respect to these. Any conclusions of human science which contradict the fundamental statements of God's Word in this matter are inconsistent with Christian faith and must ultimately be found to be scientifically false. So far as the doctrine of evolution contradicts this statement of the Holy Spirit, it must be rejected by reverent faith, as founded on false assumptions.

Within the Bible account, however, there is room for an almost boundless field of scientific research, and all its established conclusions will be found, ultimately, to be in keeping with the great facts here declared.

Right conclusions about creation are necessary to Christian faith, and fundamental to the very principle of faith, which requires us to recognize at every step the great fact of supernatural and omnipotent power, and to believe in the God who is able to exercise the power of creation, and even of resurrection.

### SECTION I—*The Creator*

There is one phrase in the opening chapter of Genesis, however, that stands transcendently above even the stupendous facts of creation. It is the first four words of the Bible, "In the beginning God." This is the one thing

11

that had no beginning. This is the one stupendous figure which stands in its divine and sublime isolation at the gateway of the great temple of truth. This is the fact which makes all other facts possible and real, and the first cause from which all effects ultimately flow. This is the overshadowing and transcendent thought that covers the whole subsequent pages of inspiration and all the confines of creation—God Himself; before all His works, Creator of all His works, and the Cause and End of all His works, "for by him all things were created" (Colossians 1:16). So let us begin our Bibles and all our purposes and works, writing on every title page, "In the beginning God" (Genesis 1:1).

## SECTION II—*Creation of the Heaven and Earth*

Coming now to the details of creation: First, we have the original creation of the heaven and the earth. It seems natural to take the sense of the word *heaven*, which is given to it in this chapter a little later, namely, the firmament, or expanse of the sky, including, naturally, all the heavenly bodies in its vast field of vision; so that the universe consists of the celestial bodies and the earth, our own planet. The number and extent of these material worlds are not intimated in the inspired account, but are growing more vast and vivid to the human mind as the discoveries of science extend our vision and unveil the secrets of nature.

As God precedes the universe, so heaven precedes the earth in the order of creation. This little self-conscious world is not the only world, or the greatest of the family of revolving spheres, although it is the theater of human destiny and the scene of God's momentous plan of creation and redemption. The story of creation, thus, in its earliest chapter, lifts our vision above the earth and makes most vivid and real to us the two greater facts of God and heaven.

### WHAT IS CREATION?

The word *create*, here used, literally means to make out of nothing, and is so used throughout the Scriptures. It is employed 54 times in the Old Testament, and always applied to God and the higher forms of His creative power. There are other words employed in this narrative, and other portions of the Scriptures, signifying to *form*, to *arrange*, etc., but this word *create* is always used to introduce a new department of creation. The apostle, in the passage already quoted, defines its meaning beyond controversy. He declares that "what is seen was not made out of what was visible" (Hebrews 11:3). That is, they were made out of nothing, and are not developments of previous forms of matter, and certainly were not eternally existent.

We are not told in what form the universe was originally created, and there is room for unlimited transformations and developments of the materials thus called into being.

## SECTION III—*Chaos*

Whether the condition described in the second verse was immediately subsequent to the original creation, or was the result of some catastrophe that followed the state of order and completeness, is not settled. But at least, at some period, either immediately after or long subsequent to the original creation, the earth was in a condition of chaos and wreck. The words used are "formless and empty" (Genesis 1:2). The two Hebrew words *tohu* and *bohu* are singularly expressive. They are very hard to translate. Literally they are rendered devastation and destruction. One is used in Isaiah 45:18, "He created it not *tohu*"—translated "to be empty." This would seem to imply that a condition of chaos was not the original state of the earth, but a subsequent wreck out of which the week of creation days was designed to reform and restore the world to its present condition as a suitable home for the habitation of men.

The revelations of geology bear ample witness to the existence of a primitive condition of convulsion and desolation. During this period, of whose length we are not informed, there was ample time for the geological formations which science has traced in the prehistoric period.

Over this darkness was the brooding presence of the Holy Spirit, and the language in which that presence is described is very beautiful, suggesting the figure of the brooding wings of a bird—the first revealing of the Heavenly Dove, who has since so graciously been manifested to dispel the darkness of earth and usher in the new creation.

## SECTION IV—*The Days of Creation*

The process of restoring the earth from a condition of chaos and preparing it for the residence of man was a gradual one, and the periods of its successive stages are called *days*. There has been much discussion as to the length of these *days*. It is enough to say that there is no necessity in the record itself to limit the word to the natural day of 24 hours. The ordinary scriptural usage of the word day is much varied. In the present passage even, it is employed in several senses. In the fifth verse it means half a day, or the period of light that came in alternation with darkness. In the end of the same verse, it means a whole day, including both evening and morning. And in the fourth verse of the second chapter, it means the whole period of the six days; while in other Scriptures, again and again, it denotes a general period of indefinite duration—such as the day of trouble, the day of prosperity, the day of visitation. In Psalm 90:4, it means a period of a thousand years. There is no grammatical reason, therefore, for limiting it to the ordinary day; and there are many things in the narrative which make it apply much more appropriately in each instance to a long period, commencing with the dark evening of still remaining chaos and wreck and ending with a brighter morning of order and higher light and life.

1. *The First Day's Work*—The work of this day was the creation of light. It is preceded by the simple sentence, "God said" (Genesis 1:3). This is next in importance to the opening sentence of the book, "God was" (1:2).

This little sentence of two words is the foundation of faith and the cornerstone of divine revelation. Back of it, also, stands the Living Word, the Person of the Son of God, who was even then the Agent in creation's work, and who is now the substance as well as the theme of the written Word.

His first creative act was the formation of light by the command "Let there be light" (1:3), and light was.

The existence of light before the appointment of the sun and the arrangement of the solar functions, which occurred on the fourth day, was long a puzzle to science and a favorite ground of objection to the Mosaic narrative. But science has recently discovered that there are more kinds of light than solar light, and that it was perfectly in accordance with the facts of nature, now fully known, that there should be light even before the sun became a luminous bearer of light for the solar system.

"God saw that the light was good" (1:4). How beautiful the beneficence of this first work of His creating love and power! The work of this day was completed by the separating of light from darkness, probably by means of the earth's diurnal revolution.

The record of the first day is closed by the declaration, "And there was evening, and there was morning—the first day" (1:5), or literally, "day one." The progress is from the lower to the higher, from darkness to light—a type of the divine order in the greater work of the new creation.

2. *The Second Day's Work*—The work of this day was the separation of the sea and the sky; of the lower and terrestrial from the upper and aerial region, here called the firmament. The word firmament (KJV) is an unhappy translation. Literally that word means something solid. The Hebrew word means, however, something elastic; the air, or the expanse of the visible heavenly arch, often spoken of in the Bible as a curtain stretched by the hand of God. The word expanse (NIV) expresses the true idea. The effect of this day's work was to separate the vapors that had hung upon the surface, and poise them in their places in the clouds, leaving the heavier masses of water to roll in the seas and oceans upon the surface. To this expanse above the surface of the earth God gave the name of heaven. This means the region of the atmosphere, and includes all the immensity above us.

**3. *The Third Day's Work***—The special work of this day was another separation, namely, of land and water. Hitherto the surface of the globe was a surging ocean. But now, whether by volcanic upheavals or supernatural forces, the continents and islands of earth are shaped, and the waters fall into their channels and basins. The work of this day is completed by the commencement of the vegetable creation, and the teeming plants of earth in all their varied forms of life and reproduction.

**4. *The Fourth Day's Work***—The work of this day included the heavenly bodies in their relation to the earth, and the adjusting of the laws which regulated the luminaries of day and night. It is not necessary to suppose that the sun was created on this day.

The word here used means appointed or set, and it is sufficient to assume that their functions were now regulated and arranged, and the laws of nature in their present operation fully established. The word "lights" literally means "light bearers." The light already created was simply deposited in these bodies for the use of man and the illumination of the earth. The sun is simply the channel of light for the solar system. Not only were they made for the purpose of giving light, but also "as signs to mark seasons and days and years" (1:14).

**5. *The Fifth Day's Work***—The fifth day's work comprised the creation of the lower forms of animal life. This was the commencement of life, and marks a new stage of great importance. There is an infinite difference between the lowest form of animal life and the highest vegetable organization. The creation of life is the divine prerogative. The literal translation of the 20th verse is, "Let the waters teem with living creatures" (1:20)—not "bring forth" (KJV), which seems to imply a spontaneous existence.

## A SECOND STAGE OF CREATION

The word *create* is here used for the second time, inasmuch as a new stage of life and being is now to be entered upon, requiring divine and omnipotent working.

The animals created upon this day include the fowls of the heaven and the fishes of the sea, regarded as alike the inhabitants of the waters, the one inhabiting the liquid air, and the other the liquid deep. The order of creation corresponds in this respect to the records of geology.

The higher character of the new world of animate beings thus created is indicated by the fact now stated for the first time, that God blessed them, and bade them be fruitful and multiply and fill the earth and air. The "great whales" described in this section mean, literally, "great monsters," and describe the mighty relics of the primitive creation whose mammoth skeletons are found in the rocky tombs which geology has unveiled—the mastodon and saurian of the primitive rocks.

**6.** *The Sixth Day's Work*—Creation now makes its highest advance, and reaches the nobler forms of animal life, the mammalia of the earth, and at last, the human family. The records of geology find the first traces of man among the remains of the higher land animals, and Moses tells us that both were created on the same day.

## SIGNIFICANCE OF MAN'S CREATION

The creation of man, however, is accompanied with circumstances of peculiar distinction and importance. It is preceded by a divine council in the Trinity, and it is not the mere command of Omnipotence, but the plan of deliberate and infinite wisdom and love. The type of this creation is nothing less than the divine image.

There is no hint of the development of this crowning form of creation out of the earlier species of life that have successively appeared, but this is a distinct act, unlike any that preceded it. And to make it still more emphatic, the distinct word *created* is for the third time now employed. In the first verse it was employed with regard to the entire universe in its original creation, in the 21st verse with respect to the first creation of life, and now here, to mark the final stage of creation—man himself. This, however, will form the subject of the next chapter more particularly, and it is enough for the present to link it with the stages in the whole work of creation.

**7.** *The Sabbath*—The last day is called the Sabbath and signalizes the consummation of God's creative work, and the higher thought of hallowed rest. It implies that God has for the present completed the material universe so far as new forms of creation are concerned. And, therefore, the word Sabbath as first employed, denotes, like the other days of creation, a long period which commenced then, and is still running its course—the seventh great age in which we now are living. It became for man the type of his Sabbath also, and so was constituted the Day of Rest, with an authority that dates from the morning of creation.

## SECTION V—*Allusions to Creation in Later Scriptures*

This wonderful story of creation is finely portrayed in the form of a series of panoramic pictures in Psalm 104. As we read it side by side with the first chapter of Genesis, it gives a vivid coloring to the simple narrative of Moses.

## THE FIRST DAY

"Let there be light, and there was light" (1:3) in the Mosaic record is answered by the Psalmist with the sublime words, "He wraps himself in light as with a garment" (Psalm 104:2).

## THE SECOND DAY

Then the separation of the expanse of heaven is thus described: "He stretches out the heavens like a tent/ and lays the beams of his upper chambers on their waters./ He makes the clouds his chariot/ and rides on the wings of the wind./ He makes winds his messengers,/ flames of fire his servants" (Psalm 104:2–4).

## THE THIRD DAY

The work of the third day, the separation of land and water, is majestically pictured in the Psalmist's vision: "He set the earth on its foundations;/ it can never be moved./ You covered it with the deep as with a garment;/ the waters stood above the mountains./ But at your rebuke the waters fled,/ at the sound of your thunder they took to flight;/ they flowed over the mountains,/ they went down into the valleys,/ to the place you assigned for them./ You set a boundary they cannot cross;/ never again will they cover the earth./ He makes springs pour water into the ravines;/ it flows between the mountains./ They give water to all the beasts of the field;/ the wild donkeys quench their thirst./ The birds of the air nest by the waters;/ they sing among the branches./ He waters the mountains from his upper chambers;/ the earth is satisfied by the fruit of his work" (5–13).

The teeming vegetable life which finished the work of the third day is exquisitely described in the Psalmist's vision: "He makes grass grow for the cattle,/ and plants for man to cultivate—/ bringing forth food from the earth:/ wine that gladdens the heart of man,/ oil to make his face shine,/ and bread that sustains his heart./ The trees of the LORD are well watered,/ the cedars of Lebanon that he planted./ There the birds make their nests;/ the stork has its home in the pine trees" ( 104:14–17).

## THE FOURTH DAY

Passing on from this beautiful picture of the newborn earth, in all its robes of verdure and beauty, he next ascends with the narrative of creation to the heavenly regions, and thus describes the fourth day's work, the appointment of sun and moon, and day and night: "The moon marks off the seasons,/ and the sun knows when to go down./ You bring darkness, it becomes night,/ and all the beasts of the forest prowl./ The lions roar for their prey/ and seek their food from God./ The sun rises, and they steal away;/ they return and lie down in their dens./ Then man goes out to his work,/ to his labor until evening" (104:19–23).

## THE FIFTH DAY

The fifth day's work brought the creation of the marine animals, and so the Psalmist's vision sweeps along the same majestic track. "The earth is full of your creatures./ There is the sea, vast and spacious,/ teeming with creatures beyond number—/ living things both large and small./ There the ships go to and fro,/ and the leviathan, which you formed to frolic there./ These all look to you/ to give them their food at the proper time./ When you give it to them,/ they gather it up;/ when you open your hand,/ they are satisfied with good things./ When you hide your face,/ they are terrified;/ when you take away their breath,/ they die and return to the dust./ When you send your spirit,/ they are created,/ and renew the face of the earth" (104:24b–30). The closing refrain, "may the LORD rejoice in his works" (104:31b), is almost an echo of the old creation decree of divine approval—"God saw . . . it was very good" (Genesis 1:31).

### SECTION VI—*Correspondence between the Bible Account of Creation and Nature*

While, as we have already premised, the Bible is not directly intended to be a revelation of natural science, and often speaks in popular terms adapted to the intellectual progress of the age when it was written, and which might not now be rigidly accurate in the light of the most advanced scientific progress, yet it never contradicts the real facts of nature; and in many things has been found to be a truly marvelous anticipation of the most remarkable discoveries of modern science. Even the statements and allusions which at one time were criticized by science as incorrect and ignorant have been found by later discoveries to be in real accord with the constitution of nature, although opposed to what was once supposed to be scientific truth.

### *LIGHT AND THE SUN*

This is nowhere so apparent as in the account of creation, and the most striking illustration of the fact just stated is the Mosaic reference to the creation of light on the first day, and the adjustment of the celestial luminaries on the fourth day. It was long thought to be ridiculous that light should be said to have been created before the sun was constituted the luminary of this planet. But the most recent discoveries have proved that this is exactly true in the order of nature, and that there are many kinds of light besides solar light.

The chief correspondence between the Mosaic account of creation and the best established results of modern science are admirably stated by Dr. Dawson in his little volume, *Nature and the Bible,* and may be summed up as follows:

*First*—Both present an exact order of creation. "The order of creation as stated in Genesis is faultless in the light of modern science, and many of its details present the most remarkable agreement with the results of sciences born only in our own day. This is a severe test for the Bible—one from which many of its friends seem to shrink; but we shall see in the sequel how it endures it, and why it was necessary that it should be subjected to it."

*Second*—Both lead us back to a beginning. "The tendency of all modern geological and astronomical reasoning has been to point by positive indications to a beginning. Geology shows us that the animals and plants which are our contemporaries did not always exist, and we can trace back animal and vegetable life perhaps to their origin on our earth. Even the rocks and continents have their geological dates, and there are none of them that we cannot assign to an origin in geological time. So in astronomy. Science, therefore, must agree with Moses in affirming a beginning of all things."

*Third*—Both begin with a condition of chaos.

*Fourth*—Both teach us of the creation of light, before the appointment of celestial luminaries. "This distinction between light and luminaries is another point on which Moses anticipates science. On any physical hypothesis of the formation of the universe, there ought to have been diffused light first, and the aggregation of this about the central luminary as a subsequent process; and the enormous lapse of time implied in this physical perfecting of our system is well shadowed forth, in its being finished only on the fourth of the six creative aeons."

*Fifth*—Both point to an early aqueous condition, and to the origination of the first animals from the waters.

*Sixth*—Both give the same account of the formation of land, and its separation from the terrestrial waters. "The greatest of all the physical changes implied in the preparation of the earth is that of the third creative day, in the elevation of the dry land and clothing it with vegetation. It is in perfect accordance with what we know from scientific investigation that the dry land should appear before the completion of the final arrangements of the bodies of the solar system. The natural cause of the appearance of the first dry land is explained by geological investigation. We left the earth at the end of the second creative aeon, with a solid crust supporting a universal ocean. But, as time advanced, the gradual cooling of the earth's mass would make this crust too small. At length it would collapse and fall into folds, giving ridges of land and shallow oceans. When rightly understood, nothing can be more thoroughly accurate than the Bible language respecting those elevated portions of the crust, arched and pillared above the waters, and in which we have our secure abode. It yet remains, however, for geology to discover the first traces of the vegetation which followed this process, and preceded the creation of the lowest forms of marine animals."

*Seventh*—Both trace the same scale of progress in the animal creation from the lower forms of life up to man. And both place man's creation among the higher orders of mammalia, and at the same stage of the work of creation. "In both records man is geologically modern, coming at the close of the great procession of animal life; and it is remarkable that geology concurs with revelation in not finding any new species introduced since the creation of man, and only a few species can be supposed to have been introduced along with him. As in the Bible record man is introduced in the same creative aeon with the higher brute animals, so in geology he is united without any break to the close of the Tertiary period of the great mammals."

*Eighth*—Both represent the most ancient men not as evolutions from former animal life of a lower order, but as a higher order of beings, forming as distinct a species as the men and women of today. "The oldest men whose remains have been found are not of a different species from modern men, but, on the contrary, are nearly allied to the most widely distributed modern race; while their great stature and physical power reminds us of the giants of Genesis. They testify, in short, to a specific identity and common descent of all men; and their great bodily development, accompanied probably with great longevity, is such as geological facts would lead us to anticipate in the case of a new type recently introduced, rather than in one which had descended through a long course of struggle for existence from an inferior ancestry."

Dr. Dawson eloquently adds: "All these coincidences cannot be accidental. They are the more remarkable when we consider the primitive and child-like character of the notices in Genesis, making no scientific pretensions, and introducing what they tell us of primitive man merely to explain and illustrate the highest moral and religious teachings. Truth and divinity are stamped on every line of the early chapters of Genesis, alike in their archaic simplicity, and in that accuracy as to facts which enables them not only to stand unharmed amid the discoveries of modern science, but to display new beauties as we are able more and more fully to compare them with the records stored up from old in the recesses of the earth. Those who base their hopes for the future on the glorious revelations of the Bible need not be ashamed of its story of the past."

## SECTION VII—*Spiritual Lessons from the Story of Creation*

### THE TRINITY

1. Creation foreshadows the doctrine of the Trinity. In the first verse of Genesis the name of God, "Elohim," is in the plural, implying surely more than the idea of dignity, and suggesting the threefold personality of the Creator. And yet to show unmistakably that the Bible does not sanction Polytheism, but reveals to us the unity of God in contrast with ancient idolatry, the verb *created* is in the singular number, thus expressing with em-

phatic clearness at once the trinity and unity of the divine Being. This prepares us for the reference in the following verses to the Word of God and the Spirit of God. And the firm conviction that this is all designed is confirmed by the strong language of the 26th verse with respect to the divine Council relating to the creation of man, "Let us make man in our image, and in our likeness" (Genesis 1:26). It is even conceivable that the constitution of man in the image of God has a reference to the trinity involved in the fact of man's own threefold nature—spirit, soul and body.

## THE WORD

2. There seems to be an allusion, at least, to the eternal Word in the third verse of the first chapter, "God said, 'Let there be light,' and there was light," compared with the first three verses of the first chapter of John: "In the beginning was the Word, and the Word was with God, and the Word was God. He was with God in the beginning. Through him all things were made; without him nothing was made that has been made. In him was life, and that life was the light of men." The Apostle Paul tells us, in the Epistle to the Colossians, that He was the Agent in the work of creation, and that "by him," or rather "in him were all things created" (Colossians 1:16). He was the living Word and the Author of life and existence.

## THE SPIRIT

3. The Holy Spirit is also distinctly foreshadowed in the figure of the *brooding wings* that hovered above the chaotic night out of which sprang the newborn earth. "The Spirit of God hovered over the face of the deep" (Genesis 1:2). This is the first picture of the Heavenly Dove whose gentle wing has ever appeared amid the darkness of earth's sin and sorrow as the harbinger of order and peace, and a beautiful type of the new creation which the same Spirit ushers in. The Scriptures elsewhere refer to the cooperation of the Holy Spirit in the work of creation. "By his breath the skies became fair" (Job 26:13). "By the word of the LORD were the heavens made,/ their starry host by the breath of his mouth" (Psalm 33:6).

## FAITH

4. The province of faith in connection with nature and the doctrine of creation is involved in this subject. In Hebrews 11:3 we are taught that the first step of faith is to believe in the doctrine of the supernatural creation of the material universe. This is not a matter merely of scientific investigation, but the distinct subject of divine testimony. God requires us to believe that the material universe was His own direct workmanship, and not a mere process of natural development or spontaneous generation. And evangelical faith must, therefore, stand firmly upon these records, and God will vindi-

cate their truth, as we have already seen He has ever done, in the face of human wisdom and the light of the most advanced science and true philosophy.

The reason God requires that faith should ever recognize Him as the Creator is because at every stage of our spiritual progress faith needs to claim the interposition of God who is still able to work with all the omnipotence involved in the first creation. Again and again in our spiritual life we come to a place where we must believe in One who can make something out of nothing, without any materials or resources except His own all-sufficiency. The thing we believe for, even in our Christian life, is often a thing which not only is not, but naturally cannot be without a divine creation. And, therefore, God constantly says to us before His mightiest promises, "Thus saith the Lord that formed it, that created it."

Therefore, in Isaiah and the other prophets, we find God constantly appealing to the works of nature as the witnesses of His power and faithfulness and the ground of His people's confidence. "Do you not know?/ Have you not heard?/ The LORD is the everlasting God,/ the Creator of the ends of the earth./ He will not grow tired or weary,/ and his understanding no one can fathom./ He gives strength to the weary/ and increases the power of the weak" (Isaiah 40:28–29).

## THE NEW CREATION

5. The story of creation is a figure and type of the new creation which God is introducing through the mediatorial work of the Lord Jesus Christ. The whole process of the six days' work is a vivid foreshadowing of the work of grace, beginning in a condition of chaos which itself was probably the wreck of primeval order. The new creation, like the old, is introduced by the Holy Spirit, and the divine and eternal Word, bringing light, order and life in due succession, revealing at length the Sun of Righteousness in the soul as its center of power and source of illumination and life, and culminating at last in "the new man" who stands complete in the glorious image of his Author (2 Corinthians 4:6; 1 Corinthians 6:17).

## THE REST OF GOD

6. The Sabbath of creation is the foundation both of the Mosaic and Christian Sabbath, each of which looks back to this as its authority. And it is also the spiritual type of the Rest of Faith, into which the soul enters when, like God, it ceases from its own works, and enters into the finished work of Jesus Christ (Genesis 2:3; Hebrews 4:3-10).

# CHAPTER 2

## THE BEGINNING OF THE HUMAN RACE

### Genesis 1:26–30; 2:7–25

#### SECTION I—*Bible Account of the Origin of Man*

##### THE CROWN OF CREATION

1. Man appears upon the scene as the last and crowning stage of the work of creation. The world has been prepared for his home, and now the occupant appears upon the field and takes possession of his fair inheritance. He is in a sense the climax and crown of the material universe. He has been called a microcosm—a little world in his own person, combining the elements and substance of the very ground he treads upon and the qualities of the lower orders of creation over which he rules, with those higher endowments which link him with the Deity and the heavens, and make him an heir of immortality.

##### THE HANDIWORK OF GOD

2. Man is the special handiwork of God. He is not the blind result of fortuitous elements and atoms, nor a mere evolution from lower forms of life. He is created by the very hand of God Himself, as a distinct order of existence, and the object of the most deliberate counsel, and all the resources of the divine wisdom and power.

Two words are used in the Hebrew language to describe the creation of man. One is the word *create*, already referred to as denoting the direct creative work of God through His omnipotence, and without any previous materials. The other is the word *formed*, which implies the existence of previous matter, and its being incorporated into his form and structure. Both of these are used with respect to man to indicate that, while the materials of the physical creation were employed in his structure and he was formed out of the dust of the ground, yet his higher nature was created by the direct fiat of the Almighty as really and completely as the universe was created in the beginning.

This act of creation does not merely apply to the spirit of man, but to the entire being; for it is used in the 27th verse of the first chapter with respect to the sexual relations of man and woman as male and female, and therefore must include the physical as well as the spiritual nature.

## HIS THREEFOLD NATURE

3. This leads us to the next fact—that man was created with a threefold nature. The language of the original distinctly implies the two elements of the spiritual and material nature of man, and it would seem that even a *psychical* life is also specified in distinction from a spiritual. Certainly we know that in the Scriptures human nature is described under this threefold division: spirit, soul and body, and it would not be strange if we should find them in the original account of man's creation. The words of the seventh verse of the second chapter, "The LORD God formed the man from the dust of the ground," describe his physical creation. The word used here for man is *Adam.* "He formed the Adam out of the dust of the Adamah," so the word Adam means one formed from the earth.

Science has shown that the chemical ingredients of the human body are the very same as those we find in the soil of the earth's surface and the limestone beneath; only it needed divine omnipotence to constitute and quicken it into life. This idea of man's formation out of the earth is familiar throughout the Scriptures, and referred to in Job 33:6, Ecclesiastes 3:20, First Corinthians 15:47 and Psalm 146:4.

There is nothing in this akin to the doctrine of evolution, which teaches not that man was made from dust, but evolved from lower brutes. The conception of the Creator taking even the chemical elements that science can classify and measure in the finest detail, but with all its wisdom cannot constitute into a living man, and by one breath from His own mouth, sending it forth a living, intelligent and immortal being, is as stupendous and divine as to create it out of nothing.

The spiritual creation of man is described in the next clause, "[He] breathed into his nostrils the breath of life" (Genesis 2:7). This is not said of any other creature. This was the imparting to man of the divine spirit, the very life of God Himself. The expression here used, "breath of life," is never applied directly to brutes. In the Hebrew it is plural; it is "breath of lives." This implies that man received more than one kind of life, not only the animal vitality, but also a rational and spiritual subsistence.

What a beautiful type of the process by which the spiritual life is again restored in the new man. It is in-breathed by the Holy Spirit. So our Lord, in leaving His disciples, breathed upon them and said, "Receive the Holy

Spirit" (John 20:22). This was the birth of the Church.

The third expression used about man's creation, "Man became a living being" (Genesis 2:7) seems to refer to his psychical nature, the department of our being to which the term *soul* is usually applied in the New Testament. The Greek word for this is *psyche*. And so it is employed in First Corinthians 15:45 with reference to this very passage. " 'The first man Adam became a living being'; the last Adam, a life-giving spirit."

This, then, constitutes the entire man, as we see again in the prayer of the apostle for our sanctification: "Your whole spirit, soul and body be kept blameless at the coming of our Lord Jesus Christ" (1 Thessalonians 5:23); and also in the picture of our Savior's childhood: "The child grew"—the physical—"and became strong"—the spiritual—"filled with wisdom"—the psychical and intellectual—"and the grace of God was upon him" (Luke 2:40).

## *IN GOD'S IMAGE*

4. The being thus created is said to have been "in the image of God." This expression is repeated in the 26th and 27th verses of the first chapter, where the word, or its equivalent, is used four times. Wherein this likeness consisted, we can only know imperfectly. We know the true and perfect man, the Lord Jesus Christ, is the perfect image of the Father. Perhaps the threefold nature of man was designed to shadow forth the personality of the Trinity. Perhaps, also, the unity of the sexual nature of man as first created, including both the woman and the offspring in the one human being originally created, was also designed to prefigure the divine relations of the Father, Son and Holy Spirit. Possibly even the face and form of man were designed in some way to represent God. Certainly we know his spiritual and moral qualities were the transcript and reflection of his Father. In the new creation we are restored to the image of God, and this is said by the apostle to consist in knowledge, righteousness and true holiness (Colossians 3:10; Ephesians 4:24; Ecclesiastes 7:29). This has been already realized in every one of His redeemed ones. "But we know that when he appears, we shall be like him, for we shall see him as he is" (1 John 3:2).

## *MALE AND FEMALE*

5. Man was created male and female. This does not mean, as would seem at first from the language, that He created the male and the female at the same time, but He created man both male and female in one person. The woman was included in the man both physically and psychically, and afterwards was taken out of the man and constituted in her own individuality. This is a strange conception of humanity. But we find traces of it even in the reasonings of Socrates and the writings of Plato, where man is represented as

originally a twofold being with four hands, four limbs and two faces, afterwards divided by the gods, and ever since each has been looking for its counterpart, and this is the explanation of the social element of human life.

This, of course, was a rude and clumsy shadow of the original and scriptural truth. Back of that truth lies the great mystery of redemption, in symbol, namely, that Christ, the second Adam, contained first in His own person the whole body of His redeemed ones, and that they have been born out of His very life as Eve was out of Adam. The fact that man contained in his own person, at first, all the race, was the reason why he acted representatively for them, and his fall involved their ruin. This natural headship of Adam is the type of Christ's headship over His new race.

The details of woman's formation are given in the second chapter, verses 21 to 24. During a deep sleep, or as the Septuagint expresses it, *ecstasy*—the same as afterwards fell on Abraham during his vision of the future (Genesis 15:12)—God separated one of Adam's ribs from his form, and "built it," as the Hebrew expresses it, into a woman, and then gave her back to him as the partner of the life from which she had sprung. Adam gave her the name woman, literally *man-ess*, and said, "This is now bone of my bones, and flesh of my flesh" (2:23).

## DOMINION

All this expresses very beautifully the natural relations of man and woman, but more profoundly the great spiritual mystery of Christ and His Church, as we shall see later.

6. Man is constituted the ruler of the terrestrial creation (1:26), "Let them rule over the fish of the sea and the birds of the air, over the livestock, over all the earth, and over all the creatures that move along the ground." And so God brought to Adam all the lower animals, and placed them under his authority (2:19). This dominion is man's primeval right, and although it has been forfeited by the fall, and is ever dependent upon his retaining the image of God, yet it shall be again restored in the fullness of redemption and the kingdom of glory.

In the eighth Psalm it is prophetically described as the transcendent dignity of man.

> What is man that you are mindful of him,
> the son of man that you care for him?
> You made him a little lower than the heavenly beings
> and crowned him with glory and honor.
> You made him ruler over the works of your hands;
> you put everything under his feet. (4–6)

In referring to this in Hebrews, the author of that epistle admits that it is not yet realized in man's actual experience; but it has all been consummated in the person of Christ, the true Man, and shall yet be shared by all His brethren in the consummation of their redemption.

Man's lordship over nature, like every other gift of the Creator, has been shamefully abused for the injury of the lower creation, and therefore the whole creation is represented as groaning and travailing together in pain, and crying out for the redemption of the body at Christ's second coming.

## INNOCENT

7. Man was created innocent and upright. The statement that "they felt no shame" (2:25) implies the perfect innocency of our first estate. This is also expressed by the "image of God." Later inspired pages declare, "God made man upright,/ but men have gone in search of many schemes" (Eccelesiastes 7:29). Man's original purity was not infallible, and yet it was faultless. It was of the same nature as the holiness of the unfallen angels. It is not the same as that to which we are restored in the new creation. That will be not human perfection, but the divine nature, and it shall be constituted infallible, through the grace of God and the eternal redemption of Jesus Christ our Lord.

## EDEN

8. The new race is placed in an earthly paradise. The name Eden means delight. The location is uncertain, but probably somewhere in the hills of Armenia, near the headwaters of the Euphrates and Tigris. Eastward means, naturally, east of Palestine. The rivers are our chief indexes in fixing the site. The first, Pison, was probably the river Halys which flows into the Black Sea. Gihon would then be the Araxes, which flows into the Caspian Sea. The latter two, the Hiddekel and Euphrates, are easily identified as the Tigris and the Euphrates, flowing southward into the Persian Gulf.

## SPIRITUAL FORESHADOWINGS

The names have a special significance: Pison meaning "flowing forth," suggesting freeness; Gihon, "bursting forth," denotes fullness; Hiddekel expressing "rapidity of motion," which is literally true of the Tigris; and Euphrates signifying "sweetness" or "fruitfulness." It is not hard to find in these four names and their place in Eden a fourfold type of the fullness of the gospel in its freeness of salvation, its fullness of grace, its power over all evil in our life and its blessed hope of the future. It is not necessary to say that the paradise of Eden finds its fulfillment and its restoration in the closing chapters of the book of Revelation.

## IN COVENANT WITH GOD

9. The human race, thus created and crowned with happiness and blessing, is placed in covenant relations and united in holy fellowship with God Himself. Therefore the name of the Divine Being Himself is changed at the commencement of the account of man's creation, early in the second chapter. This change from the word Elohim to Jehovah Elohim has been a great stumbling block to all the infidel critics of the Bible, and they have hastily assumed that it proves a double authorship of the book of Genesis.

The eye of faith and the higher spirit of Christian interpretation see in it a beautiful advance in the revelation of God. While dealing with the natural creation, He is represented under the name that expresses rather His absolute power and Godhead. But the moment that He comes to deal directly with man, His own beloved child, He changes His name and speaks to him as Jehovah, the covenant God.

The terms of the covenant into which He received our first parents are clearly stated.

There was no limitation upon the bounty and love of their Father and the fullness of their inheritance, except one simple test of implicit obedience, which involved no sacrifice of happiness and no question of love. One tree alone they must not partake of, the tree of the knowledge of good and evil. Not that this tree contained in itself any natural quality of evil, but to taste it after it was prohibited would bring the knowledge, because of the actual experience of sin.

There was no injustice in exposing man to such a temptation, for virtue is doubly valuable and doubly recompensed when it has been proved and tried; and purity without a test might not be worthy of the name. The obedience of man to this simple test would have brought to him and to his race the highest blessing. And his disobedience involved them, as well as himself, in the bitter consequences.

The relations of Adam and Eve with their heavenly parent were intimate and blessed. God Himself came to visit them in their happy home, and they met Him with unreserved confidence and unlimited delight. And so it was the type of that place and time when "the dwelling of God is with men, and he will live with them and they will be his people, and God himself will be with them and be their God" (Revelation 21:3).

## SECTION II—*Errors Contradicted by the Bible Account of Man's Creation*

### 1. *Materialism*

This is the philosophy which attributes man's nature, as well as the entire universe, to the combination of atoms of matter, through purely fortuitous circumstances and causes. The various schools of materialistic thought have as many theories, substantially agreeing in the self-existence of matter and the possibility of spontaneous life. It is enough to say that science has produced no evidence that life has ever been generated, even in its lowest form, without the contact of previously existing life. The latest conclusions from scientific researches and experiments have confirmed this fact: that life is not spontaneous or self-existent, and must be imparted from a living being. And we need not add that the entire teaching of the Scriptures is antagonistic wholly to all the principles of materialism. God is the Creator of our spirits and the Former of our bodies; and even the successive generations of men, although reproduced through natural laws and second causes, are declared to be in each individual instance the work of His creating hand. "In him we live and move and have our being; . . . we are his offspring" (Acts 17:28).

## 2. Evolution

This doctrine, which has been more systematically developed and formulated in recent years, claims to take higher ground than pure Materialism, or absolute Atheism, inasmuch as it admits the preexistence of certain lower types of life, without attempting to account for them; and then traces all subsequent species, including man, the last and highest type, from these primordial types.

Scientifically, it has only succeeded up to this time in producing a number of partial illustrations and examples of its so-called laws of development, and contents itself with weaving these together into a hypothesis whose missing links it expects yet to discover, and so complete the chain of physical facts and scientific demonstrations.

While many superior minds have adopted this theory, yet many candid and sober scientific teachers maintain that the theory is a mere hypothesis, lacking any complete or satisfactory scientific demonstration, and contradicted by some of the most inexorable facts of physiology; especially this cardinal and insurmountable difficulty that even in the present orders of the animal world, it is certain that species do not blend and propagate a new species, but that such unions always terminate with the second link, and leave it without the power of reproduction.

Apart, however, from scientific or philosophical speculations, the child of faith is left with sufficient light from God's holy Word to show him that Evolution is for him forbidden ground, and human nature a direct creation of divine power and goodness.

Man's pedigree runs thus downward into folly: "a scientist, which was the son of an ape, which was the son of a zoophyte, which was the son of a protoplasm." God's sublime genealogy is this: "A patriarch which was the son of Abraham; which was the son of Noah; which was the son of Adam; which was the son of God!"

### 3. *Original Diversity of Human Races*

The Mosaic account traces back all the families of earth to one parent stock, and all other Scriptures confirm this inspired record. In speaking to the very men and schools of thought whence all our modern philosophy has sprung, the Apostle Paul declared on Mars Hill "from one man he made every nation of men" (Acts 17:26). And the latest and soundest deductions of Ethnology and Philology all lead us back to the same conclusion, and to the simple and single origin of the human race.

### 4. *Theories of the Antiquity of Man*

The claims that have occasionally been put forth from alleged geological phenomena that the human race must have existed on the earth from an illimitable period, have been gradually reduced to a very simple sum, which in no sense contradicts a reasonable construction of the sacred record. All the oldest types of human fossils in no respect essentially differ from the men of today, and belong to a period in no respect different from that assigned to man in the records of Genesis.

## SECTION III—*Spiritual Teachings of the Account of Man's Creation*

### MAN'S DIGNITY

1. The dignity and value of man in contrast with the lower orders of creation is seen in the special attention bestowed on man's creation, and the lordship granted to him over the inferior creatures and the material world. Our Savior frequently emphasized this important truth, and based upon it the claims of man to God's providential care, and to the sympathy and consideration of his fellow men. "How much more valuable is a man than a sheep" (Matthew 12:12) was His plea on the score of simple humanity for the healing of the sufferer. "Are not two sparrows sold for a penny? Yet not one of them will fall to the ground apart from the will of your Father. You are worth more than many sparrows" (10:29, 31b) is the ground of His appeal to His disciples to trust the care of their heavenly Father and leave on Him their needless care. God is not called the sparrows' Father, but *your* Father.

This was the ground on which the life of man was guarded by God's most solemn sanctions in the covenant of Noah, in what is regarded as the first appointment of capital punishment: "Whoever sheds the blood of man, by man shall his blood be shed; for in the image of God has God made man" (Genesis 9:6). We are taught by the apostle to "show proper respect to everyone" (1 Peter 2:17), simply as men.

The value of the human soul alone was worth the sacrifice of the Son of God. Let us cherish a deeper sense of the sacredness of human life and the momentous importance of human destiny from this picture of creation.

## THE SECOND ADAM

2. Christ, the second Adam, is represented in type in the first head of humanity. From one father all the generations of earth have sprung, inheriting his curse and transmitted nature and depravity, by virtue of their oneness with him in blood and birth. So Christ, the second Adam, has also His spiritual seed and offspring, and by virtue of their union with Him they share His high place of acceptance and sonship, and partake in all the benefits of His obedience and satisfaction to the claims of justice. We were recognized in Him when He died and rose again. We were born out of Him in our regeneration. And we share with Him all His rights and destinies. "As in Adam all die, so in Christ all will be made alive" (1 Corinthians 15:22). This does not mean that all men shall be made alive in Christ, but *all men who are in Christ* shall be made alive.

## THE NEW CREATION

3. The new creation and the spiritual regeneration of man in the image of God is beautifully foreshadowed in the story of Genesis. Through the breath of God the soul is quickened into His life and likeness. All the Persons of the Trinity are united in counsel and cooperation in this supreme work of divine wisdom, love and power. And again the words are repeated in substance, "Let us make man in our image, in our likeness" (Genesis 1:26). "For we are God's workmanship, created in Christ Jesus to do good works" (Ephesians 2:10). "And have put on the new self, which is being renewed in knowledge in the image of its Creator" (Colossians 3:10). "To be made new in the attitude of your minds; and to put on the new self, created to be like God in true righteousness and holiness." (Ephesians 4:23–24).

## THE BRIDE OF CHRIST

4. The relation of the Church to Christ is unfolded in the exquisite figure of Eve's creation from the body of Adam, and then her marriage to the man from whom she had been taken. So the Church is born of Christ, and then wedded to Christ. So also the individual soul is taken from His very life and nature and given back to Him in eternal betrothal and perfect spiritual union.

This is one of the great mysteries of the gospel, which will reach at length its consummation in the marriage of the Lamb. Christ is the Husband of the Church and the Head of the body. "Just as Christ loved the church and gave himself up for her to make her holy, cleansing her by the washing with water through the word, and to present her to himself as a radiant church, without stain or wrinkle or any other blemish, but holy and blameless . . . For we are members of his body" (Ephesians 5:25–27, 30).

## MAN'S DOMINION

5. Man's kingly place as the heir of the world and the lord of the earth in the millennial age is foreshadowed in his original creation and dominion. This is one of his redemption rights, and waits its fulfillment at the Lord's coming. It is already realized in the exaltation of Christ, and shall likewise be accomplished in our expected glory. "We do not see everything subject to him. But we see Jesus" (Hebrews 2:8b–9a) exalted; and already we can sing with the redeemed: "To him who loves us and has freed us from our sins by his blood, and has made us to be a kingdom and priests to serve his God and Father—to him be glory and power for ever and ever" (Revelation 1:5b–6). And in a little while, if we but overcome, we shall sit down with Him on His throne, and share with Him the dominion of the ages to come.

## THE FUTURE PARADISE

6. The glorious hopes that await God's children in the future age are also prefigured in the happy scene of the primeval paradise. They reappear restored and inexpressibly increased in the closing visions of the book of Revelation. The earthly Eden has been exchanged for the New Jerusalem; the primeval heavens and earth, for a new heaven and a new earth wherein dwell righteousness; the happy human pair, for the great multitude which no man can number, out of all kindreds and tribes and tongues; the transient innocence and uprightness of their first estate, for the divine and perfect likeness of God, and an established and ineffable state of eternal holiness and divine perfection; and all the joys and blessings of paradise lost are multiplied a thousandfold, and secured beyond the possibility of forfeiture through the ages of eternity in a more glorious paradise restored.

## PRACTICAL LESSONS

7. Many practical lessons respecting the sacredness of the Sabbath, the sanctity of the home, and the social duties and responsibilities of life are taught us by this inspired picture of the primeval life of the human family. Man may learn the affection and respect which he owes to woman and the place of honor and equality which he should give to her. Woman may learn from her derivation from the man and her being given back to him, to live not for herself but for others, and to lose her identity in self-sacrifice and loving service. And both may learn from their own relations the intimacy of that love into which Christ receives us, in the higher bond of union of which all earthly bonds are but feeble types.

# CHAPTER 3

## THE BEGINNING OF SIN

### Genesis 3:1–19

The Bible does not reveal to us the origin of sin absolutely, but only its introduction to our own world and race through the temptation and fall of man.

### SECTION I—*The Introduction of Sin*

#### THROUGH THE SERPENT

1. It came through the serpent. How it had come to him we do not absolutely know, but that he was an already fallen creature is certain. The literal serpent was but the instrument of a spiritual personality who is more fully referred to in subsequent Scriptures. "That ancient serpent called the devil, or Satan, who leads the whole world astray" (Revelation 12:9). We know that he had been an unfallen angel at one time, and that with multitudes of others he had voluntarily left his estate of righteousness and obedience and been banished from heaven by the judgment of God.

In the 28th chapter of Ezekiel there is a sublime description of the anointed cherub who had walked up and down in the midst of the stones of fire, and was perfect in his comeliness until the day that iniquity was found in him. And of him it is said: "You were in Eden, the garden of God; every precious stone adorned you" (28:13). "You were the model of perfection, full of wisdom and perfect in beauty" (28:12b). "You were blameless in your ways from the day you were created till wickedness was found in you" (28:15). Although this is a direct reference to the prince of Tyre, yet it carries the mind irresistibly back to a higher personality and must be the description of this fallen son of light.

The serpent was not only the appropriate instrument but the expressive type of his subtlety and guile. His congenial employment is to tempt and to destroy. And his assault upon Adam and Eve is a sample of all his subsequent attacks, both on the children of men and on the Son of Man Himself.

His first approach was in the form of a question, or rather, an admission, and then a question which seemed to contradict it. "Really," is his plausible assent to all that God said, and "Did God say?" (Genesis 3:1) his devilish denial of it, in the manner least likely to be suspected. His appeal first to the woman's lower nature, then to her aesthetic taste, and finally to her higher spiritual aspirations is manifest in the three stages so definitely described: She "saw that the fruit of the tree was good for food," "pleasant to the eye" and "desirable for gaining wisdom" (3:6).

It was the same method of attack which he adopted with Christ in the wilderness, appealing first to His hunger, then to His ambition, and then endeavoring to excite Him to religious presumption. John calls this threefold process "the cravings of sinful man, the lust of his eyes, and the boasting of what he has and does" (1 John 3:16).

## THROUGH THE WOMAN

2. Sin entered through the woman. Satan did not approach Adam at first, but concentrated his forces upon the weaker nature. And often since has he used her simplicity and openness of being as the vantage ground and standpoint from which to attack and destroy man as well. The first sin was not conscious and willful, but the result of deception, and woman has often since been thus betrayed. We are to remember that the most disastrous evils may be incurred without deliberate intent of evil.

## THROUGH UNBELIEF

3. Sin entered through unbelief. Eve's first error was to listen to the devil's question about God's Word. "Did God say?" (Genesis 3:1) is always the beginning of sin. Let us take heed lest there be in us "a sinful, unbelieving heart that turns away from the living God" (Hebrews 3:12). We begin by doubting God's Word about sin, and then by doubting His Word about salvation. It was because sin entered through unbelief that salvation must come through faith.

Eve's unbelief was not the deliberate denial of God's Word, but a shadow of suspicion about the kindness of His Word. In the light of the devil's question it seemed a little hard, and her answer made it a little harder still. And then the tempter dared to deny it openly and challenge her to disobey it. "You will not surely die" (Genesis 3:4).

The doubt of divine retribution was one of the earliest forms of human sin, and it is the form which today rationalism is trying its best to inculcate into the Church of God. Again the serpent is whispering to the Church,

"You will not surely die" (3:4). Let us believe all God's words, whether spoken in warning or in promise. God's promises are always easily trusted when we fully believe and receive His commands.

## THROUGH DISOBEDIENCE

4. Sin entered through disobedience. This immediately followed unbelief, and ever does. The moment we question the exact meaning and absolute authority of any of God's words, the door is open for sin and disobedience. The essence of obedience is that it be uncompromising and unquestioning.

The very secret of the highest obedience lies in the fact that it is often blind, and without even understanding all the reasons for it. The very fact that the thing she disobeyed seemed in itself so trifling made it a more perfect test of real principle; just as Abraham's obedience to the command he could not understand was the most perfect test of the principle of his absolute obedience. These two words "unbelief" and "disobedience" are the pillars that stand at the gates of ruin, and their two opposites introduce us to the pathway of life.

## ADAM'S WILLFUL ACT

5. Sin having thus entered through Satan and through Eve, and having taken form in unbelief and disobedience, advances next to the stage of willfulness. Eve's sin was the result of deception, but Adam's sin was voluntary and deliberate. The apostle distinctly declares that Adam was not deceived, but being tempted by his fallen wife he yielded consciously; perhaps from many a lovely and plausible consideration of love to her and partnership with her in her fall, but in any case, with a full knowledge of the character and consequences of his action.

# SECTION II—*The Effects of Sin*

## THE TEMPTRESS

1. The first effect upon Eve was to make her the temptress of Adam. We cannot sin without immediately becoming influences for sin in the lives of others. Unconsciously often there will fall from us a reflection of our own spirit and the shadow of our own curse.

## THE SENSE OF SIN

2. The second effect of sin in this suggestive picture was their consciousness of it. Quick as the reflection of the shadow on the ground is the blight of sin upon the guilty soul. It carries its own witness and leaves its own record. They were ashamed. And "they realized they were naked" (3:7).

## SEPARATION

3. Separation from God is the immediate result and the loss of confidence and fellowship, so that they hid themselves from His presence among the trees of the garden. Our hearts are alienated from the love of God the moment we disobey Him. The whole human family is born under this condemnation and must first be reconciled to God before there can be peace and fellowship.

## SELF-RIGHTEOUSNESS

4. Self-righteousness next appears in the attempt to cover their shame and hide their guilt under the fig leaves which they sewed together. These stand for all the devices of man's attempts to justify or save himself, whether by false religions, sincere moralities or specious pretexts and excuses.

## SELFISHNESS

5. Selfishness and the loss of mutual love at once appear. Adam begins to blame his wife, and she excuses her sin by the temptation of another. The cruelty and harshness of Adam's answer show the sad and utter depth to which he had fallen from his former height of love and nobility. "The woman you put here with me," as though God were as much to blame as the woman, "she gave me some fruit from the tree, and I ate it" (3:12).

## JUDGMENT

6. The divine judgment swiftly follows. God is not hasty or severe, but gives the guilty ones the fullest opportunity for vindication. "Where are you?" (3:9). "What is this you have done?" (3:13). "Have you eaten from the tree, that I commanded you not to eat from?" (3:11). There is no charge. There is no anger, but calm and forbearing patience and justice, and a seeming unwillingness even to believe in the reality of their sin.

The judgment which follows begins with the serpent and henceforth makes the battle of the ages not a conflict between God and man, but between God and Satan. And that judgment is yet to be fulfilled in the complete bruising of the serpent's head and his expulsion forever to the bottomless abyss. The more gracious unfolding of mercy for man in the sentence upon Satan will come more appropriately under the next chapter. But here let us not fail to observe and realize that the battle of humanity begins with the picture of Satan as a conquered foe.

Next the sentence follows on the woman. It consigns her to a lot of suffering subjection. She had followed a false ambition and sought a forbidden exaltation "that she should be like God" (3:5), and so she is subjected to a place of subordination. And a large part of the lesson of her life is to die to her own pride and will. Her very affections are made to her the instruments and occasions of deeper suffering, and the joys and hopes of her life and destiny are all linked with the keenest pain. Woman has ever since been the suffering partner in the human family, and man's inhumanity has made the curse more bitter and hard than God designed.

On the man the sentence which comes in due time is one of toil and conflict with the stubborn earth, and ultimately of mortality, back of which there lies the shadow of a deeper and a darker death. On the race all this involved the further penalty of expulsion from Eden and from happiness; and an inheritance of death in its threefold meaning—temporal, spiritual and eternal.

### SECTION III—*Subsequent Developments of Sin in the Book of Genesis*
Genesis 4:3–11; 6:5–7; 7:21; 9:4–9; 13:13; 18:20–21; 25:34; 37:28; 42:21–22

The tree of evil soon grew into larger proportions and bore its multiplied and bitter fruit.

### CAIN

The story of Cain unfolds the fearful progression of evil. Beginning with unbelief and rejection of the blood of the sacrifice, it leads in rapid sequence to hate, murder, separation from God, devotion to worldliness, selfishness, earthy pleasure and all the dark train of issues suggested in the closing picture of the fourth chapter of Genesis.

### THE ANTEDILUVIANS

Next the antediluvians appear upon the stage as illustrations of the virulence and malignity of the poison that has entered the blood of humanity. In a few generations they have desolated the earth with corruption and violence, and only their extinction by the flood can deliver the earth from its intolerable and hideous load of depravity.

### BABEL AND THE NATIONS

The race starts anew on the other side of the deluge, and soon the elements of sin have developed again in the pride of Babel, the despotism of Nimrod and the early empires of Assyria and Babylon, with their subsequent story of cruelty, ambition and enormous wickedness.

### SODOM AND GOMORRAH

Yet again the story is repeated on a smaller scale but in darker colors in the sins of Sodom, Gomorrah and the cities of the plain, where lust so quickly matures to sin, and sin so terribly brings forth death and judgment, and the fairest scene of earth is made the very gate of hell, and a sample even of the judgment of eternal fire.

## THE PATRIARCHAL FAMILIES

And yet once more the very families of the patriarchs pass before us with the same vision of sin and its workings and consequences. We see it in the selfishness of Lot. We see it in the earthliness of Esau. We see it in the cruelty of Jacob's sons, and all the subsequent workings of Providence and conscience in their future lives. So that the book of Genesis really unfolds in almost every possible phase, the nature, malignity and development of evil, and the virulence of that fatal poison to which one simple act of doubt and disobedience opened the veins of our lost humanity.

# CHAPTER 4

## THE BEGINNING OF REDEMPTION

### Genesis 3:9–14, 20–24

#### SECTION I—*In the Story of the Fall*

Redemption begins with God and His seeking love. His tender question "Adam, where are you?" (Genesis 3:9) echoes through the ages in the shepherd's cry for his lost sheep and the father's search for his prodigal child. It is not the voice of the detective pursuing a criminal, but it is the cry of the father seeking his lost son.

#### GOD'S SEEKING LOVE

1. There is something infinitely touching in the simplicity with which God is here represented. He seems almost to have come down to the garden as at other times, not even suspecting His children's sin, nor willing to think evil of them, but treating them as though they were still His loving household, and glad as at other times to welcome His communion. Of course we do not mean that God was ignorant of their sin, but His heart seems to refuse to believe it.

This strange confidence of God and His desire to have confidence, even in spite of His people's sin, are unutterably beautiful and as high above our thoughts as heaven is above the earth. So we see Him afterwards coming down to visit the cities of the plain, to see "if what they have done is as bad as the outcry" (18:21) that had gone up to heaven, and almost hoping that there might be some explanation; "if not, I will know." So He says of ancient Israel, " 'Surely they are my people,/ sons who will not be false to me';/ and so he became their Savior" (Isaiah 63:8). And so God is still seeking lost man, and calling him through His Spirit, His Word, His Providence and all the agencies of His grace. "Where are you?" (Genesis 3:9). "Return to me" (Isaiah 44:22). "Be reconciled to God" (2 Corinthians 5:20).

The salvation of every soul begins with God. Unconscious of it at the time, perhaps, yet in eternity we shall find with adoring gratitude and wonder, the truth of His gracious words, "I have loved you with an everlasting love; I have drawn you with loving-kindness" (Jeremiah 31:3).

> Why was I made to hear His voice
> And enter while there's room,
> While others make a fatal choice
> And rather starve than come?
>
> 'Twas the same love that spread the feast
> That sweetly brought me in;
> Else I had still refused to taste,
> And perished in my sin.

### THE PROMISED SEED

2. The second stage in the development of redemption is the veiled promise of the coming Savior. This may have been but dimly understood by those who heard it first, but we know in the light of all that has followed, that the promised seed of Genesis 3:15 was none other than the great Redeemer. His humanity is distinctly foreshadowed in the description of Him as the "seed of the woman."

His sufferings and triumphs over the adversary are more distinctly implied in the words, "He will crush your head, and you will strike his heel" (3:15). His conquering feet were to be placed on the head of the dragon, but in the act of triumph He was to receive the death-blow from the serpent's sting, and for a moment sink in suffering and death as the cost of victory and salvation. But the suffering should not be vain, for the adversary should be crushed and eventually destroyed through His death and resurrection. Henceforth the picture of the coming Messiah is one of mingled victory and suffering, of glory and humiliation. The contrasted colors blend so constantly, that the picture was at length mistaken by the Jews. They saw only the coming Victor and forgot His wounds and death; and when He came, He was rejected even by His own, although we can see in their Scriptures the constant picture of His sufferings, as well as the glory which should follow.

The Church of today is in like manner forgetting the other side of the picture and losing the vision of His Coming in the shadow of His Cross.

### SATAN CONQUERED

3. The promise of the Victor carries along with it the destruction of the enemy. So the first aspect of redemption revealed in Genesis is the conflict between the serpent and the Lord. It is to the serpent that the promise of

redemption is first made, as though he were to be held primarily responsible for the fall; and his crime is to be avenged most bitterly for him by the assurance that his fiendish work should fail, and his purposes of destruction be thwarted and counteracted by divine love and grace. Henceforth the work of redemption was to be a great contest, not between man and Satan merely, but between God and Satan.

This is a standpoint from which the gospel and the New Testament constantly lead us to regard our temptations and spiritual adversaries. We are to meet them as God's enemies rather than merely ours, recognizing that the battle is not ours but God's, and defying them from the beginning as conquered foes.

Hence we find that the advent of Jesus on earth was attended by the special manifestation of Satanic power, and soon led to the personal combat between the Redeemer and the devil, which continued to the very end of His earthly ministry. On the cross He gave the adversary his death blow. His resurrection and ascension expelled Satan from access to the heavenly world, and through the Christian age He has been rescuing, one by one, His flock from the power of darkness and the kingdom of Satan; and in a little while He shall return to bind the tyrant for a thousand years, and a little later to hurl him to the bottomless pit. (See Luke 10:18; Revelation 12:9; Revelation 20, etc.)

## THE HOLY SEED

4. While we are to understand the "seed of the woman" as primarily and ultimately referring to Christ, yet the connection of the passage in Genesis, and the analogy of all other Scriptures, authorize us also to apply it to all Christ's people who are recognized as the divine seed in union with Him, and partaking of all His redemption rights and blessings. They are called a little later the seed of Abraham; and the apostle teaches us that this expression includes all the children of faith. We may give the seed of the woman as wide an application. In a still wider sense it might be applied to the whole human family, who are undoubtedly the seed of Eve.

But in this passage there is a twofold humanity. There is the seed of the serpent as well as the seed of the woman. What can the former mean except carnal, corrupt human nature, the men and women in all the ages whose moral and spiritual being are morally the offspring of Satan and of whom Jesus says: "You belong to your father, the devil" (John 8:44). The weeds were "the sons of the evil one" (Matthew 13:38). We believe therefore that these two expressions, "the seed of the woman" and "the seed of the serpent," denote respectively the two races or classes of men who from this time developed through all the succeeding dispensations, with the clearest line of demarcation, and represented the followers of the wicked one, and the covenant people of God.

Now God tells the devil in these words of Genesis that He is going to make a separation between these two classes, and keep His own people a distinct people, both from Satan and from his followers.

## A THREEFOLD CONFLICT

There is, indeed, a threefold conflict here described:

## WOMAN TO BE REDEEMED

First: "I will put enmity between you and the woman" (Genesis 3:15). That is, Eve herself and her daughters shall be saved from the unholy alliance with Satan, which he had attempted to establish, and for a time succeeded, and that Eve herself, and woman preeminently through the coming ages, should be the loyal antagonist and bitter foe of her great destroyer.

This has been gloriously fulfilled in the holy women both of the Old Testament and of the New, and it is preeminently true of the Church in every age, that not only has woman been Satan's most injured victim, but Satan's most powerful enemy, and Christ's most loving, true-hearted friend.

## THE GODLY AND THE WICKED

Then there is the second conflict between the woman's seed and the serpent's seed. This undoubtedly denotes the line of faith and godliness which runs through the Old Testament, and becomes the Church of the New Testament, in contrast with the ungodly race which commenced in the line of Cain and runs all through the ages.

## THE FAMILIES OF SETH AND CAIN

We see these two seeds first in Cain and Abel, and afterwards in Cain and Seth. We see them again in the godly members of Seth's family, such as Enoch and Noah and, on the other hand, in the descendants of Cain, and the monsters of the antediluvian wickedness, who at length overwhelmed the world with corruption, and made the destruction of the race inevitable, in order to effect the salvation of the godly remnant.

## SEPARATION IN PATRIARCHAL TIMES

We see the two seeds next in the patriarchal line of faith and covenant blessing, in contrast with the proud conquerors of Babel and Ashur, the wicked Canaanites and descendants of Lot and Esau and the pride and earthly power of ancient Egypt.

## ISRAEL AND THE GENTILES

In the later centuries we trace the two lines in the chosen people and the godly line in the kingdoms of Judah and Israel on the one hand, and, in contrast, the Gentile nations and the apostate people of God themselves. In the New Testament and through the Christian age, the lines continue as the Church and the world, and they shall be on earth when the Master comes.

## THE CHURCH AND THE WORLD

The purpose of God for these two races is separation. And the necessity of their opposite characters is irreconcilable enmity. The world has ever hated, and must hate, the spirit of godliness and the true seed. And the Church of Christ must hate the spirit of the world, although it may love its victims, and live and labor for their salvation. But it can never do this on the plane of the world itself, but on the higher ground of separation. So far as the serpent's seed remains in the individual soul, there must be the same enmity and ceaseless strife. "For the sinful nature desires what is contrary to the Spirit, and the Spirit what is contrary to the sinful nature. They are in conflict with each other, so that you do not do what you want" (Galatians 5:17).

## THE SON OF MAN

The third stage of this conflict culminates in the coming of the personal seed—the Son of Man Himself, and then the battle is changed from unequal conflict to glorious victory. Then it is that the serpent's head is bruised, and the conflict crowned with triumph. The battle of the ages is to end in His glorious coming. And the battle of the soul reaches its crisis likewise and rises to a shout of triumph when He comes in, its indwelling Lord and Victor.

## *MERCY BEFORE JUDGMENT*

5. The promise of redemption and the revelation of God's great plan of mercy are made to Adam and Eve before God proceeds to pass judgment upon them. This is infinitely gracious. And it affords us a little glimpse of His grace in His whole method of dealing with man.

How naturally we might expect Him to meet His disobedient children with indignation and severest judgment. How inexcusably had they abused their blessings, and all the kindness of His love and care! How recklessly had they thrown away their inheritance and all their hopes! How shamefully had they yielded themselves to the hands of His bitter adversary and dishonored Him before His enemy! And how utterly disappointing to His heart of love to find all of His purposes of blessing for the earth and man wrecked in a moment by the rashness and disobedience of those whom He had so richly blessed. He alone could fully understand the awful issues of this hour, the countless victims of their sin and folly, and the ages of misery and woe which they had in a moment ushered in. Surely it would have been a little thing had He stricken them in a moment from existence and indignantly closed the scene of human history forever.

But how different! Calmly, tenderly, He listens to their excuses and gives them every opportunity to justify or palliate the sin. Then He proceeds to pass judgment on the tempter, leaving for a little in abeyance their tremendous fault. And then, before one word of judgment has fallen on their heads, He unfolds, in the beautiful promise we have already explained, His wondrous plan of redeeming mercy. He does not even seem to be agitated, far less bewildered and defeated by their sin. He is perfectly prepared to meet all its emergencies. The remedy has been ready for ages, and He begins to unfold it in the hour that their sin and fall have made it necessary.

The Indians have a tradition that wherever the rattlesnake is found there always grows in the neighboring forests a little plant which is a certain antidote to the fatal sting. And so redemption springs in all its healing power amid the very earliest seeds of sin and misery, and God prepares His balm of healing even before the serpent has time to strike his fatal blow. How marvelous His resources! How wonderful His love! Nothing is too hard for the Lord. If any situation could have overwhelmed Him it was this. And the love and grace that so met and overcame it can meet all our needs and all our misery and sin.

So, again, we see this principle of mercy overcoming judgment in the story of Exodus. After God had given the law on Mount Sinai the people fell, within a few days, into the most fearful outbreak of idolatry. When Moses returned from the mount where he had been receiving the plan of the Tabernacle, he found a scene of surprising and abominable wickedness, and for a moment was utterly overwhelmed with amazement and indignation. But God, while not less displeased, was all ready for the fearful occasion. Indeed, He had for the past 40 days been wholly employed in preparing the remedy for the very thing which had now occurred, namely, the Tabernacle of mercy, which was to be to the sinning people the type of their atoning Savior, and the way of access for pardon and cleansing until His actual coming.

So still the gospel comes to sinful man along with the revelation of sin and misery, and the Spirit of grace seeks to awaken the consciousness of evil, only that He may heal it forever in the redeeming blood and grace of Christ. God does not wait until we deserve or even seek His grace, but He is "rich in mercy" (Ephesians 2:14), so that He loved us even when we were dead in sin.

## REDEMPTION THROUGH EVE

6. Redemption is revealed as to come through the woman, inasmuch as

she had been the channel of the temptation and the direct instrument of the fall. This is her high honor, and may well make her Savior doubly dear to her loving heart. Surely every woman ought to hate Satan and love the Lord Jesus Christ.

The mystery of the incarnation is distinctly foreshadowed in this promise; and the birth of Jesus, through the supernatural operation of the Holy Spirit in the womb of Mary, has lifted the humanity of Christ above the breath of human passion and earthly taint, and yet made Him the literal Brother of our race and partaker of our complete humanity in the fullest sense. It was necessary that He who bore our sins should be one of the sinful race, and that He in whom we stand as redeemed men should be Himself a man.

The perfect humanity of Christ is one of the essential foundations of redemption, and is demonstrated as completely by the story of His earthly life and the records of His infirmities and sensibilities and of all our needs and sufferings, as His deity is proved by His works of infinite wisdom and power.

## EVE'S NEW NAME

7. The plan of redemption already revealed in the words referred to, is so far understood and accepted by Adam that he gives to his wife the new name of Eve, which means "the living one," undoubtedly as an expression of faith in the promises which had been so signally linked with her seed. Accepting the hope of life through her person, and tenderly associating her with it, he calls her Eva, or *Havah*, no longer *Isha*. And thus, amid all the darkness and sorrow of the death that he had just incurred, he accepts the new hope of life, and begins to repose his trust in the coming Savior as truly, perhaps, as we do in the Savior who has already come.

## SYMBOLS OF REDEMPTION

8. God Himself now gives our first parents a number of beautiful and striking symbols of the gospel which He has already revealed in words.

### COATS OF SKINS

The first of these was the coats of skins with which He clothed their nakedness, taken, doubtless, from the sacrificial animals which they were now taught to offer in recognition of their sin and of the hope of salvation. We know that Abel offered such sacrifices soon after, and a divine warrant for the act must have been given before.

Why should it not have been just at this time? How natural that the covering of the bleeding victim, in which they saw at once the expression of their guilt and its punishment, should be made the type of their Savior's robe of righteousness.

## THE CHERUBIM

9. The cherubim of which we next read were still more significant emblems of redemption. We find that in the tabernacle and the visions of Ezekiel and John, they are linked with the representation of Christ so definitely as to leave no doubt of their being in some way types of His person and work, and of our hopes through Him.

Here they are placed at the gate of Eden to "guard the way to the tree of life" (Genesis 3:24). The idea seems to be that man was not permitted to partake of the tree of life in his natural state, through the old way of Eden, but by way of the cherubim he is to be permitted again to eat of that tree. And if this figure is the symbol of Christ and His redemption, the representation is most beautiful and instructive, teaching us that the life which man then received through natural sources, in his primeval state, shall be restored through the Lord Jesus Christ and His work of grace and salvation. So that as we receive Jesus as our life, we begin even here to partake of the tree of life, both for soul and body, and by and by, through Him, we shall receive all and more than all which Adam lost. That the cherubim did represent Christ and His complete redemption more distinctly than any mere qualities of the divine government is rendered more certain by the place which this figure occupied in the Hebrew tabernacle, as we shall see in Exodus. There the cherubic figures were formed out of the ark itself, or the mercy seat, which was the lid of the ark, being beaten out of the same piece of gold, and overshadowing it with their wings. This shows that whatever the meaning of the mercy seat and the ark is, the meaning of the cherubim must also be in keeping, and indeed identical. If the mercy seat represented Christ, as we know it did, in His propitiation and intercession, then the overshadowing figures which grew out of it must represent Christ in His exaltation and glory. How fitly this could be done by the four figures of a man, a lion, an ox and an eagle, is not hard to show. The first represented His perfect humanity; the second, His kingly majesty; the third, His sacrificial suffering and His infinite strength; and the fourth, His loftiness, His Deity and His exaltation to all the fullness of His mediatorial kingdom.

How beautiful that thus their coming Seed and Savior should be represented to the faith of our fallen parents. And if it were revealed to their apprehension, as it has been given to ours, that as He is so are we also, and that His glory is but a type of our destiny, how they must have rejoiced in that dark hour of shame and ruin to behold the vision of their future, spanning like a rainbow arch the black and gloomy cloud of that sad morning of sin and sorrow. How beautiful that God should begin the story of our race with such a vision of its future destiny. So also He begins for each of us the story of redemption, with the picture of our coming kingdom, and all the riches of His grace in His kindness towards us in Christ Jesus which, in the ages to come, He is forever to show.

## THE TREE OF LIFE

10. The Tree of Life is the last symbol of the new covenant in the garden of Eden. It had been the symbol, before the fall, of life, probably both physical and spiritual life. It is not removed even after the fall, from their view, but withdrawn from their touch, and so becomes to them the image of that new life into which they are to rise through the work of redemption.

That it should be limited to spiritual life seems arbitrary and unreasonable. Life, as we receive it in Christ, reaches our entire man, and quickens spirit, soul and body. This is Christ's great gift, eternal life; not in the sense of beginning in eternity, but in the sense of lifting us even in time into *that which is eternal* both in its nature and duration. Even here we may receive the life of the future, and receive in some measure the very breath of the resurrection morning in soul and body, through Him who is our Life, and in whom we live also, and look for deeper, fuller life forevermore. Let us cease to look for life, henceforth, through the old avenues of our fallen nature, or any of the trees of the garden. Let us seek it wholly through the way of the cherubim, and through His Person who is our new and living Way, and opens to us from the gates of Eden the way to the holy of holies, and the innermost presence of the glory of God.

This idea of the holy of holies was expressed in the ancient cherubim at Eden's gate, as well as in the tabernacle. The Hebrew word used with respect to the cherubim is the word *Shekinah*. "He placed on the east side of the Garden of Eden cherubim and a flaming sword" (3:24). It was the same Shekinah glory that afterwards shone in the inner chamber of God's sanctuary. And it represented to the faith of Adam and Eve the same conception of God's heavenly presence and glory to which henceforth fallen man is permitted to rise through the person and work of the Lord Jesus Christ.

## SECTION II—*Development of Redemption in the Remaining Chapters of Genesis*

The plan of redemption thus revealed in its simplest germs to our fallen parents, grows more distinct and full in the subsequent chapters of this wonderful book. We trace this in three particulars:

### 1. Promises
Genesis 17:7; 49:10

The promise made to Adam and Eve is renewed repeatedly in the succeeding generations.

## ABRAHAM'S GOSPEL

First we see it unmistakably in the covenant with Abraham (Genesis 17:7). This might seem to the casual reader to be simply the prediction of Abraham's posterity. But the Apostle Paul through the Holy Spirit tells us that the word "seed" was intentionally used in the singular number to denote Christ personally. "The Scripture does not say 'and to seeds,' meaning many people, but 'and to your seed,' meaning one person, who is Christ" (Galatians 3:16). And in the context he declares that God preached the gospel unto Abraham, and that our very hopes are linked with His ancient covenant. "So those who have faith are blessed along with Abraham, the man of faith" (3:9).

## THE PROMISED SHILOH

Again, the promise becomes still more definite. It is not now the seed of the woman, or even the seed of Abraham, but the seed of Judah. But it is the same faithful, victorious Conqueror that we saw in the promise of the fall, with His mighty heel on the serpent's head, the true Lion of the tribe of Judah. "The scepter will not depart from Judah,/ nor the ruler's staff from between his feet,/ until he [Shiloh, KJV] comes to whom it belongs" (Genesis 49:10).

We have passed over the testimony of Enoch, which Jude tells us was also the promise of a coming Savior, with special reference to His second advent and His millennial glory. "See, the Lord is coming with thousands upon thousands of his holy ones" (Jude 14). This, though not recorded in Genesis, was undoubtedly known to the antediluvians as the Gospel of Enoch, and reveals a much fuller knowledge of the plan of redemption than appears upon the record. We might also find a reference to Christ in the prophecy of Noah: "Blessed be the LORD, the God of Shem," and again, "May [he, KJV] Japheth live in the tents of Shem" (Genesis 9:26–27). The "he" of the King James translation is by many believed to refer to Christ rather than to Japheth.

## 2. Sacrifices
### Genesis 4:1–5; 8:20–22; 15:9–18

We have already seen that the coats of skins in Genesis 3 were connected with animal sacrifices in recognition of sin and atonement. We find the sacrificial altar henceforth at every important stage of the patriarchal history.

## ABEL'S SACRIFICE

In Genesis 4:1–5, it is the center of the first act of religious worship in the Bible, as though it were fully established and accepted as God's appointed way of access. We find Abel, "at the end of days," that is the Sabbath day, coming with his bleeding offering as an expression of his obedience and faith; and the seal of God's approval is publicly and solemnly placed upon his act of obedient faith. His offering, as well as his own subsequent death, becomes the type of the great Sacrifice of Calvary.

Cain brings far richer gifts, but they are the fruit of the sin-cursed earth and the works of his own defiled hands, and they are rejected by the Lord, and the offerer too.

## NOAH'S ALTAR

Next, in Genesis 8:20, the altar of Noah marks another crisis in the world's history, and seals the covenant which God establishes with the remnant of the race for the next dispensation. For ages the world had reeked with abominable iniquities, and after long months of judgment it had become a charnel house of death and horror. But at last the floods of wickedness had been swept away by the waves of judgment, and even these have now subsided, and Noah's little household steps forth from the sheltering ark which has carried them through the fearful crisis.

His first act is to rear an altar and offer upon it the sacrifices that he has brought from the ark. This was not the first time he had sacrificed, for the number of clean animals that he had taken in with him at the beginning implies that some of them were undoubtedly for sacrifice. But this public act receives the special seal of God's approval.

What a beautiful answer to the ignorant objections of man's carnal reasonings against the unnaturalness and harshness of a religion that is based on the shedding of blood! As the crimson stains bathe the rude altar, and as the smoke ascends up to heaven, it is finely added, "The LORD smelled the pleasing aroma and said in his heart: 'Never again will I curse the ground because of man, even though every inclination of his heart is evil from childhood' " (8:21).

It would seem as though God made up His mind to expect nothing good from man in himself, and accepted the sacrifice of His Beloved Son instead; for His sake not only forgiving, but lovingly accepting the soul that trusts Him, as a sweet savor of Christ. And then to emphasize the lesson, and honor the offering more gloriously, suddenly He spans the gorgeous arch of the rainbow, like the very smile of heaven, above the smoking altar, as a token of His covenant of everlasting love and peace.

## ABRAHAM'S SACRIFICE AND VISION

We pass on to the next period, and find the altar and sacrifice again in the life of Abraham and amid all the vicissitudes of the patriarchal tent life. The covenant with Noah was not so important as the one that here is ratified by sacrifice again. That was for temporal, but this is for enduring spiritual blessings; and it, too, is sealed by the shedding of blood, looking forward like previous sacrifices to the great atonement.

In Genesis 15:9 the sacrificial scene is vividly described. First He points to the starry heavens and renews the promise of the future. Then the victims are selected: a heifer, a she-goat, a ram, a dove and a little bird, perhaps a sparrow, in connection with which we afterwards find the most precious of the Levitical offerings. Separating them asunder, and leaving an open space between the parts, Abraham places them before the Lord, and then waits for the token of the divine acceptance. The birds of prey swoop down upon the altar, but the patriarch guards its precious deposit, and watches until the evening shadows have gathered about him. Then upon his senses there falls a deep sleep and a strange darkness, out of which the vision comes of a smoking furnace and a lamp of fire, which passes through the midst of the sacrifice as a seal of the divine acceptance and a symbol of the events which are to be connected with the future of his race, especially the furnace of Egyptian sufferings, and the pillar of cloud and fire that shall lead them forth from its trials.

Then came again the voice of God, unfolding in all the fullness of detail the promise of the inheritance, and the limits of the land which Abraham's seed shall possess. So we see that the sacrifice of Christ is the bond of our covenant and the pledge of our inheritance.

## OUR LIVING SACRIFICE

And in all this beautiful picture we may behold not only the offering of Jesus Christ, but also the consecration of the living sacrifice of our own heart and being, which we, too, must lay naked and open at the feet of our Lord, guard from the birds of temptation that would snatch it from the altar and then watch for the seal and manifestation of the Divine Presence.

This manifestation may come to us in deep darkness, and may bring the furnace of suffering, but it will be followed by the lamp of living fire, the baptism of the Holy Spirit, the covenant of God's eternal faithfulness, and all the fullness and blessedness of our land of promise, and our spiritual inheritance.

We need not dwell upon the subsequent references to sacrifice in the book of Genesis, further than to notice that the altar reappeared in the life of Isaac and the wanderings of Jacob, as the expression of their faith and the center of their religious life and worship, and was to them undoubtedly the symbol of all they knew and claimed of the coming redemption.

## 3. Types

More fully even than in the words of promise and in the sacrificial rites of the ancient dispensation, do we see the unfolding of redemption in its marvelous types. These are figures more manifest to us than they were to their own age. And the apostle implies this when he says "they were written down as warnings for us, on whom the fulfillment of the ages has come" (1 Corinthians 10:11). These types are of two classes, namely, persons and things.

## PERSONAL TYPES

### ABEL

The first of the personal types in Genesis is Abel: The child of weakness and frailty, as his name implies, the shepherd, obedient, faithful and righteous. He is called by Christ Himself "righteous Abel" (Matthew 23:35). Hated by his brother, at last slain by Cain's wicked hands because of his faith and testimony, and spilling his innocent blood upon the ground as a cry to heaven against him, he is the vivid type of Him who was born in lowliness, as "a root out of a dry ground" (Isaiah 53:2). Christ is the great Shepherd of His flock, the faithful and true Servant, the hated and persecuted Victim of His brethren, at last crucified and slain, and pouring out His precious blood as an appeal to heaven, not against sin but for the sinner, and a cry for mercy rather than for vengeance, whose blood "speaks a better word than the blood of Abel" (Hebrews 12:24).

### ISAAC

The next personal type of the coming Savior is Isaac. In two respects he strikingly foreshadows his greater Seed.

First, his sacrifice on Mount Moriah is the figure of Christ's great offering by His Father's hand and his restoration, of Christ's resurrection. He was given back from the dead in a figure, and the figure was of Christ's rising again. And secondly, the marriage of Isaac to his sole wife, with all the beautiful and typical circumstances which accompanied Rebekah's wooing and wedding, foreshadows the call of Christ's Church and the marriage of the Lamb to His Bride.

### MELCHIZEDEK

The next personal type of Christ in the patriarchal age was Melchizedek, whose figure stands out in strange isolation from his race and time like a form suspended from the sky. The apostle says he was "without father or mother, without genealogy, without beginning of days or end of life, like the Son of God, he remains a priest forever" (Hebrews 7:3). This can scarcely mean that Melchizedek was literally without parentage or descent, but that his pedigree is lost in oblivion, and that his isolation makes him a vivid type of the great Redeemer.

There are some who believe that he was literally an incarnation of Christ, the Son of God dwelling on earth for a time, even as he appeared to Abraham in the plains of Mamre in visible form, and ate and drank and talked with him. This we can scarcely accept without stronger proof than plausible inferences. But certainly he was a type of Christ, in his priesthood and kingliness and in his two gracious gifts of righteousness and peace. These four ideas were distinctly expressed by the name Melchizedek, and his two offices, as king of Salem and priest of the Most High God, Melchizedek meaning king of righteousness, and Salem signifying peace. No four words can express more fully the redeeming work and grace of Jesus: subduing and guarding us as our King; redeeming and representing us as our Priest; clothing us with His righteousness; and blessing us with His perfect peace.

## JOSEPH

The most beautiful of all the personal types in Genesis is Joseph. He represents the Lord Jesus Christ as the beloved son of his father, the victim of his brethren's hate and cruelty, betrayed, innocently suffering for the sins of others, separated from his father for long years, treated as a criminal, living a life of toil and humiliation, and suffering almost every possible privation and wrong in blameless innocence, and then suddenly and gloriously exalted to be a prince and a savior, and using his honor and power for the good of others and the salvation of the world.

Preeminently does Joseph prefigure Christ as the loving and forgiving Brother, bringing us tenderly and faithfully to the sense of our sin and then generously forgiving us and helping us to forget our faults, reconciling us by His love, receiving us to His fellowship, and sharing with us all the resources and riches of His grace and glory.

## TYPICAL THINGS

Besides these personal types of Christ in Genesis, we have several typical things that are fitted to foreshadow His redeeming work.

## THE ARK

The ark was the type of the way in which He shelters us from the judgment of sin and hides us from the storms of life, carrying us through our spiritual death and resurrection, and bearing us through the tempests of life to the shores of that blessed kingdom where the covenant of Noah shall find its full realization in the glories of the ages to come, and the new heavens and earth.

## THE DOVE AND THE RAINBOW

Not only the ark, but the other emblems connected with the ark, the dove and the rainbow, all prefigure great spiritual truths in connection with the gospel. The former represents the Holy Spirit in the several stages of His coming, both to the world and to the heart, and the latter foreshadows the vision of the Apocalypse, when the rainbow round about the throne shall be the token of accomplished redemption, and the consummation of all the hopes and destinies of redeemed humanity.

## THE MYSTIC LADDER

The ladder of Jacob is also a beautiful figure of the new and living way which Christ has come to open between earth and heaven through His own person, and which He Himself has told us is the significance of the vision of Bethel (John 1:51).

Thus even in this early form do we see the grace of God beginning to unfold. And still more fully, no doubt, it was revealed to the believers of that time. For we know that they are linked with us in the household of faith, and have risen out of the sins and sorrows of their earthly experience to the inheritance of the saints in light by the same pathway which we are treading now, and through the grace of the same great Redeemer, who has been the Hope of all the ages, and shall be the object of their adoring love, and ours, throughout the cycles of eternity.

# CHAPTER 5

## THE BEGINNING OF THE NATIONS

### Genesis 4:16–26; 6:1–5; 9:25–29; 10:1–11:26

#### SECTION I—*The Antediluvian Nations*
#### Genesis 4:16–26; 6:1–5

The human race divided immediately into two distinct families, the first and the older from the race of Cain, the second in the line of Seth. The Cainites became the representatives of the world, the Sethites, the professed followers of the true God.

### THE CITY OF CAIN

The former soon gathered into a civil community and peopled the first city of human history. It became the center of earthly culture, wealth and wickedness. There originated the earliest arts and manufactures, the first artificers in brass and iron, the first great musicians and the first proprietors of wealth and worldly estate.

### CULTURE AND CRIME

The very names of the women of the race of Cain are expressive of earthly beauty and sensuous pleasure. Ada, Zillah and Naamah signify beauty, music and sweetness; but the culmination was bloodshed and violence. Beginning with the murderer, Cain himself, we soon meet a spirit of more daring and boastful crime in his immediate descendants, in the song of Lamech, "I have killed a man for wounding me, a young man for injuring me. If Cain is avenged seven times, truly Lamech seventy-seven times" (Genesis 4:23).

In a few centuries the wickedness of this race has grown into such enormous proportions that God can no longer endure it, and the deluge comes to purge the earth of its hideous and abominable burden.

## THE FAMILY OF SETH

The race of Seth stands for a while apart from the godless world, and openly professes the name and worship of Jehovah. "At that time men began to call on the name of the LORD" (4:26), or rather "to call themselves by the name of the LORD," as the margin reads, that is, to profess the true religion, and to recognize their dependence upon the fellowship with a living and present God. This we see beautifully exemplified a little later in the most distinguished link in this line, the godly Enoch.

## UNHOLY ALLIANCE

After a few generations, however, the two races mingled in defiance of the divine purpose that there should be enmity between the seed of the woman and the seed of the serpent. The sons of God (6:2) are attracted by the beauty of the daughters of men, and the races unite in ungodly marriages, the fruit of which soon appears in a very high state of physical culture and strength, but the most desperate moral and spiritual corruption, until the earth is filled with violence (6:5). This age closes with the catastrophe of the flood, and a new generation commences afresh the story of human history on the other side.

## SECTION II—*The Family of Noah*
### Genesis 9:25–29

The race really begins anew in Noah as it had in Adam. And God renews His covenant with the patriarch not only for himself, but for his posterity, giving him the same blessings in natural things He had to Adam, and adding new promises and covenants with special reference to the security of the earth from the repetition of the awful judgment that had just engulfed it. The old benediction, "Be fruitful and increase in number; fill the earth" (1:28), is repeated, as is the old dominion given over the animal creation, with the permission to use animal food, and the most solemn sanctions in regard to the protection of human life. And the rainbow arch is made the token and seal of the promise that the flood waters shall no more destroy the race.

The three sons of Noah are constituted the respective heads of the three great divisions of the human race, which are henceforth to spread abroad to the east, the west and the south. All ethnological and philological researches lead us back to three great original races—the Aryan, Semitic and Turanian, thus confirming the threefold development of the race from the family of Noah, and from the three heads, Japheth, Shem and Ham.

## NOAH'S PROPHECY

The future of the three lines is foreshadowed by the prophecy of Noah (Genesis 9:24–27). Commencing with the family of Ham, the prophecy refers especially to the line of Canaan, his son, and pronounces upon him and his race what has ever since been literally fulfilled. The subjection and destruction of the Canaanites by Joshua, the overthrow of Carthage by the Roman power, and the sad story of the African race even down to our own time, are but instances of its wider fulfillment. The race of Shem is especially distinguished in the prophetic vision by their religious privileges. Jehovah is to be their God, and to dwell in their tents. This has been fulfilled in the selection of the seed of Abraham as God's covenant people, and the religious privileges and glorious hopes which are linked with the future of the chosen race.

The prophecy respecting Japheth indicates great national prosperity and a multiplied posterity, "May God extend the territory of Japheth" (9:27). Dr. Young translates it, "God gave beauty to Japheth." The descendants of Japheth comprise more than half of the human family, and the most cultivated, civilized and powerful nations of the earth.

The promise, "He shall dwell in the tents of Shem," may mean either God or Japheth. If the former, it has already been fulfilled in the manifestation of Jehovah to the Jewish people, and the coming of Christ to dwell among them in His incarnation and earthly life. If the latter, it signifies that which has been so literally fulfilled, the fact that the Gentiles have superseded the family of Shem in their religious privileges, and have entered their tents as the heirs of their covenant blessings, and of their worldly place and power. Even the political control of human history has passed from the Semitic race to the line of Japheth, and the tents of Shem are possessed by his brother in almost every part of the globe.

## SECTION III—*The 70 Nations which Sprang from the Family of Noah*
### Genesis 10:1–11:26

The genealogical tree of humanity, starting from the confines of the flood, spreads first into three great trunks, and then speedily becomes subdivided into 70 smaller branches which thus form the genealogical sources of the various races which have since peopled the world. This division into 70 is not accidental, but carries with it the idea of completeness, which is suggested even by the numbers which comprise it (7 x 10). The Jews were accustomed to speak of the 70 nations as comprising the human family.

The names of these several lines are preserved in the 10th chapter of Genesis and form a sort of chart of ethnology of which we have still many traces even in our most familiar geographical and historical names.

## THE FAMILY OF JAPHETH

Fourteen of these names comprise the line of Japheth. Thirty are found in the family of Ham. The remaining 26 belong to the Semitic race.

The first of the Japhetic tribes springs from Gomer. It is not hard to trace this name in the races afterwards known as Cimmerian, Cimbri, etc., and such geographical names as Crimea, Cumberland, and Cambridge.

Magog was the sacred progenitor of the Japhetic tribes, and his home was beyond the Caucasian mountains. His race is connected with the races of Tubal and Meshech in the prophecies of Ezekiel (chapters 27, 28, 29). This identifies them with the races to which those names refer, and which we know are connected with the inhabitants of Russia. These names, Tubal and Meshech, we find repeated in Tobolsk, the capital of Siberia, Moscow, Muscovite and other familiar Russian names.

Madai was the father of the Medes, Javan of the Ionians or Greeks, Tiras of the Thracians and the people of the Taurus mountains; Ashkenaz has left his name in the Euxine Sea, and, perhaps, in the continent of Asia.

Riphath reappears in the Rhiphoean mountains near the Black Sea. Elishah is the source of the word Elis or Hellas, the district of the Peloponnesus where his descendants settled. Tarshish was the colonizer of the Tartessus and Tarshish in Spain. Kittim left his name in Chittim and the islands of Cyprus and Italy. Dodanim is recognized in Dardania, a district of Illyricum, and some think in the name Rhodanus, the ancient name of the river Rhone, thus connecting his descendants with the people of France.

## HAMITIC RACE

Of the Hamites, Cush peopled the Assyrian plain and left his son Nimrod as its proud despot, and then migrating south gave his name to Ethiopia, where monuments as old as the sixth dynasty of Egypt have been found bearing his name.

Mizraim's name frequently reappears as a geographical term in Egypt. Phut is found in Nahum 3:9, in alliance with African tribes, and the city of But or Butor on the delta of the Nile perhaps retains his name. Canaan moved westward and settled in the land of Canaan, where 11 tribes are mentioned as the early inhabitants of the land. In the second and third generations of the Hamitic family, the names of Saba, Havilah, Sabtah, Raamah and Sheba are identified with regions in Arabia, and suggest many familiar names that have been derived from these early ancestors. Dedan is still found in the island of Daden in the Persian Gulf.

## NIMROD AND BABEL

A little episode now breaks the genealogical line, and the historian pauses at the name of Nimrod, who stands out as the most prominent figure of this ancient period. His name means *a rebel,* and the expression "before the LORD" (Genesis 10:9) seems to imply the proud defiance which neither regarded God or man, and finally sought in Babel's tower to entrench himself even against the heavens. It would seem at this period that God had given a commandment to the human family to disperse in various directions, and thus occupy the whole earth. We read a little later that it was in the days of Peleg that the earth was divided (10:25), and perhaps he was commanded or commissioned to deliver and execute the divine message to that effect. Nimrod, however, refused to comply with the divine order, and attempted to establish an exalted empire around the city of Babel, comprising a quadrilateral with the cities of Erech, Accad and Calneh which afterwards formed the framework of the great Babylonian empire.

His impious attempt to build the tower of Babel was frustrated by God's miraculous interposition and the confusion of human languages, compelling the rebellious tribes to obey the divine command and disperse over the unoccupied earth. Nimrod went forth from his blasted ruin and formed another empire farther east and north, around the great city of Nineveh, where the excavated mounds are today unveiling the marvelous confirmations of God's ancient Word.

Between these two centers, Nineveh and Babylon, the sovereignty of the world long alternated, and the name of Babylon has come to represent in type and mystery the last forms of the world's consolidated opposition to the kingdom of God in connection with which the last conflict of the ages shall come, between rebellious man and his righteous and long-dishonored Maker.

## OTHER HAMITIC TRIBES

Returning to the catalog of nations, the sons of Mizraim, namely, the Ludim, the Amamim, the Lehabim, the Naphtuhim, the Pathrusim, the Cashluhim, the Philistim and the Caphtorim, recall to our minds the Libyans of Africa, the names of Memphis and Pathros in Africa, the Colcheans of ancient Egypt, the Philistines, the name of Palestine and the Copts of Egypt.

## THE CANAANITES

The sons of Canaan have left their traces still more definitely on later times. Sidon founded the great Phoenician capital that bears his name. Heth was the head of the Hittites, so well known. The Jebusite was the first inhabitant of Jebus, or Jerusalem. The Amorite, in the days of Joshua, ruled seven of the great kingdoms of Canaan. The Girgasites, perhaps, have left their names in the land of the Gergashines. The Hivite, Arkite and Sinite can be traced in the region of Lebanon, in the city of Tel Arka and the stronghold of Sinas. The Arvadite is remembered by the town of Arvad in Phoenicia. The Zinite appears in Simra west of Lebanon. And the Hamathite gave his name to the great land of Hamath with the cities of Riblah, Antioch and Hamath on the Orontes.

## SEMITIC PEOPLES

Shem's descendants next claim our attention. Elam was the founder of the nations inhabiting the district that comprises Persia, which was called by the name of Assyria. Asshur was the ancient inhabitant of Assyria. Arphaxad settled in northern Assyria, and from his line came the chosen seed of Abraham. Lud was the ancestor of the Lydians of Asia Minor. Aram was the father of the Arameans and Mesopotamians; and the Syriac and Chaldaic languages are called the Aramaic. Uz, the son of Aram, was the ancestor of Job, and the name reappears in the home of this patriarch. Hul settled near the sources of the Jordan, where Huleh is still found. Gether is identified with Geshur, the refuge of Absalom, in Syria. Mash was the father of the Mysians, the people of Troy. Eber was probably the progenitor of the Hebrews. Peleg, his son, was the one through whom the earth was divided and colonized. Joktan was the progenitor of the Arabian tribes, and the names of his descendants are nearly all preserved in Arabian localities, which it is not necessary to trace in detail. Sheba, Ophir and others are made familiar by later allusions in the sacred Scriptures.

These various tribes in the line of Shem occupied a circumscribed place, compared either with the Japhethites or Hamites, being chiefly limited to Mesopotamia and Palestine; but from their narrow limits, all the world's true light has gone forth, until their brethren have been glad to dwell under its beams, and Japheth has come to reside in the tents of Shem.

## SECTION IV—*Subsequent Development of the Nations*

We have already referred to the ambitious achievements of Nimrod, and his great world empire—the founding of Babylon, Nineveh, and the neighboring cities whose monuments and ruins still attest their ancient power and glory; and also to the dispersion of the nations in the time of Peleg, probably by divine revelation and afterwards the enforcement of the divine purpose by the confounding of human languages.

## A DIVINE PLAN

All through the Scriptures we trace a distinct divine purpose in connection with the location and distribution of the various nations. The Word of God distinctly declares that when the Most High divided the nations, He placed the bounds of their habitation with reference to His chosen people and His plan of providence and redemption (Deuteronomy 32:8). In Acts 17:26–27, the apostle declared to the ethnologists of Athens that "From one man he made every nation of men, that they should inhabit the whole earth; and he determined the times set for them and the exact places where they should live. God did this so that men would seek him and perhaps reach out for him and find him, though he is not far from each one of us."

The enterprises of human ambition have been permitted and overruled by the hand of God for the working out of His will.

## THE WORLD EMPIRES

In the later centuries we find the nations crystallizing under successive empires, aspiring to universal dominion and reaching it at length. In the colossal world powers of Daniel's vision, four great empires appear arrayed against the kingdom of God. There were two others which were not included in Daniel's vision, but had already finished their career, namely, Egypt and Assyria. The next four were Babylon, Medo-Persia, Greece and Rome. The series is closed with the mystical Babylon of the visions of Daniel and John. Then shall come the kingdom of our Lord and Savior Jesus Christ and His glorified saints, which shall never pass away, and the earth at length shall be ruled in peace and righteousness and rescued from the wrongs and oppressions of the ages of the past.

## THEIR BEASTLY SYMBOLS

There is a dark figure associated with all earth's national developments. In the vision of the Apocalypse they are represented as great beasts rising out of the troubled sea, and a dragon gives to each his authority and power. They are all Satan's counterfeits, and his attempts to be a god and rule instead of God on earth.

The world will never have good government until all its monarchies and republics have been superseded by the everlasting kingdom of our God and His Christ.

## SECTION V—Hybrid Races

Several of these, sprung from the chosen seed, but not in the direct line of the Covenant, appear in the book of Genesis. First, there is the Ishmaelite race which culminates in the Arab tribes, one of the most singular peoples of human history. Next, come the wicked tribes of Ammon and Moab, descended from the unnatural daughters of Lot.

Next, we have the Edomites, who came from Esau and occupied for many centuries a prominent place in close connection with the kingdom of Judah. And later, the Samaritans arose from the mingling of the Jewish remnant after the captivity, with the population of Assyrian colonists imported by the conqueror into Palestine.

# CHAPTER 6

## THE BEGINNING OF THE HEBREW RACE

### Genesis 11:16–12:9

The time has now come when humanity is to make its third departure. The first was under Adam, the head of the entire race. The second was the Covenant with Noah. And now the third begins with Abraham, the 10th generation after Noah, who becomes the head, not of the entire race, but of a separate people, chosen out of all the families of men, to be the special depository of divine truth and the witnesses for God and the true religion throughout the coming ages; and also to form a clear genealogical line for the advent of the promised Seed.

### SECTION I—*The Origin of the Hebrews*

#### THE ANCESTRY

1. Their most distant ancestor was Eber, the grandson of Arphaxad, and the great-great-grandson of Shem, on the one side; and on the other the sixth lineal ancestor of Abraham. The name Eber has given to the race their name of Hebrews. It signifies emigrant, or one who has crossed the river, the reference being to those who had come over the river, or from beyond the river Euphrates, westward and southward.

#### THE CALL OF ABRAHAM

2. The call of Abraham was the next step. It came to him in Mesopotamia, where he had already acquired valuable possessions and occupied a position of influence. The remains which recent excavations have discovered have shown that the region of Mesopotamia, from which he emigrated, had at that time reached a very high degree of culture and wealth.

And Abraham's city, Ur, was one of the two chief centers of Chaldean civilization.

His ancestors, however, and family, were idolaters, as we learn from Joshua 24:2, "Long ago your forefathers . . . lived beyond the River and worshiped other gods. But I took your father Abraham from the land beyond the River and led him throughout Canaan, and gave him many descendants."

God came to Abraham in a special divine revelation, as we learn from the words of Stephen (Acts 7:2): "The God of glory appeared to our father Abraham while he was still in Mesopotamia, before he lived in Haran. 'Leave your country and your people,' God said, 'and go to the land I will show you.'" This call was accompanied by the promise, "I will make you into a great nation/ and I will bless you;/ I will make your name great,/ and you will be a blessing./ I will bless those who bless you,/ and whoever curses you I will curse;/ and all peoples on earth/ will be blessed through you" (Genesis 12:2–3).

## SEPARATION

3. This call involved Abraham's separation from his country, from his friends, and from his home. And henceforth the word separation is one of the keynotes of the patriarch's life, as it is the specific idea of the Jewish people. Separated first from all his former ties, he is afterwards separated, step by step, from every earthly thing: from the inhabitants of the land to which he came; from his nephew Lot; from Hagar and Ishmael; and even at last, from the child of promise, in the final sacrifice of his dearest affections and hopes on the altar of Moriah. He was thus the fitting ancestor of a people who were to embody the idea of separation from the world and dedication to God as His peculiar people.

## COVENANT

4. Next followed the Covenant promise, which included three great particulars, namely:

First, the literal seed, which should be as numerous as the sand upon the seashore (Genesis 13:16), meant, undoubtedly, to be the type of the earthly seed.

Secondly, the great Personal Seed, the Lord Jesus Christ and His spiritual offspring, including the children of faith to the latest generation, signified by the stars of heaven (Genesis 15:5).

Thirdly, the land of Canaan as an everlasting possession (Genesis 13:15). This is yet to be literally fulfilled in the restoration of Israel, and their eternal possession of the land of covenant promise (Genesis 15:18, 17:8, 24:7, 26:4; Numbers 34:12; Deuteronomy 34:4; Acts 7:5; 2 Chronicles 20:7; Psalm 112:2).

## SECTION II—*The Purpose of God in the Separation of the Hebrew Race*

### A PECULIAR PEOPLE

1. To preserve and educate a holy and peculiar people for Himself. The original purpose of God, announced in the first promise of redemption that there would be enmity between the seed of the woman and the seed of the serpent, had been constantly disregarded hitherto.

The race of Seth had soon become blended by intermarriage with the godless world, and the deluge was chiefly caused by the wickedness which resulted from this intermingling. In a little while the memories of that awful judgment were obliterated; and a knowledge of the true God, and a life of faith and godliness, seemed likely to perish from the earth in the overflowing tides of human selfishness and ungodliness.

It was, therefore, indispensable that some portion of humanity should be separated from the mass, if the true religion was to be preserved. This was for the next 2,000 years the design of the Jewish Theocracy, and this is the specific character of the Christian Church. Its very name, "Ecclesia," means "called out," and it ceases to be the Church of Christ when it becomes conformed to and mingled with the ungodly and evil world.

The Jewish people are still separated from other nations as one of the miracles of divine providence, for the further ends which are still to be accomplished in connection with the divine plan.

### THE ORACLES OF GOD

2. To receive and preserve the oracles of God, the revelation of His will, His covenants with His people, His written word, and the ordinances of revealed religion. The service rendered to future ages in this regard by the Jewish people is invaluable and incalculable. This the apostle mentions as the chief advantage of the Jews, that "they have been entrusted with the very words of God" (Romans 3:2). We owe to them the very records we are now studying, and the later Scriptures which they so reverently guarded and so zealously transmitted to succeeding generations. To them also we owe the divine law, the types and ordinances of divine worship, the holy Sabbath, and, indeed, all we know of the true and living God.

### THE LINEAGE OF CHRIST

3. To furnish an ancestry for the Lord Jesus Christ in a clear prophetic line which could be a divine credential to His heavenly character and true commission. This is the highest distinction of the Jew—that he has given to us the ideal Man, the true Head of the human race, and the Hope of all

races, the Desire of all nations; and that by his own sacred writings and the genealogical tables of the past, he has made it certain to us that this Man is the very one that has been promised from the beginning, as the true Head of humanity and the very Heir of Israel's highest honors and royal throne.

Let us never forget, as we look upon the Jew, that he is the brother of Jesus of Nazareth and has given to us our precious Savior and dearest Friend.

## THE LIGHT OF THE WORLD

4. To be not only the depository of truth and religion for future times, but also the light of the world in their own times, and throughout the dark ages of the Old Testament. From Jerusalem went forth all the light the world possessed for 10 centuries. It is probable that the teachings of Moses had a much wider influence on surrounding nations and on the ideas and philosophies of ancient heathen people than can be now fully traced, so that much of what seemed an approximation of truth in the writings of ancient literature was a reflection of the divine light which shone through God's ancient people.

The influence of their national life in its purer days under Joshua, Samuel, David, Solomon, Jehoshaphat, Hezekiah, Josiah and the results of the teaching and example of their great prophets, and even isolated individuals, such as Elijah, Elisha, Jonah, Daniel in Babylon, Esther in Persia and others like them were immeasurably important, and influenced the history of these nations to a degree of which we can form some idea from the place which Daniel occupied in Babylon, and the regard which Cyrus showed the captive Jews of his mighty empire.

## AN OBJECT LESSON TO THE AGES

5. To be a monument and an example of God's faithfulness, holiness, and mercy, and of the principles of divine government as exemplified in His dealing with this nation through all the period of their history. Even in their bitterest trials they are the divine epistle read and known of all men, showing forth to the world and the future the righteousness of God in His judgments upon sin, the faithfulness of God in fulfilling His promises, and the long-suffering and patience of God in bearing long with sin and making His grace more signal in the light of man's provocations and unworthiness.

What invaluable lessons and illustrations of truth and righteousness have been given to the world in the record of His dealing:

- with the patriarchs;
- with Israel in their redemption from Egypt and their life in the wilderness;
- with Joshua and those that entered into the land;

- amid the declensions of His people during the 400 years of the Judges;
- with Saul, David and Solomon;
- amid the innumerable vicissitudes of the later stages of the divided Hebrew kingdom down to the captivity of Judah and the dissolution of Israel, and still later in the varying scenes of the Captivity and the Restoration.

How vividly can we see the great principles of divine righteousness, the fruits of sin, the glory of true living, the mercy and faithfulness of God, as this ever-changing kaleidoscope of human character and divine government moves before the eye of faith as a drama of life and a living object lesson of a moral and spiritual teaching.

Not even the New Testament contains anything like the fullness of character teaching and personal illustration of the principles of divine truth, which we find in these records. The New Testament contains the principles which they illustrate much more fully and clearly. But we must go back to the Old for their vivid and varied illustration.

Not for themselves did these ancient generations move across the stage of time. They have been made a spectacle unto angels and unto men. For us they erred and suffered. For us they lived and died. And even their sins and sorrows have become an invaluable heritage of holy instruction for us "on whom the fulfillment of the ages has come" (1 Corinthians 10:11).

### SECTION III—*Subdivisions of Hebrew History and Subsequent Developments*

The history of the seed of Abraham has been variously divided by different expositors and historians. The following seems to be as simple and complete as any analysis that can be made:

**First**—The Patriarchal Stage, in which God dealt with them as with a family.

**Second**—The Mosaic Period, in which God emancipated them as a race.

**Third**—The Theocratic Period, from Joshua to Samuel, in which God dealt with them as a nation of which He was the direct King.

**Fourth**—The Monarchial Period, from Saul to Solomon, in which God constituted them into a human kingdom.

**Fifth**—The Divided Monarchy, from Rehoboam down to the dissolution of Israel, and the captivity of Judah, in which God suffered them to be broken into two kingdoms, and yet maintained covenant relations and dealings with both, through His prophets and messengers.

**Sixth**—The Captivity during a period of 70 years, in which God dealt with them in discipline as disobedient people.

**Seventh**—The Restoration Period under Zerubbabel, Ezra and Nehemiah, and the centuries following, which might be called the time of Expectation.

**Eighth**—The Messianic Period, during which God came to them personally in His promised Son, fulfilling the prophecies of the past and offering to them the blessings of the gospel, only to be rejected and crucified and compelled to reject His apostate people and deliver them over to the ages of judgment and sorrow, which have since been completing the record of their strange and eventful history.

## SECTION IV—*Present Condition of the Hebrew Race*

1. They are still preserved as a separate people, distinct from all other races; and manifestly preserved in their isolation for some great, divine purpose yet to be fulfilled.

2. Notwithstanding ages of unparalleled cruelty, injustice and inhumanity, they remain in undiminished numbers, one of the most vigorous races of the human family. Indeed, they are rapidly increasing, and their population today probably equals that of their most prosperous history at any period in the past, while their influence and wealth are preeminently beyond proportion as compared with the nations among whom they dwell. They are the leaders in literature and journalism in many of the European nations. They are the financial kings of the world, and they are compelling the respect, and even fear, of the Gentile communities where they are scattered abroad.

3. They are distributed in almost every nation under heaven, as an evident part of the divine plan in their future destiny. Thus they touch all the springs of modern government, know all the languages of earth, have access to all the channels of human life and influence. Should they be converted to Christianity, there is no instrumentality on earth that could so suddenly and effectually be made available for the evangelization of the entire world.

4. The great leaders of the nation still remain in unbelief, growing still more persistent in their antagonism to Christianity, or their indifference to any truly spiritual religion, and yet remaining steadfast to the faith and traditions of their ancient covenant.

5. According to the divine Word there remains and has ever existed during the Christian centuries, a little remnant according to the election of grace; a few out of the many who from time to time are led to turn from unbelief and accept the true Messiah. This number has been considerably increased in recent years. And several truly remarkable movements of entire communities toward the Christian faith have been among the most marked signs of our own times, and anticipation of the day when the entire nation

will look upon Him whom they have pierced and mourn with evangelical repentance and true Christian faith.

## SECTION V—*Future Prospects*

1. They are yet to be restored to their own land, and inherit according to the Abrahamic covenant the possession which was given as an eternal and inalienable patrimony (Romans 11, etc.).

2. They are also to be converted to the true Messiah and to accept Him whom they crucified, as their King and Lord (Zechariah 12:10).

3. They are to be severely tried in the furnace of persecution and suffering in the last days, and a large portion of the race will perish in the fearful ordeal (Zechariah 13:9; Daniel 12:1).

4. They are to be delivered by the personal coming of the Lord Jesus Christ, and to be restored during the millennial age to the sovereignty of the world as the queen of the nations, under Christ Himself, their personal and visible King. And all the glories of David's and of Solomon's throne will be fulfilled in a peaceful, righteous and happy millennial age, during which they themselves will doubtless be employed as the divine witnesses and instruments of testimony and salvation to the world, and so through them "All peoples on earth will be blessed through you and your offspring" (Genesis 28:14). (See also Zechariah 8:13; Romans 11:26, etc.)

# CHAPTER 7

## THE BEGINNING OF THE LIFE OF FAITH

The book of Genesis is especially instructive as an expression of the life of godliness and the true principles of faith and obedience. These are really the same under all dispensations. And so the apostle in the Epistle to the Hebrews, in giving us the most complete illustrations of true faith, goes back to the very beginning and chooses his highest examples from this ancient record.

The development of these various examples seems to shape itself almost into a symmetrical chain which comprises every aspect of the life of godliness.

### TYPES

The first example, Abel, as we might naturally expect in the commencement of the series, is an illustration of justifying faith. The second, Enoch, leads us a step farther to sanctifying faith. The third, Noah, teaches us the principle of testifying and separating faith. The fourth, Abraham, illustrates the obedience of faith. The fifth, Isaac, is a beautiful type of the patience of faith. Jacob, the sixth, reveals to us God's marvelous grace in the discipline and training of faith. And the seventh, Joseph, crowns the series as a monument of the trial and triumph of faith over injustice and suffering.

### CONTRASTS

All these characters have contrasts. Abel shines more gloriously in the shadow of Cain. Enoch stands out from his own generation like a silver lining on the dark cloud. Noah is distinguished from the antediluvians by his character, destiny and deliverance. Abraham has Lot as his foil. Isaac is linked with Ishmael in unequal association. Jacob is the opposite of Esau. And Joseph's loveliness is enhanced by the harshness and cruelty of his brethren.

Thus light and shadow move on together, and both reveal more perfectly the picture of truth and true living.

## SEVEN PAIRS

These seven pairs stand for great principles, quite as much as the individual characters already referred to. Abel and Cain represent the opposite principles of grace and nature. Enoch and Lamech stand for holiness and worldliness. Noah and the antediluvians represent the ideas of separation on the one hand and judgment on the other on all who become allied to the evil world. Abraham and Lot perfectly express the conceptions of faith and sight. Isaac and Ishmael are declared by the apostle to be types of grace and law. Jacob and Esau represent respectively the spiritual and the fleshly man. And Joseph and his brethren illustrate the triumph of innocence and suffering on the one hand and the ultimate retribution of selfishness and sin on the other.

Let us, however, look a little more in detail at each of these personal types of life and character.

## SECTION I—*Abel or Justifying Faith*
### Hebrews 11:4

### RECOGNITION OF SIN

1. We see the faith of Abel in the recognition of sin implied in his sacrifice. This was the chief distinction between his offering and Cain's. The latter came to God as one on equal terms, acknowledging no need for expiation, or sacrifice, and presenting his offering as a friend to a friend.

Abel took the place of a guilty sinner, deserving the death which he witnessed in his substitute, and from which he claims exemption only through the vicarious sufferings of that substitute and sacrifice.

Cain refused all this, and so he lost the forgiveness which Abel found, and Abel lost the sin which he confessed. The latter knelt a penitent, and rose a justified and righteous man. The former began by saying, "I have not sinned," and ended by the bitter cry, "My sin is greater than can be forgiven." This is ever the gateway to heaven, "If we confess our sins, he is faithful and just and will forgive us our sins" (1 John 1:9). "Only acknowledge your guilt" (Jeremiah 3:13). God can forgive anything, but He cannot pass over a farthing in His book of accounts. He never ignores or cancels the account. It must be fully acknowledged, and then it must be fully satisfied through Christ's atonement. Then, though it be written in scarlet, and be a debt of 10,000 talents, the promise is forever true, "Whoever confesses and renounces them finds mercy" (Proverbs 28:13).

### THE BLOOD

2. Abel's faith not only recognized sin, but all the divine provision for its

expiation through sacrifice. He did not expect acceptance because of his personal character or his works, nor did God make these the grounds of his acceptance. The apostle says, "God spoke well of his offering" (Hebrews 11:4). He was a poor, worthless sinner, but his offering was the type of God's own perfect Son, and carried with it all the value of the person and work of the Lord Jesus Christ. Therefore Abel was justified just as we are, on account of the blood and righteousness of Jesus Christ. God has already testified of this gift, what He has of no other, "This is my Son, whom I love; with him I am well pleased" (Matthew 17:5). And all who bring it and identify themselves with it, will share that commendation and benediction. God will say of them, "My Son, whom I love; with him I am well pleased." "All beautiful you are . . . there is no flaw in you" (Song of Songs 4:7). This is the meaning of the apostle's language, "Which he has freely given us in the One he loves" (Ephesians 1:6), and of the Savior's prayer, "That the love you have for me may be in them and that I myself may be in them" (John 17:26).

### BELIEVING AND RECEIVING

3. Abel's faith not only recognized the sin and the sacrifice, but also the efficacy of the sacrifice, and his acceptance on account of it. He believed that he was accepted and justified, and so entered into all the joy and rest of a full assurance of faith. Hence we are told by the apostle, "By faith he was commended as a righteous man" (Hebrews 11:4). It was not by feeling; it was not by the subsequent fruits of his life; it was not by inferential reasoning; but it was by simply believing God's testimony to his offering.

So the sinner must still not only acknowledge his sin and accept his Savior, but he must fully and firmly believe that he is accepted, justified and admitted to the place of sonship and perfect blessing in the love and grace of the Father. We must take this assurance by simple faith. We must believe the record which God has given us of His Son. We may weep and pray, but all will bring no rest until we honor God by simply believing His own testimony concerning His Son, and concerning our place of acceptance when united to him.

Notice what Abel believed. Not only did he accept the place of forgiveness, but he obtained witness that he was righteous. He stood in the place which man had occupied before he fell, as fully justified as though he had never sinned. Nay, more, the sinner is as fully justified when he accepts the righteousness of Christ, as though he had performed the very acts of righteousness which the Lord Jesus fulfilled in his stead. This is the New Testament doctrine of justification by faith. It is as old as Eden. And Abel fully understood it and experienced it.

This was the pathway of life for all the Old Testament saints. This was the message of Habakkuk, for all to read in its vivid and vehement characters, even as they run, "But my righteous one will live by faith" (Hebrews 10:38). This was the glorious theme of Paul. This was the keynote of the Reformation. This was the turning point of Whitfield's life and the great message of his marvelous ministry. This is still the only gospel that can save sinners, and the only solid ground on which sinners can build for sanctification, for the fullness of the Christian life, and for the hope of glory.

May we all know the faith of Abel, and stand with him at last as he shall lead the everlasting song in the choirs of the ransomed: "Worthy is the Lamb, who was slain" (Revelation 5:12), "and with your blood you purchased men for God" (5:9).

## SECTION II—*Enoch, or Sanctifying Faith*
### Hebrews 11:5

Some men's biographies are greater than the lives they record. But one sentence tells the story, in the case of Enoch, of a life whose loveliness and sublime issue has never been approached by any mere human experience, whether we consider the glory of his character, or the grandeur of his destiny.

"Enoch walked with God" (Genesis 5:22). "One who pleased God" (Hebrews 11:5). "He was commended" by faith, "as one who pleased God" (11:5). "Then he was no more, because God took him away" (Genesis 5:24). "He was taken from this life, so that he did not experience death" (Hebrews 11:5).

### NOT ENOCH, BUT GOD

The personality most prominent in Enoch's life was not Enoch but God. He was more remarkable for his Companion than for himself. This is the glory of true holiness; it hides us in the presence of our God. This is the true meaning of godliness. This is the true secret of divine holiness. It is not mere Christ-likeness, but it is Christness—Christ in us. Such a life alone can please God. The only thing that can meet the requirements and expectations of God's law is the Spirit, the nature, the very life of His dear Son, reproduced in us. Therefore "the love you have for me" shall "be in them, and that I myself may be in them" (John 17:26). Would we, therefore, please God? Let us receive the very Person of His dear Son, and offer Him to God as the one unceasing burnt offering and frankincense of our life. Then shall we also have the testimony that we please God, for the Spirit always bears witness to Jesus and His glory. Then shall we be able to believe that we please God, without any fear of exalting ourselves, and claim the very highest place in Christ, while we hold ourselves ever in the lowest abasement and self-renunciation.

Then, too, may we know that we shall be with God forever, and Christ in us shall become the Hope of glory. Then shall we be robed and ready for the Bridegroom when He comes, and have the wedding garment which Rebekah wore—even her husband's robes to cover her person and hide her face.

## HOLINESS AND TRANSLATION

Divine holiness, therefore, is linked very closely with that which Enoch's translation sublimely foreshadowed, the second coming of Christ and the rapture of His waiting people as they meet Him in the air. Enoch's life was animated by this hope, and it was his special testimony to his own generation. "See, the Lord is coming with thousands upon thousands of his holy ones" (Jude 14). Therefore, God signalized it in his own experience, by making him the first glorious illustration of it. Let God's people hear today the solemn whisper, "Behold, I come like a thief! Blessed is he who stays awake and keeps his clothes with him" (Revelation 16:15). "For the wedding of the Lamb has come,/ and his bride has made herself ready./ Fine linen, bright and clean,/ was given her to wear./ (Fine linen stands for the righteous acts of the saints)" (19:7–8).

## SECTION III—*Noah, or Separating Faith*
### Genesis 7:1; Hebrews 11:7

We have already seen that the cause of the deluge—or rather of the corruption which necessitated the deluge—was the mingling of the godly and the worldly seed and the failure of the descendants of Seth to preserve that line of separation which God had indicated at the beginning.

Noah stands out, however, as a distinguished exception to this universal conformity to the world, and for this cause he and his family are preserved from the common corruption and judgment.

The same tendency is sweeping away the Church today, and the issue will be, not a flood of water, but a flood of fire. The lessons of Noah's life are, therefore, peculiarly timely and important at this crisis. For our Lord has said that in the days of the Son of man it shall be precisely as it was in the days of Noah.

## HE BELIEVED

We see the faith of Noah manifested in his believing the Word of God with respect to the coming judgment on the old world. The reason that God calls us to give up this present world is because it is doomed. Like Christian in *Pilgrim's Progress*, we are in the city of destruction, and we are fleeing from its impending flames. The world will not believe this, but is making its calculations in defiance of divine warnings, and looking forward to an unbounded future. But true faith looks through its glass at the splendid palaces and monuments, and lo, each of them has become a sepulchre; nay, its magnificence is driven like ashes in the whirlwind of the last conflagration. And it turns away from things so transient and uncertain to seek a city that has foundations, and find in heaven a better, even an enduring substance.

Noah looked upon the world around him in the light of a century later, and saw it all a hideous wreck of perishing millions. The men around him laughed and scorned because they saw no sign of any such catastrophe in sea or sky. So the Apostle Peter tells us that in our day there will come scoffers who shall say, "Where is this 'coming' he promised? Ever since our fathers died, everything goes on as it has since the beginning of creation" (2 Peter 3:4). It is the philosophy of blind, cold naturalism. God's answer to it is the gospel of His Second Coming, the message of warning which proclaims the doom of all earth's pride and power. Nothing will more help us to separate ourselves from the world, and rise above its pride and power, than the belief and realization of this great and portentous truth. "The world and its desires pass away" (1 John 2:17). "The Lord is coming" (Jude 14).

### HE PREPARED

2. Noah not only believed in the coming catastrophe, but prepared for it, and built the ark of refuge according to the divine prescription and specifications. And then at the appointed time, when there was no portent on the cloudless sky, and no sign of the coming tidal wave of judgment on the earth or sea, he entered into his refuge and shut the door upon all that seemed substantial and real around him. His faith was practical. He did something. He did it all his life long. And he did it up to the very end. For 120 years he continued to build the ark, and when it was finished he showed his faith by committing his family and all his belongings to it, even when to others it may have seemed the height of folly and fanaticism.

So faith not only separates itself from the present world, but it lays hold upon the hope of the future, and prepares most practically, patiently and persistently, according to God's plan for the issues which it foresees.

Christ is our Ark. But there is a sense in which although that ark is finished, we have to practically build it into the structure of our entire life. Our whole Christian experience, like Noah's work, is the putting on of Christ, the building up of the house of faith and holiness of which Jesus is the substance, with the imperishable materials of His grace, and by the agency and energy of His Holy Spirit, so as to stand the test of that coming day.

### HE SEPARATED HIMSELF

3. Noah not only prepared for the future, but he also separated himself from unholy association with the men and women of his own generation.

And not only by his life did he stand thus apart, but by his testimony he bore fearless and faithful witness against their wickedness, and warned them of the coming retribution. The Scriptures call him "a preacher of righteousness" (2 Peter 2:5). And the apostle says in Hebrews that "he condemned the world and became heir of the righteousness that comes by faith" (Hebrews 11:7). We cannot bear effectual witness against the world until we get above its life, and out of its evil influences. We cannot do men good so long as we are on their level. Separation is indispensable to successful service.

But even success is not necessary to acceptable service. Noah's preaching seemed the most fruitless that mortal ever attempted. For 120 years he labored in vain. Nor was he alone. For the Spirit of God also strove with men all those years. It is not a sign, therefore, that our work is not divine because sometimes the fruit is delayed and men even grow more obdurate in their rejection of our message.

At last the message and the messenger were abundantly vindicated. The time came when the world would have given all it was worth for the lowest place in Noah's house of safety; but it was too late.

Noah let them have their farms and stores for a little while, and then God gave it all to him as he came down from Ararat that glorious morning under the magnificent arch of the rainbow and looked once more upon the loveliness of earth—it was all his own. There was no rival to dispute his title to any of its ample fields and vast estates. Noah had become the heir of the world, simply because he had given up the world.

The day is coming when we, too, shall understand how he that loves his life shall lose it, and he that loses his life for Christ's sake, shall find it and keep it unto life eternal. And no man who has left houses or lands or possessions for Christ, shall fail to receive a hundred fold in the times of restitution when the Son of man comes.

Let the world have its real estate, its mansions, its stocks and bonds. Christ is keeping it all for His waiting people who can afford for a little while to let the world go by. "Blessed are the meek, for they will inherit the earth" (Matthew 5:5).

This is the true secret of separation from the world. We do not want its old title, for it is defective. We are going to get it all with a better deed from the original owner, in a little while. And therefore we refuse to invest our money in the poor life interest the present usurper can only give us.

## THE FLOOD A TYPE

4. But we need to be separated, not only from the society of the world, but from its spirit, by a true death and resurrection, in our inner life, with the Lord Jesus Christ.

The flood was the type of this spiritual experience. The Apostle Peter says of Noah that he and his family were saved by water. "And this water symbolizes baptism that now saves you also—not the removal of dirt from the body but the pledge of a good conscience toward God. It saves you by the resurrection of Jesus Christ" (1 Peter 3:21). That is, the flood which buried the sinful world, and thus saved Noah from the engulfing waves of sin, is the type of our death to sin with the Lord Jesus now, and our resurrection life through Him to a new world of purity such as was prefigured by the new dispensation upon which Noah entered after the flood.

We may go out of the world all our days, and yet have the world in us, all the more idolatrously just because we are denied its enjoyments. It is in the heart that the world must die. The true world that we are to hate and shun is the love of the world. Therefore the apostle says that by the Cross of Christ "the world has been crucified to me, and I to the world" (Galatians 6:14).

It is only as we really know in our spirit the meaning and the experience of that death, and rise with Him to the new nature and the new inheritance, that the world can attack us no more. Risen with Christ, "set your hearts on things above, where Christ is seated at the right hand of God" (Colossians 3:1). "For you died, and your life is now hidden with Christ in God. When Christ, who is your life, appears, then you also will appear with him in glory" (3:3–4).

### SECTION IV—*Abraham, or the Obedience of Faith*
Hebrews 11:8–10, 17–19; Genesis 12:4; 13:8–9;
14:14–16; 15:5–6; 17:1–5; 22:1–3, 10–18

Abraham's faith has about it a many-sided fullness which makes it difficult to classify under any single aspect, in conjunction with other types. For in some sense it embraces the features of all the other types, and is indeed, the archetype of faith for all time. Hence the patriarch has been called "the father of all who believe" (Romans 4:11).

And yet its lessons come with great propriety after the three types already presented, as showing the fullness and entirety of the spiritual life into which God will lead His obedient children when they have learned with Abel, Enoch and Noah, the threefold secret of justification, sanctification and separation.

We have called the special feature of Abraham's faith, obedience, simply because the Holy Spirit has used this word as the first emphatic lineament in the picture of the patriarch's faith. "By faith Abraham, when called to go to a place he would later receive as his inheritance, obeyed" (Hebrews 11:8). Following the divine picture we notice:

## FAITH OBEYING

1. In Abraham we behold faith obeying God's command. Faith meets us in the very beginning, as an act of obedience. It is not optional with us whether we shall believe God or not. "And this is his commandment: to believe in the name of his Son, Jesus Christ" (1 John 3:23). This makes faith our highest service. This also takes from the act of faith the personal responsibility, and places it upon God. If we are simply obeying His orders, He will be responsible to carry us through.

This gives to faith a very practical character. It ceases to be an intellectual assent and becomes a real act and a decisive committal of our will and all the forces of our being. Hence we find in all great results of faith in God's Word that it was connected with decisive and courageous action, and it was in the *doing* that the blessing came. Israel must go forth before the sea could divide. Naaman must wash in the Jordan before he could be clean. The paralytic must take up his bed and walk before he could be healed. And James sums it all up in the impressive words: "Show me your faith without deeds, and I will show you my faith by what I do" (James 3:18). Abraham's faith would have been an idle dream, if he had not done something that involved the risk and committal of his whole life to Him whom he believed.

## FAITH TRUSTING

2. Faith believing in God personally, before it believes even God's promise, is faith trusting. Abraham believed God. His faith rested in the bed-rock of God's own personal character and faithfulness, before it even leaned upon the pillars of promise that rose from the foundations of that rock. True faith is not believing in words merely, even divine words, but believing ON the Lord Jesus Christ.

How beautifully we see it in the Syrophoenician woman, who had nothing but Christ Himself, and yet clung to Him before she had a single word from His lips, and then believed it just because it was His word. This was the reason why Abraham could trust even in the dark hour when God's very words seemed somehow contradicted by the command to offer Isaac. He did not understand, but he still trusted.

This personal aspect of faith, the leaning of our heart upon the living God Himself, is best expressed in the simple word *trust*. What an awful significance it gives to unbelief that it is refusing to believe God; not merely the rejection of the statement or a truth, but a direct assertion of want of confidence in God Himself.

## FAITH TRUSTING IN THE DARK

3. Faith is trusting God in the dark. "Abraham . . . went, even though he

did not know where he was going" (Hebrews 11:8). Later the way gradually became more precisely determined, but at first it was indefinite and dark.

This is faith without sight, and this is essential to faith. When we can see things clearly, it is often mere reasoning, and not faith at all. How wondrously the navigator sails by what he calls "dead reckoning." Day by day he marks his path upon the chart, as if following a chalk line upon the sea. And at last he knows just when the head lands are coming into view, and yet he has seen no point of land. His calculations are all from above.

And so faith looks up and sails on in the light of heaven upon the trackless sea, content to know:

> He knows the way He taketh,
> And I will walk with Him.

## FAITH BELIEVING THE PROMISE

4. Faith, next, is believing the divine promise. Having learned to go without exact light, it must now learn to receive the light of promise and fully credit it, even long before its fulfillment; and, indeed, when that fulfillment seems most improbable on natural grounds.

God promised Abraham a son, and yet He withheld for a long time the fulfillment, while in the meantime every natural cause seemed to render it impossible. But Abraham believed, as the apostle expresses it, "against all hope" (Romans 4:18), and "being fully persuaded that God had power to do what he had promised" (4:21).

So we must take God's divine Word when He gives it, specifically believe it, and expect it to be accomplished, whether it be the word of pardon, of sanctification, or of answered prayer in any other particular.

## FAITH CONFESSING

5. Faith is not only believing, but confessing its confidence. Not only did Abraham believe God would give the child of promise, but he began immediately to act as though God had given what He had said. Therefore we are told that his faith called "things that are not as though they were" (4:17).

So we must not only claim, but confess our blessings, and regard the things which are still future as accomplished in God's purpose. "Whatever you ask for in prayer, believe that you have received it, and it will be yours" (Mark 11:24).

## FAITH SURRENDERING

6. Faith is yielding up the world because it has a better inheritance, and a better title even to the world itself. Therefore when a strife arises, Abraham surrenders his personal rights to selfish Lot, and lets him choose the best;

and then that same night God appears to Abraham, and tells him that it is all his own.

So our faith can let the world go and know that God will give it to us in a better way, by an eternal, inalienable title.

## FAITH CONTENDING

7. Faith is contending for its inheritance when the enemy disputes it. Abraham yielded everything to Lot; but when the Eastern kings invaded the land, and took Lot a prisoner, Abraham went against them and resisted them in the name of the Lord, as the true heir and king of Canaan. By one of the most astonishing campaigns of all history, more wonderful even than Joshua's invasion of Canaan, he utterly out-generalled them and recovered all the spoil.

It was the type of our faith resisting the devil when he comes to dispute our new inheritance. We will be tolerant and patient with men so far as our personal rights are concerned. But when Satan disputes our standing, and puts his foot upon our inheritance, we will arise in the name of the Lord against the most tremendous odds, and claim the victory through Jesus Christ, by that aggressive and authoritative faith which treads on scorpions and serpents, and triumphs over all the power of the enemy; saying even to the mountain, "Go, throw yourself into the sea" (Matthew 21:21), and withering the fig tree of evil in His name.

## FAITH TESTED AND TRIUMPHANT

8. Faith tested and yielding, perhaps, for a time to the infirmities of nature, will ultimately triumph and enter into rest and complete victory.

The earlier trials of Abraham's faith developed sometimes a spirit of timidity, and an undue eagerness to hasten God's promise. But at least when the supreme trial came, and the child of promise and all the hopes connected with him had to be yielded into God's hands, the grace of God enabled him grandly to meet the test. Faith so allowed Abraham to trust in God's faithfulness, wisdom and love, and to hold fast to his confidence that somehow the promise would be fulfilled, that he committed all obediently and unreservedly into his Father's hands. And then he beheld His marvelous working, and received the sign of His divine approval and of all His promises restored to him as from the dead.

### SECTION V—*Isaac, or the Patience of Faith*
Genesis 21:3–9; 22:2–12; 26:12–25

The life and character of Isaac touch at many points the commonplace lives which comprise the great mass of Christian experience.

He is an actor in no great public events, but moves in a passive sphere, yielding and suffering, rather than aggressive and strong.

More than any other of the patriarchs he teaches us the lesson of the death of self, and the life of self-renunciation, weakness and patient endurance.

1. He is the first example of the rite of circumcision, the divine symbol of self-crucifixion. And his whole life is a commentary upon the covenant act of consecration, of which he was the infant subject on the eighth day of his life.

2. His childhood and youth were one long scene of endurance and self-denial from the persecutions of Ishmael.

3. These were followed by a still more searching self-renunciation, namely, his offering on Mount Moriah at the hands of his father, as a living sacrifice. This must have been to Isaac as real a death as it was to Abraham, and from this time his life was a surrendered one, and really a resurrection life in its true spirit.

4. Isaac's marriage involved the consecration of his affections and the renunciation of his will. His bride was chosen for him, not by his own caprice, but by the will of God, and sweetly accepted in the spirit of perfect obedience.

5. In the trials of his life, described in detail in the 25th chapter of Genesis, we see him envied by the Philistines, robbed of his wells of water, pressed from place to place by his jealous neighbors, and yet meekly yielding at every point, and, like his Master, going to another place.

6. His last trials and self-renunciation were with respect to his children. His personal preference for his eldest son had to be abandoned, and with the same sweet submission he yielded to the disappointment of his cherished affections, accepting the will of God concerning Jacob, and gave his blessing to the one who had so deceitfully wrung it from his hand.

Thus, from infancy to age, Isaac becomes the type of self-surrender, submission to the will of God, passive obedience, and what we have already called the patience of faith, and, indeed, might also call the love that "always protects, always trusts, always hopes, always perseveres" (1 Corinthians 13:7).

### SECTION VI—*Jacob, or the Discipline of Faith*
Genesis 25:23, 27–34; 28:10–22; 32:24–31; 33:1–5;
47:9; 48:15–16

There is very little that is naturally attractive in the character of Jacob. Humanly speaking, he was the most unpromising and unworthy subject of divine grace in all the patriarchal history. And yet, for this very reason, he was the best example of divine grace—that grace that is founded, not on human merit, but which triumphs over man's meanness and worthlessness, and, where sin abounds, makes its riches to abound the more.

We trace five great stages in the life of Jacob:

## HIS CHOICE

1. The first was his choice of the blessing. It was undoubtedly an act of faith. And it was probably founded upon his mother's teachings regarding the promise that had preceded his birth, and designated him as the head of the chosen race.

Everything naturally seemed against him. Esau was the firstborn, and the favorite of Isaac. But notwithstanding the natural difficulties, he believed the thing promised and set his heart upon securing the covenant blessing.

Had his faith been more perfect, he would have avoided the restless and deceitful policy by which he tried to help God to fulfill His promise. But notwithstanding the means he employed, the motive was in its essential character a true one, and God accepted that which was good in it, and then, by the discipline of suffering, purged out the refuse and the dross. Jacob's choice was the spiritual one, while Esau's sole concern was for that which was earthly and temporary.

## THE REVELATION OF GOD

2. The next stage of Jacob's life is the manifestation of God to him, confirming His choice and revealing His covenant in the vision of Bethel (Genesis 28).

This corresponds to the time in our Christian life when, having chosen God, He personally reveals Himself to the soul and brings us into conscious covenant relations with Him.

This was followed in Jacob's case by many years of vicissitude and spiritual unsteadiness, during which he made little progress in his religious life, and showed in his dealings with Laban that the old natural spirit of self-acting and carnal wisdom was still there in all its activity.

## VICTORY AND PENIEL

3. At length we come to the third stage of his life, and that is his deeper religious experience and consecration, which begins in the scene at Peniel (Genesis 32), where, crushed with anxiety and impending danger, his own resources fail him at last, and he is driven to cast himself helplessly upon the strength of God. In that night of agony and prayer, which has become the type of many a spiritual crisis since, he at length dies to his own sufficiency, sinks under the touch of God's withering hand, and rises into the victory of self-renunciation and triumphant faith, henceforth receiving the new name of Israel, in token of the transformation of his life.

This, however, was only the beginning of his consecrated life, for in the following chapter we find him still holding back from the fullness of God's will, and receiving the summons: "Go up to Bethel and settle there" (35:1). And Jacob puts away the idols which had still remained in his household, and for a time obeys the divine command. A little later, however, we find him wandering again (35:16). He even seems to have forgotten the full meaning of the divine command to dwell at Bethel, and probably this was the cause of all the troubles that followed in his later years.

### THE DISCIPLINE OF TRIAL

4. The next stage of Jacob's life is the discipline of trial, which is at last to burn out the selfishness and earthliness, and prepare him for the fullness of the blessing that God has already bestowed in covenant, to be the head of Israel's future tribes, and even give his name to its lasting and illustrious history.

These trials began in the death of Rachel at Ephratah, followed by the unnatural crimes of Jacob's sons, and, at last, the mysterious and terrible tragedy of Joseph's loss and the years of agony and suspense that at length filled the bitter dregs of his cup of affliction.

### THE TRIUMPH OF FAITH

5. The last stage of Jacob's life is the triumph of faith, and the issue of his suffering in the happy reunion with his long-lost son, and the grateful testimony, "The Angel who has delivered me from all harm" (48:16), and then the dying confession of victory and satisfaction, "I look for your deliverance,/ O LORD" (49:18).

## SECTION VII—*Joseph, or the Victory of Faith over Suffering and Wrong*
### Genesis 37:3–28; 39:1–6, 20–23; 41:30–43; 42:3–8; 45:1–15, 25–28; 50:22–26

Jacob was the type of suffering, largely caused by his own sinfulness, and designed to sanctify him from the life of self. Joseph's sufferings have a different purpose, and are intended to show how the providence of God can overrule the most trying dispensations, and at length deliver His trusting children from the darkest and most mysterious trials, and crown them with glory and blessing.

1. The first chapter of Joseph's faith had reference to his early visions of the future and the revelation to him of the will of God for his own destiny.

It was because he believed this, and rested in the divine faithfulness, that he was persecuted by his brethren; but for the same reason, also, he was sustained in all the trying scenes of future years.

2. We see the trials of Joseph's faith. First, came the cruel envy of his brethren, and their heartless crime and next, the false accusings of his mistress, and his languishing in prison amid neglect and humiliation for weary, hopeless years as it seemed, at least, to natural reasonings.

3. We see Joseph's faith under trials, bravely meeting them with courage and manliness, making the best of his situation, and so conducting himself that he rose to the highest place, both in the household of Potiphar, and in the prison of Pharaoh.

The secret of this was his fidelity to conscience and his unfaltering faith in God.

4. Joseph's faith was recompensed at last with complete deliverance and glorious triumph. The height to which he rose was greater than the depth to which he had sunk. And so it ever is in the story of true faith and obedience.

5. We see in Joseph next the faith which works by love. He did not use his triumph for his own selfish aggrandizement or enjoyment. Rather, he used his triumph first for the salvation of the entire world from famine and death and next, for the welfare of the very brethren who had so wronged him, forgiving their sin, receiving them to his love, and sharing with them his wealth and honors.

6. We see next in Joseph a faith that looks back upon trial in the light of God's wisdom and love. He saw the hand of God in all his sufferings, and above all his wrongs, and could say, "You intended to harm me, but God intended it for good" (Genesis 50:20).

This is faith's after-view of trial. And only as we thus contemplate it can we endure it without bitterness or discouragement.

7. We see in Joseph, finally, the faith that looks out upon the future with an eternal hope. He saw something better than Egypt's throne. He saw the coming deliverance of his people under Moses and Joshua and still later the final resurrection of the dead, and the eternal inheritance of glory. And so his last act was to give commandment concerning his bones, and to make sure that his dust should have a part in the glorious hopes that awaited his people in the ages to come.

How completely his life foreshadows all the highest aspects of the life of faith and godliness, as well as the sufferings and glory of that greater One who is for us not only the Example, but also, the Object, the Author and the Finisher of our faith.

# EXODUS

# INTRODUCTION

## SECTION I—*Contents and Divisions*

The book of Exodus is called in Hebrew *Ve-eleh shemoth*, which is the first sentence in the book, meaning "These are the names" (Exodus 1:1). The name Exodus was given by the Greek translators in the third century B.C., and it literally means "the out-going," thus denoting the chief theme of the book, the departure of the Israelites out of Egypt. This, of course, is not the only theme in Exodus, which gives also the subsequent history of Israel in their journey to Sinai, and the account of the covenant at Sinai, and the Law, the Tabernacle and the Priesthood.

The usual division of the book is in two portions. First, from chapter one to the end of chapter 19, which treats of Israel's deliverance from Egypt and the events which immediately follow. Second, from chapter 20 to the end of the book, containing an account of the giving of the Law and the Tabernacle and other institutions of Moses. A more detailed division, however, is found in the form and structure of the book itself, which is divided into paragraphs of sufficient length to each form a single reading for congregational worship. There are 17 of these sections or paragraphs which may be classified as follows:

1. Oppression of Israel and birth of Moses. (1:1–2:25)
2. The call of Moses, and the people's acceptance of his mission. (3:1–4:31)
3. Moses' appeal to Pharaoh and its failure. (5:1–23)
4. The increased oppression of the people. (6:1–27)
5. The first nine plagues. (6:28–11:10)
6. The 10th plague, the Passover and the departure of Israel. (12:1–42)
7. Ceremonial directions about the Passover. (12:43–13:16)
8. Israel's march from Succoth through the Red Sea, and Pharaoh's destruction. (13:17–14:31)
9. The song of Moses and Miriam. (15:1–21)

10. The march of Israel from the Red Sea to Sinai. (15:22–19:25)
11. The Decalogue and the book of the Covenant. (20:1–23:33)
12. The ratification of the Covenant and the ascent of the mount by the elders of Israel and Moses, with Moses remaining there 40 days. (24:1–18)
13. Directions for the Tabernacle and the Ark. (25:1–30:38)
14. Call of Bezalel and others to build the Tabernacle; appointment of the Sabbath as a sign, and delivery of the two tablets of stone to Moses. (31:1–18)
15. The people's sin and its forgiveness. (32:1–33:23)
16. Renewal of the tablets and the Covenant. (34:1–35)
17. The construction of the Tabernacle. (35:1–40:38)

## SECTION II—*Development of the Gospel in the Writings of Moses*

In the Mosaic Dispensation, we begin with:

First, the evil seed. We find it enthroned in the world's oldest, proudest empire, with Satan as its god. We see it later in Amalek, Israel's first foe in the wilderness. And then in Edom, Moab, Midian and Balaam, the wisest of them all. And, it is not long until we find it in Israel too, in the mixed multitude that followed them from Egypt, the idolaters of Sinai, the rebels of Korah's company and the generation that refused to enter the promised land and fell in the wilderness.

Second, the chosen seed is also here. We see them redeemed from bondage by judgment and by blood, led by God's own guiding hand, healed by His direct presence, fed by manna from heaven, refreshed by water from the rock, conducted to victory by God Himself, and saved from all their enemies. They are educated and disciplined by the Law of Sinai, the types of the Tabernacle and the providence in the wilderness, and finally led across the Jordan to the full possession and conquest of the Land of Promise.

Third, all these things were types of the gospel of Christ. With a clearness and vividness not seen before, Jesus shines forth in all the institutions of the Mosaic age. These might be comprised under four classes:

*Typical Places*—Egypt represents the world; the Red Sea, our separation from it by our death and resurrection with Christ; the wilderness, the failure of life; the Land of Promise, the full inheritance of faith; and the Tabernacle, God in Christ meeting sinful man with atonement, cleansing, the supply of all his needs, communion, light and at length eternal glory.

*Typical Persons*—The High Priest represents our great Redeemer and High Priest, Jesus Christ. His official robes symbolize Christ's grace and fullness.

The common priests represent the household of Christ in their access to Him. The Levites set forth the practical side of Christian life and the idea of service. The Nazarites stand as the embodiment of separation to God.

*Typical Things*—The manna and rock point to the one supply for all our spiritual need. The four great offerings unfold the fullness of Christ's one sacrifice. The rites of cleansing, especially the provisions for leprosy, set forth the sanctifying grace of the gospel. The brazen serpent lifts our eyes to the great Healer and antidote to sin and death. The two silver trumpets remind us of the twofold Word of God. The pillar of cloud and fire is the glorious symbol of the Holy Spirit, our Guide and Comforter.

*Typical Times*—Two sorts of times were set apart, namely, the Sabbath and Sabbatic times. The Sabbath was a memorial of creation and a type of redemption and the rest of faith. The Sabbatic times were the Sabbatic Week, or the 50th day after the Passover to Pentecost; the Sabbatic Month, the seventh month of the year, occupied with the great typical feasts; the Sabbatic Year, every seventh year; and the Sabbath of a week of years, or the Jubilee. The great feasts filled up the first seven months of the year, and were all typical of Christ: the Passover, of His Cross; Pentecost, of the Spirit's descent; Trumpets, the proclamation of the gospel; Atonement, the reconciling of the world; Tabernacles, His glorious coming and millennial reign.

And so the gospel was never more wonderfully set forth than by Moses. Indeed, we must go back to these ancient symbols to get our truest conception of its depth and fullness.

# GENERAL PLAN AND SCOPE
# OF THE BOOK

Exodus is the book of redemption, the inspired record of Israel's deliverance from Egypt and the bondage of Pharaoh, and their entering into the theocratic government with Jehovah at Mount Sinai, through the law and the ordinances connected with the Tabernacle and the Priesthood.

It is the great spiritual type of the redemption of the people of God, through the Lord Jesus Christ, and the gracious covenant into which He receives them under the gospel.

We may trace five great stages in the development of this type: bondage, redemption, pilgrimage, law and grace.

# CHAPTER 1

## ISRAEL'S BONDAGE

### SECTION I—*The Scene of Their Bondage*

Egypt, the world's first great empire, was the scene of Israel's bondage and the first of those mighty world empires which became arrayed in succession against God and His people.

Territorially it was one of the smallest of countries, comprising a narrow strip on each side of the Nile, a few miles wide and perhaps 500 miles long. It consisted of two provinces—upper and lower Egypt—with their respective capitals, Thebes and Memphis, whose colossal ruins still tell of their ancient magnificence. The people were not an African race, but emigrants from Asia, and highly advanced in culture and civilization.

It was a powerful kingdom in the days of Abraham, and more than 15 dynasties of kings had already occupied its throne before the time of Joseph. Thirty dynasties altogether can be traced from the earliest times until the close of the Egyptian sovereignty. The first 14 of these were native sovereigns. The next three were the Hyksos or shepherd kings, an invading race who came in from Asia at the head of nomadic tribes, and for a time held the Egyptians under their sway. The last 12 dynasties were the restored native sovereigns.

It was during the reign of the shepherd kings that Joseph and the Hebrews entered the land. They found favor with the king, but were told that shepherds, as they themselves were, were an abomination to the Egyptians who had been conquered by them.

The other king, who afterward rose up and knew not Joseph, was undoubtedly the head of the 18th dynasty of native Egyptian sovereigns who superseded the Hyksos, and naturally were hostile to their Hebrew friends and allies, whom they perhaps regarded as another pastoral race, who in due time would threaten the subversion of their dynasty, as the shepherd kings had done before.

## SECTION II—*The Entrance of the Hebrews into Egypt*
Exodus 1:1–8; 1 Chronicles 4:21–23

The residence of Israel in Egypt was a part of God's providential plan revealed to Abraham in a vision centuries before. It occupied a period of about 215 years; the whole interval of 400 years, mentioned in Genesis 14 and Acts 7, included, no doubt, the previous patriarchal period beginning with the time of the vision. Their home, Goshen, was in the northern province and many of the places have been identified in connection with recent researches and excavations. For a time they were a prosperous and favored colony, and rapidly increased in population and probably also in wealth and influence.

Several incidents of this part of their history are narrated in the opening chapters of the book of Chronicles (1 Chronicles 4:21 and 7:21). One of them was related by marriage to the king, and several of them occupied influential positions in the royal household. The region which they occupied was near the royal city of Zoan, and the two chief cities of Goshen were Rameses and Pithom.

## GOD'S PURPOSE

The design of God in permitting them to enter Egypt was, no doubt, to prevent their intermingling with the tribes of Canaan, as they surely would have done in a little while, in the second or third generation, had they remained in the land. But this was rendered impossible in Egypt by the antipathy between the Egyptians and the Israelites, and by their separate colonial establishment. It was really the next stage in their separation as God's peculiar people. It was also designed to prepare them by the discipline, which followed at a later period, for their national history.

Another reason assuredly was to bring the power of God into direct contact with the proudest form of heathenism, and give an opportunity for the triumph of Jehovah over the world's most ancient and mighty pretensions. A still further reason undoubtedly was to afford a type of our spiritual bondage and redemption. It was for the same reason that our Lord went down into Egypt in His infancy, that He might be our Forerunner in coming out of the world and becoming the separated people of God.

## SECTION III—*Israel's Oppression*
Exodus 1:8–22

There seems to be no doubt that the race of kings who changed the Egyptian policy towards the Hebrews into bitter hostility and cruel oppression was the dynasty that expelled the Shepherd kings, and that the chief figure in this oppression was the greatest of Egyptian sovereigns, known to us in the native records as Rameses II, and in Grecian history as Sesostris. A few years ago his sarcophagus was discovered, and his remains have been unveiled and placed on exhibition in the celebrated museum at Bulak. It is one of the transformations of history and an example of the vanity of human greatness, that the figure which was the terror of the world and the tyrant of the children of God is a helpless and impotent specimen today, in a glass case in an Egyptian museum.

The reasons for the severe measures adopted by the Egyptian rulers were undoubtedly political, and designed to prevent the danger of a powerful rebellion or, at least, a party that might at any time become a threatening power in case of rebellion or foreign invasion. The new Hebrew community had become numerous enough to be a dangerous element, and would naturally take sides with one of their kindred races. The Egyptian government, therefore, determined to reduce their strength and numbers, and at the same time utilize their industrial resources, in great public improvements and enormous architectural works. Many of the previous kings had been great builders, but the greatest of Egyptian monuments belong to this period.

The latest discoveries have confirmed in every particular the Bible account of the vast treasure cities which the Hebrew captives were employed to erect. And the hieroglyphic pictures of the taskmasters are true to the Bible narrative in every detail.

## SECTION IV—*Spiritual Lessons*

We pass, however, to the deeper spiritual import of these facts and incidents.

### THE DEVIL

1. Pharaoh is a type of the devil, our adversary. He is represented throughout the Scriptures as the prince of the kingdom of darkness and the god of this world, holding under his oppressive sway the entire human race, and imposing upon them the cruel bondage of sin and its miserable slavery. The spirit of Pharaoh, through his entire career, is the very spirit of Satan. And the judgments which came upon him and his people were manifestly designed to emphasize this fact, and foreshadow and unfold the ultimate destruction of the principalities and powers of spiritual darkness. The gods of Egypt were but impersonations of devilish principalities and powers. The magicians of Egypt were evidently the subjects of Satanic possession and, to a certain extent, of supernatural Satanic power.

The judgments inflicted through Moses were aimed directly at the deified forms of natural life and the things which the Egyptians worshiped. It was against the gods of Egypt that God said He would be avenged. "On that same night I will pass through Egypt and strike down every firstborn—both men and animals—and I will bring judgment on all the gods of Egypt. I am the LORD" (Exodus 12:12).

The final infatuation and destruction of Pharaoh is a vivid type of the doom which is ultimately to come upon the prince of the power of the air in his eternal overthrow. And so the whole series of transactions is a spiritual panorama of the powers of evil in conflict with the kingdom of God, and the victory which at last is to come, through the Seed of the woman, over the serpent and his brood.

## THE WORLD

2. Egypt is a type of the world, as our place of bondage. It is called by the apostle, "the present evil age" (Galatians 1:4). We are warned against its spirit and power just as strongly as we are against Satan and sin. Our Master teaches us that we are not of the world, even as He is not of the world, and that the love of the world is incompatible with the love of the Father.

The very design of our redemption by the sacrifice of the Lord Jesus Christ was "to rescue us from the present evil age, according to the will of our God and Father" (1:4).

All through the later prophets, Egypt is the type of the world. And the warnings of Hosea and others, against going down to Egypt, have the same simple spiritual meaning as the New Testament exhortation: "Do not love the world" (1 John 2:15); or "Cursed is the one who trusts in man,/ who depends on flesh for his strength" (Jeremiah 17:5). "You cannot serve both God and Money" (Matthew 6:24).

## THE BONDAGE OF SIN

3. Their bondage in Egypt was the type of the slavery of sin from which the Lord Jesus Christ delivers His people.

Our Lord taught this to the proud Hebrews of His own day when they ignorantly and falsely boasted: "We . . . have never been slaves of anyone" (John 8:33). They seemed to have strangely forgotten the story of Egypt and the captivity of Babylon. Our Lord might easily have reminded them of this, but He rather seeks to show them the deeper slavery and heavier bondage under which their souls were held. "I tell you the truth, everyone who sins is a slave to sin" (8:34).

So again, the Apostle Paul uses the same figure: "Don't you know that when you offer yourselves to someone to obey him as slaves, you are slaves to the one whom you obey—whether you are slaves to sin, which leads to death, or to obedience, which leads to righteousness? But thanks be to God that, though you used to be slaves to sin, you wholeheartedly obeyed the form of teaching to which you were entrusted" (Romans 6:16–17). "But now that you have been set free from sin and have become slaves to God, the benefit you reap leads to holiness, and the result is eternal life. For the wages of sin is death, but the gift of God is eternal life in Christ Jesus our Lord" (6:22–23).

## BEGAN IN BLESSING

4. The bondage of Egypt began with them in apparent blessing, but it soon became an iron chain and a furnace of suffering. So man's life on earth began in the innocence and happiness of Eden. But soon another king arose, and the god of this world became the antitype of Egypt's cruel oppressor.

It is not that the world in itself is essentially wrong, but the spirit of the world has become evil, and that which might have been in innocency a home of perfect happiness, has now become, through sin and Satan, a place of bondage and a snare of evil.

## SLAVES

5. Our spiritual bondage, like that of Egypt, has its heavy tasks and its hopeless servitude. Satan imposes upon his dupes far heavier toils than the brick fields of Zoan required. And like those monsters of cruelty, he, too, refuses to give his toiling victims even the straw for their bricks. He demands of men what they cannot do, and then lashes them with his cruel scourge when they do not do it.

One of his chief torments is an accusing conscience, which holds the poor guilty heart to the full standard of duty, but gives it no power to perform it, and no palliation or mercy for its fault, but goads it on by the terrors of remorse and despair. Looking upon these poor victims, the Master said with tender compassion, "Come to me, all you who are weary and burdened, and I will give you rest" (Matthew 11:28). Sin is a heavy task and a weary slavery, and truly the way of transgressors is hard.

## TASKS

6. Satan employs his captives like old Rameses, in building his treasure cities. It is true he makes them think that they are laying up treasures for themselves, and building their own houses. But when with weary toil their work is accomplished, he executes upon them the cruel decree of death, and their treasures remain for others to enjoy.

The materials of these ancient cities were striking types of the transitoriness and perishableness of the world's riches and glories. Sand and straw are God's own images of the instability of earthly things. The houses of sand,

and the wood, hay and stubble tell us of the destruction which is surely coming in the testing fires of the great day. And so all the weary work of the worldling is doomed to transitoriness and dissolution, and shall disappear like ashes in the whirlwind in the flames of a dissolving world. "Man is a mere phantom as he goes to and fro:/ . . . he heaps up wealth, not knowing who will get it" (Psalm 39:6). "Each man's life is but a breath" (39:5).

> Their tombs will remain their houses forever,
>    their dwellings for endless generations,
>    though they had named lands after themselves.

> But man, despite his riches, does not endure;
>    he is like the beasts that perish.

> Like sheep they are destined for the grave,
>    and death will feed on them.
> The upright will rule over them in the morning;
>    their forms will decay in the grave,
>    far from their princely mansions. (49:11–12, 14)

> The foolish and the senseless alike perish
>    and leave their wealth to others. (49:10)

> For he will take nothing with him when he dies,
>    his splendor will not descend with him. (49:17)

## REFUSES TO RELEASE US

7. Like the ancient oppressor, our spiritual tyrant refuses to relax his hold upon his captives. Pharaoh held on to his victims with a death grip.

It is interesting to notice the stages of that conflict in which the grasp of his cruel fingers is unlocked by the wrenching hand of God, as it were, inch by inch. "Let my people go," was the divine command, "so that they may hold a festival to me in the desert" (Exodus 5:1). His defiant answer was: "Who is the LORD, that I should obey him and let Israel go? I know not the LORD and I will not let Israel go" (5:2).

## A LITTLE WAY

After the first judgments fall he relaxes a little, and concedes this much: "Go, sacrifice to your God here in the land" (8:25). How like the spirit of the world. At first it absolutely refuses to yield its claims in the slightest degree at the command of God. But compelled by His power, at last it consents to let men have a little religion, but it must not involve any real separation from the world. Serve God "in the land" (8:25). Moses refuses this; and then Pharaoh makes a further concession: "I will let you go to offer sacrifices to the LORD your God in the desert, but you must not go very far" (8:28).

The world may even consent to let us go a little distance from it, but it wants to keep us in sight. The fast of Lent is all right if we will not forget to come back again to our old master with the Easter carnival.

## OUR CHILDREN MUST STAY

In the next stage of the conflict he consents to let them go, but they must leave their little ones as hostages (10:10–11). So Satan holds multitudes of people through their children, either by foolish parental indulgences in things which they themselves would not do, or through the idolatry of their affections, by which multitudes are held in his power.

## OUR PROPERTY

The final consent is, "Go, worship the LORD. Even your women and children may go with you; only leave your flocks and herds behind" (10:24). The world is willing to let us have our creeds and churches, if it can only hold our possessions. And multitudes of God's children are just in this position, serving the Lord after a fashion with their intellects and emotions, but wholly immersed in the riches and pleasures of earth, and really holding all they claim to own in the spirit of worldliness and selfishness. Thus our master holds us with persistent grasp, pursuing us even unto death, as Pharaoh pursued the Hebrews to the very waters of the Red Sea, and only relaxing his grasp at last, in the throes of dissolution.

## OUR LIFE

8. Like Pharaoh, the world, our tyrant, demands at last our very life. The Egyptians did not merely compel the unrequited labor of the Hebrews, but the climax of the oppression was the decree of death upon every male Hebrew child. Nothing less than their destruction could satiate their masters. And so, "the wages of sin is death" (Romans 6:23), and the ultimate purpose of our adversary is our destruction, both soul and body forever.

The story is related of a vindictive man who desired to wreak a terrible revenge upon his enemy. He waited until he could combine every extreme of devilish cruelty in his horrible revenge. He heard that his enemy had become a Christian. Fearing that this would rob him of his sweetest triumph, namely, the ruin of his soul, he resolved, if possible, to compel him to abjure his faith. And so one day in a favorable opportunity, he sprang upon his victim and threatened him with instant death unless he denied his Lord. In his sudden terror the poor man promised to do so if he would spare him. No sooner had he said this than his enemy, with a scornful and satanic laugh ex-claimed: "Now I have my revenge complete. I have both your soul and your body." And with one cruel blow he struck him to the earth, with the diaboli-cal consciousness that he had ruined him utterly and irretrievably both for time and eternity.

So our relentless enemy seeks our complete destruction. And often, when he has his victim bound in the snares of sin, with his cruel hand he hurls him swiftly into eternity, lest he might lose, at last, the prize of his immortal soul. Oh that men would realize that sin is the huntress that seeks the pre-cious life, and that Satan's only happiness is the task of making other souls as wretched as himself. May it be true of all who read these lines, "But thanks be to God that, though you used to be slaves to sin, . . . you have been set free from sin and have become slaves to God, the benefit you reap leads to holiness, and the result is eternal life" (Romans 6:17a, 22).

# CHAPTER 2

## REDEMPTION

The deliverance of Israel from the bondage of Egypt is the type of man's redemption from the power of sin and Satan.

### SECTION I—*The Redeemer*
Exodus 2:1–15; 3:1–18; 4:1–17; Deuteronomy 18:15–18

Our great Redeemer is typified by Moses, who himself declared that one greater than he was to arise from among his brethren and lead them into their spiritual inheritance. "But when the time had fully come, God sent his Son . . . to redeem those under the law, that we might receive the full rights of sons" (Galatians 4:4–5).

*MOSES A TYPE OF CHRIST*

The points in which Moses was the figure of Christ are numerous and striking. Among them we may briefly notice.

1. Like Christ he was born of an oppressed race (Exodus 2:1–2). So our great Redeemer was born of a woman, made under the law, our kinsman and brother and the sharer of all our human infirmities and sufferings. "Since the children have flesh and blood, he too shared in their humanity" (Hebrews 2:14).

2. Moses was not only a slave-born child, but also a prince of royal dignity, an heir to Egypt's very throne. So the Lord Jesus is the Heir of all power, and the Prince of glory by eternal right (Exodus 2:10; Philippians 2:6; Hebrews 1:2).

3. Moses gave up all his honors and dignities to share the sufferings of his brethren and save them from their cruel bondage. And so our great Redeemer became partaker of our human nature, and its lot of suffering, shame and death. "Who, being in very nature God, did not consider equality with God something to be grasped, but made himself nothing,

103

taking the very nature of a servant, being made in human likeness. And being found in appearance as a man, he humbled himself and became obedient to death—even death on a cross" (Philippians 2:7–8; see also Hebrews 11:25–26).

4. The rescue of Moses in his infancy, from the cruel decree of Pharaoh, reminds us of the bloody attempt of the cruel Herod to destroy the life of the infant Jesus, and His deliverance through the marvelous providence of God, by His flight into this very land of Egypt, where His infancy was sheltered, even as Moses' was (Exodus 2:3; Matthew 2:14–16).

Moses' retirement for 40 years into the wilderness of Midian, and his quiet preparation there for his future work, resemble the early preparation of Jesus for His future ministry, and even more distinctly foreshadows His 40 days of conflict with the devil in the wilderness before He entered upon His public ministry (Exodus 2:11–25; Matthew 4:1–11).

5. Moses' work began with a terrific conflict with the devil-gods of Egypt. And so the ministry of Jesus was preceded with the conflict of Satan, and involved at that stage a direct conflict with the powers of darkness whom He came to destroy (1 John 3:8).

6. The character of Moses was typical of the spirit and character of Jesus (Exodus 3:11; Matthew 11:29). Moses was the meekest of men, and his gentleness of spirit was continually tested and exemplified through all the provocations of his trying position (Numbers 12:3). So of our Lord Jesus it was said: "He will not quarrel or cry out; no one will hear his voice in the streets. A bruised reed he will not break, and a smoldering wick he will not snuff out" (Matthew 12:19–20).

7. The work of Moses is typical of the great work of the Lord Jesus Christ. He was the founder of Judaism; so Christ was the Founder of Christianity. He gave Israel the law; so Jesus has given us the gospel (John 1:17). He was the great prophet of the old dispensation; so Christ is of the new (Deuteronomy 8:15–18; Acts 7:37). He was the deliverer of his people from Egypt; so Christ is our Redeemer (Revelation 5:9). He was the founder of the system of sacrificial offerings; so Christ is the great sacrifice (Hebrews 9:12). He was the builder of the Tabernacle; so Christ Himself is the true sanctuary (Hebrews 8:1–2; 9:10–12). He was the mediator between God and Israel; so Jesus Christ is our one way of access to the Father (Exodus 20:22; Galatians 3:19; 1 Timothy 2:5).

Yet Moses was but the figure of Him who was to come. When Jesus appeared on earth, Moses came to the Mount of Transfiguration and laid his testimony at the feet of Jesus, acknowledging Him as the true substance and end of all His glorious dispensation, while the voice from heaven proclaimed, "This is my Son, whom I love; . . . Listen to him" (Matthew 17:5). No voice so loudly as Moses' witnessed to the preeminence and glory of Jesus Christ. And in all the preaching of Christ and His apostles, they always began with Moses as they unfolded the things concerning Him in the ancient Scriptures. And the song of redemption on the shores of the sea of glass, at last, shall have as its deepest note, the song of Moses blending with the song of the Lamb.

## SECTION II—*The Redeemed*
### Exodus 1:13–14; 2:23–25; 3:7–8; 4:19–31; 5:4–21

1. Their condition was helpless and hopeless (Exodus 3:7, 9). "The LORD said, 'I have indeed seen the misery of my people in Egypt. I have heard them crying out because of their slave drivers, and I am concerned about their suffering' " (3:7).

2. They at first refused their deliverer and seemed incapable even of understanding the divine purpose in their deliverance (Exodus 2:14). So "he came to that which was his own, but his own did not receive him" (John 1:11). And the story of every redeemed soul surely begins in the same record of unbelief, indifference and neglect.

3. As their deliverance drew near, the rigors of their bondage increased, until at last it was unsupportable (Exodus 5:9). So when God is about to awaken His people to a sense of their need, and prepare them for their deliverance, their burdens become heavier, and their case more desperate. The Hebrews expressed this fact by a proverb which is full of significance for all our lives: "When the tale of brick is doubled, then cometh Moses." "The darkest hour is just before the dawn," is our modern translation. It is when men are lost that they become saved. It is when the prodigal is ruined that he is nearest home. It is when we have no help or hope that the Lord is at hand.

4. At length they lifted to heaven their cry of distress: "The Israelites groaned in their slavery and cried out, and their cry for help because of their slavery went up to God. God heard their groaning and he remembered his covenant with Abraham, with Isaac and with Jacob. So God looked on the Israelites and was concerned about them" (2:23–24).

It is the story of prayer and its answer. It was but a groan and a cry, but God hears the sighing of the prisoner; and the Spirit's mightiest prayer is oft a groaning that cannot be uttered. It is still as true, God "said [not] to Jacob's descendants,/ 'Seek me in vain' " (Isaiah 45:19).

5. At length they not only pray, but believe. So their redemption begins like ours, with faith. "Aaron told them everything the LORD had said to Moses. He also performed the signs before the people, and they believed. And when they heard that the LORD was concerned about them and had seen their misery, they bowed down and worshiped" (Exodus 4:30–31).

## SECTION III—*The Redemption*

1. *Began in Judgment* (Exodus 7:1–6, 19–25; 8:5–7, 16–24; 9:22–26; 10:12–17, 21–23, 28–29; 11:1; 12:29–36).

Israel's redemption began in judgment as man's redemption at Eden had begun in the sentence upon the serpent. Moses' first work was to break the power and pride of Pharaoh and prove the supremacy of the God of Israel over the idols of Egypt. So Christ's redeeming work began in judgment on sin and Satan. So in the prophetic vision of His coming it is said, "For the day of vengeance was in my heart,/ and the year of my redemption has come" (Isaiah 63:4). We see here again the great principle of salvation by destruction, which we saw in Eden and in the Flood, of which the cross of Calvary was the solemn symbol, and the closing scene of the Christian dispensation will be the sublime culmination.

### THE PLAGUES

The plagues of Egypt were especially significant as types of divine judgment on Satanic power as well as human wickedness. They were 10 in number, denoting by the symbolical significance of this number the completeness of the divine judgment on the evil of which this was the expression. The immediate subjects of these visitations were especially fitted to humble the idolatry of Egypt, and prove the impotence of their gods, in contrast with Jehovah. All things that to them were most sacred and, indeed, symbolical of their deities, were involved in the common humiliation and judgment, and proved their utter helplessness to defend or avenge themselves.

### THE NILE

The waters of the Nile were the first to be smitten, and they were not only of vital necessity to the health and comfort of the people, but were especially sacred as symbolical of the life-sustaining power of nature embodied in their majestic river, which was the source of physical life and fertility to the soil, but now became a stream of death. It was the more significant because it was into this very river that Pharaoh had ordered the Hebrew children to be cast.

### FROGS

The second plague, known as the plague of the frogs, was similarly aimed at Egyptian idolatry. The frog was the symbol of human life in embryo. The creative or formative principle among the Egyptians was a frog-headed god. This creature was made to die at the word of Moses, as an expression to its blind worshipers that its very life was at the command of Israel's God.

## GNATS

The plague of gnats, which followed, was not only still more trying and painful, inasmuch as it touched the very persons of the Egyptians, which had not hitherto been the case in the other visitations, but it also humiliated the most sacred objects of their false worship. It appeared in both man and beast, infesting all classes without distinction, covering even the persons of the priests, so that they were made unclean and could not enter their temples, and swarming upon the very animals that were most sacred, and degrading them as the helpless victims of this defiling and disgusting nuisance.

## FLIES

The fourth plague, of flies, was an awful visitation not only upon the persons of men, but upon all the produce of the land, consuming and destroying every green thing, and reducing the inhabitants to the horrors of famine. It had also the same religious significance as the previous plagues. The beetle, one of the flies of Egypt, was a sacred emblem, representing the sun, and its being turned into a scourge and a curse, which they were glad to have removed as a horrible nuisance, was a most vital blow at their favorite form of devil worship.

## ON LIVESTOCK

The plague on livestock swept with one destructive blow over all the cattle of Egypt, destroying both the sacred animals held in such reverence, and also the beasts of burden and the animals for the food of the people without discrimination.

A distinction now begins between the Israelites and the Egyptians, which continues through all the remaining judgments.

## BOILS

The plague of boils which follows leaves the inoffensive cattle free, and now attacks only the human form, covering the person with a filthy, eruptive disease, and driving at length the very magicians from the presence of Moses with humiliation and horror. They not only acknowledged the finger of God, but fled in dismay from the stroke which they themselves had at length felt.

## HAIL AND LIGHTNING

The plagues that follow grow more terrible. The seventh is a terrific storm of hail, with thunder and lightning, in wild and awful commotion, devastating the land, terrifying the people, and even the proud king. For a moment he is awestricken, and asks a reprieve, but speedily repents of his weakness and returns to his obduracy.

## LOCUSTS

And then follows the eighth plague, one of the most awful forms of calamity known in the Scriptures—the swarming of locusts, which suddenly cover all the land and devour whatever has remained from the former judgments, leaving the whole land a waste of desolation.

## DARKNESS

The ninth plague is a vivid culmination of the third series of three, and has a special religious significance about it. In fact it carried to the Egyptian mind a significance even greater than we can understand. It was the visitation of preternatural darkness continuing for three days, so dense that it could be felt. Something like this may have been familiar to the Egyptians in the awful simoom of this land, which often darkens the air for days; but this was a gloom unknown before, coming suddenly at the divine command, so intense that it seemed almost palpable to the touch, and covering only the land of Egypt, Goshen being exempt. The religious import of the plague is heightened by what we know of Egyptian worship. The sun was, perhaps, the chief object of worship, under the name of Amun Ra. The very name of Pharaoh signifies the sun, and represents the king as in some sense connected with it, and entitled to divine honors.

The darkness, therefore, adds to all the previous judgments this final humiliation to the very highest of the objects of their nature worship, and proclaims the true God as supreme above everything in both earth and heaven. Pharaoh is, at length, alarmed and dismayed; he sends in haste for Moses and grants permission to the people to depart, making only one restriction—that their cattle shall remain behind. This Moses peremptorily refuses, and then, in a fit of infatuation, Pharaoh dismisses him from his presence, forbidding him to see his face again, and hardening his heart for the last fatal resistance.

## THE DEATH STROKE

The last blow in the series of divine judgments was a death-blow at the very life of the nation. The death of the firstborn son, while not the extinction of the entire race, is significant of the sentence of destruction upon the entire race, thus cut off in its hope and flower. From this judgment Pharaoh's own home is not exempted. The peculiar meaning of this judgment is found in the fact that it would have fallen upon the Hebrews, too, had they not been protected by the redeeming blood of the Paschal Lamb. It seems, therefore, to stand as the very type of God's eternal judgment on the whole fallen race represented by Egypt as the type of the world, and from which the children of faith were saved, not even by their national immunities and privileges, but only by appropriating faith in the blood of redemption. Falling upon Pharaoh and his people with unmitigated and irremediable severity, it tells of the wrath of God which is revealed from on high against all unrighteousness of men, and which for those outside the covenant of grace and the blood of Jesus, hangs as a dark and fiery cloud of eternal death.

## CLASSIFIED

The 10 plagues of Egypt have been ingeniously arranged by interpreters, as old as the Jewish Rabbis, in several series; the first nine forming three clusters of three each, and the last one standing in awful isolation as the climax. At the end of the first three, the magicians of Pharaoh acknowledge the finger of God. At the end of the second three, they fly in terror from His presence. And at the end of the third three, Pharaoh refuses to see the face of Moses again, and is given up with hardened heart to the inexorable judgment of God.

In the first three there is no distinction between the Hebrews and the Egyptians. In the last seven the Egyptians only suffer, and the Hebrews are divinely exempted. These last seven are the peculiar types of the judgments which are to fall in the last day upon the godless and anti-Christian world. They point forward to the last seven plagues which the angels of judgment are to pour out upon the earth, and from which the saints of God shall be probably exempt. In the vision of these judgments in the book of Revelation, the song of Moses is strangely introduced, intimating a close relation between the incidents we are now relating and the apocalyptic vision.

The entire 10 plagues suggest the judgments of God upon Satan, upon the world, and upon the antichrist in the last days, and present the shadow side of God's great redeeming work, which follows as truly as the shadow follows the light.

2. *Redemption by Blood* (Exodus 12:1–28, 43–51; 13:1–4).

The redemption of Israel was accomplished through the blood of the Paschal Lamb. And so our redemption is effected through the blood of Christ. On the night when Egypt's first-born were slain and Israel's homes were spared the touch of the destroying angel, there was another death in Goshen's tents. It was the Paschal Lamb, whose sprinkled blood became the substitute for Israel's first-born, and the type of the vicarious and sin-atoning Savior. All the details of this solemn ordinance are arranged with special fullness and spiritual significance, and for 3,000 years the children of Israel have preserved this ancient memorial with but little change, as one of the most remarkable monuments of the truth of their wondrous history.

## THE BEGINNING OF MONTHS

It is really the first of the typical ordinances of the great Mosaic system of ceremonial rites. It was to mark a new era in Israel's history, and therefore to be to them the beginning of months, the first month in the ecclesiastical year (Exodus 12:2), even as the sacrifice of Christ is the beginning of the Church's history and the hour when the soul accepts His atonement, the beginning of its spiritual record.

## THE LAMB

The circumstances connected with the selection of the lamb, and its death, are strikingly typical. The lamb was to be without blemish, even as Christ was holy, harmless, undefiled and separate from sinners. It was selected the 10th day of the month, and kept until the 14th, that all might observe its perfect blamelessness and have their attention fixed upon its significance and prepare for its sacrifice. The period that elapsed from its separation until its death was exactly typical of the duration of Christ's public ministry, counting a day for a year. In His 30th year He was publicly set apart, and in His 34th year He was crucified, after an interval of between three and four years, during which He walked in the light of all men and demonstrated to all men His fitness for the work of man's redemption.

## THE HOUSEHOLD

The lamb was taken, not for the individual, but for the household, to show that Christ is the Redeemer, not of any individual or race exclusively, but of the whole family of God. Provision was made for the entire household, adding another if its own circle was too small, suggesting thus to exclusive Israel that they were to share their lamb with their Gentile neighbors (12:3–5).

## SLAIN

At the appointed time the lamb was to be slain by the whole assembly of the congregation of Israel, in the evening. And so the Lord Jesus Christ was delivered by the Jewish Sanhedrin, and publicly crucified about the time of the evening sacrifice (12:6).

## THE SPRINKLED BLOOD

The sprinkling of the blood vividly expresses the application to our hearts of the death of our Lord Jesus Christ, and our acceptance of and dependence upon His offering for our salvation. It is not enough that Christ has died for us; we must appropriate the efficacy of His death to ourselves. The place where the blood was sprinkled may suggest that Christ's blood bears witness not only to us, but to the world around and to the heavens above, of our redemption.

## THE FLESH

The next thing was the eating of the flesh of the lamb. This expresses our participation in the life and strength of Christ, and our taking Him as the very substance and subsistence of our new life, both for soul and body. He Himself has expounded this spiritual mystery in the sixth chapter of the Gospel of John, with deeper fullness, and taught us that His own very life must be imparted to all who would fully live in Him. They were to eat the flesh on the same night that the blood was shed and sprinkled; so our participation in the life of Christ must begin the moment that we accept Him. We cannot live on mere justifying faith, but must have His abiding communion from the moment of our conversion. We cannot take Christ merely for our forgiveness, but the same night we must also take Him for our spiritual life.

## THE FIRE

The flesh of the lamb must be roasted with fire. So Christ must be prepared for and presented to our spiritual apprehension by the Holy Spirit, not as a raw, naked conception, but as a warm, living personality. It must not be sodded with water. Perhaps this means the vain and empty words with which man often soaks the precious truth of God, until it becomes of none effect through the dilutions of human wisdom.

## THE WHOLE CHRIST

The whole of the lamb was to be eaten, with his legs and the purtenances thereof (12:9–10), and nothing of it was to remain until the morning. Thus we are to partake of the complete Christ, accepting not only His blood for our redemption and His flesh for our life, but His head for our thought and wisdom, His legs for our walk and guidance and all the purtenances thereof for all that pertains to our entire existence, even to the most commonplace need of our daily life. No part of Christ or His fullness must be lost or left unclaimed.

## UNLEAVENED BREAD

It was to be eaten with unleavened bread and bitter herbs. The former tells of our separation from sin. The latter of the deep and painful experience through which the Holy Spirit leads to the renunciation of self and sin, and the full acceptance of Jesus, the tears of penitence and the death of self, in all its pains and wholesome self-renunciations (12:8).

## PILGRIMS

They were to eat with their loins girded, their shoes on their feet, their staves in their hands and in haste. The girded loins, the sandalled feet and pilgrim's staff, proclaim their pilgrim life, and mark the beginning of their journey and their readiness to obey and follow (12:11). And so the blood of Jesus separates us from the past, and sends us forth on our heavenly pilgrimage, strangers henceforth to the world, followers of Jesus and ready for His service and will, wherever He may call.

We, too, must eat this holy feast in haste. There is no time for lingering and hesitating. Ere midnight the destroying angel will have passed, and he that loiters may be lost forever. Over the gateway of mercy the inscription burns in letters of fire: "Flee from the coming wrath" (Matthew 3:7). "I tell you, now is the time of God's favor, now is the day of salvation" (2 Corinthians 6:2).

## THE FIRSTBORN

The next chapter more fully unfolds the deeper meaning of the ordinance in regard to the firstborn of Israel, who were to be holy unto the Lord in token of their redemption (Exodus 13:2). The application to us is connected with the use of this expression, firstborn, as descriptive of our place in the family of God. We are all recognized as His firstborn, in the sense of heirship with Jesus Christ. He is the Firstborn of the Father, and therefore the Heir of all things. By His death He redeemed His brethren, and by our union with Him we enter into His place of full inheritance and thus are all God's firstborn sons.

This ancient ordinance of the redeeming blood has passed like a crimson line through all the later teachings of the Scriptures, and given name, shape and color to almost every sentence of apostolic teaching and every song of the heavenly worship. "For you know that it was not with perishable things such as silver or gold that you were redeemed . . . but with the precious blood of Christ, a lamb without blemish or defect" (1 Peter 1:18–19). "Because you were slain,/ and with your blood you purchased men for God/ from every tribe and language and people and nation./ You have made them to be a kingdom and priests to serve our God" (Revelation 5:9b–10a).

### 3. *Redemption by Faith.*

Israel had to enter upon their redemption by a step of bold, decisive faith. And so we are redeemed not only by blood, but saved by faith.

Their first step of faith was their departure from Rameses. For a time their path was circuitous and perplexing. God did not lead them by the direct way of the land of the Philistines, which was much nearer, but around by the

Red Sea, and afterwards through the wilderness of Arabia (Exodus 13:17). So, in leading the soul to its inheritance, God frequently takes the most perplexing way in order to bring it into a deeper knowledge of Himself, and a more thorough death to itself and the world, and teach it by such discipline the lesson of faith.

It was not long before the faith of Israel was sorely tested. They soon found themselves shut in between the surrounding mountains, the sea in front and the pursuing armies of Egypt behind. They seemed shut up to destruction; but they were really shut up to faith and to God. Yet out of their desperate straits came the most glorious chapter of their national history. And so many of us have come to the place of perplexity and even despair, and then found it the very gate of heaven.

First, they must show, however, their own miserable unbelief and worthlessness. In the hour of peril they completely break down, and begin to reproach Moses and Aaron with their cruel misfortunes (14:10–12).

## *STAND STILL*

Next they must get quiet, and cease from all their unbelieving fears and restless activities and efforts at self-deliverance. "Do not be afraid. Stand firm and you will see the deliverance [of] the LORD. . . . The LORD will fight for you; you need only to be still" (14:13–14). God cannot save a soul until it stops trying to save itself, and ceases from its own works and also from its fears.

## *GO FORWARD*

Next comes the advance step of faith: "Tell the Israelites to move on" (14:15). The troubled heart must now act—not in its own strength, nor for its own deliverance, but in dependence on God's promise and salvation. It must accept His word and step out upon it, even in the dark—even into the very waters of the flood. Perhaps their feet are suffered even to touch the waves for a moment, as they advance, as we know was the case when afterward they crossed the Jordan. But the next moment the hand of God has interposed, the waters roll asunder and the path stretches across the angry sea, and leads them on to victory and redemption.

So must we believe and follow, stepping out in faith into the uncertain future, and expecting God to clear and lead the way.

## *THE WAY OF FAITH*

This initial act of faith is subsequently repeated again and again in the experiences of life in other things. And therefore the deliverance of Israel has come to mark the various deliverances of God's people in the trying places of their experience. But in every case the steps of faith are the same. The first is our failure. The next, the cessation of our struggles, fears and activities. And the third, the simple obedient steps of faith, taking God at His word, stepping out in the dark and finding His faithfulness and providence opening our pathway. This is the aspect of faith which the apostle emphasizes in the great picture gallery of Hebrews 11:29: "By faith the people passed through the Red Sea as on dry land."

This is the kind of faith which the natural heart in vain assays to imitate. The Egyptians, assaying to do what the Hebrews did, were drowned. To the eye of sense they did the same thing, but they failed in it. Two persons may perform the very same act, apparently, and in the one case it may prove a miserable attempt at faith which can only bring disaster. The Church is full of these miserable assays at faith, mere make-believes, which involve no real risk of ourselves, or committal to God. Man can believe a good deal when he sees the evidence and has somebody walking before him on dry ground, as Pharaoh's hosts had. But to step out in the dark like one who walks on the sea, with no evidence but God's naked word and the risk of ruin if He fails us, in the faith of God, which flesh and blood hath not revealed to the natural man—this is the faith which brings any great deliverance, whether it be the forgiveness of sins, the sanctifying presence of God, the healing power of Christ or answered prayer in any great emergency. The apostle has expressed it in the simple words: "We live by faith, not by sight" (2 Corinthians 5:7). And Christ has pronounced upon it this benediction: "Blessed are those who have not seen and yet have believed" (John 20:29).

4. *Redemption through the Holy Spirit* (Exodus 13:20–22; 14:19–20).

Israel's redemption was accompanied by the presence and protection of the pillar of cloud and fire, to us the symbol of the Holy Spirit and His part in leading the soul from bondage to redemption. The moment they set forth from Egypt, the Divine Presence preceded their march, and henceforth led them all the way. It was the old symbol of fire, accompanied by the cloud of glory which also appears in almost all the manifestations of God, both in the Old and New Testaments. It is the sublime emblem of that blessed Spirit who becomes the guide and guardian of every child of God, from the beginning of his pilgrimage to the consummation of his complete redemption.

## THE TWOFOLD MANIFESTATION

We observe two stages of this manifestation, even in the first chapter of Israel's new experience.

First, God went before them until they reached the edge of the divided sea, but then He instantly passes through the camp, baptizing them as He passed, no doubt, with the enveloping cloud, and went behind them, marching like a wall of fire between them and their foes. It is not fanciful to apply this to the twofold experience by which the Holy Spirit leads the soul that follows Christ. First, He leads it to faith in Christ as one who goes before, as a presence with us, and yet not fully in us. And then, when we make a full committal and pass through the crisis of absolute surrender and death and resurrection with Christ, He comes nearer to our hearts, passes through and into our entire being, baptizes us and possesses us with His personal presence, henceforth becoming the very element of our being, before us, behind us, within us, above us, beneath us forever more. The first of these experiences might be expressed as the teachings and leading of the Spirit. The second is the baptism and indwelling of the Spirit. His glorious personality must also become real, as well as the Savior, in the experience of every redeemed soul. We must know the Paschal Lamb and the Pillar of Cloud and Fire as a personal presence, the beginning of our entire spiritual life.

The third chapter of the Gospel of John describes the first stage of this spiritual experience. The second chapter of the Acts of the Apostles describes the second and deeper baptism of the Holy Spirit. Often it is in the hour of some crisis like the very floods of the Red Sea that the soul enters into this more intimate fellowship with the Holy Ghost. Let us not fear to follow His guiding presence even into the darkest and most trying place; and when we reach the depths, then we shall find our Guide encompassing us with His loving arms, covering us with His overshadowing wing and standing not only before us but behind us as our glorious reward and our wall of fire around about.

### 5. *The Principle of Death and Resurrection.*

The passage of the Red Sea is the great symbol of the principle which runs through the whole plan of redemption, namely, death and resurrection. The Red Sea was to them a seeming grave; as much so as Isaac's sacrifice on Mount Moriah was his yielding up to death. Their coming forth on the shores of Paran was a vivid type of our stepping into the resurrection life, through our union with the Lord Jesus Christ, in His death and resurrection. It is true that death was not as thorough as it had afterwards to become. And so 40 years later we meet with a new figure of the same principle, namely, the passage of the Jordan, setting forth our more thorough and complete deliverance from the old life and quickening into the life of the Spirit.

### THE TWOFOLD DEATH

Corresponding to this in the redeemed soul, there is often the double experience of death and resurrection: the first, when we turn our backs upon the world in our conversion and die to our former life; the second, when we turn our back upon ourselves and die to the inner life and the entire natural self. Even the first experience, however, is supremely important, and the soul should be taught to recognize all its blessed reality and to count itself so identified with Christ in His crucifixion that it is as one already executed for its own crimes, and thus completely justified in the sight of God through the death of our Substitute.

There is no reason why the deeper death should not also be experienced at the same time, unless it be that the soul has not yet fully realized what it has to die to. Perhaps it needed the experience of the wilderness to show Israel the worthlessness of themselves and the necessity of their crucifixion. Sometimes God has to reveal to us in our subsequent experiences after conversion the fact that in us "nothing good lives" (Romans 7:18), that we may be driven to put off the old man with his deeds, and accept the Lord Jesus in His fullness as our perfect life.

This principle of death and resurrection is the real philosophy of the plan of salvation. God does not pass over our former sin, but He judges it and punishes it in the person of Christ, with whom we are recognized and so identified that His death is practically our execution. This is the ground of our justification. God does not pass by our sin, but fully deals with it and slays us for it, and the soul that enters into life is counted a new-born soul that never participated in the sins of the past.

So also with regard to the question of righteousness. God does not accept our imperfect obedience, but repudiates it, and takes instead Christ's perfect obedience as if it were ours, and thus regards us and treats us as if we had perfectly obeyed His entire law. So again with respect to sanctification. It is not the improvement of our old nature, it is not the gradual perfection of self, but it is the repudiation and death of our old nature, and the imparting of a new and resurrection life, which is wholly supernatural and divine, and literally Christ "has become for us wisdom from God—that is, our righteousness, holiness and redemption" (1 Corinthians 1:30).

On the other side of the Red Sea, God recognizes His people as a new race; and so, "if anyone is in Christ, he is a new creation; the old has gone, the new has come" (2 Corinthians 5:17).

## A FIGURE OF BAPTISM

Hence this transaction is connected in the language of the New Testament with the ordinance of baptism, in a remarkable way. The Apostle Paul, speaking of this event in First Corinthians 10:2, says, "They were all baptized into Moses in the cloud and in the sea." We know that the word baptism is preeminently figurative of death and resurrection, and so used again and again with respect to our union with Christ. "All of us who were baptized into Christ Jesus were baptized into his death" (Romans 6:3).

## THE CLOUD AND THE SEA

Their being baptized, therefore, in the cloud and in the sea, expresses the idea of their being delivered to death, and brought forth to a new life: the sea expressing the idea of death and judgment; the cloud, the descending life of heaven. How beautifully the same two ideas are combined in the baptism of our Lord Himself, as He stepped into the waters of the Jordan and was baptized with water; and then even as the cloud, which of old passed through the hosts of Israel as they went through the sea, came the descending Holy Spirit from the open heavens, and rested upon Him, and He was baptized henceforth both in the cloud and in the sea. So we see the two same thoughts in Peter's language on the day of Pentecost: "Repent and be baptized . . . in the name of Jesus Christ" (Acts 2:38). That is the baptism in water—the sea. "And you will receive the gift of the Holy Spirit" (2:38). That is the baptism in the cloud. This is the ever true and full significance of Christian baptism. It is not merely the baptism of water, which is only the sea, but it ought ever to be accompanied with the baptism of the Holy Spirit, which is the baptism of the cloud. And when the soul truly yields itself to this ordinance, as an act of self-crucifixion with Christ and entire consecration to the union with Him, then, indeed, that blessed Presence itself passes like the ancient cloud through its entire being, and becomes henceforth the divine element in which it lives and moves and has its being.

6. *The Redemption Song* (Exodus 15:1–21).

Israel's redemption was celebrated by the song of Moses and Miriam. And so our redemption must also be confessed and commemorated by the spirit of praise. The song of Moses is the keynote of all the songs of redemption that fill the Bible, and reaches its full chorus in the song of the Lamb, by the sea of glass, and the choirs of glory. We shall never know the full joy of salvation until we begin to praise. This is the first evidence of faith, real faith, and is ever the support and inspiration of faith. "He put a new song in my mouth,/ a hymn of praise to our God" (Psalm 40:3). "I will praise you, O LORD./ Although you were angry with me,/ your anger has turned away/ and you have comforted me" (Isaiah 12:1). This is the language of the forgiven soul, and the more we praise, the more we shall ever have to praise for.

7. *The Memorial of Redemption* (Exodus 13:5–16).

The redemption of Israel was commemorated by a memorial ordinance, the Hebrew Passover. So our redemption is celebrated by the Lord's Supper, designed to show forth Christ's death till He comes, and therefore dear to every heart that loves the Redeemer and values His precious blood.

The deeper fullness of our redemption is unfolded in many succeeding types of the book of Exodus, but these we reserve for our last theme in the division of the book; even as God deferred them until the people were prepared for their fuller revelation, by the experience which immediately followed their crossing of the Red Sea.

# CHAPTER 3

## CHRISTIAN PILGRIMAGE AS PREFIGURED IN THE BOOK OF EXODUS

The events that immediately followed the crossing of the Red Sea furnish a beautiful picture of Christian experience, especially in its earlier stages.

### SECTION I—*Divine Guidance*
### Exodus 13:21–22

"By day the LORD went ahead of them in a pillar of cloud to guide them on their way and by night in a pillar of fire to give them light, so that they could travel by day or night. Neither the pillar of cloud by day nor the pillar of fire by night left its place in front of the people" (Exodus 13:21–22).

Divine guidance is one of the first experiences of the Christian life. And it is finely expressed in the symbol of the pillar of cloud and fire which led the Hebrews in all their journeyings. Not only did the Divine Presence bring them to and through the sea, but it henceforth became their Guide through all the journey of the wilderness, moving when they moved, and waiting when they rested. So, still: "Those who are led by the Spirit of God are sons of God" (Romans 8:14); "I will instruct you and teach you in the way you should go;/ I will counsel you and watch over you" (Psalm 32:8) is God's voice to the pardoned soul.

Nor has the Master left us without His own personal confirmation of this precious truth: "When he has brought out all his own, he goes on ahead of them, and his sheep follow him because they know his voice" (John 10:4). "I am the good shepherd; I know my sheep and my sheep know me—just as the Father knows me and I know the Father" (10:14–15). "But the Counselor, the Holy Spirit, whom the Father will send in my name, will teach you all things and will remind you of everything I have said to you" (14:26). "He will guide you into all truth" (16:13).

## SECTION II—*Trial*
### Exodus 15:22–24

"Then Moses led Israel from the Red Sea and they went into the Desert of Shur. For three days they traveled in the desert without finding water. When they came to Marah, they could not drink its water because it was bitter. (That is why the place is called Marah.) So the people grumbled against Moses, saying, 'What are we to drink?' " (Exodus 15:22–24).

The next chapter of their new experience is trial. They were led immediately, not into a smiling paradise, but into the dreary wilderness. "For three days they traveled in the desert without finding water. When they came to Marah, they could not drink its water because it was bitter" (15:22b–23). Here we have not only trial, but the failure of all earth's sources of comfort in trial. Not only is there the desolation of the wilderness, but the very springs which ordinarily refreshed the traveler are to them fountains of bitterness.

It is thus with the child of God, even in his early Christian experience. God leads him, not into unmingled joy and circumstances of comfort and ease, but "sometimes through scenes of deepest gloom." And then, when he turns to his usual sources of comfort and help, even they become a bitter disappointment, and fail to afford their wonted sweetness. Perhaps his business becomes embarrassing, or even his dearest friends misunderstand him and disappoint him and he finds himself really alone in the world, which once had a thousand springs of enjoyment that now are all unable to satisfy. God is again showing him to himself, and making him realize more fully his absolute dependence for everything upon the divine sources of his life. The more entirely we are yielded to God, the less earth can really satisfy us, and the less we see in it.

## SECTION III—*Trial Sweetened and Sanctified*
### Exodus 15:25

"Then Moses cried out to the LORD, and the LORD showed him a piece of wood. He threw it into the water, and the water became sweet.

"There the LORD made a decree and a law for them, and there he tested them" (Exodus 15:25).

The next experience is the sweetening of Marah's waters by the branch of healing, which Moses found beside the springs of Marah, and cast into the waters until they were sweetened. This is the type, not of the removal of trial, but of the transformation of sorrow into blessing by divine grace and consolation. Moses did not find a new spring, but they drank afterwards of the same waters which at first they found so bitter. So God does not need to alter the circumstances of our life, but to add to them His presence and all-sufficiency, and they become transformed to blessings. Joseph's prison becomes a place of victory and service; Paul's dungeon becomes a sanctuary of holy song; and Bunyan's jail, a palace of vision whence he not only sees, but shows to all future pilgrims the celestial city and the land of Beulah.

Moses did not make this tree, or bring it from a great distance, but simply found it growing just beside the bitter spring.

## THE BRANCH OF HEALING

Beside every spring of sorrow, there already stands the branch of healing, the tree of promise, the Word of Life which will open fountains in the desert, and make songs to break forth in the night. The Lord showed him the tree; so when the Lord opens our eyes, how the promises grow vivid, and become living realities, streams of water, clear as crystal, fountains in the desert and sources of everlasting consolation. Paul sees one of these branches of promise, and lo, his thorn in the flesh becomes, instead of a messenger of Satan, a very angel of blessing. Jacob gets his hand upon the promise, and lo, the place of peril becomes the place of power, and the darkest hour of his life, the very turning point of victory and transformation.

And so the myriads about the throne, who have come out of great tribulation, shall forever tell how,

> Sorrow, touched by God, grows bright
> With more than rapture's ray,
> As darkness shows us worlds of light
> We never saw by day.

### SECTION IV—*Divine Healing in Its Earliest Ordinance and Statute*
Exodus 15:25–26

"There the LORD made a decree and a law for them, and there he tested them. He said, 'If you listen carefully to the voice of the LORD your God and do what is right in his eyes, if you pay attention to his commands and keep all his decrees, I will not bring on you any of the diseases I brought on the Egyptians, for I am the LORD who heals you" (Exodus 15:25–26).

God here undertakes to be the Guardian of His people's physical health and strength, by His own direct power and continual interposition.

The last clause literally should read, "I, the LORD thy God, am healing you," intimating a continual exercise of His healing love and power.

## THE COVENANT

It is frivolous and trifling to apply this passage merely to their exemption from the plagues of Egypt. There would have been no meaning in such a promise, for they had no reason to fear that these plagues should come upon them. They had been exempt from them in Egypt, even before they knew God's covenant fully, and there never had been any intimation that they would be exposed to them. The references were, no doubt, to the diseases which were common to the Egyptians, and which they themselves had seen, and, perhaps, experienced in their Egyptian life. In referring to this subject in Deuteronomy, He again repeats the promise: "The LORD will keep you free from every disease. He will not inflict on you the horrible diseases you knew in Egypt, but he will inflict them on all who hate you" (7:15). The most casual reader would naturally apply these words to ordinary sickness, and such diseases as fall in the experiences of life upon the people of the world, and which they themselves had known by personal experience in Egypt. He promises to do this by His own personal and continual power, care and keeping. The faithfulness with which He fulfilled this promise is touchingly shown in the testimony of the Psalmist: "And from among their tribes no one faltered" (Psalm 105:37). He promised this continual deliverance to them by a divine covenant, which He also terms a "decree and a law" (Exodus 15:25).

## THE CONDITIONS

And like every covenant, it was connected with certain requirements on their part, especially with their diligent hearkening to His voice, and their prompt obedience to His commands. These are some of the conditions of God's healing presence with His people. It is only as we abide in Him, hearkening to His voice and quickly responding, that we can avoid the causes of physical suffering, and maintain the unbroken communication of His life in our physical being. These words, "decree and law," place the promise of divine healing upon a very substantial and enduring basis. And unless we can prove that this ancient ordinance is revoked, it still remains the basis of our trust in His healing life and word.

That God should thus early reveal Himself to them as their physical Healer, immediately upon their crossing the Red Sea and entering upon their new life, proves that He expected them to depend upon Him in the fullest sense, as the supply of all their needs, present and future. No doubt the land of Egypt had many human resources for the healing of disease, for we know that they had reached a somewhat high stage in medical as well as other arts and sciences, but none of them were henceforth to be employed by His peculiar people. God alone was to be their Physician and their Life; and all through the Mosaic institutions we find no provisions for natural or medical healing, but the constant recognition of God Himself as the Keeper and Healer of their bodies, and of their physical strength as intimately and inseparably connected with their holiness and obedience.

## OUR REDEMPTION RIGHT

Now we know that "these things occurred as examples" (1 Corinthians 10:6) to us, and that they, in all this, were but the types of God's redeemed people under the new covenant. What right have we to ignore this part of their experience, and yet apply the story of the manna and the rock to our spiritual experience? Surely, the one is intended to be as real and permanent as the other, and the ordinance of healing to have its counterpart in the New Testament as truly as the manna is fulfilled in the Living Bread. Such is indeed the case, for our Lord's ministry began, just like their experience, in the manifestation of His healing power, and He is still the "same yesterday and today and forever" (Hebrews 13:8). He reveals Himself throughout the ages as a Living Presence, who can sustain our entire being from His own life, and who Himself "took up our infirmities . . . and carried our diseases" (Matthew 8:17) as well as our sins.

Why should the gospel be deprived of its mightiest credential before an unbelieving world? Why should the unbelief of the Church put away these ancient promises, and neutralize so large a part of our redemption? Why should not the young disciple receive at the very commencement of his pilgrimage, in implicit faith, the covenant promise: "I am the LORD who heals you" (Exodus 15:26)?

## SECTION V—*The Springs and Palms of Elim*
### Exodus 15:27

"Then they came to Elim, where there were twelve springs and seventy palm trees, and they camped there near the water" (Exodus 15:27).

These are types of the times of refreshing and rest that come to the children of God after scenes of trial (15:25). "Weeping may remain for a night,/ but rejoicing comes in the morning" (Psalm 30:5). There are sweet arbors on the king's highway, and green oases on the wide desert. There is a land of Beulah, as well as a valley of Baca. And He knows best when to lead us amid its palms and fountains, and when to test our faith and love in the howling wilderness.

There are 12 wells, or rather springs, of water for one fountain of Marah. There was a well for every tribe. And so God has for each of us a fountain of comfort and blessing, as well as a cross and a thorn. There is a fresh well for each of the 12 months of the year, and a new palm tree for each of the 70 years of life.

The 70 palms signify a yet more abundant and delightful provision for rest and shelter from the heat of trial, and the rich and abundant fruits of divine love and bounty. "He makes me lie down in green pastures,/ he leads me beside quiet waters,/ he restores my soul./ He guides me in the paths of righteousness/ for his name's sake" (Psalm 23:2–3).

## SECTION VI—*The Manna*
### Exodus 16:1–5, 14, 25

They must next be fed and taught whence their provision comes in their wilderness journey.

### THEIR MURMURING

First, therefore, they were made to feel their need, and to understand that the wilderness affords no natural supply for that need. So God has to teach us that earth can no longer fill the soul, and that our spiritual nourishment must wholly come to us from Him. As usual, the result in their case is failure; failure that becomes the occasion for God's richer grace.

### MET BY MERCY

They murmur because they have no bread, and their carnal hearts turn back again to Egypt. But their murmuring is met by God's mercy, and becomes the occasion for the commencement of the supply of manna which henceforth meets their daily wants through all the desert journey for 40 years.

Travelers tell us of a substance that bears this name, and somewhat resembles the miraculous manna of Exodus, which is still found in small quantities in certain portions of the desert, but confined to special locations, and almost always found under the tamarisk tree. It is not necessary to show that no mere natural substance could have supplied in sufficient quantities the wants of three million people; and besides, the regularity of its fall, the systematic interruption of it on the Sabbath and the fact that it was confined to no certain locality, but followed them all through their desert march, are sufficient to show that it was a wholly supernatural provision.

### THE LIVING BREAD

It is a type of God's spiritual provision for His people's deeper need in their Christian pilgrimage. Our Lord unfolds the mystery of this living bread in the sixth chapter of the Gospel of John, and teaches us that He is Himself His people's life.

The manna was a very simple form of bread, not ministering to the stronger appetites of the body, but simply satisfying and completely supplying all its needs.

So the grace of God comes to us in great simplicity, not ministering to the self-life, but supplying all our real spiritual needs, and containing the substance of everything which our entire being requires for its nourishment and growth.

The manna needed to be daily renewed. We cannot live on former experiences, but must abide in continual fellowship in the source of our life.

The manna fell on the morning dew. And so the Holy Spirit must bring to us the fresh supplies each moment of Christ's sustaining life and grace.

When the hearts of the people grew carnal, they became weary of the manna; and so the world has no taste for Christ, and the worldly minded Christian takes no delight in His communion and His Word. The manna was in no sense a natural growth, and the worldly minded Christian cannot appreciate it. It came from heaven, and God is likewise ever teaching His children that their spiritual life cannot feed on the things of earth, but must be supplied from Himself.

The reason why multitudes of Christians are so famished and feeble is because they are trying to live upon the husks or the fruits of the world. They are longing for the flesh pots of Egypt or the quails of lust and are weary of the simple bread of God. They feed on men's philosophies, the protoplasms of materialism, the sentimentality of naturalism, the prurience of the playhouse, the sensationalism of the novel, the filthy hash of the newspaper or the husks of the market and stock exchange, instead of the pure, sweet, sustaining Word of God.

## SECTION VII—*The Living Water from the Stricken Rock*
### Exodus 17:1–7

This is the type of God's provision for our spiritual refreshing through the indwelling and continual influence of the Holy Spirit.

### *THE HOLY SPIRIT*

The manna represents Christ as the source of our life; the water, the Holy Spirit. They came to Rephidim, which signifies rest, and there, no doubt, they expected rest and refreshing. But nature has still no supply for the spiritual life. The old sources of our strength will ever fail us, until we learn to draw it alone from God. The wells of Rephidim are dry, and a great cry of bitter disappointment and anger goes up against Moses and against God. But again the resources of grace are sufficient, and murmuring is met once more by mercy. The rock is stricken by the rod of the Lawgiver, and from its riven bosom a living well pours its overflowing tide, until the people and cattle drink to repletion, and the stream flows on, it would appear, through all their desert pathway. For the Psalmist declares that it ran in the desert like a river; and the apostle tells us that "[They] drank from the spiritual rock that accompanied them, and that rock was Christ" (1 Corinthians 10:4; see also Psalm 78:15).

Our Savior has given us the sweetest commentary on this passage in His words to the woman of Samaria; "If you knew the gift of God and who it is that asks you for a drink, you would have asked him and he would have given you living water" (John 4:10). "Everyone who drinks this water will be thirsty again, but whoever drinks the water I give him will never thirst. Indeed, the water I give him will become in him a spring of water welling up to eternal life" (4:13–14). " 'If anyone is thirsty, let him come to me and drink. Whoever believes in me, as the Scripture has said, streams of living water will flow from within him.' By this he meant the Spirit, whom those who believed in him were later to receive. Up to that time the Spirit had not been given, since Jesus had not yet been glorified" (John 7:37–39). The water of Horeb, therefore, is a type of the Holy Spirit; and the rock of Horeb, of Christ, from whose stricken bosom the Spirit has come forth, since the day of Pentecost, to satisfy the thirst of sinful and suffering men.

### HOREB AND KADESH

It is important to contrast this scene with the later incident at Kadesh, recorded in the book of Numbers, where Moses struck the rock again, but in so doing displeased God, who had commanded him only to speak to it, and the water would come forth. It was struck once, and henceforth open forever. And so, the death of Christ cannot be repeated. Once for all, His sacrifice was sufficient and complete, and all the resources of grace are now at the command of the penitent and believing soul, and the word of simplest trust. The rock is struck; the Spirit is given; heaven is opened; "Whoever wishes, let him take the free gift of the water of life" (Revelation 22:17).

## SECTION VIII—*The Conflict with Amalek at Rephidim*
### Exodus 17:8–16

Hitherto Israel has had no battles to fight, and has met with no adversaries since the destruction of the Egyptian host. All their trials have come from the wilderness and from themselves. So, often for a while in our early Christian life, we are exempt from severe conflicts. But now their first battle must come to teach them the secret of victory. "The Amalekites came and attacked the Israelites at Rephidim" (Exodus 17:8). This battle is the type of Christian warfare in one of its aspects: "The LORD will be at war against the Amalekites from generation to generation" (Exodus 17:16), implies that the conflict is not ended yet.

## THE FLESH

Amalek was the type of the flesh. He was descended from Esau; and Esau represented the carnal nature. The apostle explains this in Galatians 5:17: "For the sinful nature desires what is contrary to the Spirit, and the Spirit what is contrary to the sinful nature. They are in conflict with each other, so that you do not do what you want."

## A FIGHT OF FAITH

But it is not to be a battle in their own strength. He who leads the battle in the plain below, Joshua, is himself the type of the Lord Jesus Christ. And the secret of even his victory is the uplifted hands of Moses on the mount above. These uplifted hands tell not only of prayer, and continual prayer, but of the prayer of victory and faith. The uplifted hands are not merely raised in intercession, but also in triumph holding up the name of Jehovah as the banner and afterward signalizing the victory by the name of *Jehovah Nissi,* "the LORD is my Banner" (17:15). So we say, "This is the victory that has overcome the world, even our faith" (1 John 5:4). The only secret of triumph in the conflict with the flesh is, "Live by the Spirit, and you will not gratify the desires of the sinful nature" (Galatians 5:16). And the only song which we shall ever sing on this battlefield as a song of triumph is, "Thanks be to God! He gives us the victory through our Lord Jesus Christ" (1 Corinthians 15:57).

## THE HAND ON THE THRONE

The marginal reading of the 16th verse of Exodus is: "Because a hand was against the throne of the LORD." This expresses the attitude of faith, grasping the very throne of power and authority, and triumphing in the strength of God.

What a comfort in our spiritual conflict it is to know that it is the Lord that will have war with Amalek, and not the poor weak heart of man; and also to remember the decree of extermination which we may claim: "I will completely blot out the memory of Amalek from under heaven" (17:14).

We may so triumph over the flesh in abiding union with the Lord, that we shall reckon ourselves dead indeed unto sin, and treat the life of self as something that is all buried in the oblivion of our Savior's grave.

## SECTION IX—*Order and Government*
Exodus 18:5, 13–26

The 18th chapter of Exodus gives us an account of the visit of Jethro, Moses' father-in-law, and the results of his counsel to Moses, which led to the organization of the eldership, and a systematic plan for the oversight and government of the people.

This also has its spiritual significance in our Christian life and in the history of the Church; teaching us the necessity not only of a true spiritual experience and a life of interior communion with God, but of a proper and systematic adjustment of our external life, the necessity of order and government in the Church of Christ and proper habits in the regulation of our religious life and work. God has, therefore, given to us the institution of the family, of the Church, and of civil government, and the various spheres and ministries of social and business life and Christian work. They all involve their several responsibilities and obligations to which we cannot be indifferent any more than to the claims of our more spiritual relations to God Himself.

### A PICTURE OF GRACE

What a beautiful picture these chapters present of the life of God's ancient people, following the leadership of His personal presence in helpless dependence, as a flock would follow a shepherd through the wilderness or the little child would follow its mother's lead as she guided it through the unknown pathway. How fatherly and tender the divine love and care! How gentle and forbearing the attitude of God! And how impatient and imperfect, often, the spirit of His petulant and murmuring children. Every word of impatience on their part, every impetuous fear, every outcry of disappointment and dread is met by some new expression of His infinite patience, forbearance, gentleness and boundless grace.

### A STARTLING CHANGE

But suddenly all this is changed. In a moment they are called to meet Him in an aspect so different that at first they are overwhelmed with awe, and beg to be permitted to fly from His presence. This leads us to the next chapter.

# CHAPTER 4

## THE DISPENSATION OF THE LAW

Exodus 19:1–25; 20:1–21

This is introduced about two months after the crossing of the Red Sea. They have now reached the base of the Sinaitic mountains, and God calls Moses apart into Mount Sinai, announces to him that He is now about to lead His people into a solemn covenant, and bids them prepare for the manifestation which God is about to make to them. "You yourselves have seen," He says, "what I did to Egypt, and how I carried you on eagles' wings and brought you to myself. Now if you obey me fully and keep my covenant, then out of all nations you will be my treasured possession. Although the whole earth is mine, you will be for me a kingdom of priests and a holy nation" (Exodus 19:4–6a). "The people all responded together, 'We will do everything the LORD has said' " (19:8).

### THE PREPARATIONS

They were then commanded to prepare themselves most solemnly, separating their persons from all defilement, and assembling on the third day around the base of the mount, but charged most emphatically to stand apart from it, and not even to touch it, on penalty of death.

On the third morning, Jehovah appears enthroned upon the mount in awful majesty and glory. Thick clouds of murky blackness hang around the lofty brow of Sinai, and vivid lightnings cleave asunder the awful darkness, and re-echo themselves in incessant thunderings, while out of the darkness and fire there issues the piercing sound of the trumpet, growing loud and long, until all the people tremble, and even Moses is filled with irresistible awe and fear.

At length, God summons Moses into the darkness, and he disappears from the sight of the trembling people into the midst of the mount of fire. Then follows the living voice of God in the ears of all the people, and the proclamation of His mighty law. Sentence after sentence they fall from the

129

mount; every word of those 10 commandments, which become to the ages the summary of righteousness and duty, in its twofold completeness, with respect both to God and all the subordinate relationships of life.

As a token of their authority and permanence, these words are afterward written by the finger of God on tables of stone, and preserved in the Ark of the Covenant, and the very shrine of the Hebrew Tabernacle.

Many different names have been given to this divine message. They are called the Decalogue, the Ten Commandments, the Words of the Covenant, the Tables of the Covenant, the Testimony, the Tables of the Testimony and, also, the Law. Another account of the same events is given in Deuteronomy 5:22–31, slightly modified in some subordinate expressions. Our present purpose simply requires that we shall explain the meaning of this dispensation of law in its relation to their spiritual life and ours.

## SECTION I—*The History of the Law*

1. It was given at Mount Sinai in the third month after the departure of Israel from Egypt as a proclamation of God's covenant with His people.

2. It was given with great majesty and terror (Exodus 20; Hebrews 12:18–21).

3. It was given through the mediatorship of Moses (Galatians 3:19–20), and so is called the Law of Moses (John 1:17).

4. It was given through the ministry of angels (Acts 7:53; Galatians 3:19).

5. It was spoken by the voice of God Himself (Hebrews 12:26).

6. It was administered by the Lord Jesus Christ, and the Angel of the Covenant (Exodus 23:20–21; Acts 7:38; Malachi 3:1).

7. It was written by the finger of God on two tables of stone (Deuteronomy 5:22; Exodus 31:18).

8. It was broken by the people, and the first tables were broken in the hands of Moses; perhaps as a token of the fact that the contents of the tables had already been broken by their disobedience and the sins of men (Exodus 32:15–19).

9. It was rewritten by God and renewed in the second and more gracious covenant, and then deposited in the Ark of the Covenant to be there preserved, perhaps as a type of the fact that Jesus Christ has brought us into a new covenant with God, and He keeps for us the law under this new covenant, and also keeps it in our hearts, as our indwelling sanctifier (Exodus 34:1-28; 40:20).

10. It consisted of three parts, namely, the moral, contained in the 10 commandments; the ceremonial, having reference to the ceremonial types; and the judicial, having reference to the social life and the civil government of the people.

## SECTION II—*The Design of the Law*

### *THE HOLINESS OF GOD*

1. It was intended to reveal the holiness of God. They had just come out of the darkness of Egypt, and had no true conception of God. Again and again had they shown in their short pilgrimage their disregard of His authority and law. They must learn His absolute righteousness and infinite holiness. Without this His very mercy would be abused.

So in our life God must reveal Himself in His majesty and purity, as well as His love. So He came to Job, until he abhorred himself in the light of God. So He came to Isaiah, until he fell at His feet as unclean and cried out for purity. So He comes to every soul before it can rightly understand sin or holiness. The simplest faith will ever be the most reverent. The more we know His purity, the more will we prize His love. And so even under all the grace of the gospel, we are taught that we must have grace "and so worship God acceptably with reverence and awe, for our 'God is a consuming fire' " (Hebrews 12:28b–29).

### *THE STANDARD OF CONDUCT*

2. The next design of the law was to reveal to man the perfect standard of duty and righteousness, under that period of divine revelation. It was a marvelous embodiment of all the essential principles of righteousness and virtue.

Beginning with God Himself, it first presents Him as the supreme object of worship. Next it teaches the method of worship; then the spirit of worship; and then the time of worship.

Coming, secondly, to man's relative duties, it begins first with the family, the root of society; next it touches our obligation to human life; then to social purity; then the rights of property; and then of reputation; closing in the 10th commandment with the very spring of action and character, our desires and motives, and demanding for them absolute righteousness and purity.

It has well been called, even by eminent jurists, "A miracle of ethics," transcendently in advance of the very highest productions of human thought in any age or land.

### *TO REVEAL SIN AND LEAD TO CHRIST*

3. It was designed to reveal man's sin and lead us to Christ for salvation and sanctification. This was perhaps its chief design: "I would not have known what sin was except through the law" (Romans 7:7); "Therefore no one will be declared righteous in his sight by observing the law; rather, through the law we become conscious of sin" (3:20). God Himself declares: "God has come to test you, so that the fear of God will be with you to keep

you from sinning" (Exodus 20:20). God knew His people would break the law, and never expected them to be saved by their own obedience to it; but rather to see through its demands their helpless and lost condition, and thus be driven to accept the atonement and righteousness of the Lord Jesus Christ. "So the law was put in charge to lead us to Christ that we might be justified by faith" (Galatians 3:24). So it must come to every soul, to reveal self, to convict of sin, to prostrate at the feet of mercy, "that every mouth may be silenced and the whole world held accountable to God" (Romans 3:19). And then, when He has included all under sin, He has mercy upon all who believe.

A poor slave lay dying. His master came to see him and took him gently by the hand. The slave kissed the hand and said: "Blessings on this hand." "Why, Sam," said the master, "how can you say that? That hand never did you anything but harm; it has beaten and bruised you a hundred times; how can you bless it?" "Yes, blessings on that hand," replied the poor slave. "It was that which drove me for comfort to my precious Jesus; He soothed my sorrows, and made my heart so glad that I can only say blessings on the hand of hard old master, for driving me to Thee."

So the law is a hard old master; it can only condemn and smite, but drives us to the cross and the Savior, and we should only bless it, too.

Not only does the law show us our guilt, and thus drive us to Christ for our salvation, but at a later stage in our experience it reveals to us ourselves and our utter sinfulness, and also drives us to Him for sanctification.

The first operation of the law in convicting a sinner and leading him to Christ for pardon is set forth in Romans 3:9–31. But there must come a second working. The soul must see its inherent wickedness and discover that "nothing good lives in me, that is, in my sinful nature" (Romans 7:18), but it will receive Christ in His fullness, for its inner purity and life.

This operation of the law is evidently described in Romans 6 and 7. For a while, like Israel in the earlier part of their journey, the soul has gone on in joy and confidence; but suddenly the sky is overcast. It comes to Sinai; it hears the voice of the law; it finds that within which is neither able nor willing to obey; it readily cries, "We will do everything the LORD has said" (Exodus 19:8), and then it fails, sins and despairs and falls under condemnation.

What is there in all this to sanctify? Why, it is the very root of sanctification. It is finding out our helplessness. It is coming to the end of self. And when, discouraged and defeated with its vain endeavors and its broken vows and purposes, it cries in despair, "What a wretched man I am! Who will rescue me from this body of death?" (Romans 7:24). Then it finds the same blessed Friend who set it free from guilt, standing again by its side, and offering to save it from self and sin by His indwelling life and power; and it cries in joyful deliverance, "Thanks be to God—through Jesus Christ our Lord" (Romans 7:25).

Again the law has been its schoolmaster to lead it to Christ—this time for sanctification. And now it learns that even for this evil heart, as well as for its wretched past, He has paid the full penalty; that it may look on its old self as no longer a real self, but dead with Christ, through His cross, and know that the law of the Spirit of Life in Christ Jesus does set it free from the law of sin and death, and that the righteousness of the law is fulfilled in it, as it walks in the new resurrection life, not after the flesh, but after the Spirit.

## SECTION III—*The Place of the Law Under the Gospel*

### REDEEMED FROM ITS CURSE

1. Christ has redeemed us from the curse and penalty of the law by being made a curse for us (Galatians 3:13), so that the believer is now in the position of one who has been already executed for his own sin in the person of his Substitute, and the law has no more demands against him.

### CHRIST HAS KEPT IT FOR US

2. Christ has earned for us its promises by keeping its precepts, and thus puts the believer in the position of one who has obeyed the commandments and deserves their recompense. This is the meaning of His righteousness (Romans 10:4).

### CHRIST HAS REENACTED IT

3. Christ has reenacted the law in His own precepts and commandments, and in His own example and life where we find the true and perfect rule of our Christian life. It is not that the law is abolished, but uplifted and reenacted with greater fullness, sweetness and spirituality. It is very much the same as the issuing of the second edition of a book, containing important additions and corrections, and taking the place of the former edition. Therefore, Christ's commandments, "these words of mine" (Matthew 7:24), as He calls them, are the Christian's final law. And Christ's own beautiful life is the exposition and object lesson of that law:

> A life in which the law appears
> Drawn out in living characters.

The law of Christ is therefore more complete, more comprehensive, more searching and reaches a higher standard than the law of Moses. Its first word is, "Love the Lord your God with all your heart and with all your soul and with all your mind and with all your strength" (Mark 12:30). And its second, "Love each other," not as yourselves, but "as I have loved you" (John 15:12).

## THE LAW IN THE HEART

4. The Holy Spirit writes this new law upon our hearts and disposes and enables us to keep it. He does this by revealing in us and uniting to us the very person of the Lord Jesus Christ, who becomes our indwelling righteousness, and so lives in us His own pure and perfect life of love and obedience, as we receive Him and yield to His voice and will. Hence the Holy Spirit came on the anniversary of the giving of the law, the day of Pentecost, thus suggesting to us that He would henceforth be to every believer the very substance of the law, and the power to perform it. This was the ancient covenant: "after that time . . . I will put my law in their minds and write it on their hearts" (Jeremiah 31:33). This is how the Spirit sanctifies us; and how "because through Christ Jesus the law of the Spirit of life set me free from the law of sin and death" (Romans 8:2). When He enters the life and controls it, the righteousness of the law is fulfilled in us, as we "do not live according to the sinful nature but according to the Spirit" (8:4). This also is a reason why Jesus Christ is represented as our righteousness, "who has become for us . . . holiness" (1 Corinthians 1:30). He Himself enters and occupies our heart, and becomes in it the spirit of righteousness.

All this was beautifully expressed and set forth in Exodus, by the second covenant of the law, accompanied by the gracious words of Moses: "The LORD, the LORD, the compassionate and gracious God, slow to anger, abounding in love and faithfulness" (34:6); and still more vividly by the fact that this law thus renewed was not left in the hands of the people, but enshrined in the ark and thus kept and carried in their midst.

Now we know that the ark was a type of Christ. So the figure speaks to us of Jesus keeping for us the divine law, and then entering and abiding in us, and keeping it also in us, as our life and righteousness.

# CHAPTER 5

## THE REVELATION OF GRACE IN EXODUS

We have already seen that the story of Israel's redemption was designed to prefigure the plan of redemption and the grace of God which brings salvation to all men. But now, after the revelation of the law, we have a much fuller development of the principles of the gospel and the grace of the Lord Jesus Christ in meeting the conscious need which the law reveals, and fulfilling its righteousness in our hearts and lives.

### SECTION I—*The Mediation of Moses*
Exodus 20:19–21; 32:30–35; 33:1–17

Even amid the terrors of Sinai, we behold the beautiful illustration of the mediatorial work of the Lord Jesus Christ, in the intercession of Moses between God and the terrified people. "Speak to us yourself," they cried to Moses. "But do not have God speak to us or we will die" (Exodus 20:19). In great condescension God grants their request, and so Moses enters into the thick darkness and fire, and becomes the medium of communication between God and His sinful people, and the great type of a greater Daysman who dwells amid the glories of God's ineffable holiness, and yet meets us in our own humanity as a merciful and faithful High Priest in things pertaining to God.

### THEIR SIN
This character is maintained by Moses, not only in the covenant of the law, but again throughout the period of their wilderness life. Most beautifully does it appear in the dark and awful hour when the people broke their covenant, and turned the sacred scenes where God had manifested His presence into a place of idolatrous revelry; provoking, at first, their meek and gentle leader even to break the very tables of the covenant in his haste and displeasure, and for a time threatening to turn away the presence of God al-

together from their midst. Then it is that the depth and strength of his character shine out with a grandeur which only finds its parallel in the priesthood of the Lord Jesus Christ. Throwing himself on his face before God, he cries, "Oh, what a great sin these people have committed! They have made themselves gods of gold. But now, please forgive their sin—but if not, then blot me out of the book you have written" (32:31–32). And as Jehovah for a little reserves His forgiveness, and speaks of sending an angel instead of His own personal presence before His rebellious people, the faithful intercessor ventures to plead again: "If you are pleased with me, teach me your ways . . . Remember that this nation is your people. . . . If your Presence does not go with us, do not send us up from here. How will anyone know that you are pleased with me and with your people unless you go with us? What else will distinguish me and your people from all the other people on the face of the earth" (33:13, 15–16). His prayer prevails, and the promise is renewed.

## THEIR SECOND FAILURE

Yet again is their sin repeated in the 14th chapter of Numbers, when the unbelief of the spies and the congregation holds them back from entering the land of Canaan at Kadesh Barnea, and the Lord is again provoked to cut them off in His wrath. Once more the faithful intercessor is on his face before God, crying: " 'In accordance with your great love, forgive the sin of these people, just as you have pardoned them from the time they left Egypt until now.' The LORD replied, 'I have forgiven them, as you asked' " (Numbers 14:19–20).

So for us the Lord Jesus ministers before the throne, and therefore "he is able to save completely those who come to God through him, because he always lives to intercede for them" (Hebrews 7:25).

## SECTION II—*The Altar of Earth*
### Exodus 20:24–26

At the foot of Sinai, and in the chapter which records the giving of the law, we find this beautiful provision for the frailty and sin of the covenant people, and for the very transgressors who were so soon to break that law, and need its blessed atonement. "Make an altar of earth for me and sacrifice on it your burnt offerings and fellowship offerings, your sheep and goats and your cattle. Wherever I cause my name to be honored, I will come to you and bless you. If you make an altar of stones for me, do not build it with dressed stones, for you will defile it if you use a tool on it. And do not go up to my altar on steps, lest your nakedness be exposed on it" (Exodus 20:24–26). How simple, how full of Jesus is all this.

## *OF EARTH*

It was to be an altar of earth, which the poorest could erect, and for which the materials could be found in any spot, however remote from the Tabernacle or the mount. So Christ needs no costly offering from the helpless sinner, but anywhere, and everywhere, whosoever will, may come boldly to the throne of grace. If it should be more convenient to make an altar of stone, it should not be of hewn stone, teaching us that no work of our own righteousness is needed to justify the soul, or will be suffered to mingle with the righteousness of Christ.

## *NO TOOL*

If we lift up our tool upon that finished work, we have polluted it. "To the man who does not work but trusts God who justifies the wicked, his faith is credited as righteousness" (Romans 4:5).

## *NO STEPS*

And then, most beautiful of all, there were no steps to this altar. It is not above the level of the humblest and most desperate sinner. It needs no wrought up condition of feeling or merit to bring us into saving contact with Jesus Christ. We need not say in our heart, " 'Who will ascend into heaven?' (that is, to bring Christ down)" (10:6). We need not wait until we have raised ourselves to the highest morality or religious feeling, but He meets us on our level, and saves us as we are, in the fullness of His all-sufficient grace. Indeed, the moment we try to get up to the highest place of personal merit, or self-effort, we only show our nakedness. The process of salvation is a going down, and the condition of mercy is to come at last where we actually accept Him as the Author and Finisher of our faith. Blessed altar of earth! Blessed type of Calvary, sweetly proclaiming, "Whoever wishes, let him take the free gift of the water of life" (Revelation 22:17).

## SECTION III—*The Ordinance of the Hebrew Servant*
### Exodus 21:5–6

"But if the servant declares, 'I love my master and my wife and children and do not want to go free,' then his master must take him before the judges. He shall take him to the door or the doorpost and pierce his ear with an awl. Then he will be his servant for life" (Exodus 21:5–6).

This is also a beautiful type of the mediatorial and redeeming work of Christ. This servant might have claimed his freedom and enjoyed it alone. But his wife and children were still in bondage, and he refused to go free until he could also claim their liberty. He was also attached to his master, and unwilling to leave him. He was allowed, therefore, by the Hebrew law, to return to bondage, and consecrate himself anew to his master's service, and share the lot of his family, by the second ceremony of boring his ear, and fastening him by it to the door post of his master's house, in token of perpetual servitude. The word of God has not left us in any doubt about the meaning of this type. In Psalm 40:6, it is applied to the Lord Jesus Christ, the Father's Servant, who might have retained His freedom from suffering and humiliation. But He, for His Father's honor, and for the sake of His Bride, the Church, stooped to the place of subjection and indignity; undertook the fearful task of procuring our redemption; gave Himself joyfully to do the will of God as a servant; shared in the fullest measure the bondage and suffering of His beloved people; and has saved us forever from the servitude of sin and the miseries of our lost estate.

## SECTION IV— *The Blood of the Covenant*
### Exodus 24:4–11

A few days after the giving of the law at Sinai, God enters into covenant with His people by a series of beautiful and significant rites. The scene stands in striking contrast with Sinai and its terrors. And the one secret of all the difference is that the blood is the ground of acceptance and communion, and the token and seal of the covenant that is now ratified. Accompanied by Aaron and his sons and the 70 elders of Israel, Moses again approaches Mount Sinai, in the presence of the assembled people. The covenant is solemnly proclaimed in their hearing and written down by the hand of Moses, and then the altar is built under the hill, and sacrifices of burnt offerings and peace offerings solemnly presented before the Lord. The blood of the victims is carefully gathered in basins; one-half is sprinkled on the altar and the rest upon the people.

## THE TWOFOLD ACTION
The significance of this twofold action concerning the blood cannot be too carefully marked and remembered. The blood which was poured upon the altar represents the death of Christ for our sins. Blood is ever a token of life in the Old Testament, and so the blood poured upon the altar is the life of Christ poured out *for* man. But the other half of the blood preserved in basins and then sprinkled upon the people, represents something very different, namely, the resurrection life of Christ and the continued efficacy of His intercession and indwelling to sanctify and keep us in fellowship with God, and enable us to fulfill the divine covenant. The shed blood is the death on Calvary. The sprinkled blood is the resurrection life of Christ, shed

abroad in our hearts, and so cleansing, sanctifying, and sustaining our spiritual life. The one is *His life for us*, the other *His life in us*.

## FELLOWSHIP

Next, notice the effect of this offering and application of the blood. They were at once brought into the immediate presence and fellowship of God, as we are brought nigh by the blood of Christ. They "saw the God of Israel. Under his feet was something like a pavement made of sapphire, clear as the sky itself. But God did not raise his hand against these leaders of the Israelites; they saw God, and they ate and drank" (Exodus 24:10–11). There is no vengeance, for sin is out of sight. There is no cloud, but all is clear as the sapphire heaven, for He has blotted out as a thick cloud all their transgressions. There is the vision of His presence, the fellowship of His love, and the very feast of His glorious provision. So we have boldness by the blood of Jesus to enter into the holiest of all. So we may receive the new covenant in His blood. So we may sing "To him who loves us and has freed us from our sins by his blood, and has made us to be a kingdom and priests to serve his God and Father—to him be glory and power for ever and ever! Amen" (Revelation 1:5–6).

## SECTION V—*The Tabernacle*
### Exodus 25–26

"The LORD said to Moses, 'Tell the Israelites to bring me an offering. You are to receive the offering for me from each man whose heart prompts him to give. . . . Then have them make a sanctuary for me, and I will dwell among them. Make this tabernacle and all its furnishings exactly like the pattern I will show you' " (Exodus 25:1–2, 8–9). This is the grandest of all the Old Testament types of Christ. It is all one great object lesson of spiritual truth. In its wonderful furniture, priesthood and worship, we see with a vividness that we find nowhere else, the glory and grace of Jesus and the privileges of His redeemed people. And as in the architect's plan we can understand the future building better, even than by looking at the building without the plan. So, in this pattern from the mount, we can understand as nowhere else, that glorious temple of which Christ is the cornerstone, and we also, as living stones, are built up in Him "a spiritual house to be a holy priesthood, offering spiritual sacrifices acceptable to God through Jesus Christ" (1 Peter 2:5).

### The Form and Structure of the Tabernacle
It was an oblong structure, about 45 feet long and 15 feet wide and high;

very similar in size and proportions to the double parlors of an ordinary dwelling house. It was constructed of boards of shittim wood, a peculiarly indestructible material, overlaid with gold, and fastened with sockets and tenons of silver, brass, etc. It was covered with three tiers of skins, and a final interior lining of most costly curtains, embroidered and adorned with symbolical figures of the highest beauty and spiritual significance. The external covering of the roof was of rough sea cows' skins, to protect it from the inclemency of the weather. The exact form of the roof is a matter of dispute, some believing it to have been pitched at an angle, and some an arched or a flat surface.

## THE HOLY OF HOLIES

The Tabernacle itself was divided into two unequal chambers by magnificent curtains called *The Veil.* The inner chamber was a perfect cube, 15 feet square. It contained the ark of the covenant, over which was the mercy seat, which was its lid, and consisted of a solid plate of gold. Then, springing from this, and formed of the same piece of solid gold, hovered the cherubim, symbolical figures representing the faces of the four typical forms of the animate creation—the man, the ox, the eagle and the lion. Between the meeting wings of the cherubic figure shone the Shekinah, or visible divine glory, the luminous cloud of transcendent brightness, which, perhaps, arose and expanded into the pillar of cloud and fire that hovered above the Tabernacle, and led the march of Israel. This chamber was the Holy of Holies, God's especial presence chamber and throne of grace and glory. None ever entered it except the high priest, and he only once a year.

## THE HOLY PLACE

The other division was twice as large, 15 feet by 30, and was called the Holy Place. It was open to the ministering priests only, but not to the common people, and it was separated from the outer court by *The Door*, a curtain, also of blue, purple and scarlet, which none but cleansed and consecrated priests might pass. Its articles of furniture were: the golden lampstand, which was its only light, there being no windows at all; the table of the bread of the Presence, covered with 12 loaves, crowned with pure frankincense, which were offered to God for one week, and then eaten by the priests, and renewed from Sabbath to Sabbath; and the golden altar of incense, with its accompanying censer, where pure frankincense was continually offered, and from which, once a year, on the great Day of Atonement, the high priest with the golden censer took burning coals and smoking incense in his hands, passed through the mysterious Veil, entered alone the Holy of Holies, and there made atonement for the people in the immediate presence of God.

## THE COURT

Surrounding the Tabernacle was another court, an enclosure 87 by 175 feet, with an opening on the eastern side called *The Gate*. Into this court all the people might come.

Two objects of ceremonial worship stood here. Near the gate was the brazen altar of burnt offering. Here the sacrifices of burnt offering were presented, the blood sprinkled and the fire kept ever burning, from which the altar of incense was supplied. All parts of the Tabernacle had to be sprinkled with blood from this altar. It was the only way of access to the presence of God. Farther in was the bronze laver, a vast basin, perhaps with polished exterior, forming thus a mirror as well as a fountain, made from the metal mirrors of the women of Israel, and so enabling the priests at once to see their uncleanness in the metal, and then to wash it away in the water which it contained. It was for the purification of the priests as they entered the sanctuary, and no one could pass through the door until he had washed in this fountain. The gate of the enclosure was always open. It had no hangings, like the two inner doors. All might freely come into His courts and bring their offerings for sin and uncleanness.

## OUTSIDE THE CAMP

Outside the gate was the camp of Israel, forming a square around the Tabernacle of vast extent, three tribes on each side, the tribe of Judah being on the east, opposite to the entrance of the Tabernacle gate. And just beyond, still farther out, there continually burned *the fire outside the camp*, where the bodies of the sin offerings were consumed, and also the refuse of the camp.

Such was this simple and wonderful structure, God's first sanctuary, and the type of all that is sacred and precious in the person and work of Christ, and the privileges of our heavenly calling.

*The Erection and Subsequent History of the Tabernacle*

## PLANNED

First, we have the Tabernacle as it was planned in heaven, and shown to Moses on the mount as a pattern (Exodus 25 to 31). This is the type of Christ set forth from eternity in the counsels of divine love, our Redeemer prepared for us from before the foundation of the world, and revealed in successive types and prophecies long before His actual incarnation and life on earth. Moses built the Tabernacle according to an actual model which God had shown him during the 40 days on the mount. So Christ was born, lived and died, in exact accordance with the prophetic picture of previous ages of revelation.

## INTERRUPTED

Then, in Exodus, there is the dark interval of sorrow and rebellion (chapters 32 and 33), during which the people transgressed the covenant they had just entered into, and showed most painfully the need of the salvation which God had just been preparing. This is the type of man's fall and his failure under the Old Dispensation. Christ had been already provided, but man must feel the need of the divine salvation, by the actual experience of sin. It is touching beyond degree to know that all the time that man was rebelling against his God, *God's remedy was waiting in that mount of grace.*

## BUILT

Then, in chapter 34, we come to the second stage in the history of the Tabernacle, its actual erection according to the divine plan already shown, and through the freewill offerings of the people, and the skill and workmanship of the men whom God had specially endued for this purpose. Two men were particularly called and qualified by the gifts of the Holy Spirit in sacred art to originate and execute all its symbolic decorations; and the women of Israel were similarly prepared and enabled to make ready its costly materials. So its entire erection was through the supernatural gifts of the Holy Spirit, as well as the divine plan which was revealed to Moses.

## ITS HISTORY

During the 40 years of their wilderness life it was borne from place to place in succession by the faithful hands of the Levites, who were appointed for this special ministry. After their entrance into Canaan, it remained for a time at Gilgal, and afterward was established at Shiloh, which became the religious center of the national worship for a long time. During the period of the Judges we lose sight of it for a season through the subjugation and humiliation of Israel. But we find it afterward in Nob, in the neighborhood of Jerusalem, in the reign of David. And finally it was established on Mount Zion through the piety of this good king, where it remained until superseded by the more magnificent Temple of Solomon, which was, however, only a more splendid edition of the same building, containing all the essential features of the Tabernacle, only adding a higher degree of splendor, and so typifying the future glories as the Tabernacle typifies the grace of Christ and His redemption.

### Spiritual and Typical Significance of the Tabernacle

It was designed to represent and prefigure the most important teachings of the Scriptures with reference, first, to Christ, secondly, to the Church and thirdly, to the individual Christian. In these three aspects we shall briefly consider it.

## A TYPE OF CHRIST

*First: The Tabernacle as a Type of Christ.* The very word "tabernacle" is used with reference to Him in the opening chapter of the Gospel of John: "The Word became flesh and made his dwelling among us. We have seen his glory, the glory of the One and Only, who came from the Father, full of grace and truth" (1:14). The Greek word for "made his dwelling" is connected with the word for "tent/tabernacle."

Again, in the ninth chapter of Hebrews, the apostle, after describing the structure of the ancient sanctuary, applies it all to the person and work of Christ.

The points of comparison are almost unlimited. Among them may be mentioned:

(a) The location of the Tabernacle, which was entered from the camp of Judah, suggests the fact that Christ was born of the tribe of Judah.

(b) The materials of which the Tabernacle was constructed, namely, indestructible wood and pure gold, suggest His perfect humanity on the one hand, and His supreme divinity on the other.

(c) The colors which were so constantly mingled in the Tabernacle, especially the prevailing hues of white, blue, scarlet and purple, all point to qualities in Him: the white, His spotless purity; the blue, His heavenly origin; the scarlet, His sufferings and death; and the purple, His kingly glory.

(d) The external plainness in contrast with the internal glory of the Tabernacle; the sea cows' skins without, and the gold and Shekinah glory within, proclaim the lowliness of Christ's earthly state, and yet the beauty and glory of His character and inner presence, as He reveals Himself to the soul that abides in Him.

(e) The contrast between the Tabernacle and the Temple, the one a shifting tent, exposed to constant vicissitude and humiliation and the other combining in itself all the glory of earth and heaven, suggests to us: first, the earthly life of our Lord; and second, His exaltation and the kingly glory of His millennial reign.

(f) Because the Tabernacle was the place of God's manifestation of Himself to Israel, and the place where He revealed the symbols of His immediate presence, it reminds us of Him who is Himself the image and manifestation of God, and whose very name, Immanuel, means "God with us."

(g) The Tabernacle was God's meeting-place with Israel. "There, above the cover between the two cherubim . . . I will meet with you" (Exodus 25:22), were His own words; and there they heard the voice of God speaking from between the cherubim. And so the Lord Jesus Christ is the only way of access to the Father, and fellowship with heaven. "If anyone loves me, . . . My Father will love him, and we will come to him and make our home with him" (John 14:23).

(h) The Tabernacle was the place of sacrifice. Its most vivid spectacle was the flowing and the sprinkled blood, and it tells us in every part of the sacrifice of Christ.

(i) Not only was it the place of sacrifice, but also the place of cleansing; the blood atoned and the water washed away the stain of defilement. So Christ is the Fountain for sin and for uncleanness. He "gave himself up for her [the Church] to make her holy, cleansing her by the washing with water through the word, and to present her to himself as a radiant church, without stain or wrinkle or any other blemish, but holy and blameless" (Ephesians 5:25b–27).

(j) The Tabernacle was the place where the guilty might freely come to the altar of atonement; and Jesus Christ is the propitiation not only for our sins, but also for the sins of the whole world.

(k) The Tabernacle had inner chambers. And so it speaks of the deeper life, and the fuller blessings into which those may enter who are willing to abide in Christ. "I am the gate" (John 10:9), He says, and "I have come that they may have life, and have it to the full" (John 10:10). He is our Life, our Bread, our Light, our Altar of prayer, our Open Veil of access even to the innermost presence of the holy God.

(l) The Tabernacle was the place where the law was enshrined in the bosom of the ark, and ever covered by the sprinkled blood which proclaimed the sinner's acceptance. So Jesus keeps for us the divine law; then keeps it also in us, by His indwelling life and presence, and so becomes our perfect righteousness.

(m) The cherubim of glory in the Holy of Holies were types of Christ's exalted glory; of His humanity, crowned with the strength of the ox, the majesty of the lion and the loftiness of the eagle's flight. All this is the pledge of our future glory.

All this and much more we see in this ancient object lesson concerning Him of whom Moses and the prophets did write, and which He has come Himself to fulfill, with a fullness which He will yet enable us more fully to understand in every detail respecting this pattern in the mount.

## A TYPE OF THE CHURCH

*Second: The Tabernacle as a Type of the Church.* That which is true of Christ the Head, is also true of His body, the Church. Among other points of instruction which the Tabernacle suggests in this connection, it may be noticed:

> (a) Like the Tabernacle, the Church has been planned by God Himself, and is in no sense a human institution. It should in every respect be organized, constituted, built up and equipped according to the pattern which Christ has shown us Himself, "Teaching them to obey everything I have commanded you" (Matthew 28:20).
>
> (b) The Church requires the same divine anointing through the Holy Spirit, on the part of all who, like Bezalel and Oholiab, are engaged in her spiritual upbuilding. Not the gifts of intellectual brilliancy, but the wisdom of the Holy Spirit, and the endue- ment of His power; these alone can accomplish definite and eter- nal results, and all else will wither and drift away in the fiery blasts of the great ordeal.
>
> (c) The Church, like the ancient Tabernacle, should have her chief beauty within; not in costly decorations, but in the glory of the indwelling God and the exhibition of a crucified and sin- cleansing Savior. Without this she can only be what Israel's temple was when the Master and the Shekinah departed, and the avengers came with fire and blood. Without this His word can only be, "your house is left to you desolate" (Matthew 23:38), or, as it was to the Church of the Laodiceans, "Because you are . . . neither hot nor cold—I am about to spit you out of my mouth" (Revelation 3:16).
>
> (d) Like the ancient Tabernacle, the Church should have her inner chambers for deeper teaching and closer fellowship in the holy place, in the light of the sevenfold lamp of truth, and at the table of the heavenly bread; while the sweet fragrance from the golden altar fills all the place with the breath of heaven, and the rent veil just beyond reveals and opens up to her vision even the innermost chambers of heaven itself, from which ever shines the Shekinah of His abiding presence.

(e) Like the ancient Tabernacle, the Church should be the repository of the world's true light and living bread, the light of the world and the stewardess of the mysteries of God.

(f) Like the ancient Tabernacle and Temple, the Church has her earthly and her heavenly life, the time of desert wandering and vicissitude, but the prospect also of a glory greater than that of Solomon's temple, when the Lamb shall gather His redeemed on Mount Zion, and the universe shall come to gaze on the glories of the New Jerusalem, prepared as a bride adorned for her husband.

## A TYPE OF CHRISTIAN LIFE

*Third: The Tabernacle as the Type of Christian Life.* What is true of Christ, is true in our individual measure of each one of His people. "In this world, we are like him" (1 John 4:17). Let us not fear, therefore, to claim the fullness of our great salvation.

## CONDEMNATION

The first chapter in every Christian's existence is the dark, sad chapter of condemnation. This was vividly set forth in the ancient camp of Israel by the fire that ever burned outside the camp, suggesting the wrath of God revealed from heaven on all unrighteousness of men. That fire consumed the offering to which sin had been transferred, and it must likewise consume all whose sins are not transferred to that burnt offering. If He, in the place of the sinner, suffered this vengeance, how shall we escape if we dare to stand before God covered with our guilt and corruption? "For if men do these things when the tree is green, what will happen when it is dry?" (Luke 23:31). Our Lord has not quenched this fire, but left it still burning outside the gate of the gospel for all who reject Him. "Whoever believes in him is not condemned, but whoever does not believe stands condemned already because he has not believed in the name of God's one and only Son" (John 3:18).

## SALVATION

The next stage in the believer's life is salvation. So we now enter the gate and stand within the court. We may freely come. There is no barrier, not even the fold of a curtain, intervening. We hasten through the inviting entrance, and stand before the smoking altar which tells us of the cross and the blood through which we have redemption from sin. We place our hand upon the head of the sacrifice, and we become partakers of the great expiation. Next, the laver speaks to us of the Holy Ghost, whose power regenerates and cleanses the soul from sin. We wash in its fountain, and are qualified and authorized to enter into the inner presence, and into the more intimate fellowship of the Holy Place.

## SANCTIFICATION

The Tabernacle also tells us of the next stage of Christian experience and life—communion, consecration, sanctification and abiding fellowship with Christ. That inner chamber just beyond the open court is only for God's priests. How, then, may we dare to intrude? Thank God, we are all admitted to the place of priesthood, if we will accept it. He "loves us and has freed us from our sins by his blood, and has made us to be a kingdom and priests to serve his God" (Revelation 1:5–6). Not a few, now, but all are "a royal priesthood, a holy nation, a people belonging to God" (1 Peter 2:9). So we may boldly enter in, but not until we have washed in that cleansing laver, as well as sacrificed at the altar. We must accept His sanctifying as well as justifying grace. Even to Peter, who had been "bathed," that is, justified, Christ said: "Unless I wash you, you have no part with me" (John 13:8). Although we have boldness by the blood of Jesus even to enter into the holiest, yet we must come with "hearts sprinkled to cleanse us from a guilty conscience and having our bodies washed with pure water" (Hebrews 10:22b). Thus, divinely cleansed, "let us draw near to God with a sincere heart in full assurance of faith" (10:22a). Our great High Priest is standing within, and sweetly saying, "I am the gate; whoever enters through me will be saved. He will come in and go out, and find pasture" (John 10:9).

What pasture! There is the sevenfold lamp which speaks of Christ and the Holy Spirit: our perfect Light; the light of truth; the light which reveals Himself; the light of heavenly vision; the light which brings sight as well as light to our dull eyes; the light of guidance and direction amid the perplexities of life; His own continual presence and voice as the Shepherd as well as the Door, and the light which will shine through us and from us as the light of men.

Next the Tabernacle tells of the living bread; the table with its 12 loaves, one for each of us, made from the finest of the wheat, ever renewed with each returning Sabbath. Not only bread, but frankincense like honey out of the rock; all the sweetness of His consolations as well as the strength of His life; bread that nourishes both soul and body, and becomes our perfect life and sustenance. Then, not only is there the bread, but all that is implied in the altar of incense. This includes all that is involved in a life of prayer and communion with God, through Jesus Christ. That incense, together with the anointing oil, was the most sacred thing in all the Tabernacle service. It might not be imitated by mortal art, but was consecrated sacredly for the service of God alone. It was compounded of many ingredients; and some of it, we are told, was beaten very small, and then was burned with sweet spices on that pure altar (Exodus 30:34–38).

So that spirit of prayer must be born from above, and cannot be imitated or counterfeited by merely human effort. It springs from the combination of all the circumstances of life and qualities of our Christian character. It is the flower of piety, and the fragrance of the heart; distilled like perfume, indescribably delicate, pure, and heavenly. Nothing is too small to enter into it, and become an occasion for it. The incense of prayer may be beaten very small, and arise from a thousand trifles in our life which we may so consecrate to God as to become a sacrifice of sweet smelling savor. Our little trials and trifling ministries, laid on this golden altar, become to Him like the fragrance of spring and the breath of Aaron's censer; and He treasures them in heaven in "bowls full of incense, which are the prayers of the saints" (Revelation 5:8). But in order to be divinely fragrant, they must be set on fire by the Holy Ghost, the true Intercessor and Advocate on earth, as Christ is the Advocate on high, making intercession "for us with groans that words cannot express" (Romans 8:26). The sweet incense of the holy place penetrated through the veil and filled the Holy of Holies. So the spirit of prayer makes both earth and heaven one. The altar stood at the very entrance to the inner chamber; and so when we are rapt in fellowship with God, we are at the gate of heaven and almost within the veil. We can hear the voices and catch the breath from those inner chambers. Happy are they who thus abide in Him, in the atmosphere of ceaseless communion and peace. The most trying place will be fragrant, like odors of heaven, and the most lonely spot a little sanctuary where all heaven will seem to be around us with its almighty protection, its blessed companionship, and its unspeakable joy.

## GLORY

The innermost chamber in the Hebrew Tabernacle was the Holy of Holies. It speaks to us of heaven itself, the immediate presence of God, and the glory which awaits us at His coming or our translation within the gates. It tells us of a heaven not far off and shut from our vision, but near and open. The veil is rent in twain from top to bottom, and the Holy of Holies sheds its light and glory all round us even here, so that translation itself is scarcely a change of companionship, although it may be of location. That inner chamber tells us of the place where our prayers can enter now in sweet incense, and be accepted in His name. Our eyes can look through the veil and see heaven open and Jesus standing at the right hand of God. There the sprinkled blood on the mercy seat is ever pleading for us, and claiming our perfect and perpetual acceptance. There the ark within the veil, with the unbroken law within its bosom, is the symbol of the perfect righteousness which we share with Him, and in which we stand accepted in Him, even in the immediate presence of God. There the cherubim of glory are the patterns of the dignity and royalty which our redeemed humanity has already attained in Christ, its illustrious Head, and which we shall share in its fullness when He shall appear. As we look through, we know that our spirits, too, shall follow, and be with Him where He is. The feet that tremble and falter shall walk through the gates of day; and the very body of our humiliation shall be like Him when He shall appear, and shall be changed into the image of the body of his glory.

And all this we have even here, not only in vision and prospect, but in foretaste.

> The holy to the holiest leads;
>   To this our spirits rise,
> And he who in His footsteps treads
>   Shall meet Him in the skies.

*Fourth: The Anointing of the Tabernacle.* After the Tabernacle had been fully completed, according to all the pattern shown on the mount, it was solemnly dedicated to God, and the entire tent and its furniture were anointed with oil, specially prepared according to the divine prescription, and consecrated to this exclusive purpose, and then the manifestation of the Divine Presence appeared upon it. The pillar of cloud spread its curtains above it, and the Shekinah glory took its place between the cherubim and filled the tent so effulgently that even Moses was not able to enter the holy place. Moses had simply and perfectly obeyed God's directions, and now God accepted his work, and put His seal upon it. This was symbolical of the anointing of Jesus Christ with the Holy Ghost, and of the same anointing which comes upon every consecrated heart when it has obeyed the divine directions, and presented itself a living sacrifice to God. God will so fill such a soul that there shall be no room for self and sin. This, indeed, is the true secret of sanctification and self-crucifixion. The expulsive power of the Holy Ghost and the Divine Presence are the only true antidotes to the power of self and Satan.

Henceforth the Tabernacle becomes the seat and center of the divine manifestation. We thus observe three stages of the manifested presence of God in Exodus, namely: First, the pillar of cloud and fire that went before; next, the presence from the mount; and now, the presence of Jehovah in the Tabernacle. We trace the same three stages in the Old Testament: First, the Spirit of God as manifested in the patriarchal dispensation; secondly, the revelation of God under the law; and thirdly, the revelation of God in Christ, the true Tabernacle. "In the past God spoke to our forefathers through the prophets at many times and in various ways, but in these last days he has spoken to us by his Son, whom he appointed heir of all things, and through whom he made the universe" (Hebrews 1:1–2). Hence we find God in the very first verse of Leviticus, speaking to Moses no longer out of the mount or cloud, but *out of the Tabernacle.* So we may find in Christ the continual presence and guidance of our covenant God. "If anyone loves me," Christ says, "he will obey my teaching. My Father will love him, and we will come to him and make our home with him" (John 14:23). Let us only do what Moses did, yield ourselves fully and implicitly to the divine will, hand ourselves over as the property of Christ, and we shall also be possessed and filled with a glory as divine as the Shekinah, and as enduring as the life and love of God (Exodus 40).

Henceforth this event, the setting up and anointing of the Tabernacle, becomes a landmark of time. It was to begin the second year of their national history and was on the first day of the first month. The first year had begun with the Passover, but this forms the next great era of their existence.

And so the moment when the soul is dedicated and anointed by the Holy Ghost is an eternal era in its history, as important as the hour of its new birth; the beginning of months and years, from which all its experiences and hopes are henceforth measured. Have we entered upon this second year? Have we begun it, like them, with the sacrifice of our being in implicit obedience, on the altar of God? And have we received the descending fire, and the abiding Comforter henceforth to speak to us, not from the heavens, or even from the tables of stone, but from the inner chambers of His sanctuary in our hearts?

## SECTION VI—*The High Priest*
### Exodus 28:1–43

The next great type of the gospel, unfolded in Exodus, and closely connected with the Tabernacle, is the ministry of the high priest, and his robes, functions and consecrations. These are described in detail in the very midst of the account of the Tabernacle, just after the description of the altar of burnt offering (Exodus 27), and before the description of the altar of incense and intercession, which comes in chapter 30.

The place where the account of the high priest is introduced is very significant in connection with its typical import. It prefigures Jesus Christ as our great High Priest at the right hand of God in the heavens. And it is most natural and beautiful that it should be introduced just after the altar of burnt offering, which represents His sacrifice on Calvary, and just before the altar of incense which represents His intercession in heaven.

It is not necessary to prove to any intelligent Christian that the Hebrew high priest was the special type of the Lord Jesus Christ, as our Mediator and

Advocate with the Father. He is represented in this office with great frequency and fullness in the New Testament. The apostle calls us to "fix your thoughts on Jesus, the apostle and high priest whom we confess" (Hebrews 3:1), and adds, "Therefore, since we have a great high priest who has gone through the heavens, Jesus the Son of God, let us hold firmly to the faith we profess. For we do not have a high priest who is unable to sympathize with our weaknesses, but we have one who has been tempted in every way, just as we are—yet was without sin.

Let us then approach the throne of grace with confidence, so that we may receive mercy and find grace to help us in our time of need" (Hebrews 4:14–16). His person and work were prefigured by the functions, garments and consecration of Aaron.

## 1. HIS FUNCTIONS

(a) Reconciliation.—It was his province to deal with the question of sin, and settle it between God and the transgressor. It was his to take the sacrificial blood, and bringing it within the Holy of Holies as an atonement for the sins of the people, open the way between the guilty sinner and his offended God. This he did once in the year, and this he alone could do; no other dare enter that awful presence. So Christ has come to offer both gifts and sacrifices for sins, and to make reconciliation for the guilty. And so He "was sacrificed once to take away the sins of many people" (Hebrews 9:28). "But now he has appeared once for all at the end of the ages to do away with sin by the sacrifice of himself" (9:26). And "when this priest had offered for all time one sacrifice for sins, he sat down at the right hand of God" (10:12).

It is Christ's business and His alone, to deal with sin, and settle it for the sinner. No one but He can redeem us from sin, and reconcile us to God. We can do nothing about sin, but simply commit it to Him and leave it with Him. He has already offered the atoning blood, and opened the way into the holiest for all who come unto God by Him, and we may freely bring to Him our guilt and infirmities, for pardon and cleansing.

How prone the heart is to keep away from Christ our burden of sin, and wait until we have somehow fitted ourselves by some sort of penance, reformation, or self-atonement. How foolish and useless! The very business of the priest is to receive sinners and put away sin.

(b) Intercession.—The office of the high priest was not only to prefigure the complete atonement of Christ, but also to set forth

His continual ministry of intercession for us at God's right hand.

It was his to carry the names of the congregation on his breast and shoulders, as a memorial before God; thus representing all their wants at the source of blessing, and claiming for them all the grace and help they needed. So Christ makes continual intercession for us. "Christ Jesus, who died—more than that, who was raised to life—is at the right hand of God and is also interceding for us" (Romans 8:34). He is represented as encompassed with infirmity, and instinctively sensitive to our suffering and need. His intercession is the ground of our continual acceptance, and the plea of all our effectual prayers. Coming in His name, we are accepted even as He is; and our very standing before the Father is the same as His own. He represents us as our Head, and holds for us the place which He is preparing as our eternal home. The incense of His perfect intercession mingles with our imperfect prayers, and brings back to us the fullness of the divine acceptance and blessing.

(c) Benediction.—It was his privilege after he had made reconciliation and intercession for the people, to come forth and bless them in the name of the Lord, saying: "The LORD bless you and keep you; the LORD make his face shine upon you and be gracious to you; the LORD turn his face toward you and give you peace" (Numbers 6:24–26).

And so our Great High Priest, when He had accomplished the work of reconciliation and presented His perfect offering to God, completed His ministry on earth by the same beautiful act of benediction. Having led them out as far as Bethany, "he lifted up his hands and blessed them. While he was blessing them, he left them and was taken up into heaven" (Luke 24:50–51). The last sight the earth had of Jesus was with outstretched hands and parted lips, pronouncing blessings upon our heads. He is the Priest of blessing. The first word of His first sermon was "blessed"; the last utterance in the last book of the Bible is "blessed"; and the scroll of prophecy closes with this gracious benediction: "The grace of the Lord Jesus be with God's people. Amen" (Revelation 22:21).

In addition to these three great ministries of reconciliation, intercession and benediction, there are several other functions which seem to have belonged to the high priesthood. It was his to inspect and pronounce upon the leper, and cleanse him from his defilement. So Christ is our great Healer. His death released the one accused of murder in the cities of refuge (Numbers 35:25). And so Christ's death released the prisoners of hope under the ancient dispensation and opens the gates of liberty and heaven to all true believers.

## 2. GARMENTS OF THE HIGH PRIEST
These are described in full detail in Exodus 28 and were all symbolical.

(a) His personal robes of pure white linen were typical of Christ's sinless humanity (28:39, 42). He was holy, harmless, undefiled and separate from sinners, and needed not to offer any sacrifice for Himself; but was perfectly qualified through His personal righteousness to be a substitute for the sins of others.

(b) The ephod was made of blue, purple, scarlet and fine linen: the blue, telling of His heavenly origin; the purple, His royal dignity; and the scarlet, His sufferings and atoning work. Connected with the ephod were the shoulder plates which consisted of two onyx stones, each containing the names of six tribes of Israel, and borne continually on his shoulders, as a symbol of Christ's upholding His people with all the strength of His omnipotence and love, unwearied with our weight, or even carrying our weakness with His everlasting might, even as the good Shepherd bare His lost lamb on His shoulders rejoicing.

The government of the universe He bears on one shoulder; but He gives both to the upholding of His people. "Underneath are the everlasting arms" (Deuteronomy 33:27).

(c) The breastplate was borne upon his breast, and contained 12 precious stones, set in gold, in which were engraved separately the names of all the tribes of Israel. The exquisite significance of this every consecrated heart knows by the most tender and thankful experience. It is the picture of Christ's personal love and sympathy; not to His people collectively, but to each one of us individually.

When it comes to His heart, each of us has a separate place. He does not love us by sixes or twelves, but one by one. "I have loved *you* with an everlasting love" (Jeremiah 31:3). Our names are not written or painted upon His breast, but cut in imperishable lines, and in the living Rock. "I have engraved you on the palms of my hands" (Isaiah 49:16). "Can a mother forget the baby . . . ?/ Though she may forget,/ I will not forget you" (49:15). The most precious jewels are the tokens of the value He sets upon us; not because of our intrinsic worth, for a jewel is in itself useless, but simply as an expression of affection altogether out of proportion to our utility or worthiness (Exodus 28:29).

(d)  The robe of blue which covered the person of the high priest was hung with bells and pomegranates. It was significant of His heavenly character, while the bells typified the sweet assurance which the Holy Spirit brings to our hearts, of the presence and intercession of our High Priest for us, on high; and the pomegranates signify the precious fruits which flow from His priestly work (28:31–34).

(e)  The Urim and Thummim (28:30), two words which signify *lights* and *perfections*, are supposed to have been precious stones, which in some way, perhaps through their changing colors, gave intimation of the divine response to the inquiries of the priest respecting the will of God. They denote in the person and work of Christ the perfect righteousness and infinite wisdom which He imparts to those who trust Him. He becomes their wisdom and righteousness.

(f)  The golden waistband which bound together the flowing robes of the high priest was a symbol of the ceaseless ministry of our great High Priest, whose exalted glory at the Father's right hand is not a selfish triumph, but a place of service. John beheld Him girded with the golden sash, engaged in a ceaseless activity on our behalf (Exodus 28:8; Revelation 1:13).

(g)  The turban of gold and blue, with its inscription on the brow of the high priest, was the crowning emblem of his symbolical robes. Not only on His shoulders and on His breast, but also on His brow, does Jesus carry His beloved people. Upon the plate of gold surmounting the high priest's turban these words were inscribed: "HOLY TO THE LORD" (Exodus 28:36), and he was commanded to wear it continually when he went into the holy place, that he might bear the guilt of their holy things. What a wonderful way it was to bear their guilt, so that it was not only hidden from God's sight, but so covered by the righteousness of the High Priest, that we appear in the sight of the Father, as "HOLY TO THE LORD." "Who will bring any charge against those whom God has chosen? It is God who justifies. Who is he that condemns? Christ Jesus, who died—more than that, who was raised to life" (Romans 8:33–34). How wondrous those words in Jeremiah 23:6, "This is the name by which he will be called:/ The LORD Our Righteousness." But how much more wonderful the words in Jeremiah 33:16: "This is the name by which [we] will be called:/ The LORD Our Righteousness." We are covered with His righteousness, bear His

very name, and so are accepted in the Beloved, and loved even as
He is loved.

## 3. THE CONSECRATION OF THE HIGH PRIEST
(Exodus, and more fully, Leviticus, chapters 8 and 9)

We shall refer more fully to this in its place in Leviticus. It is sufficient for
the present, to observe that the consecration of Aaron and his sons was accompanied by all the offerings of the Levitical law, and by their anointing
with oil as the symbol of their enduement with the power of the Holy Spirit.
Then they were separated for seven days in the Tabernacle, and on the
eighth day came forth to the people in connection with special sacrificial offerings when God appeared in glory. All this is symbolical of Christ's setting
apart to His great work, and its successive stages of development, ending at
last with His second and glorious appearing; and also, of our partnership
with Him in His priesthood, and in the glory of His second coming.

The sons of Aaron represent the priesthood of Christians; while Aaron
stands for Christ, our High Priest, and the Head of His priestly house.

Have we understood all these things, and their marvelous pictures of grace
and of Christ? Have we found our abiding place in that living Tabernacle,
claimed our privileges as a holy priesthood, and received upon our heads the
anointing oil and the priestly benediction?

> Oh, may we stand before the Lamb,
> 　When earth and seas are fled,
> And hear the Judge pronounce our names
> 　With blessings on our head.

# LEVITICUS

# GENERAL PLAN AND SCOPE
# OF THE BOOK

$A$s Genesis is the book of beginnings and Exodus the book of redemption, so Leviticus is the book of reconciliation and fellowship. It brings us into the tabernacle, and opens to us all the privileges of access to the presence of God, and our place of blessing as His priestly household.

There are seven main divisions into which the chapters of this book naturally fall.

1. The four offerings (chapters 1–7).
2. The priesthood (chapters 8–10).
3. The rites of cleansing (chapters 11–15).
4. The great day of atonement as the type of reconciliation (chapters 16–17).
5. The statutes of holiness (chapters 18–22).
6. Fellowship with God as typified in the great feasts (chapters 23–25).
7. Obedience and faithfulness (chapters 26–27).

# CHAPTER 1

## THE FOUR OFFERINGS

Strictly speaking, we have five offerings described in these chapters, namely: the burnt offering (chapter 1); the grain offering (chapter 2); the fellowship offering (chapters 3); the sin offering (chapters 4, 5); and the guilt offering (chapter 5). Practically, however, the last two are identical in their main significance, both being of the nature of expiatory offerings to take away the guilt of sin, and its penal consequences. The sin offering was the fundamental one, prefiguring the great principles involved in Christ's propitiation for sin, the guilt offering seeming to refer rather to the provision made in Christ's death, for special acts of transgression and disobedience.

### THE ORDER OF THE OFFERINGS

The order of Leviticus is at first sight very strange, commencing with the very highest aspect of Christ's sacrifice, and the one into which we are the last to enter, and closing with the simpler phases of His redeeming work, and those which we become first acquainted with in our experience in justification. The explanation is that God is moving outward in this progression, and therefore commences at the interior of the tabernacle, where He is at length to bring us, and ends outside the gate, where He finds us poor, helpless and guilty sinners, and then returns with us through all the stages of His gracious plan of salvation, as here unfolded.

We shall, therefore, invert the order of these sacrifices in discussing them, not because we question the divine order and its extreme beauty, but because we desire to lead the reader through the stages of his own experience, and then return with him in the divine order backwards, to contemplate all the riches of grace in Christ Jesus.

### SECTION I—*The Sin and Guilt Offering*

### THE SIN OFFERING

We shall commence with the sin offering (Leviticus 4:1). It represents

Christ's death for us, as God's propitiation for sin.

We find three pictures of this sacrifice:

## FOR THE PRIEST

1. It was to be offered for the priest (4:1–12).

This, however, was not necessary in the case of Christ, who was sinless and needed no atonement for His own person (Hebrews 7:27).

## FOR THE PEOPLE

2. It was offered for the whole congregation (Leviticus 4:13–21).

This represents the death of Christ for all men. The several stages of this sacrificial act are full of spiritual significance. The sacrifice was to be offered by the elders of Israel (4:15), and by the laying of their hands upon the head of the victim. So Christ was officially delivered to death by the council of the elders of Israel, as a sacrifice for the entire nation. And Caiaphas, the high priest, was even inspired to announce to the people the necessity for this substitution.

Then the bullock was slain, and its blood sprinkled seven times before the Lord, and before the veil (verses 16, 17). This denotes the death of Christ and the offering of His life to God in place of our forfeited lives, and the perfection of this offering as meeting His claim upon our lives.

Next, the fat of the bullock was separated and offered to God as a pure sacrifice, implying that there was something in Christ which was directly presented to God, and had no connection with our sin; that is, that His death was an act of obedience to the Father, as well as a vicarious offering for the guilty (verse 19).

Then came the most impressive part of the service. The body of the bullock as an unclean thing was carried outside the camp, and burned to ashes as something unfit for sacrifice, and worthy only to be consumed. So Christ was borne outside the camp, and crucified in ignominy as an accursed thing under the judgment of heaven, and the bane of earth, and literally "made him who had no sin to be sin for us" (2 Corinthians 5:21). Indeed, the word for offering in this passage literally means sin. So for us the sinless One became as it were, a mass of sin, and an accursed thing (Hebrews 13:12; 2 Corinthians 5:21).

## FOR EVERY INDIVIDUAL

3. For each individual, the sin offering must also be separately presented. It was not enough that it should have been offered by the whole congregation, but each one must separately present an offering for his own sin (Leviticus 4:22–31).

So it is not sufficient that Christ has died for the sins of the whole world, but each one of us must appropriate His sacrifice for our own sins. Two classes are here specified, namely: a leader, verse 22, and one of the common people, verse 27. But with great emphasis it is shown that both must come in the very same way. There is no royal road to mercy. "There is no difference, for all have sinned and fall short of the glory of God" (Romans 3:22–23). Then both must lay their hands on the head of the sin offering, and thus transfer their guilt to him (verses 24, 29). Both must receive atonement and forgiveness through the priest (verses 26, 31). In both cases the sprinkling of the blood seven times is omitted, for that was done once for all in the one sacrifice on Calvary; and all that the individual needs to do to be a partaker of the benefits of the sin offering is to recognize his sin, transfer it to the victim and appropriate his forgiveness and cleansing.

There are some most vivid and instructive features in this offering, on which for a moment we should dwell.

It was the most realistic in its representation of the hideousness of sin of all the Hebrew offerings.

## THE LAMB OF SACRIFICE

Standing before the worshiper was an innocent snow-white lamb, bowing its gentle head at his touch. His soul is stained with guilt and sin, but the lamb had done no wrong. And now he lays his hand on that gentle head, and confesses over it all his guilt. Instantly the sin is transferred to the substitute, and it becomes, as it were, a mass of blackness, loathsomeness and hideous wickedness. Its little life is stricken out as by the blow of vengeance. Its body, laid open—a hideous mass of uncleanness and laceration—is dragged from the tabernacle as an offensive and unhallowed thing, and actually called by the very name of sin. It is treated as something unfit to remain for a moment longer in the presence of God or His people, and hastily borne outside the camp to the fires where the filth of the camp is consumed, and there is hurled upon the flames and consumed to ashes as a spectacle of vengeance.

## THE LAMB OF GOD

Transfer all this to the person of Jesus, and behold Him in the place of this suffering lamb, and we have some idea of what is involved in His being "made . . . sin for us" (2 Corinthians 5:21). Standing in our place, "the LORD has laid on him/ the iniquity of us all" (Isaiah 53:6), and immediately He became, as it were, a mass of inconceivable wickedness, and an accursed thing in the sight of earth and heaven. The judgments of God fell upon His head. The anathemas and insults of men were not too cruel for His deserving. He was treated as though He had committed every abominable crime that man has ever committed, and as a thing unfit for either earth or heaven. He was nailed to the cross between the heavens and the earth, as a spectacle of shame and horror, until, consumed by the fires of death and judgment, with Him our sin was also consumed forever. This is the meaning of the act of appropriating faith. As we lay our hand upon His innocent head, our sin passes over to His person, and henceforth recognized as consumed and extinguished in the ashes of His dissolution. Our guilt, therefore, is declared to be put away and remembered no more, and our very sinfulness may be thus laid upon Him, that "the body of sin might be done away with" (Romans 6:6).

What a precious foundation this offering lays, not only for our perfect justification, but for our complete sanctification, and for our deliverance from all the power of evil.

## THE GUILT OFFERING

The guilt offering, as we have already observed, was a modification of the sin offering, having reference rather to particular acts of transgression. The laws respecting it are given (Leviticus 5:14–6:8). Many important lessons are involved in these prescriptions, with reference to the provision which Christ has made for our forgiveness and cleansing.

## IGNORANCE

1. Ignorance is no excuse for sin (5:17). "If a person sins and does what is forbidden in any of the LORD's commands, even though he does not know it, he is guilty and will be held responsible." Ignorance may be an extenuation of sin, but God holds us responsible to know His will as well as to do it. And his ignorance requires to be forgiven as well as his sin. "The priest will make atonement for him for the wrong he has committed unintentionally" (Leviticus 5:18).

## RESTITUTION

2. Confession and restitution must be made, whether it be sin against God or man, and the transgressor must add a fifth part to the original amount. God's mercy is founded on righteousness and requires on the part of the transgressor a repentance which is thorough and practical, and proves its sincerity by its fruits. Many souls who are involved in spiritual darkness, will find the remedy in this divine requirement and no matter what it may cost, it is the only true way to obtain real and lasting peace and blessing (5:16; 6:4–5).

## SACRIFICE

3. Having made confession and restitution, the sin offering must next be presented. This prefigures our appropriation of Christ's blood and

righteousness as the ground of our forgiveness.

## GOD'S ESTIMATE OF SIN

It is added in connection with the sin offering that it is to be according to the priest's estimation, and not the sinner's (5:14–6:6). This suggests that man's estimation of sin is sure to be wrong, and that God only can judge it, and provide a ransom of sufficient value to atone for it. We are to take God's estimate of it and not our own. And if we see it in His light, we shall feel that nothing less than the inestimable value of the Savior's blood can ever expiate its guilt (6:2–5).

## ALL KINDS OF SIN

4. These requirements apply to two classes of trespasses, both those against God and those against our neighbor. The standard of sin is made very thorough and searching, and sin against our neighbor is recognized also as sin against the Lord.

The trespasses provided for in this offering included sins in the holy things of the Lord, disobedience to any of the commandments of the Lord, falsehood against our neighbor, breach of trust, violence, the deceiving of our brother, the withholding of that which has been found and false swearing.

The offering presented in connection with this sacrifice was probably the same as the ordinary sin offering. In both these offerings the sacrifice might be either a bullock, a lamb or a dove, according to the ability of the offerer, God's requirements being tenderly adjusted to the lot and circumstances of each; teaching us that Christ's sacrifice is within the reach of every sinner, however lost and helpless.

## SECTION II— *The Fellowship Offering*
### Leviticus 3:1–17; 7:11–16, 32–34

The special significance of this sacrifice has reference to Christ in His offering of Himself to God as the ground of our peace and communion with the Father.

## THE SACRIFICE

1. The first part of this sacrifice was similar to the other offerings, comprising the selecting of an unblemished animal, the imposition of hands, the slaying of the sacrifice and the sprinkling of the blood. All this was symbolic and was intended to foreshadow the blood of Christ as the ground of our reconciliation to God, and our justification.

    . . . through him to reconcile to himself all things, whether things on earth or things in heaven, by making peace through his blood, shed on the cross.

Once you were alienated from God and were enemies in your minds because of your evil behavior. But now he has reconciled you by Christ's physical body through death to present you holy in his sight, without blemish and free from accusation. (Colossians 1:20–22)

## THE FEAST

2. The special features of the fellowship offering are exceedingly beautiful and instructive. They were intended to express the idea of our communion with God, through the offering and intercession of the Lord Jesus Christ. They consisted chiefly of two attractive symbolical acts, the one expressing God's part in this divine fellowship, the other, man's.

The whole figure is that of a feast at which two parties sit down together, namely: God and His accepted child, while the heavenly bread on which they both feed is the person of Jesus Christ Himself.

## GOD'S PART

First, God receives His portion. This was expressed by the offering of the fat and the inwards of the sacrifice exclusively to God. In harmony with this the Jews were prohibited under any circumstances from eating the fat, or drinking the blood of animals. The first was regarded as the Lord's and expressive of God's part in the sacrifice of Christ.

And the second was the token of Christ's atoning life. The fat of the fellowship offering and the inwards represented the innermost life and love of Jesus Christ, and that which was highest and divinest in Him; all of which was offered in absolute devotion and perfect consecration to His Father.

## THE BREAD OF GOD

There was much more in Christ's death than the atonement of men. Beyond all that it involved for us, there were elements in His sacrifice which supremely relate to God alone, and meet and satisfy His claims and His affection. In this sense Jesus Christ was an offering to God, as well as a sacrifice for man, and so became the very bread of God, as well as of the believing soul. Therefore when we come to God in communion, we bring to Him as set forth in this sacrifice the Lord Jesus Christ, as His part in the feast. Not only are we accepted on the ground of His finished work, and perfect righteousness, but we offer afresh to God in active and living faith, and worship, His loveliness, and the sweet incense of His person and character. And if He is living in us, we offer to God not only the historical Christ, as the abstract embodiment of virtue and goodness, but His actual and living

Spirit, as the very life of our being, and the incense of our hearts, and are delightfully conscious that what we present to God is not our own love or devotion, but the Spirit of Christ living and loving and springing within us. So "we are to God the aroma of Christ" (2 Corinthians 2:15) and are "accepted in the Beloved" (Ephesians 1:6, KJV).

## OUR PART

This is God's portion in the feast of the fellowship offering. But this having been offered, we next receive our portion from His hand. This was also expressed in the ancient fellowship offering by the portion of the sacrifice which was given to the priests as their part in the banquet. These priests represented all consecrated believers under the gospel.

## THE STRENGTH OF CHRIST

After the priest had offered the fat and the sacrifice, he also sat down to partake of the right shoulder and the breast of the lamb (Leviticus 7:32–34). The former prefigured the strength of the Lord Jesus Christ, which becomes the very life and strength of the consecrated heart, and on which we may sweetly feed, and thus put on His strength, and so become "strong in the Lord and in his mighty power" (Ephesians 6:10).

## THE LOVE OF CHRIST

The breast signifies the love of Jesus. This also becomes our life. All the tenderness of His affection, all the sweetness of His sympathy, all the intimacy of His friendship, all the blessedness of His care, all the power of His indwelling life and love are thus made our own. Feeding upon His breast, not only do we enjoy His love to us in all its fullness, but we absorb and assimilate into our very being His own nature which is love—His spiritual life, His holy will, His devotion to God, His tenderness, His meekness and patience. This is the secret of holiness. This is true sanctification. Thus only can we love the Lord our God with all our heart and our neighbor as ourselves. Thus only can we love one another as He has loved us. This is the feast to which He invites His people.

"Here I am! I stand at the door and knock. If anyone hears my voice and opens the door, I will come in and eat with him, and he with me" (Revelation 3:20). This is the secret of His inner fellowship, which the men of Capernaum could not understand and would not receive. "I am the living bread that came down from heaven. . . . Whoever eats my flesh and drinks my blood has eternal life, and I will raise him up at the last day. . . . Just as the living Father sent me and I live because of the Father, so the one who feeds on me will live because of me" (John 6:51, 54, 57).

## SPIRITUAL FRESHNESS

There were minute features in this beautiful offering, which shed still fuller light on these profound lessons. The flesh of the fellowship offering was to be eaten the same day that it was offered (Leviticus 7:15); teaching us that there can be no stale experience in a true Christian life, but our fellowship with Christ must be continually renewed and we must abide in Him by living faith, moment by moment, and not live on old memories and experiences.

## THE SPIRIT'S QUICKENING

The fellowship offering also was always made by fire. And so the Holy Spirit alone can quicken and make real our communion with Christ and our participation in His life.

## LEAVEN

There was one singular provision in connection with this sacrifice, permitting the offering of leavened bread in connection with the thanksgiving oblation (7:13). Unleavened cakes mingled with oil were first to be offered, and then leavened cakes were mingled with them. When we remember that leaven was the type of sin, it looks very strange that such an expiation should be permitted. But it seems to imply that even the soul that is not yet fully sanctified may enjoy this communion with Christ. At the same time it gives no tolerance to known or indulged sin. For it is expressly provided in the 20th verse of the same chapter, that the soul that ate of the flesh of the sacrifice of fellowship offerings, in uncleanness, "must be cut off from his people."

It would seem to show that even a soul not yet freed from the leaven of natural corruption may come into the sanctuary and offer to God the perfect sacrifice of Christ, and feed upon it, notwithstanding his own worthiness, provided that all known sin has been acknowledged and renounced, and his uncleanness laid over upon the sin offering and renounced in his repentance and renewed obedience.

## SECTION III— *The Grain Offering*
### Leviticus 2:1–16

## THE HUMANITY OF CHRIST

This offering signifies Christ in His perfect human life, as the satisfaction of His Father, and the supply of His people's needs. It was a bloodless offering, but after the institution of the fellowship offering, it was usually connected with that offering, showing us that the life of Christ is not to be separated from His death, but becomes our true bread, as it is connected with His atonement, His mere teaching and example requiring the addition of His blood to form the perfect supply of our spiritual need (see 7:12).

## THE FLOUR

1. The grain offering consisted of fine flour, typical of Christ's perfect humanity (2:4; 1 Peter 2:22). There was something exquisitely and infinitely perfect about Christ's whole person. Every fiber of His being was fine and infinitely sensitive to suffering, joy and every touch of His Father's will.

## THE OIL

2. The fine flour of the meat offering was mingled with oil, which was typical of the Holy Spirit's union with Christ, both in His birth, His baptism and His entire ministry (Luke 1:35; 3:22; 4:1).

## FRANKINCENSE

3. The grain offering consisted also of frankincense, which was typical of the intense devotion of Christ's heart to the glory of His Father and of the sweetness and love which characterized His Spirit (John 8:27; Ephesians 5:2).

## NO LEAVEN

4. The grain offering was accompanied by unleavened cakes, the absence of leaven implying the perfect purity of Christ's character and life (Hebrews 7:26; 1 Corinthians 5:7).

## NO HONEY

5. The absence of honey in the grain offering strikingly expresses the freedom of His Spirit from all mere human sweetness, whether of sentiment, passion, self-indulgence or earthliness of any sort; the sickly sweet which many persons mistake for spiritual loveliness, and which belongs to much which is merely earthly and human (Leviticus 2:2; John 2:4; Luke 9:59; Mark 3:35; Matthew 12:50).

## SALT

6. The grain offering was mingled with salt (Leviticus 2:13). This is expressive of that quality in Christ's character which may be best expressed, perhaps, by the term wholesome; the intense practical wisdom and sense which kept Him from committing Himself to any man, from ever being weak or foolish, or in any way betraying Himself to His enemies. The same quality is expressed by the apostle in his counsel to us: "Let your conversation be always full of grace, seasoned with salt, so that you may know how to answer everyone" (Colossians 4:6).

## FIRE

7. The grain offering was offered with fire, perhaps suggesting Christ's suffering life and also the quickening influences of the Holy Spirit.

## WORSHIP

8. The grain offering was first presented to God and then partaken of by the worshiper. So Christ's life was God's bread and thus becomes also ours, as we have already seen in the deeper teaching of the fellowship offering. This entire offering thus represented the beauty and purity of Christ's life as the satisfaction of God, the strength of our life, and in conjunction with the fellowship offering, the supply of our spiritual need.

## SECTION IV—*The Burnt Offering*
### Leviticus 1:1–17

## ENTIRE CONSECRATION

This was the crowning sacrifice of the Levitical economy and expresses the highest elements in the offering of the Lord Jesus Christ and the believer's entire consecration.

Its highest import was to express and prefigure Christ's spotless, sufficient and complete self-sacrifice to God. It proceeded on the assumption that the sin had already been expiated by the sin offering, and hence a sinless sacrifice was laid upon the altar and consumed to ashes as a sweet savor, every part acceptable to Jehovah, to whom it was wholly dedicated. It was thus an offering to God, rather than for man.

The very name used to describe it literally means "to ascend," suggesting this thought of entire dedication to Jehovah. It becomes, therefore, a type of Christ offering Himself to the Father in our stead, and then offered by us in faith and full consecration.

## UNBLEMISHED

1. It must be without defect (1:3). The very essence of Christ's sacrifice for us involved the condition of His absolute sinlessness. Presenting Him to God we know that our offering must be accepted, and that the Father will say, "with him I am well pleased" (Matthew 3:17).

## VOLUNTARY

2. It must be willingly given. So He came crying, "Here I am, . . . I desire to do your will, O my God" (Psalm 40:7a, 8a). "No one takes it from me, but I lay it down of my own accord" (John 10:18). When they came to arrest Him, He showed by His miraculous power in prostrating the officers by

a look that He might easily have escaped had He wished; but He offered Himself to die in our stead, a willing sacrifice.

## UNTO GOD

3. It was slain before the Lord (Leviticus 1:5). So Christ yielded up His life, not only in the sight of men, but before the Lord. "Yet it was the LORD's will to crush him and cause him to suffer,/ and though the LORD makes his life a guilt offering . . ." (Isaiah 53:10). Like Abraham's sacrifice of his son, so the Father was the chief Actor in the scene, and also the chief Witness. And He looked upon that bleeding cross and dying Victim, and He knew that there was nothing withheld.

## THE SPRINKLED BLOOD

4. The blood was sprinkled round about the altar. This expresses the presenting of Christ's life, of which the blood was ever the symbol, as a ransom for sinful men, whose lives had been forfeited because of sin, and have been redeemed by the precious blood of Christ (Leviticus 1:5).

## CONSECRATION IN DETAIL

5. The sacrifice was next flayed, and cut into pieces, and thus exposed in every part, naked and open for inspection in every particular (1:6). This was intended to show that Christ's life was fully disclosed to the keenest inspection of His Father's eye, and offered to God in all the minute details of His being, His consecration extending to every thought, every moment and every issue of His existence. His whole life was a burnt offering, and in His death every detail was wholly consecrated and held upon the altar until the sacrifice was complete.

This is the reason why the last sufferings of our Lord are so fully described, and why the scene of agony was so protracted and minute. It was the cutting of the burnt offering into its innumerable pieces, and the presenting of each in detail, until there was nothing that could be added to the cup of pain, and the sacrifice of love. So our consecration must be specific and explicit, covering the minutest details of our life and actions.

## CONSUMING FIRE

6. The burnt offering was next laid upon the altar, over the wood and the fire, and wholly burnt to ashes (1:7–9). This was fulfilled in the consuming fire of Christ's sufferings both in life and death, under the hand of God and in the ascending flames of His own entire self-sacrifice and love. The entire burnt offering was consumed on the altar, and so Christ was wholly given to God.

All His life was offered, and every drop of His blood shed through the spear wound in His side. It is the completeness of the offering that makes it a perfect type of our consecration.

## THE CEASELESS FLAME

7. The burnt offering was to be continually kept upon the altar (6:9–13). So Christ's sacrifice was as unceasing as His life. Indeed, it has not ceased, in the sense of His entire consecration, even with His death.

## THE SWEET-SMELLING SAVOR

8. Christ's offering thus wholly made was perfectly accepted by the Father, and is called "a fragrant offering and sacrifice to God" (Ephesians 5:2). The whole idea of the burnt offering is that of sweetness and acceptance. There is not any odor of sin about it, but it breathes the very incense of sweetness and love; and God delights in it and requires that its fragrant breath shall continually ascend before Him.

So the Lord Jesus Christ has fully satisfied all the claims of the law and all the expectations of the Father. For ages God had been looking down in vain to find in the human race one in whom He could completely delight. "I looked for a man," He says, "but I found none" (Ezekiel 22:30). At length His heart rested on His beloved Son. In Him He found, for the first time, one of whom He could say, "with him I am well pleased" (Matthew 3:17), and for His sake He has loved and accepted sinful man ever since.

It is most important that we should recognize God's rights and claims in the work of redemption, as well as the necessities of lost men. Even if no mortal should ever be saved, God was entitled to obedience and love from those whom He had created at such cost. And even if Christ's life and death had never brought a soul to heaven, it has at least satisfied the claims of heaven upon the human family and honored the character and law of God.

## THE HANDS ON THE HEAD

9. One of the most vital acts in the sacrifice of burnt offering was the imposition of hands on the part of the worshiper (Leviticus 1:4) by which he identified himself with the sacrifice and so became accepted in its acceptance. This is a figure of the act of appropriating faith by which we accept the Lord Jesus Christ as our righteousness and present Him to God as the ground of our acceptance, and so are made accepted in Him even as He is accepted.

## OUR CONSECRATION

10. This beautiful offering not only typifies the sacrifice of Christ, but also becomes the pattern of our true consecration to God. From each of us God rightly claims, in the light of His most searching presence, the willing

and entire surrender and dedication of our entire being, and the consecration of every detail of our life. Like Him, too, our whole life should be a continual ascending flame of love and service on His holy altar, so that the Father can say of us as of Him; "My Son, whom I love; with him I am well pleased" (Matthew 3:17).

The only way in which we can ever make this offering is by receiving the Lord Jesus Christ into our very life and being, and becoming so identified with Him that we can continuously present Him in our heart of hearts as the very life of our life. This was what He Himself meant when He said: "For them I sanctify myself, that they too may be truly sanctified" (John 17:19). It is only as He thus lives in us that we can be truly consecrated, and that God can ever take pleasure in us.

## PRESENT YOUR BODIES

The 12th chapter of Romans is God's exposition of the burnt offering, as the sixth chapter is of the sin offering.

Let us hear the divine call afresh in beautiful type: "I urge you, brothers, in view of God's mercy, to offer your bodies as living sacrifices, holy and pleasing to God—this is your spiritual act of worship" (Romans 12:1). And in order that we may fulfill this consecration, let us receive Him who has already fulfilled it as our indwelling life and righteousness; and then we shall give back to God that which is but His own, and which He has already accepted in the person of His beloved Son.

# CHAPTER 2

## THE PRIESTHOOD

### *Leviticus 8–10*

The functions and garments of the high priest have been already described in the book of Exodus. The Scripture referred to above gives us an account of the consecration of the high priest, and also of his sons.

#### SECTION I—*Aaron and His Sons*

Aaron represents the Lord Jesus Christ as our Great High Priest. In this office He has no successor, and in the specific functions of His high-priesthood none of His people, of course, can participate.

The sons of Aaron, however, represented the priesthood of all believers, who are called by the apostle in Hebrews a house—that is, the priestly house of Christ (Hebrews 3:6; 1 Peter 2:9; Revelation 1:6). There is no special priesthood now in the New Testament Church. We are called to enter into the holiest by the blood of Jesus, and to minister in the most intimate fellowship and the most exalted service at His altar. In all except the special functions of the high priest, Aaron's sons shared his separation and consecration, as we also are made partakers of Christ in the fullness of His grace and glory.

#### SECTION II—*The Consecration of Aaron and His Sons*

*THE SACRIFICE*

Leviticus 8:1–4

1. This act is accompanied by the offering of all the sacrifices of the Levitical service. The sin offering, the burnt offering, the grain offering and the fellowship offering are all included in the holocaust of this impressive ritual, implying that the priesthood of Christ in our behalf is connected with

His perfect sacrifice and the completion of His redeeming work.

## THE ENROBING
### Leviticus 8:7–12

2. Aaron himself is first robed with his special garments.

This was the type of Christ's being set apart to His messianic work. Like Aaron He was anointed with holy oil, alone in the first instance, as the figure of His baptism by the Holy Spirit when He began His public ministry and officially assumed His priestly work.

## AARON'S SONS
### Leviticus 8:13

3. The sons of Aaron are next separated and robed.

They were robed, not with the same garments as the high priest, but with their simpler vestments of pure white linen; but they were not anointed at this stage. This represents the calling of Christ's disciples prior to His death and resurrection, and to the outpouring of the Holy Spirit on the day of Pentecost. They, too, were separated to be priests unto God, and clothed with the garments of their divine calling and their special character, but their full baptism from on high did not come until after His sacrifice was complete.

So likewise, in Christian life there is often an interval between our conversion and our entire consecration.

The garments of Aaron's sons were threefold, namely: their coats represented our Christian character, their sashes were expressive of service, and their bonnets or head coverings suggested the consecration of our intellects to Christ and the laying of our thoughts in captivity at His feet.

## THE GREAT SACRIFICE
### Leviticus 8:14–21

4. Next follow the sin offering and the burnt offering.

These represent the two great aspects of Christ's sacrifice, as the expiation of our guilt and the ground of our acceptance and justification through the atoning death of the Lord Jesus Christ.

All this followed in beautiful order in the development of Christ's actual work in the three stages so clearly indicated up to this point, namely: Christ's baptism and consecration to His work, the calling of His disciples and the offering of His great sacrifice.

## THE CONSECRATING BLOOD
### Leviticus 8:22–25

5. Next comes the ram of consecration, and the application of its blood to

Aaron and his sons. It was sprinkled upon the right ear, the right thumb and the right toe, both of Aaron and his sons, to intimate and prefigure the blood of Jesus Christ becoming the price of our redemption, and purchasing us and setting us apart as God's peculiar property in an entire consecration. The application of the blood to Aaron first implies the dedication of Christ's resurrection life to the Father and to the work of redemption. This blood represented not only His death, but also His life; not only the life given for man, but the life taken again and given anew to God and His people. It was of this consecration that He Himself said just before His death and resurrection, "For them I sanctify myself, that they too may be truly sanctified" (John 17:19). And it is this of which the apostle speaks, "Both the one who makes men holy and those who are made holy are of the same family" (Hebrews 2:11).

Christ's life in heaven is as fully consecrated as ours is required to be on the earth. Therefore His right ear is sprinkled with the blood; and so He hears with consecrated ears our every cry of need and the Father's slightest wish. His right hand is ever held at the service of His people, and His feet are dedicated as fully as when He walked through the fields and villages of Galilee to the finishing of His mighty work.

The blood of redemption was next applied to the ear and the hand and the foot of each of the sons of Aaron, implying our participation in the consecration of Christ and the redemption of all our powers for His service and glory. The blood not only expresses the idea of redemption, but also of resurrection life. In the book of Leviticus the blood is always the life, and the application of the blood to the members of the body suggests at once their purchase and also their quickening life.

## THE WAVE OFFERING
Leviticus 8:26–29

6. This was followed by the wave offering.

It was a beautiful ceremony, in which the priest took in his hands the offering of bread and oil with the fat of the sacrifice, and waved them before the Lord for a sweet savor, in token of the yielding up unto God in acceptable service of all that was involved in these gifts. It was fulfilled in Christ's presenting His complete offering to the Father in the heavenly places, and our yielding our members and all the fullness of Jesus Christ in us in consecrated service unto God. It stands as an object lesson of offered service.

## THE ANOINTING OIL
Leviticus 8:30

7. This was next followed by the anointing of Aaron and his sons with oil mingled with blood from the altar.

Now for the first time the sons of Aaron partake of the anointing. In the previous ceremony Aaron only was included, but now he shares it with his house.

This is a beautiful picture of the outpouring of the Holy Spirit which followed the complete sacrifice of Christ.

The baptism came first upon Jesus Himself, our ascended High Priest, and then from Him upon His Church and people. The apostle expresses it in these beautiful words in the Acts of the Apostles (2:33): "He has received from the Father the promised Holy Spirit and has poured out what you now see and hear."

The anointing which came upon Aaron's sons was mingled with the blood. And so the Holy Spirit comes upon us, the priests of God, as the spirit of Christ and of Christ's resurrection life; and in exact correspondence with this idea He is called in Romans 8:2 the Spirit of life in Christ Jesus. This is the exact meaning of the oil and the blood—the Holy Spirit bringing to us the life of Jesus Himself.

This anointing came not only upon the persons of Aaron's sons, but upon their garments. These represent our Christian graces, and teach us that they must ever spring from the life of our Lord and the abiding presence of the Holy Spirit.

## THE FELLOWSHIP OF LOVE
### Leviticus 8:32

8. All this is followed by what seems a combination of the grain offering and the fellowship offering. It was the priestly feast upon the flesh of the offerings and the bread of the meat offering, and vividly sets forth our participation in the life and strength of the Lord Jesus Christ, and the divine provision for our spiritual nourishment when we are engaged in His priestly service. Not only does God call His people to minister at His altar, but He also feeds them upon the very richest gifts of that altar, and makes them to be abundantly satisfied with the fatness of His house and to drink of the rivers of His pleasures.

## THE ABIDING LIFE
### Leviticus 8:31–36

9. The chapter closes with the most significant of all the symbols of His service. This was the dwelling of the priests for seven days with Aaron within the tabernacle until their consecration was complete. These seven days represent, of course, the idea of completeness, and typify the entire period of our Christian life, during which we, too, are to abide in the secret place of the Most High, and dwell in the tabernacle with our Great High Priest in unceasing fellowship and unbroken consecration.

## THE EIGHTH DAY—THE COMING GLORY
**Leviticus 9:1–24**

10. The crowning act of the whole service of consecration.

It came upon the eighth day, when Aaron and his sons, after renewing the sacrifices in all their fullness came forth from the tabernacle, and with uplifted hands the high priest blessed the people, and the glory of the Lord suddenly appeared to all the congregation amid the shouts and prostrations of the assembly. This has been correctly applied, we have no doubt, to the coming day when our priestly ministry shall end and our Great High Priest shall come forth from the right hand of the Father and be revealed amid the glories of the advent to the wondering gaze of His people; and all that was meant in that ancient benediction which closed this scene shall be realized in the ages of blessing which are to crown the millennial world. Then shall these words be literally fulfilled in the happiness of a sinless and tearless earth.

> The LORD bless you
> and keep you;
> the LORD make his face shine upon you
> and be gracious to you;
> the LORD turn his face toward you
> and give you peace. (Numbers 6:24–26)

This is implied symbolically in the eighth day, which represents the beginning of a new week. This means a new dispensation.

It is also suggested by the reference to Aaron's coming down from offering the sin offering, the burnt offering and the fellowship offering, and the appearing of the glory of the Lord, and the fiery tokens of His majestic presence.

This word "appear" is constantly used to denote His second coming. It is beautifully linked in the ninth chapter of Hebrews (verses 20–26) with the three aspects of His redeeming work to which this entire section refers: "But now he has appeared once for all at the end of the ages to do away with sin by the sacrifice of himself" (verse 26). That was His first appearing. "He [Christ] entered heaven itself, now to appear for us in God's presence" (verse 24). That is His present ministry, represented by the abiding of the priests for seven days in the tabernacle. "And he will appear a second time, not to bear sin, but to bring salvation" (verse 28). That is the third appearing, toward which the ceremonies of the eighth day in the Levitical anointing service so significantly looked forward.

## SECTION III—*Warnings and Judgments*
### *Against False Priesthood and Strange Fire*

### *NADAB AND ABIHU*
**Leviticus 10:1–12**

The consecration of the true priesthood is followed immediately by the awful example of Nadab and Abihu, significantly intended, no doubt, to show the contrast between the false and the true priesthood, and to foreshadow the counterfeits which the enemy would try to substitute, and their inevitable rejection and punishment. The sin of the two sons of Aaron seems to have arisen partly from a sudden temptation to indulgence in strong drink, because it is immediately followed in the eighth verse by the most rigid warnings with regard to the use of wines on the part of those who come near in the service of the tabernacle.

### *STRANGE FIRE*

It is further represented as an act of disobedience in that they offered incense and strange fire, which had been forbidden. It represents the methods of approach to God by any other way than that which He has prescribed and appointed. The application of the warning is as various as the different forms of false religion and worship which Satan has palmed off upon his deluded followers. These include all the forms of mere natural religion: the offerings of idolatry and self-righteousness, and their vain attempts to satisfy the claims of a holy God by man's works; worship without the Holy Spirit, the only true fire; worship without the recognition of Christ and His death and intercession as the ground of our acceptance; the fire of mere intellectual sacrifice, or aesthetic culture; worship which consists in religious sentiment, fine art, musical ecstasies, emotional feeling, unhallowed, unsanctified motives and all except that which springs from the spirit of Christ, and is identified with His name, life and glory.

The judgment which fell upon the false worshipers in this case foreshadows the consuming fire which must destroy every unholy thing that presumes to intrude into the presence of God. It may not always break out in judgment here, but " 'Surely the day is coming; it will burn like a furnace. All the arrogant and every evildoer will be stubble, and that day that is coming will set them on fire,' says the LORD Almighty. 'Not a root or a branch will be left to them' " (Malachi 4:1).

### *THE SPIRIT OF FEAR*
**Leviticus 10:16–20**

In the closing verses of the chapter there seems to be a hint that this fearful warning might lead the priests to the extreme of undue fear, and it may have been from this cause that they omitted to eat the sacrifice of the sin offering in the holy place, according to the divine provision. Perhaps the terrors of that awful manifestation had made them afraid to venture even upon their rights and privileges. Moses sharply reproves them for it, and commands them to guard against repeating the neglect. So while we serve with reverence and godly fear, and while He still is a consuming fire, we must not hesitate, also, to come boldly to the throne of grace, and enter into all the fullness of our redemption rights and privileges.

# CHAPTER 3

## THE ORDINANCES OF CLEANSING

### Leviticus 11–15

Let us not fail to notice the beautiful order in the successive developments of truth in this wonderful book of gospel teaching. First and best of all, we have the offerings, unfolding the perfect sacrifice of Christ as the ground of our access to God. Next we have the priesthood, which prefigures the way of access through the person and intercession of the Lord Jesus Christ, and our priesthood in Him. And now we have in this third section the condition of access, namely; our cleansing from sin and defilement. This is set forth in a number of ceremonial provisions with regard to uncleanness, culminating in the most significant of all these ordinances, namely: that respecting the leper.

### SECTION I—Clean and Unclean Animals
#### Leviticus 11

These various distinctions are specified in the 11th chapter of Leviticus. While they were, no doubt, to a great extent purely ceremonial, and may seem to us somewhat obsolete and are no longer binding, yet they were intended as simple object lessons to lead the thoughts and consciences of the people, step by step, to the conception of the moral difference between right and wrong.

God was teaching His people as we would teach a little child, or an irrational animal, first by symbols and then afterwards by deeper moral intuitions and convictions. The fact that certain things were permitted and certain others prohibited as articles of food would prepare their minds for the more important prohibitions respecting their deeper spiritual life.

## SECTION II—*Uncleanness in Connection with Birth*
### Leviticus 12

It is not necessary to explain in detail the various provisions for the cleansing of the young mother from the defilement contracted through the birth of her offspring. These ordinances received a beautiful illustration in the rites of purification connected with the birth of our Lord Himself; and the offering of the turtledove and the two young pigeons at the hands of His humble mother was not deemed unworthy of being fully chronicled in the story of His life.

In these ordinances also there was a certain symbolical allusion to great spiritual and moral conceptions; perhaps the idea lying back of all was the radical depravity of human nature, and the transmission and taint of sin by the very law of heredity. Was not this what David meant when he cried: "Surely I was sinful at birth,/ sinful from the time my mother conceived me" (Psalm 51:5)?

## SECTION III—*Leprosy of Person*
### Leviticus 13:1 46

This was the special type of sin as separating us from God and the companionship of the holy and marking its traces even in our physical diseases and infirmities. It was the most realistic type of sin and its inherent consequences in the Old Testament.

1. It was incurable by human means, and so a type of the malignity and hopelessness of sin.

2. It excluded from the presence of God, and the fellowship of His people. The victim dwelt apart, and no man dared to touch his contaminating person. So sin inevitably separates the soul from the presence of God, and from the good and holy; and even in heaven itself the unsanctified heart would be more intolerably wretched and isolated than in the abyss of woe.

3. It was a constantly increasing sore, gradually spreading from joint to joint, and limb to limb, until the whole body became a putrefying mass and a living death. So sin is never stationary. "Evil men and impostors will go from bad to worse, deceiving and being deceived" (2 Timothy 3:13). And there will be an eternal progression in the ages of the future, more terrific even than the developments which we have seen on earth.

4. It suggested the connection between sin and its physical consequences. It was the outward mark of the inward plague. Therefore it becomes peculiarly expressive of the meaning of disease in the economy of God's moral government, not as the token of special punishment for special sin,

but in general as the effect of sin, and the mark upon our body of our fallen state, and our separation from the perfect life of God and holiness. Consequently the healing of disease was always associated with spiritual cleansing and quickening in the ministry of Christ; and this has ever been the first principle in the scriptural experience of divine healing.

5. Leprosy was a disease involving unspeakable wretchedness, shame and misery, and looking forward to a future of hopeless despair. The very Hebrew word for leprosy means "the stroke or wound of God." So sin involves more than we have yet seen of its fearful possibilities and issues, for it shall yet pass under the final judgment of a righteous God and be banished to its own place without alleviation or limitation of its fearful virulence and avenging.

## SECTION IV—*The Cleansing of the Leper*

### CONVICTION AND CONFESSION
**Leviticus 13:12–13**

1. The inspection and discrimination of the victim.

He must be brought to the priest, who alone could pass judgment upon the case. So Christ alone can be the true judge of sin. If the plague was working secretly or in spots, the leper was pronounced unclean. But if the plague was exposed and the leprosy covered all his person, it was a singular provision of the Mosaic law that he might be pronounced clean. This was designed to teach us that conviction and confession of sin bring immediate forgiveness, but if it is hidden it involves inevitable condemnation. The moment the tax collector cries, "God, have mercy on me, a sinner," the Savior declares, "This man . . . went home justified before God" (Luke 18:13–14). The moment Job exclaims, "I despise myself" (Job 42:6), the Lord pronounces him righteous. "Only acknowledge your guilt" (Jeremiah 3:13), He cries. Stand like the ancient leper who was required to cry, "Unclean! Unclean!" (Leviticus 13:45), and "the blood of Jesus, his Son, purifies us from all sin" (1 John 1:7). "If we confess our sins, he is faithful and just and will forgive us our sins and purify us from all unrighteousness" (1:9).

### SEEKING THE SAVIOR
**Leviticus 14:2**

2. The leper must be brought unto the priest.

He perhaps was not able to go without help, perhaps would not have gone if he had not been kindly led. So God brings us to Himself, sometimes directly, as He called Philip and Saul, by His Holy Spirit and His sovereign grace, and sometimes through the instrumentality of Christian friends.

## SEEKING THE LOST

### Leviticus 14:3

3. The priest next goes out to meet the leper outside the camp.

What a lovely picture of the Savior as He stoops to the sinner's lowest level and meets him on his own plane of unworthiness and helplessness. So we read in the Gospels that Jesus put forth His hand and touched the shrinking leper, and said: "I am willing, . . . Be clean" (Mark 1:41). We have a Great High Priest who "is able to deal gently with those who are ignorant and are going astray, since he himself is subject to weakness" (Hebrews 5:2). No man need say in his heart, " 'Who will ascend into heaven?' (that is, to bring Christ down) 'or Who will descend into the deep?' (that is, to bring Christ up from the dead). But what does it say? 'The word is near you; it is in your mouth and in your heart' " (Romans 10:6–8).

We do not need to work ourselves up to a point of special consecration or feeling in order to receive the divine blessing; we have only to turn to God where we are and put ourselves at once into His all-sufficient hands. He sees the first movement of our heart toward Him and comes to meet us. "While he was still a long way off, his father saw him and was filled with compassion for him; he ran to his son" (Luke 15:20).

So the Savior is already moving toward the sinner with all the tenderness of His welcoming love. "For the Son of Man came to seek and to save what was lost" (19:10).

## DEATH AND RESURRECTION

### Leviticus 14:4–7

4. The next step in the cleansing of the leper was the selection of two birds, one of which was sacrificed and the other sprinkled with its blood and set free in the open field, as a type of the twofold fact of Christ's death and resurrection.

The slain bird set forth His crucifixion and the loosed one His resurrection. This is the basis of every sinner's cleansing. "The blood of Jesus, his Son, purifies us from all sin" (1 John 1:7); and His blood means His life shed for us and imparted to us. These two birds also imply our death and resurrection with Christ. The first prefigures our old life yielded up to Christ; the second, our new life springing forth into freedom, emancipated from the power and the penalty of sin, and like the liberated bird soaring and singing in the light of heaven.

It will be noticed here that at this stage the priest is to "pronounce him clean" (Leviticus 14:7)—the sinner's justification in contrast with his sanctification next described.

## SEPARATION
**Leviticus 14:8–9**

5. The next stage is the actual working out of all this in the leper's experience.

First his person and his garments must be completely washed, denoting the putting off of all the filthiness of the flesh, both in his nature and in his deeds. This was followed by the shaving of his entire body, even to the hair of his eyebrows. Everything that could be a figure of the old life was cut off and laid aside in entire self-renunciation.

## CONSECRATION
**Leviticus 14:14**

6. The next act is full of beautiful significance.

It is the thought already expressed in the consecration of the priest; his right ear, hand and foot were touched with the blood of the sacrifice as a symbol of their complete redemption and dedication to God. The ear represents our receptive faculties, the hand our active faculties and powers, and the foot our habits and walk. All these are thus redeemed and consecrated by the recognition of Christ's death for us, and the communication of His life to us.

## THE SPIRIT'S ANOINTING
**Leviticus 14:15–17**

7. The final act in this beautiful ceremony was the baptism of these same three members with the holy oil of anointing.

This was significant of the Holy Spirit, by whom we become possessed when we have made the consecration already described. The Spirit of God now takes possession of our ears, our hands and our feet, and controls and endues them with His abiding presence and power.

## THE FULLNESS OF THE SPIRIT
**Leviticus 14:18**

Then "the rest of the oil" was poured upon the leper's head, implying that even after the Holy Spirit has fully possessed us there is an infinite reserve still awaiting us, and that all His immeasurable fullness also belongs to us. How much the rest of the oil means only eternity can show. Poured on the head, of course it overflowed to the rest of the body. Perhaps it implied that the sinner's head needed a fuller baptism than any other part of his being, to keep his own reasoning suppressed and his busy brain pervaded and possessed only by the Holy Spirit.

## SECTION V—*Mildew of Garments*
### Leviticus 13:47–59

As leprosy of person refers to the depravity of our nature and personality, mildew of garments has respect to the sinfulness of our acts and habits of life. Clothing in the Old Testament is a figure of the conduct and conversation of man. The word *habit* itself originally meant a robe. It still describes a kind of costume, and by figurative application, also, the course of one's life. Not only are we intrinsically depraved, but the whole course of our life has been sinful. Referring to both these facts, the prophet with intense vividness declares, "All of us have become like one who is unclean,/ and all our righteous acts are like filthy rags" (Isaiah 64:6).

The only remedy for mildew of garments was to wash them, and, if this failed, to burn them altogether. There are some habits of life which are not essentially evil, but which can be cleansed and truly consecrated; there are others, however, which can only be wholly renounced and destroyed. No one but the priest could detect the degree of the plague or apply the true remedy; so the Lord Jesus Christ alone can cleanse our ways, as well as purify our hearts.

## SECTION VI—*Mildew of House*
### Leviticus 14:33–53

The house represents the Church of God, and the teaching is that even Christ's own spiritual temple needs to be guarded from the taint of sin. How true this is will be quickly seen if we but remember the sad and solemn story of the Christian centuries. How quickly the eyes of the Great High Priest detected, even in the seven churches of Asia, already the taint of awful mildew; and how soon it spread until Christendom was a corrupt mass of spiritual loathsomeness and disease.

The remedy was to be adapted to the degree of the contamination. In some cases it might be cleansed without the destruction of the house, but where it had spread into the very walls and timbers the building must be torn down and carried away bodily and destroyed. So in the Church of God there are evils which are only superficial and confined to the few, and may be healed by faithful discipline; but there are others which become intrinsic and essential, and for which God's only remedy is the dissolution of the very system which bears His name by unhallowed claim. Hence He says of some of the apostolic churches, "If you do not repent, I will come to you and remove your lampstand from its place" (Revelation 2:5). But concerning the others He decrees, "I am about to spit you out of my mouth" (3:16). And of the great ecclesiastical system which has become an apostasy and an anti-Christ, He declares that "the Lord Jesus will overthrow [the lawless one] with the breath of his mouth and destroy by the splendor of his coming" (2 Thessalonians 2:8).

## SECTION VII—*Personal Uncleanness of the Flesh*
### Leviticus 15:1–33

This chapter refers to a number of personal and physical defilements, all of which refer to the necessity of our bodies being sanctified and preserved in sacredness and purity in all their members, as the temples of God and the instruments of His service.

# CHAPTER 4

## THE DAY OF ATONEMENT OR COMPLETE
## RECONCILIATION

### Leviticus 16–17

These chapters stand in the center of the book of Leviticus and are expressive, above all other ceremonial rites, of the great principle of our perfect reconciliation to God through the Lord Jesus Christ. The day was called *Kipporim*, meaning "the atonement," and the rabbis have given it the distinguishing name of *Yoma*, or "the day," thus distinguishing it from all other days. It was sometimes called the festival of feasting. To us it is significant of the finished work of redemption through the Lord Jesus Christ. The word atonement finely expresses this thought by its very structure: it means literally, "at-one-ment," and expresses the great fact of our reconciliation to God.

### SECTION I—*The Day*
### Leviticus 16:29–34

This was the 10th day of the seventh month, both numbers being symbolical and both expressing the same idea of completeness. The seventh month was the culminating month of the Hebrew calendar. Its imposing rites terminated with the Feast of Tabernacles, the very crown of all the festal year in its joyous significance. It was the Sabbatic month of the first seven, and the 10th day added a still higher emphasis to the idea of completeness which this whole service symbolized. Its highest spiritual teaching with respect to the redemption of Christ might be expressed in the words "Once for all;" Christ's own dying cry, "Finished," signalizes the same victorious fact. It denotes the eternal accomplishment of His redeeming work, by the one complete sacrifice. There is nothing to be added to it. His finished transaction made an end of sin and brought in everlasting righteousness (Daniel 9:24), and the sinner has only to enter upon His accomplished work and receive the salvation of God so fully prepared for him.

It was kept as a fast day as well as a feast day, and the Jews were required to observe it as a Sabbath of rest and to afflict their souls and do no servile work therein (Leviticus 16:29–31). It was thus to be marked by a deep sense of sin, and also by an entire cessation from all their own works; and so it expressed the two great spiritual thoughts of repentance and of absolute trust in the finished work of Christ, with the renunciation of all our righteousness and the works of the flesh. The apostle expresses the same truth in Romans 4:5, "To the man who does not work but trusts God who justifies the wicked, his faith is credited as righteousness."

## SECTION II— *The High Priest*

### CHRIST'S SOLITARINESS
**Leviticus 16:17**

1. The high priest alone was allowed to perform the sacrificial and priestly offices of this day, no man being permitted in the tabernacle when he made atonement. This implies the absolute solitariness of our great Redeemer in the hour of His suffering and the fact that He is the only Savior, and unaided by us or any other creature, has Himself accomplished the mighty task of man's eternal salvation. There is a touching solemnity in the thought that on that great day the sanctuary which was usually crowded with priests was deserted by all but the single form of the high priest alone. It was a solemn type of that awful hour when the Redeemer trod the winepress alone, and in the anguish of the garden and the desolation of the cross there was no man at His side, and even the Father had for a moment deserted Him.

None but He might enter the Holy of Holies. Those mysterious curtains barred every other visitor from entering, on penalty of instant death, beneath the consuming fire of God's holy presence. The strain of sin is on every human spirit, and no breath of evil can live in the presence of the Holy God. But on this day the high priest entered even this innermost shrine, because his person had been cleansed in the symbolical water, and he held in his hand the blood of the sacrifice and the incense of the golden altar, which proclaimed complete propitiation for the sins which He represented. He stands as the representative of our Great High Priest. His is the only figure that the eye of faith can behold in the hour of its conscious guilt and the only one on whom the eye of God can gaze with complacency and acceptance. The Father beholds Him and is satisfied. The sinner beholds Him and is saved. In the center of this ancient picture we behold one form and hear but one name, "Jesus only" (Hebrews 9:24 and 10:20).

## ONCE FOR ALL
**Leviticus 16:1–2**

2. Only once in the year might even he enter those sacred precincts, namely: on this appointed day. This was the divine foreshadowing of the fullness of the time when our great Sacrifice came to redeem His sinful people, and of the fact that His sacrifice, as already shown, was complete and final. The Hebrew year stands for the entire Christian age, and this one sacrifice represents the moment when on Calvary Jesus made entire and complete reconciliation for us. For unbelief or superstition to question this, or attempt to throw a doubt upon the efficiency of this sacrifice, or to renew the offering of the atoning blood, is to insult the very blood and crucify the Lord afresh. This is what Romanism does in the sacrifice of the mass, which is an ignorant, profane and blasphemous renewing of the sacrificial death of Christ in symbol, as it was done in the ancient Jewish rites. It was right that they should renew the sacrifice from year to year, because the great Victim was not yet offered; but when He actually consummated His one sacrifice, the hand of God rent in twain the veil of the temple from top to bottom, and showed that the work was done, and that no other high priest should ever enter officially this sacred enclosure again, as the prophet Daniel had predicted. He made the sacrifice and the oblation to cease by the "everlasting righteousness" which He Himself now brought in (Daniel 9:24, 27; Hebrews 9:26–28).

In the experience of the believer there ought also to be the same definiteness, completeness and once-for-all-ness in the committal and acceptance of appropriating faith. Our Lord's blessed Word has authorized this decisive trust and everlasting rest of faith and its full assurance. "I tell you the truth, whoever hears my word and believes him who sent me has eternal life and will not be condemned; he has crossed over from death to life" (John 5:24). "I write these things to you who believe in the name of the Son of God so that you may know that you have eternal life" (1 John 5:13).

## HIS SPOTLESS PURITY
**Leviticus 16:4**

3. The high priest first arrayed himself in the plain linen robes, which consisted of a linen coat, undergarments, turban and sash, differing but slightly from the garments of the other priests. They were expressive of our Savior's personal holiness. The figure was still further enhanced by the symbolical act of washing his flesh with water before he put them on. The whole representation expresses the personal purity and perfect sinlessness of our Lord Jesus in His human character and life before He suffered as a sacrifice on Calvary. This was indispensable to the efficacy of the sacrifice. "Such a

high priest meets our need—one who is holy, blameless, pure, set apart from sinners, exalted above the heavens" (Hebrews 7:26).

## THE HIGH PRIEST'S PERSONAL OFFERING

4. Having thus arrayed himself in his personal robes of immaculate purity, the high priest next offered the sacrifice prescribed for his own personal sins. This consisted of a bullock by which he made atonement for himself (Leviticus 16:3, 11). This of course was unnecessary in the sacrifice of Christ. He had no personal guilt to expiate by His sufferings. And yet may it not be that the personal atonement made by Aaron was designed to prefigure the fact in our redemption that the Lord Jesus Christ recognized our sins the same as if they were His own, and that "God made him who had no sin to be sin for us, so that in him we might become the righteousness of God" (2 Corinthians 5:21).

## THE TWO GOATS
**Leviticus 16:5, 7–25**

5. Having presented his own personal offering, the Hebrew high priest next selected the offering for the people's sin. This part of the ceremony contains the very essence of the whole type, and requires our most careful attention and intense interest, and the very anointing of the Holy Spirit that we may both apprehend and spiritually apply it. This offering required two sacrificial animals in order to embody the whole meaning that was to be afterward fulfilled in one person. It was necessary to express the two thoughts of Christ's offering to God and also His substitution for the sinner. And so two goats were chosen, the Hebrew language in which they are described literally meaning, "two shaggy he-goats." The rabbis tell us that both were required to be exactly alike, of the same age, color, size and appearance in every way. They were not intended to represent two Christs, but two aspects of the one Christ.

The first of these goats is described as the goat "for the LORD" (16:8). This represents the aspect of Christ's death which has reference, primarily, to the claims of God, His justice and holiness. The Lord Jesus Christ came to satisfy these, even if no sinner ever should be saved. He gave Himself as an offering and a sacrifice unto God as well as for men. The successive steps with regard to this sacrifice are very significant.

## THE SIN OFFERING

First, the goat was slain as a sin offering. Then its blood was brought within the veil, accompanied with the incense from the golden altar and sprinkled upon the mercy seat under the very eye of the fiery Shekinah which represented the immediate and holy presence of God. This whole act vividly prefigured the death of Jesus Christ on the cross, and then the offering of His life as a pure and perfect gift in the immediate presence of the Father. Was this what He meant when He said to Mary, "Do not hold on to me, for I have not yet returned to the Father" (John 20:17)? Was He on His way to lay that precious life before the throne as a ransom for His people, and as an answer to all God's demands and rights? Or had He done so in the interval between His death and resurrection? We know, at least, that in some way at this time He passed within the veil and through the eternal Spirit (perhaps that means in His own eternal and spiritual life) offered Himself without spot to God (Hebrews 9:14).

## THE SCAPEGOAT

Having presented the first of these two goats, the high priest next took the other goat, which is described in our version as the scapegoat, but literally in the Hebrew as the goat for *Azazel.* Laying both his hands upon its head he confessed over it all the sins of the children of Israel, and all their transgressions in all their sins, putting them on the head of the goat; then he sent it forth into the wilderness by the hand of a selected person, and the goat was to bear upon it all their iniquities into the land not inhabited, and so to be let go into the wilderness. This was intended to denote the fact that Christ, having died on the cross for our sins, has thus borne them away, no more to return to us, any more than the goat returned from the solitude of the desert. Christ took our guilt into the depths of His bottomless grave, and there it is sinking still and will never rise again.

This idea of eternal redemption is the specific thought of the day of atonement. "The Lamb of God, who takes away the sin of the world" (John 1:29). "As far as the east is from the west,/ so far has he removed our transgressions from us" (Psalm 103:12). "I have swept away your offenses like a cloud" (Isaiah 44:22). "[I] will remember their sins no more" (Jeremiah 31:34). "Search will be made . . ./ for the sins of Judah,/ but none will be found" (50:20). "For I will forgive their wickedness/ and will remember their sins no more" (Hebrews 8:12). "[I] will hurl all [their] iniquities into the depths of the sea" (Micah 7:19). These are some of the figures in which the significance of this solemn ceremony is amplified throughout the Scriptures. It is blessed to know that the goat carried the sins of Israel into a land not inhabited. They never fell on anybody else, and it is blessed to know that the sins we lay on Christ are so canceled that not only shall we be saved from their consequences, but no other shall bear them for us.

## AZAZEL

But what is the meaning of that strange expression "Azazel"? Who was "Azazel"? This has been one of the controversies of exegetical theology. The word occurs nowhere else in the Old Testament, and probably should have no translation. The most judicious authorities apply the word to a personal evil spirit, to be understood as the opposite of Jehovah. This is the natural construction of the language. One goat was for the Lord, the other for the other person. Origen held that Azazel denoted the devil. We know that evil spirits are believed to inhabit desert places, and the root of the Hebrew word seems to be connected with the sense of banishment and separation. Is it taught by this awful figure that Christ was delivered up in the hour of His crucifixion to absolute and unlimited malignity of the very prince of wickedness and cruelty? Was there a sense in which, for a moment, our Substitute was handed over to the torments which we should have borne and should eternally have suffered in the world of the damned? Is the sinner the subject of Satan's awful dominion, and entitled to the torments of his power and hate? And did our Lord take our place in this real sense, when He entered the regions of the kingdom of darkness, that He might rescue us from the tyrant who had enslaved us? What a lurid light these very questions cast upon the dark hour of His sorrow! Truly,

> None of the ransomed ever knew,
> How deep were the waters crossed;
> Nor how dark the night that the Lord passed through
> Ere He found the sheep that was lost.

## RESURRECTION ROBES
### Leviticus 16:23–24
6. The next act of the high priest was the changing of his garments, the washing of his flesh in water and the putting on of his garments again.

This very beautifully and truly represents the putting off of Christ's robes of flesh by His literal death, and then the putting on again of the garments of His humanity through His glorious resurrection. All this accompanied the sending forth of the scapegoat, and so is spiritually associated with the consummation of Christ's sacrificial work. It was after He had borne away our sins that He put on again His resurrection body.

## THE SACRIFICE ACCEPTED
### Leviticus 16:24–25
7. The crowning act of all these sacrifices immediately followed and consisted of the sacrifice of the burnt offering and the fat of the sin offering on the altar of the tabernacle. This was expressive of the acceptance of the sacrifice as a sweet smelling savor in the presence of God, and the complete obliteration of all the guilt of the people and even the very consciousness of their sin.

## SECTION III—*The Meaning of the Blood*
### Leviticus 17:11–14

The 17th chapter of Leviticus expounds with great fullness and beauty the reason why the blood is so constantly emphasized in this and all other Levitical sacrifices, for "without the shedding of blood there is no forgiveness" (Hebrews 9:22), and almost all things were purged with blood.

To the coarse sensibilities of the merely natural mind all this is offensive and seems to be unworthy even of a great God or a refined nature. But the Holy Spirit explains to us that the blood means the life (Leviticus 17:11–14). For this cause they were prohibited from eating or drinking blood. It was separate and sacred as a special token of this idea of atonement, and the reason was that the blood was recognized as the life, the very vital element of the human body. The shedding of blood, therefore, represents the idea of the laying down of life. So Christ's blood means the sacrifice of Christ's life instead of ours. Our life was forfeited, both in the natural and spiritual sense; and for us He gave His own as a ransom, thus purchasing back our spiritual and also our eternal life.

The blood was not only shed, but also sprinkled; not only was it poured out upon the altar outside of the holy place, but also sacredly gathered again and carried into the most sacred precincts of the inner sanctuary, and there kept in drops of sprinkled freshness on the mercy seat between the cherubim. This sacrifice is the second great aspect of the blood of Christ, namely: His life taken up again in His resurrection and presented to God as a living and perpetual sacrifice in the Holy of Holies. Not only is it presented to God, but it is also imparted to us as our life; so that the blood of Christ applied to us is not merely His death for us, purchasing us back from condemnation, but it is His life in us, continually applied as our true life and imparting to us in our very being a continual spring of purity, peace, power and even physical vitality if we will so receive it.

It is in this higher sense that the blood of Jesus Christ keeps cleansing us from all sin; and it is in this sense that His flesh is meat indeed and His blood is drink indeed. "Whosoever eats my flesh and drinks my blood has eternal life, and . . . remains in me, and I in him" (John 6:54, 56). All this has come to us through Christ's one offering.

We need only add that our Great High Priest has not only entered, like Aaron, into the holy place and presented His precious blood as a ransom for our perfect salvation, but He has left the door forever open; and as we drink that blood and receive that indwelling life, we too may enter in where He is gone and dwell in the perpetual fellowship of His abiding love and the Father's benignant Presence.

Let us conclude with God's own commentary on the meaning of this ancient type.

> It is impossible for the blood of bulls and of goats to take away sins, . . . For this reason it can never, by the same sacrifices repeated endlessly year after year, make perfect those who draw near to worship. If it could, would they not have stopped being offered? (Hebrews 10:4, 1–2)

> But when this priest [Christ] had offered for all time one sacrifice for sins, he sat down at the right hand of God. Since that time he waits for his enemies to be made his footstool, because by one sacrifice he has made perfect forever those who are being made holy. (10:12–14)

> Therefore, brothers, since we have confidence to enter the Most Holy Place by the blood of Jesus, by a new and living way opened for us through the curtain, that is, his body, and since we have a great priest over the house of God, let us draw near to God with a sincere heart in full assurance of faith, having our hearts sprinkled to cleanse us from a guilty conscience and having our bodies washed with pure water. (10:19–22)

# CHAPTER 5

## HOLINESS

### Leviticus 18–22

After the revelation in the preceding chapters of our reconciliation to God and access to His immediate presence through the sacrifice and priesthood of Christ and the cleansing of His blood and Spirit, it follows in logical order, that the life and conversation of God's separated and reconciled people should be prescribed and unfolded. This is the true divine order: first, reconciliation, then holiness. It is not only that we are brought near to God through the blood of Christ, but that through Him we can also walk in His commandments. And it is required of those who have been redeemed at such cost and brought into this place of privilege, that they should be holy even as He is holy. Therefore the Apostle Peter, in his profound epistle, connects our holiness immediately with our redemption and separation to our spiritual priesthood.

> Be holy, because I am holy. (1 Peter 1:16)

> For you know that it was not with perishable things such as silver or gold that you were redeemed from the empty way of life handed down to you from your forefathers, but with the precious blood of Christ. (1:18–19)

> But you are a chosen people, a royal priesthood, a holy nation, a people belonging to God, that you may declare the praises of him who called you out of darkness into his wonderful light. . . . Live such good lives among the pagans . . . that by doing good you should silence the ignorant talk of foolish men. (2:9, 12, 15)

The four chapters from Leviticus 18–22 contain a great number of

199

promiscuous injunctions and precepts with regard to the personal, domestic and social purity and righteousness of the people; and while not presenting a complete or systematic code of morals, yet they embrace the most essential principles and practices of a truly upright and holy life.

## THE GROUND OF HOLINESS

1. This section is preceded by that which is the ground of all true holiness, namely: a reminder of the covenant relation of the people to God as their covenant God, expressed by the special name of Jehovah.

"The LORD said to Moses, 'Speak to the Israelites and say to them: "I am the LORD your God" ' " (Leviticus 18:1–2).

"I am the LORD your God" occurs no less than 19 times in the 19th chapter, and repeatedly in the others (18:2, 4, 30; 19:2, 4, etc.). The similar expression, "I Jehovah am holy," is also repeated many times in these chapters. These two together express the two great truths of God's covenant relation and of His personal holiness as the ground of our holiness.

This is really the New Testament conception of holiness, and the one which throughout this entire series of scriptural expositions we shall endeavor to unfold; that we are not sanctified by law or conscience, or our own efforts or works, but by the grace of God and the imparted holiness of the personal Christ Himself. The two grounds of holiness are: Be holy, because I am your covenant God and, "Be holy, because I am holy." In the same spirit the apostle says to the disciples at Rome, "Therefore, I urge you, brothers, in view of God's mercy, to offer your bodies as living sacrifices" (Romans 12:1). That is the same as if he said, "I urge you by the fact that God is your covenant God and Redeemer." The other truth, God's holiness as the pattern and source of ours, is a still more profound and emphatic teaching of the New Testament. We can only become holy through the holiness of God. It is not merely that we imitate Him; we must receive Him and then reflect His own life and nature in our lives. "It is because of him that you are in Christ Jesus, who has become for us wisdom from God—that is, our righteousness, holiness and redemption" (1 Corinthians 1:30).

## SEPARATION

### Leviticus 18:3

2. The next element in the life of holiness, as here revealed, is Israel's separation from the spirit and character of the nations of Egypt and Canaan.

So we are called in the New Testament to be a peculiar people, separated from the spirit of the world even as Christ is not of the world. There can be no holiness without this. Therefore, in exactly parallel order, the apostle follows the call to consecration with the injunction, "Do not conform any longer to the pattern of this world, but be transformed by the renewing of your mind. Then you will be able to test and approve what God's will is—his good, pleasing and perfect will" (Romans 12:2). The telegraph wire can only retain the celestial fluid as it is insulated, and the soul can only keep its purity when separated from the touch of the world.

## OBEDIENCE
### Leviticus 18:4–5

3. They are next required to obey the judgments, ordinances and statutes of the Lord. These are described as intended for their good, rather than merely to gratify God's despotic will. The habit of implicit obedience and recognition of God's absolute authority and the sacredness of all His commandments constitute the very groundwork of a holy life. To Joshua it was enjoined as one of the conditions of victory: "Be careful to obey all the law my servant Moses gave you; do not turn from it to the right or to the left, that you may be successful wherever you go" (Joshua 1:7). And so the Lord Jesus Christ has made this the chief condition of His fellowship and blessing:

If you love me, you will obey what I command. (John 14:15)

Therefore everyone who hears these words of mine and puts them into practice is like a wise man who built his house on the rock. (Matthew 7:24)

He who does not love me will not obey my teaching. (John 14:24)

It is not a new condition of self-righteousness or legal obedience. Our salvation is not earned by it, but, being saved by His very grace and received to the fellowship of His love, He expects it from us as the service of loving children, and it is the practical test of true holiness. "But if anyone obeys his word, God's love is truly made complete in him" (1 John 2:5).

## PURITY
### Leviticus 18:6, 17–30

4. Personal purity in all our habits and social relations is next required under the most solemn sanctions.

This is amplified in a great number of particulars, which at first sight might seem to shock our finer sensibilities; but that they are mentioned implies the necessity of the warning and of our ceaseless vigilance, if we would maintain our character and life unspotted and unblamable. In keeping with this thought is the admonitory fact, that in the most elevated and spiritual of the New Testament epistles, the picture of our innermost communion with God and our partnership in the exaltation of our risen Lord is followed by the most explicit warnings to the very persons who had been thus represented as sealed by the Spirit and seated with Christ in heavenly places to watch against lying, anger, lust, covetousness and the most gross and abominable sins (Ephesians 5:3–18). These warnings were the more necessary because of the gross licentiousness and unnatural wickedness of ancient heathen nations (Leviticus 20:10–21).

## IDOLATRY AND SORCERY
### Leviticus 19:4, 26, 31; 20:1–6, 27
5. They are next warned against idolatry and sorcery.

And this was one of the most deeply rooted and widely prevalent enormities of ancient times. Sorcery was connected with every form of paganism, and constituted, in chief part, the very religion and worship of the heathen. It was really the literal worship of the devil and a counterfeit of true religion. It was always associated with the sin referred to in the previous paragraph, sanctioning the most abominable impurities and even consecrating them to religious worship. Its power was the greater because it could lay some claim to supernatural manifestations and was undoubtedly accompanied in many instances by the miraculous working of Satan. It was the same in kind as modern spiritism. It was called necromancy even by Moses (Deuteronomy 18:10), and this word literally means communing with the dead. It is the most portentous form of Satanic power in the world today, and it is to continue with more marked developments down to the latest ages, and break out in unprecedented energy just before the coming of Christ (Revelation 16:14).

There is still much need to caution those that have entered upon a deeper spiritual life against the subtle counterfeits that follow spiritual illumination and deep emotion. The Adversary is always watching to lead the susceptible into these perils which become the more dangerous the more light we have. Through humble vigilance and holy faith and obedience we shall always be safe in His keeping (1 John 2:26–27).

## BENEVOLENCE
### Leviticus 19:9–10, 33–34
6. Kindness and benevolence toward the poor, the suffering and the stranger are next required.

This is the law of love. It is developed in the New Testament with still greater fullness, as a constant test of our true love to God (James 1:27; 1 John 3:17–19).

## HONESTY
**Leviticus 19:35–36**

Strict integrity and honesty in all our commercial dealings with others were part of the ancient code of holiness.

7. It is indispensable to anything that presumes to bear the name of righteousness and practical Christianity in the present day. The apostles continually insist upon the commonplace virtues of industry, uprightness and strict integrity between man and man (Leviticus 19:35–36; Romans 12:17; 13:7–8; Ephesians 4:28; 1 Thessalonians 4:6).

More than 18 centuries have made no advance on the beautiful statutes of love and righteousness which we find in this ancient code. "When you reap the harvest of your land, do not reap to the very edges of your field or gather the gleanings of your harvest. . . . Leave them for the poor and the alien. . . . Do not defraud your neighbor or rob him. Do not hold back the wages of a hired man overnight. . . . Do not pervert justice; do not show partiality to the poor or favoritism to the great, but judge your neighbor fairly" (Leviticus 19:9–10, 13, 15).

## LOVE
**Leviticus 19:16–18**

8. Brotherly love one to another and love even toward enemies are next required.

How much is expressed in these few sentences, "Do not go about spreading slander among your people. Do not do anything that endangers your neighbor's life. . . . Do not hate your brother in your heart. Rebuke your neighbor frankly so you will not share in his guilt. Do not seek revenge or bear a grudge against one of your people, but love your neighbor as yourself" (16–18). What a heaven the Church would be if she would even return to the simplicity and purity of this life of primitive piety decreed nearly 15 centuries before the day of Pentecost.

## REVERENCE
**Leviticus 19:32**

9. Reverence for the aged is another of the beautiful traits of the ideal life of the ancient covenant. "Rise in the presence of the aged, show respect for the elderly and revere your God. I am the LORD" (19:32).

It would seem as if God made the aged His own representatives, and the spirit of reverence toward men a steppingstone toward the higher veneration we owe to God. Is not this true of the loss of this spirit in our time, through the overgrown license of modern democracy? It is one of the most appalling signs of the times of degeneracy, and harbingers of the age of lawlessness which is to close the tragedy of time.

## STEWARDSHIP
**Leviticus 19:23–25**
10. The recognition of God's ownership in their property, and of their stewardship in their earthly substance, was another important ingredient in their consecrated life.

## FILIAL PIETY
**Leviticus 20:9**
11. Reverence and honor to parents was not only embodied in the Decalogue as the first commandment in the second table, but was also included in those detailed prescriptions respecting the practical life of the people, and the severest penalties were visited upon disrespect to the father or mother. The parental relation, even more than the place of the aged, was regarded as the very type of the divine relationship.

## PURITY OF THE PRIESTS
**Leviticus 21:1–23**
12. Peculiar holiness on the part of the priests in their domestic relations and their personal purity was emphasized at great length in the 21st and 22nd chapters.

The priest was to be married only to a pure virgin; their families were to be holy; they themselves must avoid all uncleanness, and not even defile themselves by mourning for the dead, except only for their immediate relatives. This of course, refers to the priesthood of Christians and teaches us the necessity of entire sanctification, if we expect to walk in priestly fellowship and abiding communion with Jesus Christ. It was also required that the priests must be free from all blemishes and physical defects, even as the offerings of the people must be without blemish. This would seem to imply that Christ both requires and will supply perfect strength and soundness to those who minister to Him (Leviticus 21:17–23; 22:1–21).

In the closing book of Malachi it is represented as the shame and sin of using blind and the lame animals for sacrifice (Malachi 1:8). The blemished priest was cared for and fed, but he might not minister before the Lord. So God has provided for His feeblest children and will not cease to love and keep them, but He requires power on the part of those who minister for Him (Leviticus 21:16–23). "None of your descendants who has a defect may come near to offer the food of his God. . . . He may eat the most holy food of his God, as well as the holy food; yet because of his defect, he must not go near the curtain or approach the altar, and so desecrate my sanctuary. I am the LORD who makes them holy" (21:17, 22–23).

## SERVICE VOLUNTARY

**Leviticus 22:18–22**

13. And finally, the person and offerings of the priesthood must not only be unblemished, but they must be voluntary.

So our service must be the service of the whole heart; we must cry, like our Great Master, "Here I am—it is written about me in the scroll—/ I have come to do your will, O God" (Hebrews 10:7). "Whatever you do, work at it with all your heart, as working for the Lord, not for men" (Colossians 3:23).

# CHAPTER 6

## *FELLOWSHIP AS ILLUSTRATED IN THE ANCIENT FEASTS*

### *Leviticus 23–25*

This also follows in natural order: redeemed, reconciled, cleansed, sanctified. We enjoy the divine communion, and sit down with our Father and His household in the blessed fellowship typified by the ancient feasts of the Levitical service.

This is the flower and the fruit of the consecrated life. Very sweetly and gloriously is it foreshadowed in these ancient festal ordinances which made Judaism to a great extent a more joyous ritual, at least in its outward form, than the simpler worship of what we call Christianity. Although it was what was called the age of their minority and almost of servile bondage, yet it is astonishing how ample the provision that was made for the expression of gladness and the enjoyment of repose and recreation.

### SECTION I—*The Sabbatic Feasts*

There were four of these altogether, reaching from the Sabbatic week to the Sabbatic week of years.

#### *THE WEEKLY SABBATH*

1. "There are six days when you may work, but the seventh day is a Sabbath of rest, a day of sacred assembly. You are not to do any work; wherever you live, it is a Sabbath to the LORD" (Leviticus 23:3).

Already this had been instituted at creation, as the memorial of God's rest from His finished works (Genesis 2:2). We find it observed by Abel (Genesis 4:3), and by Noah in the intervals of sending out the dove. It was recognized in the giving out of the manna (Exodus 14:22), as an institution already known and observed among them. It was reenacted in the fourth commandment, and recalled by the word "remember," in that commandment (Exodus 20:8). It was recognized as a memorial of creation (Exodus 20:11), of their deliverance from Egypt (Deuteronomy 5:15), and as the sign of God's covenant with His people (Exodus 31:13–17). It was to be kept not only with sacredness, but with joy as the symbol of rest from the bondage of the law. And so it already anticipated the spirit of the New Testament Sabbath, as a day of delight and triumph (Isaiah 58:13–14). Our Savior has reenacted the Sabbath (Mark 2:28) by declaring that "the Son of Man is Lord even of the Sabbath." And He has given it a new significance as the Lord's Day, and new prescriptions respecting its observance in the spirit of larger and holier liberty and love (Revelation 1:10; Mark 3:4).

It has become to us the memorial of Christ's resurrection, and so has passed from the seventh to the first day of the week, as was proper in an institution signalizing now the beginning of redemption rather than the end of creation. But the change of time involves no change in the essential principle of permanent application of the day and the ordinance.

## THE SABBATIC MONTH

2. "Say to the Israelites: 'On the first day of the seventh month you are to have a day of rest, a sacred assembly commemorated with trumpet blasts' " (Leviticus 23:24).

The seventh month was the most sacred of all the Jewish calendar, and the crowning month of every ecclesiastical year, the remaining five months having been left blank, perhaps because they were to be filled with a more glorious future for Judaism which is yet to be revealed. This month began with the Feast of Trumpets, followed by the Day of Atonement, and reached the climax of rejoicing in the Feast of Tabernacles (23:24–44).

## THE SABBATIC YEAR

3. The seventh year was also a Sabbath, and was exempt from all servile labor.

The land rested from sowing and reaping, the previous year having produced double. All debts were suspended and the year was devoted to sacred convocations. A neglect of the Sabbatic year and its provisions was the sin of the later Jews, and the Babylonian captivity was sent in some measure because of this neglect, that the land might enjoy for 70 years the Sabbaths which the people had refused to redeem from their selfish avarice (Leviticus 25:1–8, 20–22; 26:25–35; 2 Chronicles 26:21).

## THE SABBATIC WEEK OF YEARS

4. The Sabbatic week of years, or the year of Jubilee, was the climax of this series, and the most imposing and joyous of all their feasts.

Consecrate the fiftieth year and proclaim liberty throughout the land to all its inhabitants. It shall be a jubilee for you; each one of you is to return to his family property and each to his own clan. The fiftieth year shall be a jubilee for you; do not sow and do not reap what grows of itself or harvest the untended vines. For it is a jubilee and is to be holy for you; eat only what is taken directly from the fields. (Leviticus 25:10–12)

During this year forfeited inheritances reverted to their original owners, slaves received their freedom, gladness filled their hearts and homes, and the glorious age which Christ is yet to bring in the times of restitution of all things was sublimely prefigured. Christ's earthly ministry began with the announcement of the year of Jubilee.

The Spirit of the Lord is on me,
  because he has anointed me
  to preach the good news to the poor.
He has sent me to proclaim freedom for the prisoners
  and recovery of sight for the blind,
to release the oppressed,
  to proclaim the year of the Lord's favor.

... "Today this scripture is fulfilled in your hearing."
  (Luke 4:18–19, 21)

## SECTION II— *The Five Annual Feasts*

### 1. THE PASSOVER
**Leviticus 23:5–14**

This came on the 14th day of the first month. It was also the Feast of Firstfruits, signified by the first sheaf, presented immediately afterwards (Leviticus 23:10). The Passover was typical of our redemption by the blood of Christ, therefore it was the beginning of their ecclesiastical year, as Christ's death inaugurated the Church, and our acceptance of His blood is the initial act in the religious history of every soul.

The single sheaf waved in connection with this feast 50 days before Pentecost, prefigured Christ the firstfruits. The Passover was thus not only a type of His death and resurrection before the Church was gathered through the Pentecostal outpouring, but it also prefigured the blessing which comes to the soul in the very moment of its acceptance of Jesus; the single sheaf of blessing is followed later by the fullness of the Spirit and all His abiding fruits.

## 2. PENTECOST OR THE FEAST OF WEEKS
**Leviticus 23:15–21**

This was called the Feast of Weeks because it came 50 days after the Passover. It was introduced by all the sacrifices. It was specially significant of the first, or grain harvest, but was also the anniversary of the giving of the law at Mt. Sinai.

These two facts enable us to understand its spiritual significance; viz: the first ingathering of the church at Pentecost, and the coming of the Holy Spirit as the inner law of our Christian life instead of the mere letter written in stone. This is the second great chapter of the believer's history. After he has received the Lord Jesus Christ in His atoning blood, the Holy Spirit becomes the personal occupant and indwelling presence of his inner life, the very law written upon his heart, the revelation of the divine will and also the power to obey it and the spring and source of all the fruits of Christian life. God's own Word is the best commentary upon all this.

> "The time is coming," declares the LORD,
>   "when I will make a new covenant
> with the house of Israel
>   and with the house of Judah.
> It will not be like the covenant
>   I made with their forefathers
> when I took them by the hand
>   to lead them out of Egypt,
> because they broke my covenant, . . ."

> "This is the covenant I will make with the house of Israel
>   after that time," declares the LORD.
> "I will put my law in their minds
>   and write it on their hearts.
> I will be their God,
>   and they will be my people."
>       (Jeremiah 31:31–33)

> Because through Christ Jesus the law of the Spirit of life set me free from the law of sin and death. (Romans 8:2)

> But the fruit of the Spirit is love, joy, peace, patience, kindness, goodness, faithfulness, gentleness and self-control. Against such things there is no law. (Galatians 5:22–23)

## 3. THE FEAST OF TRUMPETS
**Leviticus 23:23–25**

This came on the first day of the seventh month. It ushered in the Sabbatic month. Perhaps it was typical of the idea of the permanent proclamation of the gospel which succeeded the day of Pentecost, and ushered in the Christian age. More especially it prefigured the wide diffusion of the gospel of the kingdom which is to usher in the last ages, the seventh month of time, and the advent of the Lord Himself. This gospel of the kingdom, our Savior tells us, must be preached among all nations, and then shall the end come (Matthew 24:14). It would seem that we are already in the beginning of this great evangel, and that the tongues of Pentecost are once more proclaiming on the mountain tops of earth that the Feast of Tabernacles and the year of Jubilee are close at hand.

## 4. THE DAY OF ATONEMENT
**Leviticus 23:26–32**

We have already examined in detail the spiritual significance of this great feast as it respects the great central truth of the gospel, and the experience of our Christian life.

It occurred on the 10th day of the seventh month, and was typical of the reconciliation of the soul to God through the Lord Jesus Christ and His complete atonement. Its fullest meaning, however, can only be realized when this atonement has become effectual in the actual reconciliation of Israel and the children of God in all nations. Therefore it comes not in the first or second month along with Pentecost or the Passover, but away down in the seventh month, when God's ancient people are to be brought nigh and their reconciliation is to be to the world as life from the dead (Romans 11:12–15).

## 5. THE FEAST OF TABERNACLES
**Leviticus 23:33–44**

This was the crowning joy of all the Hebrew year. It commenced on the 15th day of the seventh month and lasted through eight days, beginning and ending with the Sabbath. During this time the people dwelt in booths, constructed from branches of young trees, festooned with flowers and hung with fruits and decorated with palms and willows of the brook. It was designed to celebrate their wandering in the wilderness, and also the complete ingathering of all the fruits of the earth in the final harvest. In later times several beautiful ceremonies were added to its observance. Water was carried by a procession of priests from the pool of Siloam and poured out upon the altar in the temple, and great lights were hung up in the court of the women in the temple. It was to these that our Lord referred in His allusions in John 7:37–38 and 8:12, when he cried: "If anyone is thirsty, let him come to me and drink. Whoever believes in me, as the Scripture has said, streams of living water will flow from within him." And again: "I am the light of the world. Whoever follows me will never walk in darkness, but will have the light of life."

Personally the Feast of Tabernacles voiced its fulfillment in the fullness of the Spirit's indwelling and the fruits of love and service in our deeper Christian life. It expresses, generally, the idea of free salvation, of full salvation and of triumphant gladness. Its dispensational meaning, however, is still more glorious, as it points forward to the ingathering harvest of the Church and the world, the completing and homecoming of all God's redeemed ones, both Jews and Gentiles, and the great rejoicing over which prophecy lingers with rapturous vision in such pictures as this:

> I looked and there before me was a great multitude that no one could count, from every nation, tribe, people and language, standing before the throne and in front of the Lamb. They were wearing white robes and were holding palm branches in their hands. . . .

> > "Never again will they hunger;
> >   never again will they thirst.
> > The sun will not beat upon them,
> >   nor any scorching heat.
> > For the Lamb at the center of the throne
> >   will be their shepherd;
> >   he will lead them to springs of living water.
> > And God will wipe away every tear from their eyes."
> >   (Revelation 7:9, 16–17)

We find in connection with this that the observance of the Feast of Tabernacles is mentioned by the prophet Zechariah, as one of the features of the millennial times. "Then the survivors from all the nations that have attacked Jerusalem will go up year after year to worship the King, the LORD Almighty, and to celebrate the Feast of Tabernacles" (Zechariah 14:16).

## SPIRITUAL ERAS

These great ancient feasts mark two important progressions. First, spiritually in our individual Christian life, we begin with the Passover and the cross of Calvary. Next we have the first sheaf, and the beginning of the fruits of faith and salvation. A little later we come to Pentecost, and the first rich harvests of spiritual life and blessing abundantly follow. But sometimes there comes a long interval of reaction. There are five blank months in the Hebrew calendar, and oh, how many Christians can remember a Pentecost which followed their earliest love, but which soon began to disappear like rivers in the desert, in the long, weary period of declension and barrenness that followed. Then comes the Feast of Trumpets. Does it not herald a higher stage of experience? Perhaps it tells of more than our blessing, even the blessing of service for others. This is the time when we begin to testify for God and lift up our voice like a trumpet to proclaim His grace and goodness. The Day of Atonement may be a type of that deeper reconciliation in which we learn the secret place of the Most High, and enter the house of God to lead henceforth a life of abiding fellowship which shall know no more reactions, declensions and mournful falls. This is followed by the Feast of Tabernacles, the full indwelling and fruition of the Holy Spirit, and a life of unceasing and overflowing joy, victory and service for others. It is not the water flowing in, now, but flowing out in rivers of blessing to the world. Our place henceforth is with palms of victory in our hands, and a continual gladness, for our sun shall no more go down nor our moon withdraw its shining.

But, secondly, these five feasts tell of the order of the dispensations. The Jewish ecclesiastical year began with the Passover, and in ancient times they followed this order in their calendar. The civil year of the Jews, however, began with the Feast of Tabernacles, and was followed by the five silent months that immediately succeeded the feast. The modern Jews have adopted this later calendar, and consequently have inverted the order of blessing which God designed. They commenced with rejoicing and pride, and they got into darkness and sorrow all the weary centuries of their exile and retribution, and it is not until they come back in the order of the ages to the Passover month and accept the blood of redemption which their own hands shed on Calvary, that their year shall begin to roll in its cycle of blessing, and the Feast of Tabernacles shall come in its divine order.

The divine order is the reverse of Israel's calendar. Beginning with the Passover, which represents the cross of Jesus and is followed by Pentecost and the power of the Holy Spirit, and then by the great consummation of the seventh month as their religious year foreshadowed, their history would have been as blessed as their own ancient feasts. In this progression God is leading His own chosen Church; she has come to the blood of the cross, and received the descending fire at Pentecost; she has gone forth with the trumpet call to the nations; she herself has entered into the holy place, and is gathering the world in reconciliation to a reconciled God; and in a little while the last great feast shall come with all its rejoicing, and with Him, its chief joy, and the heavens and the earth shall unite to celebrate the glorious harvest of the ages and the triumphal march of the Lamb.

# CHAPTER 7

## THE DIVINE COVENANT, OR FAITHFULNESS TO GOD

The closing chapters of Leviticus (24–27) are chiefly occupied with the promises, precepts and penalties of the divine covenant between God and the nation, and also on the part of individuals.

### SECTION I—*National Faithfulness to God's Covenant*

#### IDOLATRY

This is the subject of the 26th chapter.

**1. Warnings against idolatry.**

"Do not make idols or set up an image or a sacred stone for yourselves, and do not place a carved stone in your land to bow down before it. I am the LORD your God" (Leviticus 26:1).

This was the most glaring form of national unfaithfulness and apostasy; and it was through this fearful sin that both Judah and Israel at last sank into declension and degeneracy, and were in consequence delivered to the judgments of God and the power of their enemies. Idolatry was the open rejection of the true God and an act of deliberate apostasy from their covenant. It was thoroughly cured by the Babylonian captivity, and never afterwards became a national sin, or even, apparently, a temptation.

#### THE SABBATH

**2. Renewal of the Sabbatic laws and the prescriptions respecting the sanctuary worship.**

"Observe my Sabbaths and have reverence for my sanctuary. I am the LORD" (26:2).

The Sabbath was always recognized as a sign of God's covenant with Israel, and it was because of their unfaithfulness to it that the Lord sent the

Babylonian captivity of 70 years as a great national Sabbath, to remind them of the Sabbaths that they had robbed Him of. The Sabbath and the sanctuary were designed to be the very anchor of the national faith, continually holding them, by the stated seasons and systematic habits and ordinances of worship, to their sacred obligations.

It is still true that the Lord's day and the Lord's house are the safeguards of religion in every land, and that according to the reverence and sacredness with which these are observed the spirituality and the morals of the people can be gauged.

## OBEDIENCE
### Leviticus 26:3–13
### 3. Obedience and the promise of blessing connected with it.

All the subsequent history of Israel hinged upon these solemn words. As long as they obeyed Jehovah they were happy and prosperous; but when they disobeyed, disaster and ruin ever came to them. This was the prime condition of victory, announced even in the minutest particular, to Joshua 40 years later; and the moment they infringed it, by the sin of Achan, their armies were ignominiously defeated. This was the reason that Saul was rejected at a later period, because he would not absolutely obey the Word of God through Samuel. This was the reason David was chosen, because with all his faults he was a man after God's own heart, of whom God could say, "he will do everything I want him to do" (Acts 13:22). This was the turning point of Solomon's life, of Rehoboam's reign, and was, ultimately, the cause of Zedekiah's fate. It was the cry of Isaiah, "If you are willing and obedient,/ you will eat the best from the land;/ but if you resist and rebel,/ you will be devoured by the sword" (1:19–20). It was the imploring appeal of Jeremiah, "Obey me, and I will be your God" (7:23). And it is, too, the inexorable condition of the blessings of the gospel, and of the abiding communion and approval of Christ: "You are my friends if you do what I command" (John 15:14).

The promises to the obedient in Leviticus 26 are fivefold.

1. National wealth and abundance, fruitful seasons and rich harvests from field, orchard and vineyard (verses 4–5).
2. National peace, both from human enemies and from beasts that afterward became the scourges of the accursed land (verse 6).
3. National victory in war: "Five of you will chase a hundred, and a hundred of you will chase ten thousand" (verse 8).
4. A multiplied population: "I will . . . make you fruitful and increase your numbers" (verse 9).
5. God's manifest presence among them: "I will walk among you

and be your God, and you will be my people" (verse 12).

## DISOBEDIENCE
### Leviticus 26:14–39
#### 4. Disobedience and its penalties.

This is a very remarkable passage, and is a literal prediction of the mournful later history of disobedient and apostate Israel.

First, we have the picture of their disobedience: "If you will not listen to me and carry out all these commands" (verse 14). Then it grows still darker as it discloses the utter corruption of their spirit and affections: "If you reject my decrees and abhor my laws and fail to carry out all my commands and so violate my covenant" (verse 15). And again: "If after all this you will not listen to me" (verse 18). And yet again: "If you remain hostile toward me and refuse to listen to me" (verse 21). And still later, as their obduracy grows more intolerable: "If in spite of these things you do not accept my correction but continue to be hostile toward me, I myself will be hostile toward you and will afflict you for your sins seven times over" (verses 23–24).

How true all this became, as the national declension passed from the neglect to hearken, to open disobedience and even scornful and defiant rebellion and apostasy, as written in the story of the wilderness, the Judges, the life of Saul, the pride of Rehoboam, the profanity of Jeroboam, the wickedness of Ahab, the transgressions of Ahaz and Uzziah, the last days of Israel and their awful extinction, the fall of Zedekiah, and, last of all, the rejection of Jesus of Nazareth by the entire nation, and their fearful ruin by the Roman power.

## FIVE PERIODS

It will be noticed that this picture of wickedness consists of a number of paragraphs like scenes in a panorama, describing, apparently, the special developments of Israel's national history of wickedness which afterwards actually occurred. There are five of these distinct periods thus described. The first, from verse 14 to 17; the second, from verse 18 to 20; the third, from verse 21 to 22; the fourth, from verse 23 to 26; and the fifth, from verse 26 to 27, or the end of the chapter. These may describe the successive declensions in the wilderness, during the period of the Judges, during the later days of the kingdoms of Israel and Judah, after the Restoration, and finally, during Christ's personal ministry, culminating in the crucifixion of their Messiah.

## JUDGMENTS

Secondly, we have the vivid picture of God's judgments upon them. These consisted of plague, sickness (verse 16), sterility and barrenness of the soil (verse 16), hatred and disaster from the hands of their enemies, oppression and bondage (verse 17), wild beasts and desolation of the land, pestilence, siege, famine, and slaughter (verses 25–30), destruction of their cities and even their sanctuary (verse 31), captivity and dispersion among the Gentiles (verses 32–33), horrible terrors and suffering on the part of the scattered fugitives in all lands. "I will make their hearts so fearful in the lands of their enemies that the sound of a windblown leaf will put them to flight. They will run as though fleeing from the sword, and they will fall, even though no one is pursuing them" (verse 36).

How vividly these terrific pictures describe the sufferings of the seed of Abraham during the last 3,000 years, especially during the Christian centuries. The outrages and enormities practiced upon the Jews for a thousand years, during the Middle Ages, surpass all the barbarities which human history anywhere records. They have been scattered in every land, yet proscribed from almost every country as vagabonds in the earth; they have been outcast, pillaged, expatriated, robbed by the wholesale, sold into slavery, separated from their families, violated, torn upon the rack, butchered and treated as public criminals whom it was a Christian duty to torment and abuse. Surely, they have drunk to the bitter dregs this dreadful cup, and shown that not a word of this awful picture was exaggerated.

## THE SEVEN TIMES

There is one strange expression in this chapter which has received a literal interpretation by many careful expositors, that seems to be reasonably justified. It is the words "seven times." It occurs several times in the chapter. First, in verses 18 to 21, where it seems to be a comparative expression of greater and more aggravated judgments, "seven times over," referring to the increased chastisement which God was about to bring upon them. But in verse 28 it is used absolutely as a simple expression with no comparative reference to previous judgments. "I myself will punish you for your sins seven times over." If we bear in mind that this immediately precedes the last picture of judgment, which seems to be a punishment commencing at the time of the Babylonian captivity and includes the wasting of their city, and burning of their sanctuary and their dispersion among the nations, it gives additional weight to the interpretation about to be explained; that is, that the seven times denote exact chronological periods or prophetic times, corresponding to the use of this expression in the prophecies of Daniel and John, where again and again we find the words, a time, times and half a time, or three and a half times. In the fourth chapter of Daniel the same expression is used exactly as it is here. "Seven times pass by for him" (verse 16). A time denotes, naturally, the most important chronological period known, that is the year. The year consists of 360 days, according to the solar calendar and in the usual prophetic calculations, and is represented by the word time. We know that this was the case in connection with the 70 weeks which Daniel saw intervene before the coming of the Messiah. It is certain that these 70 weeks meant 490 years, which is just seven times 70 days, counting a day for a year. The establishing of this standard in this one important prophecy fixes it for others.

Applying it, therefore, to the present passage, seven times would be a week of years, comprising a total of 2,520 days, and counting each day for a year, seven times would be 2,520 years.

Now, let us put together the following important considerations:

## DANIEL'S SEVEN TIMES OF THE GENTILES

(a) Daniel declared that seven times should pass over Nebuchadnezzar's head in his madness, and at the end he should come forth restored to his reason. This, we know, was symbolical. Nebuchadnezzar represented the Gentile nations. He was the head of the image, which had already been explained to mean the four great empires that should fill up the remaining centuries of human history, and that in latter visions of this book are described as wild beasts. The meaning here is, that for seven times seven great prophetic periods this world power was to be like Nebuchadnezzar, during his insanity, debased, cruel and, as it were, possessed with madness. Such has truly been the spirit of the Gentile nations. At the end of this period these nations are to be restored, as Nebuchadnezzar was, but only through the coming and the personal reign of the Lord Jesus Christ, the true King of nations. Now these are what Christ called the times of the Gentiles. They have a definite period and are to be at length fulfilled. Previous to this the Jewish nation had been in the ascendant, but from the days of Nebuchadnezzar the world has been passing through the times of the Gentiles, and the Jewish people have been subject to their oppressions; and their own dominion has been practically suspended. Therefore the times of the Gentiles have been to the Jews times of disaster, judgment and suffering. Now, in conjunction with this fact:

## ISRAEL'S SEVEN TIMES

(b) Notice that Moses declares seven times of judgment and disaster shall pass over the Jews for their disobedience. This we see exactly corresponds with the period of the times of the Gentiles. The only question is, when were these times of Jewish calamity to begin? The natural historical epoch is the Babylonian captivity, when the city fell, the kingdom was dissolved, and the people dispersed as captives in other lands, never after to have a really independent national existence and government, for even the kingdom of Herod was subject to the permission of the Roman power. It is a delightful consideration to know that nearly 2,500 years have already elapsed since this age of calamity began, and the seven times must be nearly fulfilled. It is not ours to prophesy, but humble faith can read even behind the dark lines of their judgment the promise of the morning, while a thousand other signals on the earth and in the skies are already proclaiming to the Daughter of Zion, "Stand up and lift up your heads, because your redemption is drawing near" (Luke 21:28).

## RESTORATION
### Leviticus 26:40–46
5. The restoration of the nation after judgment and repentance.

It is indicated that at last their idolatry, disobedience and hardness of heart will be completely broken, and that the entire nation shall repent and turn to God to wander no more. And as they turn to Him with humble confession, recognizing all their calamities as divine chastenings which they have brought upon themselves, God promises that He will remember His covenant with their fathers, and will again forgive, and restore them to all their ancient privileges and blessings. This day is drawing near.

Israel has experienced a hardening in part until the full number of the Gentiles has come in. And so all Israel will be saved, as it is written:

"The deliverer will come from Zion;
  he will turn godlessness away from Jacob.
And this is my covenant with them
  when I take away their sins."

As far as the gospel is concerned, they are enemies on your account; but as far as election is concerned, they are loved on account of the patriarchs, for God's gifts and his call are irrevocable. (Romans 11:25–29)

The light of later prophecy sheds a still brighter glory over these later days. The time is coming when "I will pour out on the house of David and the inhabitants of Jerusalem a spirit of grace and supplication. They will look on me, the one they have pierced, and they will mourn for him as one mourns for an only child, and grieve bitterly for him as one grieves for a firstborn son" (Zechariah 12:10). And yet again the prophet Ezekiel describes this penitential return and restoration:

Then you will remember your evil ways and wicked deeds, and you will loathe yourselves for your sins and detestable practices. . . .

On the day I cleanse you from all your sins, I will resettle your towns, and the ruins will be rebuilt. . . . They will say, "This land that was laid waste has become like the garden of Eden." (36:31, 33, 35)

I will now bring Jacob back from captivity and will have compassion on all the people of Israel, . . . They will forget their shame and all the unfaithfulness they showed toward me . . . I will no longer hide my face from them, for I will pour out my Spirit on the house of Israel, declares the Sovereign LORD. (39:25–26, 29)

## SECTION II—*Personal Faithfulness to God*
### Leviticus 27

### *VOWS*
**Leviticus 27:1–13**

1. With respect to special vows, the special vow was a vow of consecration on the part of an individual, induced by gratitude or a sense of personal obligation, to dedicate something to God. The object dedicated might be a person, one's own child, or one's slave, or it might be an animal from his flock. It was provided that such a dedicated person or thing might be redeemed; and the estimate of its value was to be recorded, according to God's own express stipulations, or, where these were not explicit, by the estimate of the priest. It was also provided that in the case of a poor man this estimation might be reduced and the value accepted according to his ability.

All this legislation had reference to the consecration of our common life to God, and teaches us that secular things may be made as sacred as those which we call religious; and that God accepts from each one according to their ability, the dedication which they freely make of their life, their property and the dearest objects of their affection.

### *PROPERTY*
**Leviticus 27:14–25**

2. Houses and fields might likewise be dedicated and then redeemed on the same principle and the proceeds of the redemption presented to God as an offering.

This seems to teach us that in our possession of secular things we may be wholly consecrated to God, holding them as trusts for Him, and giving Him their value as tokens of thankfulness for His inestimable gifts and grace to us.

It was provided in all these ransoms, that the estimation was to be according to the shekel of the sanctuary (verse 25). This shekel of the sanctuary was the special type of Christ's redemption of His people. It was the standard of redemption money in all other respects, and it reminded them constantly that they were a redeemed people; and that all their gifts to God were to be regulated and inspired by the recognition of the price with which they had been purchased from judgment worse than that of Egypt.

## THE FIRSTBORN
**Leviticus 27:26–27**

3. There were some things which they could not dedicate to the Lord and afterwards redeem; especially was this true of the firstborn. "No one, however, may dedicate the firstborn of an animal, since the firstborn already belongs to the LORD; whether an ox or a sheep, it is the LORD's" (27:26).

It was already the Lord's as a substitute for the firstborn of Egypt, and God claimed it as a right. So our life is a redeemed life, and is already the Lord's; and our consecration is but the acknowledgment of His antecedent claims.

## UNCHANGEABLE VOWS
**Leviticus 27:28–29**

4. There were some things which could not be redeemed when once consecrated to God.

> But nothing that a man owns and devotes to the LORD—whether man or animal or family land—may be sold or redeemed; everything so devoted is most holy to the LORD.
> No person devoted to destruction may be ransomed; he must be put to death. (verses 28–29)

There was a sort of vow called *herem*, which denoted a higher kind of dedication for which no equivalent could be accepted. A man might dedicate his house, his cattle, his field and even his children to God, and then give an equivalent for their value in money, and retain them in his ordinary course of life and occupation, and feel that he had substantially fulfilled his vow. But a thing given in a sense expressed by this word could never be taken back (verse 29). This implies that there are some things in our engagements with God which are irredeemable, and in which He holds us to our sacred pledge to the letter, as He is willing to be held by His plighted word to us. There are vows and covenants which God may lead a soul to make, and which are specific and immutable, and in which our keeping faith with God is the condition on which alone we can stand approved. It was thus in the case of Jephthah. The Lord placed him among the heroes of faith, because he kept his word with God (Judges 10–12).

While we give all things to God, subject to His will concerning them as He shall show us day by day, yet there are some services and consecrations which are more definite and explicit, and wherever God has permitted us to give our word, we shall find that He will hold us to a faithfulness no less than His own. To take back a gift thus consecrated is a very serious thing. It was the sin of Ananias, and it is, no doubt, the secret of the blight which has fallen on many a Christian life. Perhaps someone who reads these lines may remember a forgotten vow made on a dying bed, a consecration as old as childhood, a promise by the deathbed of a mother, a sacrifice laid on the missionary altar, a pledge given in some great hour of deliverance which the heart has tried to make good in some other way, but for which God will accept no substitute.

## TITHES
**Leviticus 27:30–32**
5. The tithes of the land and its produce were recognized as the Lord's. These were but expressions of His ownership in everything. "A tithe of everything from the land, whether grain from the soil or fruit from the trees, belongs to the LORD; it is holy to the LORD" (Leviticus 27:30).

Among the Jews they involved a much larger proportion of the annual increase than is generally supposed. Besides the first tithe which was given for the support of the priest, there was a second which went to sustain the service of the tabernacle, and every third year there was tithe for the great annual feasts. All this, combined with the half shekel which was the ordinary offering at the entrance to the tabernacle, and the free-will offering and sacrifice, involved to every faithful Hebrew an expenditure for the cause of religion of at least three-tenths of his annual income every year. The same amount from the Christians of America would secure for the cause of Christ an annual contribution of many billions of dollars. With all our advanced light and enlarged privileges, and with the stronger motive of voluntary giving which ought ever to lead to greater sacrifice than any law of constraint, we have not yet even approached the results of systematic beneficence obtained by God's ancient people in the days of their faithfulness.

## INTEGRITY
**Leviticus 27:33**
6. The strictest honesty was required in all devoted things and all dealings with God, in the contribution of money or redemption and fulfillment of vows. "He must not pick out the good from the bad or make any substitu-

tion. If he does make a substitution, both the animal and its substitute become holy and cannot be redeemed" (27:33).

When tithes were to be redeemed and their value to be paid in money rather than in kind, one-fifth more was to be added to cover all possible cost. When tithes were to be chosen from the flocks or herds, every 10th animal was to be separated for the Lord whether good or bad. The refuse or inferior were not to be chosen for Jehovah, as sometimes modern Christians dispose of their poor coin, but the strictest integrity was to mark their dealings with the Lord. A spirit of equal conscientiousness now would revolutionize the practical working of modern Christianity.

# NUMBERS

# GENERAL PLAN AND SCOPE
# OF THE BOOK

W*ilderness* is the first Hebrew word in the book of Numbers, and it aptly expresses the spiritual teachings which underlie that strange history. It unfolds the wilderness life of the Christian, as does no other book of the Bible. It is the story of wandering and failure. Its counterpart is the book of Joshua, which is the story of victory, inheritance and rest.

The history of the book of Numbers comprises a period of about 38 years, but the close of those years finds the people of Israel at nearly the same point at which they were in the beginning of that period. They had spent almost half a century in traveling the futile circles of the trackless desert, which only had served to furnish a grave for the generation that had crossed the Red Sea and to teach their children the lessons which were to save them from their fathers' unbelief and bring them into the inheritance which their fathers had refused to claim.

This book has always been regarded as typical of Christian experience in its lower and more defective forms, and so it is full of instruction, spiritual warning and quickening for our own time, which affords, we fear, a true and faithful counterpart, in many respects, of the unbelief, disobedience and disappointment so vividly set forth in the story of the wilderness.

# CHAPTER 1

## THE ARMY

The book of Numbers opens with the picture of an army of more than 600,000 men, marshaled for victorious warfare, and organized and equipped in perfect form with all the accompaniments necessary for their successful advance.

We find in this great host all the elements which constitute the army of the Lord in the Church of the New Testament.

### SECTION I—*Sons*
### Numbers 1:1–54

The first thing required in the marshaling of the host was that everyone should declare his pedigree and should be enrolled according to the house of his fathers. It is thus in our spiritual life, and it teaches us that before we can be true soldiers, we must know that we are sons of God. The reason why many Christians fail in their tests and their service is because they do not know their place in the divine household, and have not entered fully into the blessed assurance of a full divine sonship. Therefore God required of His ancient people that they should know and declare their pedigree, before they could put on their armor. We also may know that we have eternal life and are the sons of God, and so be able to bear an unequivocal testimony to the world and stand with unfaltering front before the Adversary.

Our Lord received in like manner the witness to His Sonship, before He went forth into the wilderness to meet Satan, and then afterwards into the world to overcome him in others. This was what the devil tried his best to unsettle: "*If* you are the Son of God" (Matthew 4:3). But Christ overcame him in the confidence of His Father's love and His high calling. So let us, as we read these ancient records, make sure of our pedigree and fully claim our sonship. "Yet to all who received him . . . he gave the right to become children of God" (John 1:12). "Because you are sons, God sent the Spirit of his Son into our hearts, the Spirit who calls out, 'Abba, Father' " (Galatians 4:6). "The Spirit himself testifies with our spirit that we are God's children" (Romans 8:16).

## SECTION II—*Soldiers*
### Numbers 2:1–34

The next picture of the ancient host is the picture of the soldiers. Having declared their pedigree they were next required to pitch by their own standard, with the ensign of their fathers' house. Only the men of war were counted.

So God expects all His people to be soldiers. We are not registered in the heavenly roll according to our place on earthly church rolls, but according to our enlistment in the army of the living God. The order of the standards was divinely arranged according to a perfect system. There were four great divisions around the tabernacle. On the east there were three tribes, numbering 186,400 men, led by the tribe of Judah. On the south there were three tribes numbering 151,450 men, with Reuben in the front. On the west there were three tribes around the camp of Ephraim, numbering in all 108,100 men; and on the north the remaining three tribes, numbering 157,600, with Dan in the center. This was the arrangement of the tabernacle when it rested. When in motion, the tribe of Judah always led the caravan, followed by Reuben. Then came the tabernacle with the ministering priests and Levites, followed by Ephraim, Dan and the other tribes.

We may learn from this order that the Church of Christ is not a promiscuous mass of heterogeneous elements, but a divinely organized body. Christ is the living Head, and the Holy Spirit the ever-present guide, and all the divine provisions for mutual service, fellowship and cooperation we find wisely and completely defined in the New Testament and illustrated in the primitive Church.

In the center of the camp no standard was permitted; but the tabernacle and the ark were the types of Jesus Christ Himself, around whom all the ranks of God's people should ever be gathered in unity. The leadership of Judah, whose name means praise, is at least suggestive of the spirit of Christian life and warfare, which should always march out like Jehoshaphat's army with the singers and the players in the front. We shall ever find the spirit of praise to be the keynote of triumph.

Military figures occupy a very prominent place in the pictures of Christian life in the New Testament. Our life is a very real conflict, and our adversaries are not going to be set aside by our ignoring them. God's ancient people, we are told, went forth armed for battle, out of the land of Egypt; and we shall wretchedly fall amid the perils and enemies on the way if we forget that "our struggle is not against flesh and blood, but against the rulers, against the authorities, against the powers of this dark world and against the spiritual forces of evil in the heavenly realms" (Ephesians 6:12). They who fear the conflict will never have rest from it, but will be harassed by assault and defeat to the close. It is only by courageous resistance and victory that we can ever have real peace. Israel had ceaseless war during the time of the Judges, but a few brief campaigns on the part of Joshua and David brought lasting peace. After the bitterest conflicts, we always read that "the land had rest from war" (Joshua 14:15).

Let us, therefore, put on the whole armor of God, fight the good fight of faith and endure hardness as good soldiers of Jesus Christ. While we glory in our pedigree, let us also lift up our standard and write upon it—Jehovah-nissi, the LORD is my banner.

## SECTION III—*Servants*
### Numbers 3:5–51; 8:5–26

The next picture in the Hebrew host is the Levites, whose calling and functions are described in minute detail in the third and fourth chapters of Numbers. They represent the idea of service in our Christian life, as the priests did of worship, and the soldiers of conflict.

### *SUBSTITUTED AND SEPARATED*

1. They were separated unto God as an entire tribe instead of the firstborn of Israel, who were all dedicated to the Lord, and claimed as His peculiar property. As a commutation, He accepted the entire tribe of Levi instead of the firstborn of all their tribes, and set them apart to His own peculiar ministry. The dedication of the firstborn was connected with the slaying of Egypt's firstborn, and was recognized as the result of the sprinkled blood of the Paschal Lamb. It conveyed, therefore, the idea of redemption. This was confirmed by the fact that the surplus of Israel's firstborn over and above the tribe of Levi, which amounted to about 5,000 males, were redeemed by the payment of five shekels each. This was still further typical of our redemption, not with perishable things such as silver and gold, but with the precious blood of Christ.

The Levites thus took the place of the redeemed men who had been bought back from death and judgment by the blood of the Lamb, and so they express for us the great spiritual truth, that all our service must have its root in redemption, and its inspiration in the blessed consciousness of a Savior's love. A slave girl bought from the block in New Orleans, when about to fall into the hands of cruel and lustful men, was set free by her benevolent purchaser; but with every instinct of gratitude overwhelming her, she threw herself at his feet and refused to accept her freedom, begging him to take her as his servant as long as she should live, and exclaimed whenever she was asked why she was willing to endure the privations and toils of her life, "He redeemed me, he redeemed me." This is the spirit of the apostle when he says, "You are not your own; you were bought at a price. Therefore honor God with your body" (1 Corinthians 6:19–20).

## GOD THEIR INHERITANCE

2. The Levites were not only redeemed men, but they took the place of firstborn men, that is, the place of sons and heirs. The nature of their inheritance is very beautifully described in many places in the Levitical code. It consisted simply in this, that God Himself was their inheritance. They had no share in the land of Canaan except the tabernacle and its immediate precincts. To them came no worldly possessions, but it was added, "The LORD is their inheritance" (Deuteronomy 18:2). This is an expressive type, not only of the Christian's high calling and glorious prospects as an heir of God and a joint heir with Christ of all the glory of His kingdom and of His throne, but of a deeper truth, namely, that the true servant of the Lord, like an ancient Levite, must take the Lord Himself for the supply of his spiritual needs, and the strength for all his service. In this respect the Lord Jesus was a true Levite. He constantly claimed: "By myself, I can do nothing: I judge only as I hear" (John 5:30). "Just as the living Father sent me and I live because of the Father, so the one who feeds on me will live because of me" (6:57). He was constantly depending upon His Father and His resources for all His earthly ministry. And like Him the great apostle could say: "Not that we are competent in ourselves to claim anything for ourselves, but our competence comes from God. He has made us competent as ministers of a new covenant" (2 Corinthians 3:5–6a). So Peter adds: "If anyone speaks, he should do it as one speaking the very words of God. If anyone serves, he should do it with the strength God provides, so that in all things God may be praised through Jesus Christ. To him be the glory and the power for ever and ever" (1 Peter 4:11). None are so rich as they that are absolutely poor. When we have nothing else, then we have God for our inheritance, and can say: "God is able to make all grace abound to you, so that in all things at all times, having all that you need, you will abound in every good work" (2 Corinthians 9:8).

## SUBORDINATE TO THE PRIESTS

3. The Levites were subordinate to and under the direction of the priests. So Christian work must ever be subordinate to Christian worship, and our service must be under the control and inspiration of our deeper life and fellowship with the Lord Jesus Christ. Our highest service is our ministry unto

Him as priests in His presence, and all our service for others should be impelled by the spirit of higher devotion.

These two classes, the priests and the Levites, beautifully represent the two sides of Christian life, the devotional and the practical. They do not refer to two classes of men or women, some of whom shall be Marthas and the others Marys, but to the two aspects which ought to be combined in all the services of the Lord—the one looking inward and heavenward, the other looking outward and around to the needs of our fellow men and the work given us to do. Both are beautifully combined in the ancient promise: "You will be called priests of the LORD,/ you will be named ministers of our God" (Isaiah 61:6).

### THREE CLASSES

4. The Levites were classified into three sections; namely, the Kohathites, the Gershonites and the Merarites. The Kohathites had charge of the sacred vessels, the Gershonites the curtains and coverings, and the Merarites the bars and boards of the tabernacle. These classes represent the various orders and spheres of Christian ministry which Christ has appointed in the Church. There are diversities of gifts, but the one Spirit; there are diversities of works, but the one God who works all in all. Some are called to be teachers, and some to be helpers; but the helpers are placed above the governments, and the least are often the greatest. The rule of preferment and honor in the kingdom of Christ is self-abasement. No ministry for Him is menial; and yet to every man His work is given, and faithfulness consists in standing in our lot.

There were some things in the tabernacle which could not be committed to careless hands. The oxen could draw the heavy boards, but the golden vessels might not be touched by any but the consecrated Kohathites. For each of us there is a work to do, which no man can be paid to do in our stead, and for which no proxy will ever be accepted. There are vessels of the Lord which our hands must bear, and cups of water which we must carry ourselves. The bearing of the tabernacle by the ministering hands of the Levites is a lovely picture of the support of the Church of Christ by the united hands of God's faithful people, each in his place and all together bearing the precious burden, in which the Lord Himself condescends to dwell.

The principle of mutual service is constantly recognized in God's Word: "One sows and another reaps" (John 4:37); and it is a heavenly and happy gift to know our places, and be able also to appreciate our brother's work. It is said about some of David's ancient warriors, in high commendation, that they could keep rank. And one of the sweetest expressions in the New Testament in commendation of the disciple is, "You, loyal yokefellow" (Philippians 4:3).

A traveler describes two laborers in Africa, working together in the sowing of their fields. The one was without legs and the other was without arms. The armless one carried his neighbor on his shoulders, while the other scattered the seed with his hands, the two together constituting one working man. So let the sons of Kohath and Gershon work together in the mutual ministry of the heavenly tabernacle.

## THEIR DEDICATION

5. The account of the Levites is closed with the beautiful picture of their solemn and public dedication on the altar of the tabernacle: "Bring the Levites to the front of the Tent of Meeting and assemble the whole Israelite community. You are to bring the Levites before the LORD, and the Israelites are to lay their hands on them. Aaron is to present the Levites before the LORD as a wave offering from the Israelites, so that they may be ready to do the work of the LORD" (Numbers 8:9–11).

What a beautiful picture of living sacrifice. This was the highest of all the Levitical offerings. It was not a bullock or a lamb, but a company of living men, solemnly dedicated by the imposition of hands, and laid as a sacrifice on the altar of the Lord. What a vividness it gives to the apostle's injunction, "Therefore, I urge you, brothers, in view of God's mercy, to offer your bodies as living sacrifices, holy and pleasing to God—this is your spiritual act of worship" (Romans 12:1).

## SECTION IV—Saints

Still another class appears in this great procession of the army of the Lord: the Nazirites, who are described at length in the sixth chapter of Numbers, and who stand as special types of saintship and separation in the Church of God. The ordinance of the Nazirites, however, is preceded by two or three other important regulations in regard to the subject of purity, culminating in the special class separated to represent this distinct idea. Their success depended upon their perfect purity, and so God made full provision for their separation from all evil.

## SEPARATION

1. Every leper, every one with an unclean issue and every one defiled by the touch of the dead, had to be separated from the camp.

"The LORD said to Moses, 'Command the Israelites to send away from the camp anyone who has an infectious skin disease or a discharge of any kind, or who is ceremonially unclean because of a dead body' " (Numbers 5:1–2).

So we must cleanse ourselves from "everything that contaminates body and spirit" (2 Corinthians 7:1), and come out from all evil, before we can be used by God in consecrated service and enter into the land of our inheritance. "Therefore come out from them/ and be separate,/ says the Lord./ Touch no unclean thing,/ and I will receive you./ I will be a Father to you,/ and you will be my sons and daughters,/ says the Lord Almighty (6:17–18). And again, "I will not be with you anymore unless you destroy whatever among you is devoted to destruction" (Joshua 7:12b).

## RESTITUTION

2. Trespasses must be confessed, restitution must be made and the sacrifice of atonement offered.

He "must confess the sin he has committed. He must make full restitution for his wrong, add one fifth to it and give it all to the person he has wronged" (Numbers 5:7).

And so our mutual or relative injuries must be met fully, that we may be victorious in our Christian warfare, and effectual in our work for God. "If a man cleanses himself from the latter, he will be an instrument for noble purposes, made holy, useful to the Master and prepared to do any good work" (2 Timothy 2:21).

So the Lord bids us to put away from our midst all causes of mutual misunderstanding, and even if a brother have aught against us to go to him in the spirit of forgiveness and love, and remove the misunderstanding if possible. "If you are offering your gift at the altar and there remember that your brother has something against you, leave your gift there in front of the altar. First go and be reconciled to your brother; then come and offer your gift" (Matthew 5:23–24).

## SUSPICION SATISFIED

3. The very suspicion of evil must be removed and prevented (Numbers 5:11–15, 24–28), and so provision is made for the trial of the suspected person by what is called "the waters of jealousy," which were to become accursed to the guilty person, but to be harmless to the innocent.

## THE NAZIRITE
### Numbers 6:1–8; 22–27

4. The highest conception of purity and separation was expressed by the law of the Nazirite.

Here we observe: (1) He was entirely separated unto God, recognizing himself, and being recognized as a dedicated life. (2) The sacrifice was voluntary and not constrained, and therefore had the sweet savor of perfect joy and love. (3) It was accompanied by a vow of special form and most sacred consecration. (4) He was to abstain from wine and all strong drink, suggesting that his life was to be free from the heat of earthly passion and excitement, and that the calm and heavenly freedom of the divine possession was ever to characterize him. (5) He must not touch the dead, not even his own immediate family. This implies that if we would be true Nazirites, we must be separated from our old fleshly nature; we must be crucified with Christ, and so risen with Him that we shall not touch even in consciousness or memory the sinful self which we have renounced and crucified. (6) No razor must touch his head or body, but he must be wholly yielded to the Lord in perfect simplicity. The hair of the human body seems in some way to be the divine symbol of power, and the design of this feature of the Nazirite's life was to suggest, as in the case of Samson, the idea of power in all the fullness of the divine enduement and indwelling of the Holy Spirit. A Nazirite thus expresses the idea of purity and power as inseparably combined. So we find that Samson was a Nazirite; and while faithful to his consecration he was possessed of the superhuman strength which God gave as the seal of that consecration. When he abandoned that he lost his strength.

Surely the lesson is not hard to find in our spiritual life. We shall be weak and sinful men as oft as we allow the world to defile us. But in holy separation we shall find boundless possibilities of God's power and fullness.

## SECTION V—*Stewards*
### Numbers 7:1–6, 11, 18, 24, 30, 36, 42, 48, 54, 60, 66, 72, 78, 84–89

The closing picture of the Hebrew camp is the presentation by the princes of Israel of their voluntary gifts in the service of the tabernacle and the consecration of the altar. This is intended to suggest and prefigure the duty of Christian stewardship, and the consecration of our means as one of the most important departments of entire dedication to God and practical Christian service. These offerings were made spontaneously and do not seem to have been even suggested by Moses, but were brought by the princes of their own accord under the pressure of their respective tribes, who seem to have contributed along with them the means for these several gifts. Moses had to hesitate and inquire of the Lord before accepting them, showing their entire spontaneousness (Numbers 7:3–5).

### CHRISTIAN GIVING
This is ever the true spirit of Christian beneficence. The consecration of their substance to God was one of the very first results of the pouring out of the Holy Spirit on the day of Pentecost (Acts 4:34) and has ever marked the measure of the Church's life and consecration. The Apostle Paul unfolded its principles and emphasized its obligations with peculiar fullness in almost all

his epistles. We find him classing it in his letters to the Corinthians among the very highest graces of the Christian life, and especially urging this spirit of heartiness and spontaneousness, as its true mode of inspiration. "But just as you excel in everything—in faith, in speech, in knowledge, in complete earnestness and in your love for us—see that you also excel in this grace of giving" (2 Corinthians 8:7). "For if the willingness is there, the gift is acceptable according to what one has, not according to what he does not have" (8:12).

The gifts of the princes occupied 12 entire days, each prince and tribe taking an entire day in succession and the services being signalized as a feast day by universal rejoicing. The services and gifts of each day are chronicled with minutest detail, embracing not only the names of the givers but also the specifications of their various gifts, and even where from day to day the gifts were the same, yet the account is repeated with equal minuteness over and over again, as if the Holy Spirit were never weary of recording in everlasting remembrance the smallest gifts of His people's gratitude and love. This is intended to teach us that God recognizes in detail our every gift and service, and has, in His book of eternal memorial, an enduring record of each.

This chapter of Numbers is the second longest chapter in the Bible, and it is not a little significant that the Holy Spirit has devoted such a chapter to the subject of Christian giving. It is but a specimen page from the larger volume which God is keeping amid the archives of the Judgment, for the day when He shall come and "his reward is with him" (Isaiah 40:10).

It is also significant that all the gifts were of equal value, teaching us that our giving should be proportionate, and that none should be unequally burdened, but together share in common the claims of Christ's kingdom (2 Corinthians 8:13, etc).

## THE NAMES

Some of the names of the princes of Israel who gave these offerings seem to possess a peculiar significance. Nahshon, the first, representing the tribe of Judah, signified an oracle, implying that very often our best way of speaking and testifying to God is through our gifts. Nethanel, the second, means God's gifts, implying that all our gifts are to be smaller recognitions of His larger bounties. Eliab, the third, signifies God his Father. Elizur, the fourth, signifies God his Rock. Shelumiel, the fifth, means God his Peace. The three together suggest that they who have learned to know Jehovah as their Father, their Strength and their Peace will count it a privilege to serve with the very best their life can offer, and that their richest gifts are little, compared with the value which they place on His inestimable grace. Eliasaph, the sixth, means God his Gatherer and implies that He will take care of the seed that lovingly give to Him. Ahiezer, the 10th, means the Helping Brother, suggesting the mutual blessings of cooperation and help in Christian work and giving. Pagiel, the 11th, signifies God meets, suggesting the favor and acceptance with which God recognizes the gifts and sacrifices of His people's love. This is beautifully expressed in the closing verses of the chapter, where we are told that after the offerings were all presented Moses entered into the tabernacle of the congregation and "heard the voice speaking to him from between the two cherubim above the atonement cover on the ark of the Testimony" (Numbers 7:89).

## GOD'S APPROVAL

It would seem as though God was so pleased with the willing gifts of His faithful people, that He came down immediately to recognize them and speak to them in the tender voice of His approval and blessing. What He said to Moses we are not told, unless it be that the next verses in the commencement of the eighth chapter (verses 1–4), commending the lighting of the lamps in the tabernacle, was the message given. If this were so, it may well teach us that the gifts of God's people, when lovingly and faithfully bestowed, will ever bring the blessing of the outpouring of the Holy Spirit in the Church of Christ, and the kindling of a light and fire in God's sanctuary and altar, which will spread its brightness afar on a dark and sin-cursed world.

In a later prophet we know that He has told us explicitly the blessing which our consecrated gifts will ever bring. " 'Bring the whole tithe into the storehouse, that there may be food in my house. Test me in this,' says the LORD Almighty, 'and see if I will not throw open the floodgates of heaven and pour out so much blessing that you will not have room enough for it. I will prevent pests from devouring your crops, and the vines in your field will not cast their fruit,' says the LORD Almighty. 'Then all the nations will call you blessed, for yours will be a delightful land,' says the LORD Almighty" (Malachi 3:10–12).

# CHAPTER 2

## THE ADVANCE

Hitherto we have seen the camp at rest, but now preparations are made for their great march. They were not to dwell forever under the shadows of Sinai or in the howling wilderness. It was but 11 days' journey from Mt. Sinai to the borders of the promised land, and within a very little while they might have been in the inheritance of their fathers. Everything was now ready; an army of 600,000 men, organized and thoroughly disciplined, had grown out of the rabble that escaped from Egypt, and the majestic presence of God was ready to lead them into glorious victory and complete possession of their national heritage. And so the signals for their advance began.

### THE PASSOVER
**Numbers 9:1–14**

1. The first of these preparations was the observance of the Passover.

This was observed at the usual time, on the 14th day of the first month, just one year after their departure from Egypt. Thus they began their advance into their final inheritance, at the same place and in the same spirit, as they had their escape from the bondage of Egypt. So we must begin every new departure of our Christian life at the cross of Jesus, whether it be, as this movement typified, our entering into the fullness of Jesus or our consecration to any special service for the Lord. We shall never get away from the necessity of that precious blood, which grows more dear to the Christian heart the more we learn of the fullness of its power, not only to pardon, but also to cleanse, to consecrate and to overcome.

There was, however, a special provision connected with this Passover, which was singular and exceptional. Certain persons came to Moses and explained that they had not been able to keep it, on account of defilements at the time through the touch of the dead. God, therefore, provided that they might keep the Passover for themselves, at a special time, on the 14th day of the second month, and it would be accepted out of season on account of special circumstances of the case. How beautifully we are thus instructed that while we are not to dispense needlessly with God's ordinary stated ordinances of blessing, yet His grace overruns all conventional boundaries and meets us under the most unusual circumstances and unseasonable times and places, when it is really necessary that He should depart from His normal methods of working.

This significant Passover was provided for members of the congregation who had become defiled, and were not prepared to participate at the usual season. So the cross of Christ meets the weakest and the most unworthy of God's children and gives them with infinite tenderness and patience, time and opportunity to recover from their failures, to be cleansed from their defilements and ultimately to take their place abreast of their brethren in full acceptance and equal blessing in the common advance.

## THE PILLAR OF CLOUD AND FIRE
### Numbers 9:15–23

2. The pillar of cloud and fire next appears as the visible guide of the march which was about to begin; and with great beauty and spiritual significance its appearance and manifestation, both in movement and repose, are described in the closing verses of the ninth chapter of Numbers.

This glorious manifestation of the divine presence finds its spiritual fulfillment in our lives in the guidance of the Holy Spirit. It is important for us to learn not only to follow the Spirit when He leads us forward, but also to wait when He holds us in silence. "At the LORD's command the Israelites set out, and at his command they encamped. As long as the cloud stayed over the tabernacle, they remained in camp. When the cloud remained over the tabernacle a long time, the Israelites obeyed the LORD's order and did not set out" (Numbers 9:18–19).

True obedience requires the spirit of great quietness, self-restraint and the suppression of all the impulsive, passionate, eager voices of the fleshly mind, as well as the prompt and courageous energy which is ready to go forward at His immediate call. Those who have best learned to wait will be most ready to run when truly called, and those who are most hasty will usually be most timorous in real danger. So we find that Joshua and Caleb, the two brave men who were not afraid to enter the land in the face of all the formidable adversaries, were also the two that could wait 40 years for their inheritance; while on the other hand the people who were afraid to go forward at God's call and occupy their promised inheritance, the very next day were rash enough to rush forward without God's command and perished miserably at Hormah (chapter 14).

Moses himself had been deeply taught this lesson of waiting by his own early experience. At 40 years of age, he, too, was ready to rush forward at his own impulse. But God sent him into Midian for another 40 years, and when he came forth he had learned to be still and let God lead (Isaiah 30:15; Acts 16:6–7). Thus we see the great apostle of the Gentiles in the commencement of his missionary work, held again and again by the Spirit from fields that he would have entered, and finally, as he tarried and obeyed, better openings for his work in other fields presented themselves, and he found the first places, at a later period, prepared for him with a fullness of blessing which would not have come if he had hastily entered them. So, on the other hand, a little later, we find him as persistently following the Spirit as he had obediently waited upon Him before. Even when the disciples around him implored him to desist from his journey to Jerusalem, he could only repel their tender pleadings and follow on after the pillar of cloud and fire which was leading his own faith forward to bonds and afflictions.

## LED OF THE SPIRIT

This blessed presence is the privilege of every consecrated believer. "Because those who are led by the Spirit of God are sons of God" (Romans 8:14). This is the only light that can lead us into the fullness of Christ, which was the special lesson of the march of Israel. He who would know the fullness of the land of promise must follow the pillar guide. It is the Spirit who "will take from what is [Christ's] and make it known to you" (John 16:15b). It is the Spirit who makes us know the things which are freely given us of God, " 'No eye has seen,/ no ear has heard,/ no mind has conceived/ what God has prepared for those who love him'—/ but God has revealed it to us by his Spirit. The Spirit searches all things, even the deep things of God. For who among men knows the thoughts of a man except the man's spirit within him? In the same way no one knows the thoughts of God except the Spirit of God" (1 Corinthians 2:9–11).

## THE SILVER TRUMPETS
**Numbers 10:1–10**
3. The two silver trumpets are next described.
These were both made of the same material and were precisely alike. They were used to summon the people to the great assemblies, public feasts, religious services, the commencement of journeys or the alarm of war. They were also used to herald the dawn of the Year of Jubilee.

## GOD'S WORD AND SPIRIT
These two silver trumpets are beautiful types of the voice of God speaking to His people through the Word and the Holy Spirit. Both made of the same material, they denote that the mind of the Spirit is always in harmony with the teaching of the Word, and that these twin voices never contradict each other. The uses of the trumpets sweetly express the precious value and the

various messages of God's Word and Spirit. They are ever leading our steps in the pilgrimage of life: warning us of danger and of enemies; calling us to work and summoning us to the battles of the Lord; wooing us to His sanctuary and speaking to us there His divine messages; bringing to us the joy and gladness of His gracious words; bringing to us the blessedness of the people that know the joyful sound and walk in the light of His countenance; and finally proclaiming to us the words of hope and promise that foretell the glad coming of our Lord, and the jubilee of millennial ages.

## THE ARK
**Numbers 10:15–36**
4. Finally, we have the ark of God represented as also leading the hosts of Israel in their first advance through the wilderness.

## A GENTLE REPROOF
Just prior to the account of this, however, we have an interesting account of the beginning of that march, and the request of Moses to Hobab, his brother-in-law, to become their guide through the desert. It is not stated whether this was authorized by the Lord, but it seems to have been an impulse of Moses' natural reason. Knowing as he did from years of experience the dangers of the wilderness and the tried experience of Hobab, it was natural that he should desire his presence and direction and think it necessary that they should have all the wisdom that could be legitimately commanded. God does not directly reprove this act of human dependence, but significantly changes the position of the ark from the center of the camp to the front, and we read that

> The ark of the covenant of the LORD went before them during those three days to find them a place to rest. The cloud of the LORD was over them by day when they set out from the camp.
>     Whenever the ark set out, Moses said,
>
> "Rise up, O LORD!
>   May your enemies be scattered;
>   may your foes flee before you."
>
> Whenever it came to rest, he said,
>
> "Return, O LORD,
> to the countless thousands of Israel." (Numbers 10:33b–36)

This second act must have made it plain to Moses, that God Himself was to be their personal Guide, and that even the wisdom of Hobab was not needed in their supernatural journey.

## CHRIST'S PRESENCE

The ark was the special type of the presence of the Lord Jesus Christ, and His direct guidance is one of the privileges of His disciples, and one of His sweetest personal promises. He is the loving Shepherd, who, "When he has brought out all his own, he goes on ahead of them, and his sheep follow him because they know his voice. But they will never follow a stranger; in fact, they will run away from him because they do not recognize a stranger's voice" (John 10:4–5).

Ordinarily the ark was in the center of the camp, as Jesus Christ is central in the hearts of His people, but in this instance it moved in front, out of its usual place; and so there are times in the Christian's experience, when the way is dark and uncertain, that our blessed Master becomes strangely manifest as the Guide of our perplexing pathway, the Leader of our timid steps, and the Captain of salvation for His struggling hosts. Sometimes He is riding before us on the white horse of victory, while His enemies flee before Him as smoke is driven, and then again resting in our midst in all the tenderness of His gracious presence.

The special form of invocation which was used when the ark set forth has become crystallized in the exquisite poetry of the 68th Psalm, which is also one of the Messianic prophecies, and finds its highest fulfillment in the triumph and ascension of the Lord Jesus Christ. It opens with the same words of Moses: "May God arise, may his enemies be scattered;/ may his foes flee before him" (68:1). And then it moves on in stately procession, like the camp of Israel in the wilderness.

> When you went out before your people, O God,
>> when you marched through the wasteland, *Selah*,
> the earth shook,
>> the heavens poured down rain,
> before God, the One of Sinai,
>> before God, the God of Israel.
> You gave abundant showers, O God;
>> you refreshed your weary inheritance.
> Your people settled in it,
>> and from your bounty, O God, you provided for the poor.

> The LORD announced the word,
>> and great was the company of those who proclaimed it:
> "Kings and armies flee in haste;

in the camps men divide the plunder.
Even while you sleep among the campfires,
  the wings of my dove are sheathed with silver,
  its feathers with shining gold." (7–13)

And then it rises to the grandeur of His ascension and His presence with His
people in the grace and glory of the gospel.

When you ascended on high,
  you led captives in your train;
  you received gifts from men,
even from the rebellious—
  that you, O LORD God, might dwell there.

Praise be to the Lord, to God our Savior,
  who daily bears our burdens. *Selah* (18–19)


## LATER HISTORY

The subsequent history of the ark of the covenant throws a beautiful light
on the personal guidance of the Lord Jesus with respect to His people. It
does not always seem to have gone visibly before the people but ordinarily to
have been carried in the center of the camp. But in times of special
perplexity and crisis, it always went immediately before. So again, when they
came to the waters of the Jordan, it was the ark which first touched the
angry billows and before whose presence they melted away and left the pathway clear for the following hosts; even as our blessed Savior leads for us the
way through the floods of death and opens the pathway of safety, victory
and glory (Joshua 3:13–17).

Thus prepared and preceded, the camp of Israel begins its forward march.

# CHAPTER 3

## THE FAILURE AND RETREAT

Their journey might have been, and should have been, a career of glorious conquest. It would have been just as easy to enter Canaan now, as half a century later; but 40 years of disaster and disappointment intervened, and at last the skeletons and skulls of all the men and women of adult age who came out of the land of Egypt were left as monuments of awful warning on the burning sands.

The stages of the unbelief and disobedience which at length culminated in their refusal to enter the land were very gradual, and are traced by the fingers of the Holy Spirit with strictest detail.

> Now these things occurred as examples to keep us from setting our hearts on evil things as they did. Do not be idolaters, as some of them were; as it is written: "The people sat down to eat and drink and got up to indulge in pagan revelry." We should not commit sexual immorality, as some of them did—and in one day twenty-three thousand of them died. We should not test the Lord, as some of them did—and were killed by snakes. And do not grumble, as some of them did—and were killed by the destroying angel. (1 Corinthians 10:6–10)

This solemn failure of ancient Israel has become the portentous warning of all the subsequent dispensations. We find the psalmist in his day recalling it to the minds of God's people with the imposing admonitions:

> Today, if you hear his voice,
>    do not harden your hearts as you did at Meribah,
>    as you did that day at Massah in the desert,
> where your fathers tested and tried me,
>    though they had seen what I did.
> For forty years I was angry with that generation;

I said, "They are a people whose hearts go astray,
   and they have not known my ways."
So I declared on oath in my anger,
   "They shall never enter my rest." (95:7b–11)

And again in the Epistle to the Hebrews, just in the midst of the last 40 years of opportunity given to Israel before the destruction of Jerusalem, the Holy Spirit again recalls the example of ancient Israel, not only as a lesson to the nation, but also as an admonition to each individual Christian, bidding him to take heed, lest by unbelief and disobedience he should miss the higher rest of which Canaan was but the type.

As has just been said:

"Today, if you hear his voice,
   do not harden your hearts
   as you did in the rebellion."

Who were they who heard and rebelled? Were they not all those Moses led out of Egypt? And with whom was he angry for forty years? Was it not with those who sinned, whose bodies fell in the desert? And to whom did God swear that they would never enter his rest if not to those who disobeyed? So we see that they were not able to enter, because of their unbelief.

Therefore, since the promise of entering his rest still stands, let us be careful that none of you be found to have fallen short of it. . . . Now we who have believed enter that rest, just as God has said,

"So I declared on oath in my anger,
   'They shall never enter my rest.' "

And yet his work has been finished since the creation of the world. . . . For if Joshua had given them rest, God would not have spoken later about another day. There remains, then, a Sabbath-rest for the people of God; for anyone who enters God's rest also rests from his own work, just as God did from his. Let us, therefore, make every effort to enter that rest, so that no one will fall by following their example of disobedience. (Hebrews 3:15–19; 4:1,3,8–11)

## MURMURING

1. The failure of ancient Israel began in their murmuring at Taberah.

"Now the people complained about their hardships in the hearing of the LORD, and when he heard them his anger was aroused. Then fire from the LORD burned among them and consumed some of the outskirts of the camp" (Numbers 11:1).

The marginal reading here is very striking. "And when the people *as it were*, complained, it displeased the Lord; and his anger was kindled and the fire of the Lord burned among them and consumed them that were in the uttermost parts of the camp. And he called the name of the place 'Taberah,' because the fire of the LORD burnt among them" (11:1, 3).

The spirit of discontent and ingratitude is generally the beginning of deeper and bolder unbelief and sin. Here we see that even before it had become fully manifest, God saw it and manifested His burning displeasure against it. For the people "as it were, murmured." This implies that kind of discontent which does not dare openly to reproach God with our troubles and misfortunes, but scolds Him through other people, and finds fault with circumstances and things, scarcely imagining that God is really blamed, or regards our murmurings as against Him. When we find fault with circumstances, we are really finding fault with God, with whose permission, at least, all things come to us. God wants us to learn that the bitterness that we tolerate in our spirit is as really sin as that which is expressed in open murder or defiant blasphemies against God, though not as aggravated. "Anyone who hates his brother is a murderer" (1 John 3:15). And unthankfulness and ingratitude toward God are the real roots of rebellion. For we read in Romans, "although they knew God, they neither glorified him as God nor gave thanks to him, but their thinking became futile and their foolish hearts were darkened" (1:21), and God gave them up to a reprobate mind, and all the aggravations and issues of sin.

## LUSTING

**Numbers 11:4–10, 18–20, 31, 33**

2. The lusting of the people and the mixed multitude at Kibroth Hattaavah.

"The rabble with them began to crave other food, and again the Israelites started wailing and said, 'If only we had meat to eat!' " (Numbers 11:4).

This spirit of earthly desire began with the mixed multitude who had accompanied them out of Egypt, and who seem to have been a sort of loose rabble of mere camp followers, having no part with God's covenant people except to be a point of contact and temptation between them and the world. Unhappily, the professing Church of God in the Christian age has been largely made up of just such camp followers. People who do not belong to the true Israel, but simply follow the camp of the Lord because of earthly attachments and advantages; and when trials or temptations come they are always channels or instruments of evil. On this occasion they began to lust after the luxuries of their Egyptian life. "We remember the fish we ate in Egypt at no cost—also the cucumbers, melons, leeks, onions and garlic. But now we have lost our appetite; we never see anything but this manna!" (11:5–6).

This would seem very disgusting if it were not so much like ourselves. It is the spirit of the flesh, and it is usually the occasion of most of our murmuring. Our Lord has given us the same sad picture of a restless and discontented world in every age. " 'What shall we eat?' or 'What shall we drink?' or 'What shall we wear?' For the pagans run after all these things" (Matthew 6:31–32a). It is the spirit of the animal in man, and it is the same in the most refined form of self-indulgence as it is in the coarse and brutal slave. The apostle calls it "the desires of the sinful nature" (Galatians 5:16). The Lord has given us physical needs and appetites, but He never designed them to be predominant in our nature; and whenever they become ends of life and objects of gratification, they drag us down into the depths of corruption.

God becomes indignant with the unholy tears and murmurings of the camp, and even Moses for a little loses his self-control and speaks with impatient haste. But the patience of God does not fail even in the hour of His displeasure. The sensual cry of the multitude was answered by the sending of a great swarm of quails, which covered the entire ground and fell to a depth of three feet for miles around. They kept the whole people a day and a night in gathering them as they fell, and they were surfeited for a whole month with the supply, until it became repulsive to them.

The judgment of God fell upon them in the midst of their gluttonous indulgence, and a plague broke out which destroyed many lives.

God has warned us very solemnly in the New Testament against the spirit of earthly indulgence, in the beautiful language which refers so graphically to our Christian pilgrimage. The Apostle Peter says: "Dear friends, I urge you, as aliens and strangers in the world, to abstain from sinful desires, which war against your soul" (1 Peter 2:11). And the Apostle John declares, "For everything in the world—the cravings of sinful man, the lust of his eyes and the boasting of what he has and does—comes not from the Father but from the world" (1 John 2:16). "Do not love the world or anything in the world. If anyone loves the world, the love of the Father is not in him" (2:15).

If we would avoid the love of the world, we must avoid the mixed multitude and maintain our separation from evil men; so we are commanded:

> Do not be yoked together with unbelievers. For what do righteousness and wickedness have in common? Or what fellow-

ship can light have with darkness? What harmony is there between Christ and Belial? What does a believer have in common with an unbeliever? What agreement is there between the temple of God and idols? For we are the temple of the living God. As God has said: "I will live with them and walk among them, and I will be their God, and they will be my people."

> "Therefore come out from them
> and be separate,
>         says the Lord.
> Touch no unclean thing,
>     and I will receive you."
> "I will be a Father to you,
>     and you will be my sons and daughters,
>         says the Lord Almighty."

Since we have these promises, dear friends, let us purify ourselves from everything that contaminates body and spirit, perfecting holiness out of reverence for God. (2 Corinthians 6:14–7:1)

## MOSES' FAILURE
### Numbers 11:11–17, 21–30

3. The next indication of declension and danger is seen in the wavering of even Moses himself in this hour of testing, when God announces to him the miracles which He is about to perform in feeding the people with flesh. It had already begun in Moses' impatience with the people's complaints, and even with the Lord for placing such a burden upon him. "He asked the LORD, 'Why have you brought this trouble on your servant? What have I done to displease you that you put the burden of all these people on me? . . . I cannot carry all these people by myself; the burden is too heavy for me. If this is how you are going to treat me, put me to death right now—if I have found favor in your eyes—and do not let me face my own ruin' " (Numbers 11:11, 14–15).

This was a fit of downright petulance, and Moses lost much by it. God took him instantly at his word, and relieved him of much of his honor and care, by taking some of the Spirit which was upon him and dividing it with the elders, who henceforth were to share the cares of the congregation with him (11:17, 25). There was more of the divine Spirit given than Moses himself had possessed, only it was shared with a large number. We are not sure that this was ultimately a real blessing. Moses might still have retained the sufficiency of God Himself, and that was all the elders had after they had received the blessing. They simply had some of the Spirit that he had had before. Moreover, this was the origin of the Hebrew eldership, and the end of it was the condemnation and crucifixion of the Lord Jesus Christ.

The spirit of impatience in Moses led to a spirit of unbelief. God's great promise of deliverance is met by him with the question, " 'Would they have enough if flocks and herds were slaughtered for them? Would they have enough if all the fish in the sea were caught for them?' The LORD answered Moses, 'Is the LORD's arm too short? You will now see whether or not what I say will come true for you' " (Numbers 11:22–23). This was the first indication of wavering in the spirit of the great lawgiver. It is not marked as severely as his later fault which excluded him from the land of Canaan, but it was probably the root even of that great and fatal error, and therefore the Lord reproved it somewhat sharply that his servant might be guarded and forewarned. "See to it, brothers, that none of you has a sinful, unbelieving heart" (Hebrews 3:12), so that we never limit the Infinite and Almighty One.

## MIRIAM AND AARON
### Numbers 12:1–16

4. The spirit of discontent next breaks out in Miriam and Aaron.

The sister of Moses had been preeminently used of God in this marvelous history as the chosen instrument in his early childhood of bringing him under his mother's nurturing care, when discovered by the daughter of Pharaoh. Afterwards she had been called by the special anointing of the Spirit. She had been selected to lead the choral songs of the triumphant people after they had crossed the Red Sea, and probably, also, afterwards in seasons of public worship and rejoicing. Being the older sister of Moses, she probably assumed a degree of authority which would be quite natural, and in this case it was carried by her to the extreme of interference in his personal matters, as good people often do. The immediate subject of her dislike and annoyance at this time was the wife of Moses. She was joined in her prejudices and evil speaking by her brother Aaron, and their combined influence threatened serious disaffection in the camp.

The description of Moses' wife has opened an unsettled controversy as to whether this was the daughter of Jethro, the wife whom he had married in Midian, or some other and second wife of whom we have no detailed account. Certainly it seems a little strange that a daughter of Midian should be called an Ethiopian. Many have found in this incident a type of the Lord Jesus Christ, and the jealousy of the Jewish people, represented by Miriam, against the Gentile bride whom He has called to share His love and honors. Certainly it is at least a solemn lesson that comes even to the best Christians when they interfere unduly in matters which are personal to others, and which the Lord alone can judge and regulate. Many have lost their peace and become separated from God by putting their hands on Jehovah's ark when they thought it needed steadying.

Miriam and Aaron seem to have carried their interference a great deal further than the mere question of Moses' domestic relations, for they even challenged his special authority, saying: "Has the LORD spoken only through Moses? . . . Hasn't he also spoken through us?" (Numbers 12:2). Perhaps they thought they had a perfect right to pass judgment upon his actions, because God had been pleased to use them in His work. In this severe trial Moses seems to have stood in the attitude of dignified and exemplary silence and meekness, for it is added immediately afterwards: "Now Moses was a very humble man, more humble than anyone else on the face of the earth" (12:3). Such an attitude will ever bring the protection and vindication of God. So we read that the Lord heard it, and spoke suddenly unto Moses and unto Aaron and unto Miriam, and came down in the pillar of cloud and stood in the door of the tabernacle, and called them forth and said: "Listen to my words: When a prophet of the LORD is among you,/ I reveal myself to him in visions,/ I speak to him in dreams./ But this is not true of my servant Moses;/ he is faithful in all my house./ With him I speak face to face" (12:6–8a). That is not merely visions and dreams, but directly, "clearly and not in riddles;/ he sees the form of the LORD./ Why then were you not afraid/ to speak against my servant Moses?" (12:8b).

The awful reproof was followed by the second withdrawal of the divine presence, and the stroke of leprosy upon the person of Miriam. Aaron falls in entreaty at the feet of Moses, and intercedes for his stricken sister, acknowledging his own equal sin; and Moses instantly intercedes for her restoration. The Lord graciously answers his prayer, but requires that she shall dwell apart for seven days outside the camp, as a token of the separation which sin ever makes between the soul and God's fellowship. It is not very long before we read of the death both of Miriam and of Aaron (Numbers 20:1–28).

In this instance we see the still lurking life of self which ever shows itself in our Christian experience in similar ways, preeminently in the spirit of judging and uncharitableness. He who has truly seen and sacrificed himself will always think very patiently and tenderly of others. Therefore we find in Christ's Beatitudes that the poor in spirit come before the merciful. And in the Epistles of Paul the great lesson of death and resurrection is fully taught before the spirit of love is unfolded.

## THE SPIES

### Numbers 13:1–31

5. The next development of the spirit of evil and the cause of subsequent failure which we trace in this book was the sending out of the spies to survey

the land and bring a report before the whole people attempted to force an entrance. The full account of this is given in the first chapter of Deuteronomy, with the immediate causes which led to it; and from this statement we see that it originated not in the first thought either of the Lord or of Moses, but in the timidity and human reasonings of the people. When they came to Kadesh Barnea, which was the entrance to the land of promise, Moses had said to them: " 'You have reached the hill country of the Amorites, which the LORD our God is giving us. See, the LORD your God has given you the land. Go up and take possession of it as the LORD, the God of your fathers, told you. Do not be afraid; do not be discouraged.' Then all of you came to me and said, 'Let us send men ahead to spy out the land for us and bring back a report about the route we are to take and the towns we will come to' " (Deuteronomy 1:20–22).

It was in consequence of this that the Lord permitted the sending out of the spies; but it only led to temptation, cowardice, unbelief and ignominious and fatal failure. The true pathway of faith is to go forward implicitly at God's bidding, and if we wait for reason to take counsel of flesh or blood after God Himself has spoken, we are almost sure to be involved in confusion and failure. Paul says: "But when God, who set me apart from birth and called me by his grace, was pleased to reveal his Son in me so that I might preach him among the Gentiles, I did not consult any man" (Galatians 1:15–16). Here we see the spirit of promptness and implicit obedience to God, irrespective of the counsels of human wisdom. When our way is not clear and our duty is not plain, it is becoming that we should take counsel of those to whom the Lord may direct us. But when God has spoken it is always dangerous to listen to the voice of man and always safe to "trust in the LORD with all your heart/ and lean not on your own understanding" (Proverbs 3:5). The spirit of human reasoning is the natural enemy of faith; and the command of God will often lead us in the face of improbabilities and seeming impossibilities. Dr. Jamieson wisely remarks concerning this: "God granted their request at once as a trial and a punishment of their distrust."

## THEIR SUGGESTIVE NAMES

The names of the spies are all suggestive of human strength and wisdom. Shammua, the first, means renown. So men today are going by the advice of the great and famous names of the Church and the world; but alas, they are not going into Canaan. Shaphat means the judge, and represents the very preeminence of human wisdom. The names of Caleb and Joshua, the two faithful ones, signify boldness and divine help. The one expresses the spirit of courageous faith, and the other the fact of almighty power which this always brings.

## REBELLION OF THE CONGREGATION

**Numbers 14:1–45**

6. The culmination of all this series of failures came at last in the shameful refusal of the whole congregation to enter the land, and their disgraceful surrender of all their hopes and privileges through cowardly unbelief and disobedience. The immediate occasion of this was the report of the spies, from which no good could have been expected and certainly none came. They could not deny the excellence of the land, the wonderful richness of the products and the soil and climate, but overtopping all these glorious prospects they could see nothing but gigantic figures of the Canaanites, the mighty Anakims and the warlike Amalekites, Hittites, Jebusites and Amorites. "We went into the land to which you sent us, and it does flow with milk and honey! Here is its fruit. But the people who live there are powerful, and the cities are fortified and very large. . . . We can't attack those people; they are stronger than we are. . . . We seemed like grasshoppers in our own eyes, and we looked the same to them" (Numbers 13:27–28, 31b, 33b).

It was in vain that the noble Caleb and Joshua stood up against their brethren and said: "We should go up and take possession of the land, for we can certainly do it" (13:30). "If the LORD is pleased with us, he will lead us into that land, . . . and will give it to us. Only do not rebel against the LORD. And do not be afraid of the people of the land, because we will swallow them up. Their protection is gone, but the LORD is with us. Do not be afraid of them" (14:8–9).

These heroic words were only met by a wail of disappointment and vexation, and a shower of stones. All that night the angry, mutinous cries of the congregation went up to heaven and soon the old and awful refrain was heard like the angry billows of the sea, If only we had died in Egypt! Or in this desert! Why is the LORD bringing us to this land only to let us fall by the sword? Our wives and children will be taken as plunder. Wouldn't it be better for us to go back to Egypt?' And they said to each other, 'We should choose a leader and go back to Egypt' " (14:2–4).

### THE CRISIS

It was indeed an awful hour and a crisis such as had never come before, and Moses and Aaron fell on their faces in the silence of a great fear, and of their utter helplessness.

### THE JUDGMENT

Suddenly the glory of God, like a lightning flash, appeared in the tabernacle in the sight of all the people, and their murmurings were hushed in terror before that fiery flame. Then, upon their leader's ear, there fell this terrific message: "How long will these people treat me with contempt? How long will they refuse to believe in me, in spite of all the miraculous signs I have performed among them? I will strike them down with a plague and destroy them, but I will make you into a nation greater and stronger than they" (14:11–12).

## THE MEDIATOR

It was then that the true spirit of this noble hero was fully revealed. He rose in this terrible hour nearer to the very height of his divine Master's self-sacrifice and priestly intercession than mortal ever approached. Utterly forgetting himself and lost only in the glory of Jehovah, he cried to God for His own name's sake to spare and pardon once more His offending and rebellious children.

> Then the Egyptians will hear about it! By your power you brought these people up from among them. And they will tell the inhabitants of this land about it. They have already heard that you, O LORD, are with these people and that you, O LORD, have been seen face to face, that your cloud stays over them, and that you go before them in a pillar of cloud by day and a pillar of fire by night. If you put these people to death all at one time, the nations who have heard this report about you will say, "The LORD was not able to bring these people into the land he promised them on oath; so he slaughtered them in the desert."
>
> Now may the Lord's strength be displayed, just as you have declared: "The LORD is slow to anger, abounding in love and forgiving sin and rebellion. Yet he does not leave the guilty unpunished; he punishes the children for the sin of the fathers to the third and fourth generation." In accordance with your great love, forgive the sin of these people, just as you have pardoned them from the time they left Egypt until now. (14:13–19)

## GOD'S GRACIOUS ANSWER

After 3,000 years we can almost hear the loving tones of that cry, and feel the warmth of that glowing heart, and the power of those burning tears. It was almost worth all the sorrow to have such a spectacle of love. We cannot wonder that He who had prompted that prayer quickly answered: "I have forgiven them, as you asked" (14:20). But in that hour there arose the vision and the purpose of a blessing, wider than Israel should ever know, even the calling of the Gentiles and the fulfilling of His mighty purpose by those who should prove more faithful than the chosen race. "As surely as I live and as surely as the glory of the LORD fills the whole earth" (14:21).

The failure of any man or any people cannot hinder the fulfillment of God's purposes. He has other instruments ready; and it is an awful thing when any man, or any church or race are excused by the Lord, or when they let another take their crown.

Israel's terrible sin has become an awful type and warning of the danger against which the Church and the Christian are so solemnly guarded in the New Testament: the danger of coming short of the fullness of their inheritance. For each of us there is a land of promise, a heritage of rest and a career of triumph and blessing, which nothing can prevent our entering but our own unbelief or disobedience. Like theirs, it is challenged by mighty enemies, and confronted by almost insuperable obstacles. But if the Lord our God delights in us, then He will bring us into this land and give it to us. "We should go up and take possession of the land, for we can certainly do it" (13:30).

In every great work and in every Christian life there comes such a crisis. God forbid that any who read these lines should fail to meet it through fear of difficulties. This is the secret of thousands of unsanctified souls today, and of hundreds of withered churches. "So, as the Holy Spirit says:/ 'Today if you hear his voice,/ do not harden your hearts' " (Hebrews 3:7). Unbelief and disobedience always go together, and have been partners since they met at the gate of Eden. The last procession of lost humanity described in the closing verses of Revelation is led down to the dark abyss by the fearful and unbelieving, and the rear is brought up by the disobedient and unholy (Revelation 21:8).

And yet, it is strange that these very sins are associated closely with their seeming opposites, and men who are afraid to follow the Lord will follow the devil in the face of certain destruction and frightful risk. The men who will not obey God can be led as very captives by Satan at his will, and by wicked men as credulous tools and subservient dupes. So we see in this very passage that the next day the people who would not go up against the land at the word of God were determined to go up when He forbade them—as rash now as they had been timid before, and as willful now as they had been recreant and disobedient.

> Early the next morning they went up toward the high hill country. "We have sinned," they said. "We will go up to the place the LORD has promised."
>
> But Moses said, "Why are you disobeying the LORD's command? This will not succeed! . . ."
>
> Nevertheless, in their presumption they went up toward the

high hill country, though neither Moses nor the ark of the
LORD's covenant moved from the camp. Then the Amalekites
and Canaanites who lived in the hill country came down and attacked them and beat them down all the way to Hormah.
(14:40–42, 44–45)

## THE FAITHFUL TWO

But God was not without His faithful ones, even in this time of national
defection. The two brave spies who had stood alone in that night of rebellion were not permitted to lose their inheritance on account of the failure of
even the whole camp. But in that hour God pledged to them their sure inheritance when the little ones at their feet should have taken the places of
the men before them. Forty years later that pledge was gloriously redeemed
in the cities of Hebron and Timnath Serah, where these heroes were permitted to crown their services and close their lives amid the complete fulfillment of all the promises of God.

So it has ever been through the Christian centuries. Amid the unbelief and
declension of the many, there have been a few names "who have not soiled
their clothes" (Revelation 3:4), and a little flock who have dared fully to
trust and wholly to follow their Shepherd Master, and to whom the inheritance has been ever given in its spiritual foretaste, and shall yet be completed in the glorious day of His appearing and His kingdom.

## REBELLION OF THE NOBLES
**Numbers 16:1–54**

7. The failure of the entire congregation is followed two chapters later by
an account of the more desperate and defiant rebellion of the nobles of Israel, under the leadership of Korah, Dathan and Abiram.

## REBELLION

Their special offense was an act of open rebellion against the authority of
Moses and Aaron, and a presumptuous claim of equal right to come into the
presence of God, both for themselves and for all the congregation. "You have
gone too far! The whole community is holy, everyone of them, and the
LORD is with them. Why then do you set yourselves above the LORD's assembly?" (Numbers 16:3). It was really an outbreak of socialism and lawlessness, a sort of typical democracy strangely prophetic of the last awful
development of human wickedness and license which is to close the present
dispensation in the coming of the *Lawless One*. More generally it represents,
however, the spirit of disobedience and self-will, refusing the authority of
God's Word, denying and defying all the claims of veneration, age, and the
sacred times and ordinances of divine religion, or human order and govern-

ment. Our own land and time are fast sweeping to the vortex of license which was opened for the fearful descent of these daring rebels against divine and human authority.

This question was soon settled by an appeal to God, and the manifestation of His terrific judgment in the entombing of these bold and wicked men, with their censers of unholy fire and their families and possessions, in the bowels of the engulfing earth, while the swiftly descending fire of God fell upon them as they went down, and its awful flame was mingled with the hideous cry of horror and anguish which arose from their midst as the earth closed over them in a living hell. Never could the people forget the sight which they then witnessed, and henceforth the authority of God and His servants was unchallenged. So will He consume with the breath of His mouth and destroy with the brightness of His coming all that oppose themselves to the name and authority of the Lord Jesus Christ, against whom, already,

> The kings of the earth take their stand
>     and the rulers gather together
> against the LORD
>     and against his Anointed One.
> "Let us break their chains," they say,
>     "and throw off their fetters."
>
> The One enthroned in heaven laughs;
>     the Lord scoffs at them. . . .
>
> "You will rule them with an iron scepter;
>     you will dash them to pieces like pottery."
>
> Therefore, you kings, be wise;
>     be warned, you rulers of the earth.
> Serve the LORD with fear
>     and rejoice with trembling.
> Kiss the Son, lest he be angry
>     and you be destroyed in your way,
> for his wrath can flare up in a moment. (Psalm 2:2–4, 9–12)

## MOSES' UNBELIEF
### Numbers 20:9–13

8. This series of mournful failures closes, alas, with the failure of Moses himself. The account of this fatal error on the part of God's faithful servant

is given in Numbers 20:11–13. The immediate occasion of it was the murmuring of the people at the fountain of Meribah, where the waters had failed, and the people again broke out, as they had innumerable times before, in bitter complaints and vehement reproaches.

For a moment Moses lost his meekness and yielded to the temptation, against which he had been warned before in a similar outbreak at Kibroth Hattaavah (Numbers 11:11). His fault on this occasion consisted in a good deal more than his angry retort to the people: "Listen, you rebels, must we bring you water out of this rock?" (20:10).

There seems to be a deeper offence implied in the fact that Moses struck the rock, whereas he was commanded only to speak to it. There was no need that the rock should be struck again, for this had been done at Rephidim in the beginning of their march, and it had been open ever since. The striking of the rock was typical of the opening of the fountains of salvation and grace through the death of the Lord Jesus Christ, once for all. Then He was stricken by the rod of the Lawgiver and from His riven side there flowed the water and the blood, which have never since ceased to be "of sin the double cure." All that was necessary now was to speak to the rock already open and ready to flow at the call of believing prayer. The rod that he used now was not the Lawgiver's rod, but Aaron's rod, the rod of the priesthood, and so a type of prayer. The purpose of this rod was not to smite, but to claim that which was already purchased and provided. Its tender buds and blossoms were not prepared for such rude blows, nor was it necessary that the willing fountain should be compelled by force to yield its flowing treasures.

Beautiful type of that gentle Spirit in His boundless fullness, opened to us by the death of Jesus, and ready to meet our need and cry at the gentlest touch of faith and prayer, but grieved when we doubt His love and try to wrest His blessings from His willing hands, as though they had to be taken by storm! It was thus that the priests of Baal prayed, cutting themselves with knives and shouting as though their god was deaf. But it was not thus that Elijah prayed. It was not thus that Jesus prayed, even at the grave of Lazarus, but with calm assurance he cried as one standing there within the holy of holies: "Father, I thank you that you have heard me. I knew that you always hear me" (John 11:41b–42a). It is not required that we shall suppress the intense emotion of the heart overflowing with the impulse of the Holy Spirit, but there is a danger that we shall still strike the rock, when we need only to speak to it in the words of simple trust which will never fail to bring the overflowing blessing that God is more willing to give than we will ever be to receive.

Let us speak to the Living Rock again and again. He has bidden us, "Whoever wishes, let him take the free gift of the water of life" (Revelation 22:17). "Receive the Holy Spirit" (John 20:22). The sin of Moses, therefore, involved the element of unbelief, as well as disobedience, haste, and even petulance and anger. It lost him the land of promise. Tenderly he pleaded with his God that it might be overlooked, and he be permitted to lead His people into their inheritance; but in vain. Even the lawgiver himself must be an example of the stern inexorable justice of the law which he had given. It is the most awful commentary upon its inflexible severity and righteousness, that it slew even the one who gave it the moment he transgressed it. "Who then can be saved?" (Mark 10:26).

Of all men, Moses cries most loudly to us from his lonely grave on this side of Jordan: "Cursed is everyone who does not continue to do everything written in the Book of the Law" (Galatians 3:10), and points us to Jesus Christ as "the end of the law so that there may be righteousness for everyone who believes" (Romans 10:4). Alas, the law made nothing perfect; not even Moses himself. But, thank God, "a better hope is introduced, by which we draw near to God" (Hebrews 7:19).

# CHAPTER 4

## GOD'S PROVISION FOR THEIR WILDERNESS LIFE, NOTWITHSTANDING THEIR FAILURE

God did not immediately reject them because of their fearful disobedience, but, at the intercession of Moses, He forgave their sin and renewed His covenant for the next generation, and even continued still to manifest His presence with the disobedient through all the period of their wilderness life. He did not permit them to enter the land of promise, for He knew that their spirit could not be trusted, and that their children must be taught by their example the fearful guilt and peril of unbelief and disobedience. So He condemned this entire generation to wander, and at length to die in the wilderness; and promised that their children who they feared would become a prey to their enemies, should be triumphantly led into the land which they had refused to enter (Numbers 14:31).

Yet even during these dreary years of fruitless journeying, His long-suffering presence still continued with them. "Neither the pillar of cloud by day nor the pillar of fire by night left its place in front of the people" (Exodus 13:22). He led them daily like a patient mother, still forgiving their continued provocations and manifesting to them, with every occasion, fresh unfoldings of His marvelous love and foreshadowings of the gospel of salvation which was afterward to be revealed.

### SECTION I—*The Sacrifices Renewed*
Numbers 15:1–41

The first of these gracious manifestations is recorded at length in the chapter immediately succeeding the account of their rebellion (Numbers 15:1–41). This chapter consists of a series of directions for sacrificial ordinances which were to be offered "after you enter the land I am giving you as a home" (15:2). These directions included the ordinance of the burnt offering, and sin offering, the drink offering, the grain offering and various oblations of thanksgiving as well as special sacrifices for disobedience and error.

## GOD'S CONFIDENCE IN THEIR FUTURE

The most striking thing connected with these renewed ordinances is the form in which they are introduced in the very first sentence of the chapter, immediately after the terrible story of their sin and exclusion from the land. The Lord begins to address them quietly as though nothing had occurred, and as if taking it for granted that they were to enter the land and that indeed it was already given to them. "The LORD said to Moses, 'Speak to the Israelites and say to them: "After you enter the land I am giving you as a home" ' " (15:1–2).

Of course He is now addressing the new generation. But when we remember that the nation was one in all its generations, the language affords an incomparably beautiful type of that transcendent mercy in which He deals with the sinner under the gospel, recognizing the sin which has been confessed and put away as something not only blotted out, but wholly ignored, and treating him in the language and reckoning of faith as a new creature, and as though, indeed, the promises of Christ were already fulfilled. God, therefore, speaks of us in the New Testament as already seated with Christ in heavenly places, and living with Him in our eternal inheritance, and He bids us thus "Count yourselves dead to sin but alive to God in Jesus Christ" (Romans 6:11).

## SECTION II— The Priesthood Renewed
### Numbers 16:46–50

The priesthood of Aaron and his sons is established anew, and the rebellion of Korah, Dathan and Abiram is met not only by their judgment, but by the most emphatic and glorious vindication of the true priesthood. This was done first by that stirring incident through which the awful plague, that had spread in the congregation after judgment of Korah, was immediately stayed by Aaron's intercession. Standing between the living and the dead with his golden censer in his hands, and the smoking incense rising from it, God recognized his typical intercession as He still recognizes the pleadings of His risen Son, our Great High Priest. The hand of judgment was arrested and the work of death instantly ceased in the terrified camp after 14,700 people had fallen under the avenging stroke (Numbers 16:49).

## THE BLOOMING AND BUDDING ROD
### Numbers 17:1–13

Next the authority of Aaron's priesthood was forcibly and vividly set forth by the public test in which each of the tribes of Israel was called to bring a rod and lay it in the tabernacle of the congregation before the Lord, that He might choose from among them in the sight of all the people the one that was to represent the true priesthood. This was accordingly done, and as the rods were laid before the Lord, lo, the rod of Aaron burst into buds and blossoms, and even as he gazed the blossoms had ripened into almond fruits. And as Moses brought out the rods and handed them to the men who had brought them, they saw, with awe and submission, the seal which Jehovah Himself had placed on the ministry of the chosen tribe and the priesthood of Aaron and his house.

This memorable sign was also designed to be for us a type of the priest-hood of Jesus, and hence the blooming rod of Aaron was ordered to be laid up and kept in the ark as the memorial for future generations. How beauti-fully this expresses to the believing heart the living priesthood of our Great Advocate. It is not a dry and withered rod, but one which is full of life and vital energy and fruitfulness. "He always lives to intercede for them" (Hebrews 7:25).

Again, Christ's priesthood, like that budding and blossoming rod, is ever fresh in its blessings. Day by day and moment by moment it brings to us new blessings as we need them. He is ever presenting us before the throne, and His mercies are new every morning as the fresh blossoms of the spring. We have not to live on stale experiences, but His unlimited resources are continually calling forth for us the fresh supply of every need from the full-ness of His Father's love and power.

What is so fragrant as the sweet breath of summer flowers? And so His prayers are ever ascending in contrast with our unworthiness and sinfulness, the odor of a sweet-smelling savor, bringing us acceptance and making us unto God a sweet savor of Christ; so that even our very prayers, when mingled with His incense, are treasured in the heavenly chambers in vases of sweet perfume before the throne.

There are, however, not only blossoms, but fruits, and so our Savior's priesthood is intensely practical, bringing us real help which is reproduced in the fruits of our holy life. "I have prayed for you, . . . that your faith may not fail" (Luke 22:32), He said to Peter. And because we have a great High Priest, we are likewise invited to "Approach the throne of grace with con-fidence, so that we may receive mercy and find grace to help us in our time of need" (Hebrews 4:16).

The fruit on Aaron's rod seems to have appeared almost instantly after the buds and blossoms. In a moment the promise was turned into maturity, reminding us how quickly the intercession of our blessed Master ripens into realization. The prayer is turned to praise and blessed fulfillment (Numbers 17:1–13).

## THE SUPPORT OF THE PRIESTHOOD
**Numbers 18:1–15**

This beautiful symbol of the priesthood was followed in the 18th chapter by a series of important ordinances respecting the priestly office, which refer to both the offerings and the provision which was to be made for their support. We have already referred to these provisions in connection with chapter 1. The Lord was to be their inheritance, and they were to have no definite part in the allotment of the land, but a recognition of their right in the tithes of the people and the sacrificial gifts, especially the wave offerings which were to be their portion.

> You, your sons, and your father's family are to bear the responsibility for offenses against the sanctuary, and you and your sons alone are to bear the responsibility for offenses against the priesthood. Bring your fellow Levites from your ancestral tribe to join you and assist you when you and your sons minister before the Tent of the Testimony. (Numbers 18:1–2)

> I myself have put you in charge of the offerings presented to me; all the holy offerings the Israelites give me I give to you and your sons as your portion and regular share. (18:8)

> I am giving you the service of the priesthood as a gift. (18:7)

> You will have no inheritance in their land, nor will you have any share among them; I am your share and your inheritance among the Israelites.
> I give to the Levites all the tithes in Israel as their inheritance in return for the work they do while serving at the Tent of Meeting. (18:20–21)

> This also is yours: whatever is set aside from the gifts of all the wave offerings of the Israelites. I give this to you and your sons and daughters as a regular share. . . .
> I give you all the finest olive oil and all the finest new wine and grain they give the LORD as the firstfruits of their harvest. All the land's firstfruits that they bring to the LORD will be yours. . . .
> Everything in Israel that is devoted to the LORD is yours. (18:11–14)

Thus the true priesthood was permanently established, and through all the wanderings of the wilderness their access to God was uninterrupted. So even the imperfect life of God's people does not prevent the blessings which flow to us from our Gracious Advocate and our access to God through Jesus Christ. The loss is immeasurable, and yet there is much left through His long-suffering grace, even for His unfaithful Church, and His erring children.

## SECTION III—*The Red Heifer*
### Numbers 19:1–22

The most impressive of all the ordinances provided for the wilderness life of Israel was that which is known as the ordinance of the red heifer, described in Numbers 19, and referred to explicitly in Hebrews 9:13, as the special type of the provision which Christ has made for our continual cleansing and keeping amid the defilements of our earthly journey.

### FOR THE WILDERNESS

1. The place where this is introduced in the book of Numbers, rather than in Leviticus or Exodus, shows that it was designed to prefigure God's provision for our wilderness life. It is not a type of our justification, but of the daily cleansing which the believer may continually claim through the constant intercession and sprinkled blood of the Lord Jesus Christ. It represents to some extent the same idea as the washing of the disciples' feet by the Master just before the passover (John 13). He there taught His disciples distinctly that this did not mean the same as their original cleansing, which had already been fully accomplished and is expressed by the word "washed," in the Greek *Louo*, which literally means to bathe the entire person; but rather that partial cleansing of the hands and feet rendered necessary by the defilement of a single day, and expressed by the Greek work *Nipto*. The language of the Apostle John, "The blood of Jesus, his Son, purifies us from all sin" (1 John 1:7), or rather, keeps cleansing us from all sin, describes this daily cleansing prefigured in the ordinance of the red heifer.

### THE TYPE OF CHRIST

2. The selection of the heifer was expressive of the person and sacrifice of Christ. She was to be red, and the rabbis tell us that there must be no single hair of any other color. She must also be without blemish of any kind, and must never have come under the yoke (Numbers 19:2). This was fulfilled in the spotless purity of the Lord Jesus, and in the fact that He was under no obligation on His own account to suffer for sin, or to take the place of the criminal; but was purely voluntary in His sacrifice, and able through His perfect righteousness to make atonement for the guilty.

The unmixed color of the living victim vividly portrays the sufferings of Christ, and the emphatic truth that His one business was to be the sacrifice for sins. His mission was all pure crimson. He had not two aims—to please Himself, and save men. He only came to redeem a lost world.

3. The heifer was next taken outside the camp and slain, so Christ was crucified outside the gate as an outcast and a criminal (Numbers 19:3; Hebrews 13:12).

4. The blood was then sprinkled seven times before the Tent of Meetings, implying the offering of Christ's life is a perfect satisfaction for the guilt of man and a complete ransom for the soul and its forfeited inheritance (Numbers 19:4; 1 Peter 1:19).

## THE BURNING

5. The heifer was then burned to ashes—every part of her body, including the skin, the flesh, the blood, the intestines. And along with her flesh were consumed cedar wood, hyssop and scarlet wool, which the priest was commanded to take and cast amid the burning of the heifer. This is an extremely beautiful part of the type and demands our close attention (Numbers 19:6).

The scarlet wool which was burned with the heifer evidently implies the sin—the sinful nature of the believer which it is our privilege to crucify with Christ and cast in the committal of faith into the flames of His burning, and know that it is reckoned dead and consumed through the power of His grace. Not only are our past transgressions put away, but our old self is thus crucified with Christ (Romans 6:6; 8:4).

But still further, the cedar wood and hyssop which were also cast into the burning represent, not the sinful part, but that which may be called the natural life in every one of us, and which the apostle expresses in First Corinthians 2:14 as the "man without the Spirit," or as it is in the Greek, "the psychical man." This is not the scarlet wool. It is not the gross and coarse flesh of lust, and yet it is human nature, which has all passed under the curse, and must all be crucified and restored as a resurrection life. The cedar represents the strongest side of nature, and the hyssop the least. The latter was the most insignificant of the plants of Palestine. So these two extremes of the natural world are introduced in the account of Solomon's writings as describing the whole extent of the natural world. We are told that he wrote of everything "from the cedar of Lebanon to the hyssop that grows out of walls" (1 Kings 4:33).

It is a lesson that we are very slow to learn that there is much more than sin to be crucified in the entire sanctification of the soul; the whole self must go, from the strength of the cedar to the frailest fiber of the climbing hyssop. The great hindrance to the consecration of many is their strong intellect and will; and the snare of others is the little clinging hyssop of their affections, or sen-

timental weaknesses; all must be cast into the fire on the altar, and the life
come forth anew, in Christ alone, if we would walk in consistent holiness.

## THE ASHES

6. The ashes of the heifer were then carefully collected and preserved, to
be laid without the camp in a clean place and mixed from time to time with
water for the purifying rite, known as the water of cleansing during their entire wilderness journeys. This represents that which the death of Christ continues to mean for us in our daily experience, in addition to its complete
atonement, once for all. There is something in the cross which throughout
all the ages is an abiding power in the sanctification of Christ's people. The
sacrifice cannot be offered anew; but the essence of that sacrifice, like the
ashes of the heifer, may be continually applied for our perpetual cleansing. It
is of this that the apostle says, "The blood of goats and bulls and the ashes of
a heifer sprinkled on those who are ceremonially unclean sanctify them so
that they are outwardly clean. How much more, then, will the blood of
Christ, who through the eternal Spirit offered himself unblemished to God,
cleanse our consciences from acts that lead to death, so that we may serve
the living God" (Hebrews 9:13–14).

So again the Apostle Peter speaks of us as those "who have been chosen according to the foreknowledge of God the Father, through the sanctifying
work of the Spirit, for obedience to Jesus Christ and sprinkling by his blood"
(1 Peter 1:2). This is something that continually accompanies our
obedience. The clean place where the ashes of Christ have been preserved
outside the camp is the right hand of God (1 Peter 1:2), whence the Holy
Spirit continually brings us the fresh cleansing of His sprinkling blood, and
we appropriate it by living faith.

## THE WATER OF CLEANSING

7. The water of cleansing which was sprinkled with the ashes implies this
very truth in connection with the Spirit's ministry. Water is always the symbol of the Holy Spirit, and the mingling of the ashes and the water teaches
us that the divine Spirit must bring to us the efficacy of Christ's death.
There is a hidden and pungent truth lying back of the figure of water and
ashes which will be quickly understood by those that have ever noticed the
effect of their combination. There is no substance in the world more intensely consuming and bitter to the taste than lye, which is just a combination
of water and ashes, and indeed, the material out of which commerce
manufactures the very substances for cleansing. All this implies that the
cleansing of the soul is not painless, but often involves the keenest conviction of sin and crucifixion of self, under the searching touch of the Great
High Priest.

He will be like a refiner's fire or a launderer's soap. He will sit as a refiner and purifier of silver; he will purify the Levites and refine them like gold and silver. Then the LORD will have men who will bring offerings in righteousness, and the offerings of Judah and Jerusalem will be acceptable to the LORD, as in the days gone by, as in former years. (Malachi 3:2–4)

## WE NEED A SINLESS SAVIOR

8. The water of cleansing was to be applied by a clean person. This certainly cannot mean any human priest or even the worshiper himself, but teaches us that our High Priest with His holy hands is ever ready to sprinkle us as often as we come in contrite faith, with His cleansing blood, and His Spirit's purifying power. And so this experience of abiding holiness and continual cleansing is connected by the Apostle John with the priesthood of Christ Himself. "My dear children, I write this to you so that you will not sin. But if anybody does sin, we have one who speaks to the Father in our defense—Jesus Christ, the Righteous One" (1 John 2:1). "If we confess our sins, he is faithful and just and will forgive us our sins and purify us from all unrighteousness" (1:9).

## DEFILEMENT

9. The causes of defilement for which this ordinance was to be applied were extremely suggestive. They were chiefly for persons who became defiled by touching the dead (Numbers 19:2, etc.). This represents the presence and influence of the carnal nature which the apostle describes as the "body of death" (Romans 7:24) hanging about the soul, unless it is wholly laid off. The corpse of the victim, as in ancient times, was chained to the body of the murderer (7:24).

A poor criminal in St. Louis told the chaplain of his prison one day, that every night in his dreams he saw the body of the man whom he had slain fastened to him by ropes and dragging him down into a horrible vortex, and that he could not shake it off. So many souls are carrying themselves as weights of corruption and death, and there are no sources of defilement so terrible as those that come to us from our sinful nature.

Sometimes the touch of the dead comes from our taking back, in recollection and reflection, our former and our forgiven sins. This always contaminates the conscience. Sometimes from not wholly leaving off the old man and reckoning ourselves dead indeed, by the habit of faith. It is only as we refuse to count him our true self that we can be free from his contagion. It is the believer's privilege to hand him over to Christ, to be by Him held and slain. But if for a moment he forgets this in the wild assaults of natural impulse, and allows a fear to assert itself and intimidate him from his new vantage ground, he will become defiled and unable to hold his victory.

More frequently the touch of the dead arises from yielding to the instigations and desires of the flesh, either willfully, or under sudden or hasty temptation. Of course, such yielding is always sin, and brings contamination and condemnation; and there must be instant cleansing, or there will be a complete loss of communion and peace.

These two considerations are the most important elements in a life of victory over the flesh, and they are both emphasized again and again in the sixth chapter of Romans, which is the very manual of this teaching. "Do not let sin reign in your mortal body so that you obey its evil desires" (6:12), is the apostle's statement of the one; and, "count yourselves dead to sin" (6:11), is the equally important direction in respect to the other. If, for a moment, either of these is disobeyed, the soul will be swept by the breath of evil, and must instantly repair to the water of separation before its purity and communion can be restored. Happy indeed are they who have learned this secret of continual cleansing.

It is further implied, however, that defilement may come unconsciously from the elements of evil that are around us constantly in a sinful world. Every open vessel which had no covering bound upon it was unclean. The air was so full of contagion that in order to avoid it even the vessels had to be closed. This is intensely true in Christian life. The soul must keep its doors locked, or it shall be continually defiled. Some natures are so open to everything that comes, that they just absorb the floating particles of evil that are in the air, even as in some manufacturing cities the purest linen absorbs the coal soot from the atmosphere. Walking as we ever do through such an atmosphere, we must just live in the blood and Spirit of Christ as the very elements of our spiritual existence, even as the pebble in the running brook is kept ever shining with the freshness of the crystal stream. This was what Jesus meant when He said to His disciples: "You are already clean because of the word I have spoken to you" (John 15:3); and then added with solemn emphasis, "Remain in me, and I will remain in you" (15:4).

## SECTION IV—*The Waters of Meribah*
Numbers 20:1–11

There was yet one more provision for the wilderness life, shadowing forth the fullness of the Spirit's grace for our Christian pilgrimage. It comes in due order, in the 20th chapter of Numbers. At first it seems to be a repetition of the miracle recorded and explained in the former passage, in connection with the smiting of the rock in Horeb (Exodus 17). On careful inspection it will be found that this is essentially different, both in the facts and in the spiritual significance. There the rock was opened for the first time by the rod of the lawgiver; here, the command was, not to strike or open the rock, but simply to speak to it, and the water would instantly flow forth from the cleft already made, once for all. As we have already seen in the previous chapter, the error of Moses consisted in disobeying this simple command, and striking instead of speaking to the rock.

## THE SPIRIT'S FULLNESS

The lesson pertaining to our present theme is the significance of this water as a type of the Holy Spirit, for the deeper and fuller supply of our spiritual need in our wilderness life. We are beautifully reminded that the fountain is still open, and that the influence of the Spirit is at the call of faith whenever the exigencies of life require His special manifestation. Instead of murmuring as they did, and as we still often do in our hours of testing, it is our privilege to come to the open fountain and simply speak the word of believing prayer and trusting confidence, and the abundant grace of the unwearied and unlimited Comforter will be poured out in all its fullness whether for cleansing, for refreshing, for enduing power, for warfare or for work.

We must also bring with us the rod of the Great High Priest, claiming blessing in the name of Jesus and in reliance upon His intercession. The Holy Spirit expects us to trust Him just as fully as we trust the Lord Jesus, and to take His gifts in the spirit of confidence, praise and rejoicing. They who do will always find Him ready to "open the floodgates of heaven and pour out so much blessing that you will not have room enough for it" (Malachi 3:10).

The abundance of the Spirit's grace is implied by the overflowing waters, which came even in answer to their complaints. The Church has never proved the fullness of divine grace and blessing as God longs to manifest it and does wherever He can find a heart large enough to trust Him for His immeasurable resources.

## THE DESERT SONG

In the following chapter another incident is added in connection with the water of Meribah, which throws a good deal of light on a subject which otherwise would be obscure.

Then Israel sang this song:

"Spring up, O well!
  Sing about it,
about the well that the princes dug,
  that the nobles of the people sank—

the nobles with scepters and staffs."

Then they went from the desert to Mattanah.
(Numbers 21:17–18)

When they came to Beer on the border of Moab, the people gathered around in a circle upon the sand, while the nobles of Israel with their staves dug a cavity in the sand and began to sing around it these words in responsive chorus, "Spring up, O well!/ Sing about it,/ about the well that the princes dug,/ that the nobles of the people sank—/ the nobles with scepters and staffs." Venturing to connect this isolated passage with the previous accounts of their supply of water and the suggestive references to this subject in the Psalms and elsewhere, it seems reasonable to assume, and indeed is almost implied by the references to this water, that the stream which flowed from the original rock never ceased to follow them through the desert. It ran beneath the sands, a subterranean river, even when its course could not be traced upon the surface; and that here, having lost the visible channel, they just tapped it through the dry sand with their staves and found it still flowing beneath their feet and springing forth at the touch of their staves and the voice of their songs, with its former exuberance and abundance. If this is true, what heavenly instruction and consolation does it administer for the life of faith.

Traveling like them over the sands of life, we often lose the sensible converse and manifest presence of the Divine Spirit. But faith may ever know that our life is still hid with Christ in God, and the hidden streams are flowing unobstructed beneath our feet. All that is necessary is for us to take the pilgrim's staff which is just the promise of God, and then sing the song of faith, "Spring up, O well," and lo, the fountains shall answer to our songs, and the desert shall blossom as the rose and we shall have the new song of answered prayer to add to the praise notes of faith.

## SECTION V—*The Bronze Snake*
### Numbers 21:4–9

This remarkable type completes the symbolical figures under which God represents to them the provisions of His grace for our spiritual needs and trials in the Christian life. Our Lord Himself has recognized it in the third chapter of John as the type of Himself. It represented to them the idea of divine deliverance from the stroke of disease and death through the sting of Satan and the malignant poison of sin. Their murmuring was visited by the attacks of fiery serpents, and death again filled the camp with horror and real cause for complaints. But the sin and need of the people only furnish, as ever before, a new occasion for the resources of grace and power.

Their sufferings were typical of the trials that come to us from the stings of Satan both in the soul and the body, and the remedy unfolds the most precious principles of the Gospel of Jesus Christ.

## CHRIST OUR DELIVERER

1. The serpent of bronze was in the likeness of the fiery serpent that had stung them. So the Lord Jesus, our Deliverer, has come to us in the likeness of sinful flesh.

2. The serpent of bronze was the figure of the fiery serpent robbed of its sting. And so the Lord Jesus Christ has despoiled the tempter of his power to harm us, and nailed him to His cross as a sort of scarecrow, merely the figure of the serpent, without life or venom or power to harm. "Having disarmed the powers and authorities, he made a public spectacle of them, triumphing over them by the cross" (Colossians 2:15).

3. The lifting up of the serpent of bronze was a type of Christ's crucifixion on the cross and His uplifting as the object of faith for the tempted and suffering soul.

## LOOK AND LIVE

4. The look by which the sufferer was brought into healing contact with the symbol is naturally fitted to be the type of living faith, and is constantly referred to as a figure of that vital contact by which we receive the efficacy of Christ's life and death. Intrinsically, the laws of vision are fitted to bring the object on which we gaze as an actual image into the eye which looks upon it. While I look at the sun, the sun is in my eye. And so, while I look at Christ, Christ is in my heart by direct reflection. Looking at Medusa's head turned the gazer into stone. Looking all night on the skeletons of the dead, the greatest of modern painters came forth to transcribe the vivid vision on his imperishable canvas. Looking on the glory of God, the face of Moses shone with its reflection. Looking constantly at a scene upon the street, it becomes so fixed upon the eye, that, if we look upon the sky, we shall see it written there. Looking at the lives of the lovely or the beloved, we grow unconsciously like them. And so, looking unto Jesus, we absorb His very life and we grow into His likeness.

The bronze snake was the type of Christ as a Savior for the guilty sinner, as a Deliverer for the tempted, as a Healer for the sick. The poor lost sinner can look up to Him and find the poison withdrawn and the serpent powerless to sting. So, also, the sick and suffering body can draw from His resurrection body, by the steadfast gaze of living trust, His resurrection and renewing life. Let us take this, as well as the fountains of Meribah and the flowing streams of Beer, as a lesson for the wilderness. And, "Let us fix our eyes on Jesus, the author and perfecter of our faith" (Hebrews 12:2), so we too shall endure the cross, scorn its shame, and sit down at the right hand of the throne of God (12:2).

# CHAPTER 5

## THE TRIALS OF THE WILDERNESS

All these provisions of grace were soon needed. As they entered upon their weary round on the trackless wastes of the wilderness, they soon found the folly and misery of their wretched choice, and repented too late, that for fear of a brave and desperate conflict, they had actually brought upon themselves a life of misery unspeakably more painful and trying, and having only the prospect of deliverance in a desert grave.

### HUNGER AND THIRST
**Numbers 20:2–25**

1. The first of these trials was the hunger and thirst of the wilderness (Deuteronomy 8:3).

There was no water for the congregation. "It has no grain or figs, grapevines or pomegranates. And there is no water to drink" (Numbers 20:5), was their cry. "He humbled you, causing you to hunger" (Deuteronomy 8:3).

So, for us, the life prefigured by their failure is a sad one. The emptiness and unsatisfied longing of the worldly Christian involves more real suffering than all the sacrifices of a consecrated life. O, the hearts that are just pining for real joy, and feeding on the husks of the prodigal, and starving on the manna, even of the Lord, for lack of power to appreciate and digest it.

### BEREAVEMENT AND DEATH

2. This came soon. Miriam dies in the desert of Zin, and Aaron at length ascends Mt. Hor, is disrobed of his garments and dies in the presence of his brother and his son.

These were but the most illustrious examples of that universal doom, which one by one passed over all their millions and made the camp of Israel one long, sad funeral procession for 40 years. Moses himself, at length, became so saturated with the spirit of this constant dying, that his sorrow grew into an immortal dirge, which has become the precious heritage of the

Church in her most ancient Psalter. The 90th Psalm is the wail of Moses over the spectacle of his people as they fell one by one by his side, and were left as bleached and mournful monuments of mortality and sin upon the sands of the desert. "You turn men back to dust," was his cry,

> saying, "Return to dust, O sons of men." . . .
> You sweep men away in the sleep of death;
>   they are like the new grass of the morning—
> though in the morning it springs up new,
>   by evening it is dry and withered.
>
> We are consumed by your anger
>   and terrified by your indignation.
> You have set our iniquities before you,
>   our secret sins in the light of your presence.
> All our days pass away under your wrath;
>   we finish our years with a moan. (90:3, 5–9)

And all this is typical, too, of our experience. True, all men, both the consecrated and the unconsecrated Christian, must share the common lot of death. But sickness and death are very different things to the soul that is wholly following the Lord, and to the man or woman whose life is afflicted and often cut off in the midst of his years because of disobedience and unfaithfulness. There is such a thing, and it is a very real and solemn thing, as suffering disease and even premature death, because we have disobeyed the law of God, or refused His call to service or consecration. There is nothing more bitter or sad than to stand by the deathbed of one who knows that his years have been cut off because he has not wholly followed the Lord, even though his soul may yet be saved. This is very clearly taught in the Scriptures. "That is why many among you are weak and sick, and a number of you have fallen asleep. But if we judged ourselves, we would not come under judgment. When we are judged by the Lord, we are being disciplined so that we will not be condemned with the world" (1 Corinthians 11:30–32). "There is a sin that leads to death. I am not saying that he should pray about that" (1 John 5:16).

The death of Miriam and Aaron did not occur until the last year of their wanderings in the wilderness, and just before their entrance to the land of promise. Aaron's death on the heights of Hor, which he ascended with Moses and Eleazar in the sight of all the congregation, was in some sense a type of the death of the great Anti-type. He was disrobed of his priestly garments and lay down to die beneath the hand of God, while his son put on his robes and came forth to complete his ministry; even as the Lord Jesus in

His human life laid down His humanity on Mt. Calvary in sight of all the world, and in His risen life came forth to wear the garments of His eternal priesthood. The essential difference, of course, was that Aaron died for his own sin, and Christ for ours.

## THE NEW HIGH PRIEST

The name of Eleazar, who succeeded to Aaron's priesthood, suggests the power and glory of Christ's ascended life and intercession. It means, "God my Helper." So God has laid help on One who is mighty—our exalted Advocate with the Father, to whom all power is given in heaven and in the earth, and who is Head over all things for His Church.

## ADVERSARIES
**Numbers 20:14–21; 21:1**

3. The hostility of the tribes on the borders of the desert, especially Arad the Canaanite, and Edom, who refused permission to Israel to pass through his territory.

They are typical of the hostility of the world to the people of God—not only the Canaanite world represented by Arad, but the religious world represented by Edom, who was the kinsman of Israel. They represent what we may expect from those that stand near to us by natural, and even by ecclesiastical ties (see also Judges 11:19; Deuteronomy 2:27).

## DISCOURAGEMENT

4. The discouragements of the long and circuitous way through which they were compelled to go in consequence of the refusal of the Edomites (Deuteronomy 2:4). "They traveled from Mount Hor along the route to the Red Sea, to go around Edom. But the people grew impatient on the way" (Numbers 21:4).

So our hearts often sink under the long and seemingly endless trials of our pilgrimage. We should remember, however, that the way was not the one that God chose for them. It was their own way, and therefore it was very hard. God had called them to go by a far more direct and glorious way, and it was their refusal and disobedience that had brought upon them all these trials. The difficulties that beset our Christian life, when we are in the will of God, are always accompanied by grace sufficient not only to overcome them, but even to rejoice in them; but the trials which we bring upon ourselves by not walking in God's way crush us, simply because God has not promised us the same grace to bear them; indeed He often makes it hard, that we may understand the blessedness of obedience, and always choose His better will. We are told that He allowed Israel to suffer from the oppressions of their enemies that they might know the difference between the service of

God and the kingdoms of those countries (2 Chronicles 12:8). " 'Your wickedness will punish you;/ your backsliding will rebuke you./ Consider then and realize/ how evil and bitter it is for you/ when you forsake the LORD your God/ and have no awe of me,'/ declares the Lord,/ the LORD Almighty" (Jeremiah 2:19).

## VENOMOUS SNAKES

5. The venomous snakes, which were permitted to torment them on account of their murmurings, represent the Satanic visitations of spiritual or physical evil which come as the result of disobedience and unbelief. "The LORD sent venomous snakes among them; they bit the people and many Israelites died" (Numbers 21:6).

There is such a thing as temptation befalling the spirit through the divine permission on account of sin. The Scriptures speak of persons being delivered over to a reprobate mind (Romans 1:28), and souls that have been delivered unto Satan for the destruction of the flesh, "and his spirit saved on the day of the Lord" (1 Corinthians 5:5).

No path is so beset with temptation as the path of cowardice and disobedience. And no souls walk in such a victory over the power of the enemy as those that dare to go forward in full obedience to all the law of God and trample on the power of serpents and scorpions. The only place where we can have power over Satan, is beneath our feet. Our attitude must be constant victory and defiance, or it will be constant harassment and torment.

This terrible visitation, however, led ultimately to a more glorious manifestation of the grace of God. And so, often, the temptations of life can be overruled for spiritual discipline and final victory. So Christ refers especially to the temptations in the wilderness, as the result of sin (1 Corinthians 10:9–10), and uses their example for our warning against all evil. But at the same time He encourages us with the most gracious promises of deliverance and protection, if we abide in humble, vigilant faith and obedience (10:12–13). "We should not test the Lord, as some of them did—and were killed by snakes" (10:9). "You cannot drink the cup of the Lord and the cup of demons too" (10:21). "So, if you think you are standing firm, be careful that you don't fall! No temptation has seized you except what is common to man. And God is faithful; he will not let you be tempted beyond what you can bear. But when you are tempted, he will also provide a way out so that you can stand up under it" (10:12–13). Not to fight the enemy in our own strength, but to look to the uplifted Christ as set forth in the bronze snake, is the instant and unfailing remedy for temptation. The secret of uniform victory is ever to look immediately to Jesus, and leave the battle in His hands. It is not the way to fight, but it is the "way to escape," which mercy opens.

## BALAAM

6. The wiles of Balaam represent the next form of their wilderness trials. They are described in very full detail, from the 22nd to the 25th chapters of Numbers.

The space given to them implies the importance of the lessons intended to be conveyed for our spiritual life. While the serpents in the wilderness represent the hostility of Satan, the divinations and enchantments of Balaam on the other hand represent the wiles of Satan. When he cannot sting us to death, he will endeavor to destroy us by guile. In order to do this he frequently employs religious instrumentalities. In this case he sent for the prophet of God. Balaam seems to have represented the traditional element of ancient piety which had lingered from the patriarchal times in all eastern lands, and yet, without a continuous revelation of God, had degenerated into superstition and become mingled with the rites of heathen divination. Balaam seems to have known the true God, but to have worshiped Him by many heathen rites, and practiced the incantations which afterwards became the symbols of devil worship, which we can trace in the custom of Hinduism, and even in the charms of spiritualism.

## THE RELIGIOUS DEVIL

The devil always prefers to use a religious agency if he can. He knew that he had control of Balaam's heart, and it was his purpose, if possible, to turn to evil account his spiritual gifts. This purpose was completely thwarted by the marvelous interposition of God, as He suffered Balaam to go far enough to show his true spirit, and then controlled him and restrained him from all power to harm His chosen people or even utter a whisper against them. And, indeed, God compelled him against his will to pronounce upon them the most signal blessings, in order that He might show to us for all time that all the hate and subtlety of hell are harmless against those who walk in obedience to the will of God and enjoy the protection of His approving and overshadowing presence. Even the oppositions of the adversary will be turned into benedictions, and the things intended against us will serve "to advance the gospel" (Philippians 1:12) and the interest of our souls. God will not only defend us Himself, but will even compel the devil to vindicate us. His word to His faithful people is: "I will make those who are of the synagogue of Satan . . . come and fall down at your feet and acknowledge that I have loved you" (Revelation 3:9).

## HIS FIRST PROPHECY

The first of Balaam's prophetic utterances was pronounced from the high places of Baal, and contained a prediction of the multiplication of Israel and their isolation from other nations (Numbers 23:8–10). "I see a people who live apart/ and do not consider themselves one of the nations./ Who can count the dust of Jacob/ or number the fourth part of Israel?/ Let me die the death of the righteous,/ and may my last end be like theirs" (Numbers 23:9–10).

## SECOND PROPHECY

His second message was proclaimed from the top of Pisgah and predicted the triumphs of Israel, not only over all the assaults of their spiritual enemies, but over all their national adversaries. It described in glowing language the presence among them of their covenant God, and His gracious vindication of them even from their own errors and sins.

> God is not a man, that he should lie,
>   nor a son of man, that he should change his mind.
> Does he speak and then not act?
>   Does he promise and not fulfill?
> I have received a command to bless;
>   he has blessed, and I cannot change it.

> No misfortune is seen in Jacob,
>   no misery observed in Israel.
> The LORD their God is with them;
>   the shout of the King is among them.
> God brought them out of Egypt;
>   they have the strength of a wild ox.
> There is no sorcery against Jacob,
>   no divination against Israel.
> It will now be said of Jacob
>   and of Israel, "See what God has done!"
> The people rise like a lioness;
>   they rouse themselves like a lion
> that does not rest till he devours his prey
>   and drinks the blood of his victims.
>     (23:19–24)

## THIRD ATTEMPT

Once more the king of Moab led him up to the heights of Moab, and from the top of Peor he looked out upon the camps of Israel, lying at his feet, and cried:

How beautiful are your tents, O Jacob,
   your dwelling places, O Israel!

Like valleys they spread out,
   like gardens beside a river,
like aloes planted by the LORD,
   like cedars beside the waters.
Water will flow from their buckets;
   their seed will have abundant water.

Their king will be greater than Agag;
   their kingdom will be exalted.

God brought them out of Egypt;
   they have the strength of a wild ox.
They devour hostile nations
   and break their bones in pieces;
   with their arrows they pierce them.
Like a lion they crouch and lie down,
   like a lioness—who dares to rouse them?

May those who bless you be blessed
   and those who curse you be cursed!
    (24:5–9).

Disappointed and indignant, Balak dismissed him in furious displeasure.

## LAST MESSAGE

But Balaam was to deliver yet one more parting message, which looked out upon the more distant future, until there rose on his vision a greater than Israel, even the Star of Bethlehem and the Mighty Seed of Jacob, and the vision faded away in broken fragments of prophecies which are even yet being fulfilled in the triumph of the European nations, the sufferings of Israel, and the national convulsions of the latter days.

I see him, but not now;
   I behold him, but not near.
A star will come out of Jacob;
   a scepter will rise out of Israel.
He will crush the foreheads of Moab,
   the skulls of all the sons of Sheth. (24:17)

A ruler will come out of Jacob
and destroy the survivors of the city. (24:19)

Yet you Kenites will be destroyed
when Asshur takes you captive. (24:22)

Ships will come from the shores of Kittim;
they will subdue Asshur and Eber,
but they too will come to ruin. (24:24)

Ah, who can live when God does this? (24:23b)

## THE DAUGHTERS OF MIDIAN

7. The crowning test and most fatal of all the trials and temptations of the wilderness is set forth in the account of the seduction of the Israelites, through the allurements of the daughters of Midian in the chapter immediately succeeding the story of Balaam (Numbers 25).

"While Israel was staying in Shittim, the men began to indulge in sexual immorality with Moabite women" (Numbers 25:1).

We know that this was brought about through the counsel and influence of Balaam himself. What he could not do through divine maledictions, he at length succeeded in doing through the fascinations of the world and the flesh. He induced his master to persuade his people to invite their neighbors to some of their idolatrous festivals. And there, through the seductions of unprincipled women and the attraction of an impure idolatry, many of the Israelites were drawn into open sin and brought upon themselves the judgments of heaven, which all the wiles of the devil or hostility of their enemies could not have caused. "They were the ones who followed Balaam's advice and were the means of turning the Israelites away from the LORD in what happened at Peor, so that a plague struck the LORD's people" (31:16).

So again we read in Revelation 2:14, that "Balaam, who taught Balak to entice the Israelites to sin by eating food sacrificed to idols and by committing sexual immorality." It would seem that this double-hearted man, finding that he had lost the bribes of Balak through refusing to curse the children of God, and bitterly disappointed at losing the splendid prize, conceived the idea of securing it yet and still keeping from any open and ostensible act of disobedience. His conscience was so distracted by avarice, that he did not see he was an accessory in the crime of the Midianites and Moabites, and therefore guilty as if he had committed it himself. The Apostle Peter gives us the key to his whole character in the words, "Who loved the wages of wickedness" (2 Peter 2:15).

## THE FLESH

The character of Balaam represents the spirit of the world, as the temptation of the Midianites stands for the lusts of the flesh. So that we have here the great trinity of evil, which still opposes and seeks to destroy the people of God—the world, the flesh and the devil. The wiles of Balak in the first instance to get Balaam to curse Israel represents the Satanic element in our spiritual temptations. The spirit of Balaam prefigures the world, and the daughters of Moab and Midian are types of the flesh in its ungodly and idolatrous tendencies in every age. Against these three which constitute the very anti-God, the counterfeit of the Divine Trinity, we must ever guard, especially as we come to the most solemn crisis of life and the borders of our promised inheritance. It was just at the gates of Canaan that they confronted Israel, and for a little almost wrecked for the second time the hopes and triumphs of the chosen people.

## BALAAM'S SPIRITUAL SIGNIFICANCE

The spirit of Balaam is so remarkable, that we may well pause for a moment and gather the pointed lessons of his character for the admonition of others.

(1) We see in him a man possessing spiritual light, without moral principle.

(2) We see in him a man whose besetting sin was the love of the world, especially avarice, which the Scriptures declare to be incompatible with practical Christianity, and to be actual idolatry.

(3) We see in him a man trying to get God's permission to do wrong, after he knows the divine will; at least, trying to have God allow him to go as near the edge of evil as possible, in order to secure the coveted prize. He stands for those who desire to obtain the world without offending God, if possible, but who want the world anyhow, and are certain in the end to sacrifice everything for it.

(4) We see in him a man whom God suffered to have his own way to a certain extent even in a forbidden path, when He saw that he wanted to take this path after he knew that it was contrary to the divine will. Pressing forward in a dangerous path in the face of the drawn sword of God's displeasure, God permitted him to go and yet met him as he went with a fiery token of His displeasure, as a solemn warning to him of the dangers that he was confronting.

(5) We see in him a man permitted and even used by God to do

much good, and yet getting none of the comfort or reward of true service, but simply knowing that he was an instrument used in spite of himself for the glory of God.

(6) We see in him a man trying to hold in check a dangerous passion and thinking that he could play with it or restrain it at his will, but finding at last that it was too strong for him, and that it became his master and destroyer.

(7) We see in him a man who had many good wishes and intentions and even longed to die the death of the righteous, and yet without any purpose or power to do right, and finally perishing, both for time and eternity in the most fearful disaster enhanced by the consciousness that he had known better all the time.

(8) We see in him a man serving the devil and yet cheated of his wages because he was afraid to go as far as his master wanted him to, and yet in the end doing all the harm that the devil meant he should.

(9) We see in him a solemn warning proclaiming to all ages that we cannot "serve God and Money" (Matthew 6:24), and that sin must not be tolerated but must be wholly crucified or it shall drown us at last in destruction and perdition.

# CHAPTER 6

## THE NEW DEPARTURE

### SECTION I—*A New Race*

The first preparation for the entering of the promised land was the death of the generation that came out of Egypt, and the coming of their children as an entirely new race who had had no part in the former rebellion. This implies a deep spiritual truth, namely: there must be a crucifixion of the natural life and we must reckon ourselves dead to sin and alive unto God through Jesus Christ with a new life just as completely as if we were not the same persons who lived the former life of sin.

This deep experience of death of self is something more than the turning from a life of sin with which our conversion begins, but involves a complete repudiation, not only of the sin, but of the nature that sinned. It is afterwards more fully set forth in the crossing of the Jordan and the rite of circumcision, when they entered the land, which were all further types of the same great fact of spiritual death and resurrection.

### SECTION II—*A New Enrollment*
#### Numbers 26:1–4, 63–65

Just as explicitly as 38 years before, the whole people were again numbered, and required to declare their pedigree as in the beginning of the book. The old enumeration would not suffice. It was found that some of the tribes had decreased and some had increased. There was a total number of 601,730 men of war compared with 603,550 men of war at the former enumeration: a decrease in all of nearly 2,000.

This foreshadows in our spiritual life a new confession of Christ which we must make as we go forward to further advance in the fullness of Christ. We cannot act on our old professions or take our former estimate of ourselves. Many Christians are really living upon their youthful memories and their early professions. God blots this out altogether unless our lives have continued in victory.

If an enrollment were made of the Church of God in its present living membership, it might show a greater reduction than the second enrollment of ancient Israel. When we press forward to a higher Christian life it is a good thing to be enrolled in some way, so that we may know, and all may know, that we are committed and fully committed as men of war, ready to stand for all that we believe or claim, and to contend earnestly for our faith against all our spiritual enemies. The secret of many a failure is a lack of full and open committal; let us get our names on the roll of honor.

Bunyan describes a scene which he saw at the gates of the Palace Beautiful, where hosts of armed men were driving back all that tried to force an entrance; but the brave soldiers of the cross were putting on their panoply and marching through the fierce hosts of hell, giving and receiving terrific blows. At length, covered with blood, they forced their way through the open gates, while harps within were heard resounding with the glorious shout, "Come in! Come in! Eternal glory thou shalt win." One brave man looking on stepped up to the man with the ink horn and roll, and said: "Sir, put down my name," and then joined the brave victors in the fearful strife. Are our names down on the roll of battle at the threshold of the promised land?

In this enrollment a special provision was made for the daughters of Zelophehad to take their place along with their brethren in sharing the common inheritance, in the absence of any male representatives of their father's house. This was referred to the Lord, and the answer was promptly given that they should have an equal share in such cases. There seems to be a deep spiritual meaning in this, the more emphatic from the fact that the men of war enrolled in the ranks of Israel included only of course the males of Israel, and the women were not numbered. The provision for the daughters of Zelophehad in this direction, however, was intended to show that woman, too, has her inheritance of faith in the conquest of Canaan, and that if she cannot be a man of war she can be at least a woman of faith. Indeed, in all subsequent ages, she has been the champion of the battles of faith and the foremost in the roll of witnesses for God and truth. Christianity has owed as much to her faith and love as it has given to her in exalting her liberty and honor.

## SECTION III—*A New Leader*
### Numbers 27:12–23

The solemn message comes at last to Moses that even he must die. The spirit of his law is inexorable and since he broke it he must become a victim of its penalty. To the very borders of the Land of Promise he brings the people, but another must lead them in. There was a deep spiritual reason for this. The law made nothing perfect, but "a better hope is introduced" (Hebrews 7:19). Moses could lead no soul into sanctification or victory; He only, of whom Joshua was the type, could do this.

Therefore, in the order of the revelation of truth and grace, Moses must leave us before we possess the full inheritance. He could show it to us; he could see it himself, in the distance; from the heights of Pisgah, the law could survey the whole extent of the life of holiness, but it could not give it to us. This is not through any inherent fault of the law, for it is holy, and just, and good (Romans 7:12). "For what the law was powerless to do in that it was weakened by the sinful nature, God did by sending his own Son in the likeness of sinful man to be a sin offering. And so he condemned sin in sinful man, in order that the righteous requirements of the law might be fully met in us, who do not live according to the sinful nature but according to the Spirit" (8:3–4).

## SECTION IV—*A New Covenant*
### Numbers 28:1–8

In these chapters we have the renewal of all the ordinances respecting the sacrifices, feasts and consecrations. It would seem that even the old enactment of these would not suffice for the new life just before them, and the new race about to go forward on their great national campaign.

So as we enter on fresh advances, and especially upon the life of entire consecration which their Canaan experiences symbolize, we must enter into a new covenant; we must receive even the old gospel with new freshness, and we must take Christ anew and in all His fullness.

The first sacrifice, in this new enactment of the covenant, is the burnt offering. This seems to imply that our deeper experience must begin with that which the burnt offering so grandly expressed, our entire consecration to God.

Then we have the feasts of the Lord very fully referred to in this enumeration, implying that we must enter into the most intimate fellowship with God in the enjoyment of His love and grace if we would be strengthened and enabled to war a good warfare, and stand amid the conflicts and tests of such a life and experience.

The entire book of Deuteronomy is literally an amplification of this thought, being, as its name implies, a repetition and rehearsal of the national history and covenant in the ears of the new generation as it had been delivered 40 years before to their fathers.

The Holy Spirit has given us with great sweetness and fullness the new covenant into which He brings us when we pass from the dispensation of the law to that of grace, and from the life of the wilderness to the life hid with Christ in God in rest and victory.

> "The time is coming," declares the LORD,
>   "when I will make a new covenant
> with the house of Israel
>   and with the house of Judah.
> It will not be like the covenant
>   I made with their forefathers
> when I took them by the hand
>   to lead them out of Egypt,
> because they broke my covenant,
>   though I was a husband to them,"
>       declares the LORD.
> "This is the covenant I will make with the house of Israel
>   after that time," declares the LORD.
> "I will put my law in their minds
>   and write it on their hearts.
> I will be their God,
>   and they will be my people.
> No longer will a man teach his neighbor,
>   or a man his brother, saying, 'Know the LORD,'
> because they will all know me,
>   from the least of them to the greatest,"
>       declares the LORD.
> "For I will forgive their wickedness
>   and will remember their sins no more."
>   (Jeremiah 31:31–34)

Twice in the New Testament is this quoted and applied to believers under this dispensation to meet the possible objection that it is something purely Jewish and future. It is the new covenant into which the Holy Spirit desires to bring every Christian under the present dispensation, and under this covenant alone can we have victory over sin and the fullness of our spiritual inheritance (Hebrews 8:7–13; 10:14–17).

## SECTION V—*A New Campaign*

They do not wait until they are across the Jordan to begin hostilities against their enemies and prove their faith and courage or the power of Jehovah's promise of victory over all their enemies, but they begin at once to meet the adversaries immediately around them, and long before they cross the Jordan they have a splendid record of glorious triumphs.

## SIHON AND THE AMORITES
### Numbers 21:21–35

The first of these was their victory over Sihon the king of the Amorites, who forced the battle upon them himself by refusing to allow them to pass through his territory as the Edomites had already done, and even by openly attacking them.

The result was a decisive and glorious victory, followed soon after by the conquest of Og, king of Bashan, and the whole territory on the east side of the Jordan. Other references to this most important campaign will be found in Judges 11:19–21; Deuteronomy 2:32–33; Psalm 135:10–11; Amos 2:9.

These were no mere desert tribes, but mighty sovereigns of numerous and wealthy nations established in fortified cities of great variety and extent and almost impregnable defenses. The region over which they ruled covered the whole country east and southeast of the Jordan known as Bashan, Gilead and the country of the Amorites. Even in the present day it is a land of almost unequaled beauty, fertility and luxuriance. Modern travelers have discovered the ruins of hundreds of mighty cities, evidently as old as the time of Moses, and bearing abundant evidence to the truth of all the allusions to the strength of these fastnesses which we find in the inspired record (see Dr. Porter's *Ruined Cities of Bashan,* etc.).

This victory at once placed Israel in possession of a vast and fruitful region second only in importance to Palestine itself, and at the same time it gave them a prestige in the eyes of the surrounding nations and the Canaanites themselves, which is well described in the fears of the king of Moab in his message to Balaam: "A people has come out of Egypt; they cover the face of the land and have settled next to me" (Numbers 22:5b). And so fear had fallen upon the people because of the children of Israel.

This first campaign of Israel represents the conflicts and victories upon which we may enter the moment we consecrate ourselves fully to the Lord and even before we have passed through the deeper spiritual experiences that await us farther on. It is not necessary that we should wait for any future inheritance, but there are adversaries before us that we may rise up and immediately challenge and in the strength of God overcome at once, and subsequent victories will chiefly depend upon our spirit of prompt obedience and courage in matters that confront us now.

It need not intimidate us that these adversaries are giants like Og and Sihon. The battle is not ours, but the Lord's, and the message is the same that they received: "Do not be afraid of him, for I have handed him over to you" (21:34).

## THE MIDIANITES

### Numbers 31:1–8

The conquest of Og and Sihon was followed a little later by the destruction of the Midianites, who had seduced the people through the counsel of Balaam and who were doomed in consequence to extermination.

It is specially added that in the destruction which followed Balaam was also slain and met the retribution of the crime of which he was the chief instigator. The destruction of the Midianites has its spiritual parallel in every true and permanent Christian life. The things which have overcome us must be met and overcome by us. There is such a thing as the spirit of revenge, in a true and holy spiritual sense. Speaking to the Corinthians about the sincerity of their repentance the apostle says: "Your sorrow led you to repentance" (2 Corinthians 7:9). "See what this godly sorrow has produced in you: what earnestness, what eagerness to clear yourselves, what indignation, what alarm, what longing, what concern, what readiness to see justice done. At every point you have proved yourselves to be innocent in this matter" (7:11).

It was thus that Peter took revenge upon his headlong and impulsive nature by hanging upon his Master's cross with downward head, and laying in the dust the self-life that had once denied his Savior and Lord. And it is thus that we may be revenged upon the things in ourselves and in the world which have betrayed us in the past, but which God will permit us to meet again and slay in holy avenging.

All these enemies on the borders of Canaan were special types of our spiritual foes. The Amorites were the descendants of Lot, and thus, in a very special sense, they represented the flesh. The Midianites belonged to the same race, and were well affiliated with the daughters of Lot from whom they had descended, and the horrid lusts of Sodom and Gomorrah out of which they were born. These gigantic passions, tall of stature as Sihon and Og, and seductive as the beauty of the daughters of Midian, must be slain without mercy while we stand in victory above the ashes of our accomplished sacrifice and shout: "May I never boast except in the cross of our Lord Jesus Christ, through which the world has been crucified to me, and I to the world" (Galatians 6:14).

### SECTION VI—*The Division of the Inheritance*
### Numbers 32:1–33:6

This passage discusses the beginning of their inheritance, and directions for the division of the land among the tribes.

Even before they cross the Jordan they enjoy the foretaste of their future inheritance in some measure, and three of the tribes receive their portion on certain conditions. The tribes of Reuben and Gad, and the half tribe of Manasseh came to Moses to ask to be assigned the fertile regions that had already been subjugated on the east of the Jordan. Their request was granted somewhat reluctantly, on account of the selfish spirit which it displayed, and the danger it seemed to intimate of their withholding from their brethren their cooperation in the conflicts that still awaited them. However, on their promising to stand by the tribes until the land of Canaan should be all subdued, and simply leaving their families in the cities of their inheritance, consent was given and the conquered territory was allotted to them.

Their act is a true picture of the spirit of many Christians in becoming contented with a mere attempt at consecration and spiritual warfare and a half accomplished victory. They are willing to subdue some of the enemies on this side of Jordan, but they are content to accept an inheritance that is only on the borders of the promised land, and lies hard by the surrounding world. They do not care to go through the waters of death and enter the resurrection life, or at least, if they do, they are willing to leave their wives and little ones in the world and cross for a season of Christian work, and then come back again and enjoy the fair pastures of Bashan. God let them have their way and gave them a measure of blessing in it, but when the great conflicts of succeeding ages came the Syrian and Assyrian armies came sweeping over the eastern plains and they were the first to be overrun by the invasion and led away into captivity.

## THE OTHER TRIBES
### Numbers 33:50–56

In connection with the inheritance of Reuben, Gad and Manasseh, explicit directions are given for the division of the land among the other tribes, as soon as it should be subdued (chapter 33:50 to chapter 36).

They were particularly enjoined to see that the Canaanites were wholly exterminated, with the solemn warning that if they failed to do this they would themselves be enslaved by the former inhabitants of the land whom they might leave in their hiding places. Then the boundaries of the land were given and the arrangements prescribed for allotting it to the remaining eight and a half tribes. The tribe of Levi was to receive no inheritance, the Lord Himself being their portion.

Explicit provision was made against the intermarriage of the tribes, so that the inheritance of no family should be lost, but the title in each inheritance was made inalienable. Forty-eight cities were set apart for the use of the Levites in all the various tribes, and six cities of refuge were appointed, three on each side of the Jordan, where the fugitive manslayer could repair when pursued by the avenger.

All this will be more fully explained and applied in the book of Joshua. Meanwhile, it is sufficient generally to observe that it was all typical of the unfolding of our fuller inheritance, as the Holy Spirit opens it to our hearts and calls us to go forth to its enjoyment and possession. The apostle declares that "We have . . . received . . . the Spirit who is from God, that we may understand what God has freely given us" (1 Corinthians 2:12). "The Spirit searches all things, even the deep things of God" (2:10). And He shall take of the things of Christ and shall show them to us. Thus He is trying to unfold to the faith and hope of the longing believer the riches and glory of his unoccupied possessions and press him onward to apprehend all that for which he is apprehended of Christ.

The inheritance to which He calls us has not only its allotments adapted to each of us, but it has also its Levitical cities, with provision for consecrated service, and the divine arrangements for our love and care for a lost and sinful world, for whose rescue we are to provide and to labor as earnestly as for our spiritual enjoyment and privileges.

### SECTION VII—*Itinerary of the Journey*
### Numbers 33:1–49

A little before the close of the book of Numbers, a brief itinerary of all their journeyings in the wilderness is recorded, commencing with their departure in Egypt from Rameses and closing with their camp in Moab on the east side of Jordan.

So God is keeping a record of every human life, and these records are but sample pages from the great volume which will yet be opened as an eternal memorial of the past. It is very solemn and significant, however, that the record of those seasons of Israel's history which were spent out of communion with God is very brief, and that, as in Exodus, the centuries of their bondage are covered by a single sentence, so in Numbers the whole 38 years of their wandering in the wilderness are passed over in complete silence, coming in somewhere between the 13th and 14th verses of the 20th chapter of Numbers, and having no record elsewhere except this simple itinerary in Numbers 33.

O, what long blanks will cover whole lifetimes in the eternal annals, and what crowded pages will spread over brief hours of faithful service and suffering, when the books shall be opened.

> He liveth long who liveth well,
> All other life is short and vain;
> He liveth longest who can tell,
> Of living most for heavenly gain.

# DEUTERONOMY

# *INTRODUCTION*

## SECTION I—*Contents and Subdivisions of Deuteronomy*

The book consists of four parts:

1. An introductory address delivered by Moses on the plains of Moab, containing a recapitulation of the principal events of the history and closing with a solemn charge of obedience and faithfulness to God. This is recorded in the first four chapters, commencing with 1:6, and closing with 4:43. This might be called retrospective.

2. Then follows a long address from 4:44 to 26:19, which might be called didactic and hortatory. This consists of a summary of the principal precepts of the Law, and a collection of important statutes and laws, with respect to their national and individual life; especially when they enter the Land of Promise. This is interspersed with several brief narratives respecting a portion of their wilderness life already past.

3. Then follows a shorter address from 27:1 to 30:20, mostly prospective in its character: referring, especially, to the inscription of the Law on pillars of stone on Mounts Ebal and Gerizim, with the blessings and the curses after they should enter the land. This is followed by a solemn declaration of the punishments and recompenses which will most surely follow their disobedience or obedience to the commandments of God, and a solemn appeal to them, as a people, to choose the way to obedience and life.

4. The last section of Deuteronomy, comprising chapters 31–34, contains a brief account of the closing scenes of Moses' life, including the appointment of Joshua, provision for the reading of the Law, the song of Moses and his parting blessing upon the tribes, closing with the account of the death, burial and eulogy of the great lawgiver. Such, in brief, is the structure of this book.

## SECTION II—*Mosaic Authorship*

The question of its Mosaic authorship has already been generally referred to in our introduction to the Pentateuch. The following additional particulars may be added with reference to this special book.

1. Jewish and Christian traditions are all in favor of its Mosaic authorship.

2. The testimony of our Lord and His apostles is very strong. Some of Christ's most important quotations from the Old Testament were directly from the book of Deuteronomy. He uses the authoritative expression, "It is written," as He quotes from Deuteronomy 8:3; 6:13, 16, on two important occasions (Matthew 4:4, 7 and 10). So, again, Matthew 22:24, compared with Deuteronomy 25:5. So again, Matthew 19:7–8; Mark 10:3–4; John 5:46–47. Again in Acts, Peter quotes from this book (3:22–23); Stephen also (7:37); and Paul (Romans 10:19; 12:19; Galatians 3:10). Our Lord's citations from this book are the more conclusive from the fact that He was arguing with the Jews from the law of Moses, and had this not been one of his writings His citations would have been invalid.

3. The next argument for the Mosaic authorship of Deuteronomy is the evident antiquity of the book. Commencing with the close of the prophetic chain we can trace back allusions to it through the whole line of Hebrew testimony. Jeremiah is so full of such references that it is perfectly certain that the author of the one book was familiar with the other. So striking is this, that the critics have reversed the order and claim that Deuteronomy is based on Jeremiah. However, if we can trace it in earlier prophets this will become conclusive as to which is the original composition. We have no difficulty whatever in doing this. Many allusions to it have been found in Isaiah, of which these are samples: Isaiah 1:2, compared with Deuteronomy 32:1. Isaiah 1:10 with Deuteronomy 32:32. Isaiah 1:6 with Deuteronomy 28:27. Isaiah 27:11 with Deuteronomy 32:28. Isaiah 46:8 with Deuteronomy 32:7. Isaiah 50:1 with Deuteronomy 24:1. Isaiah 58:14 with Deuteronomy 32:13. Isaiah 59:10 with Deuteronomy 28:29. In Amos compare chapter 4:6–10 with Deuteronomy 28:15–22. Compare Amos 6:12 with Deuteronomy 29:18. Amos 9:14–15 with Deuteronomy 30:3, 5, 9. So, again, in Hosea. Compare Hosea 4:14 with Deuteronomy 23:17–18. Hosea 5:10 with Deuteronomy 19:14. Hosea 6:1 with Deuteronomy 32:39. Again, compare First Kings 8:51 with Deuteronomy 4:20. First Kings 18:40 with Deuteronomy 13:15; 17:5. Second Kings 14:6 with Deuteronomy 24:16. Second Kings 18:6 with Deuteronomy 10:20. Second Samuel 7:23 with Deuteronomy 7:8. First Samuel 2:6 with Deuteronomy 32:39. First Samuel 15:2 with Deuteronomy 25:17. First Samuel 28:3 with Deuteronomy 18:10–11. So, again, even as far back as the book of Judges, compare Judges 1:20 with Deuteronomy 1:36. Judges 2:2 with Deuteronomy 7:2. Judges 2:18 with Deuteronomy 32:36. Judges 4:14 with Deuteronomy 9:3. Judges 5:4 with Deuteronomy 33:2. Ruth 4:2–12 with Deuteronomy 25:5–10. Ruth 4:10 with Deuteronomy 25:6.

Again the language is archaic, and the phrases peculiar in many instances to the Mosaic writings. Besides, numerous allusions in the book imply an ancient date; for example, the prohibition of intercourse with the nations of Canaan, which would be unreasonable if the book were written in the time of Jeremiah. The allusion to Amalek would have been equally absurd, for Amalek had ceased to exist as a nation. The reference of 7:24 to the time when they would desire a king would have been an anachronism in the days of Jeremiah, when the kingdom had not only been introduced but was just about to pass away. Again, the directions for inscribing the blessings and curses of Mounts Ebal and Gerizim could have had no meaning after the time of Joshua. So, also, the recent memory which Moses refers to of the passage of the wilderness, as something which his hearers had themselves experienced.

4. The whole structure of the book is in harmony with the Mosaic time. The references to the wilderness, to their recent life in Egypt, to the experiences of their journey, are so direct and personal that, without the most glaring literary fraud, it cannot assume any other position for the writer than that of a contemporary with the events described.

5. It is distinctly declared to contain the addresses of Moses himself and to have been written by him (1:1; 29:1; 31:1). If this be not true then the book is a forgery and cannot be the Word of God and entitled to a place in the sacred writings of the Jews. Indeed, it is inconceivable how they could have given it this place if they had no such idea.

# GENERAL PLAN AND SCOPE OF THE BOOK

The fifth book of Moses is named in the Hebrew canon by its two initial words, contracted so as to form the word *Debharim*. The word Deuteronomy was given to it by the translators of the Septuagint. This seems to be the translation of the term *Mishneh Ha-torah*, which literally means "Iteration of the Law," a term which the Rabbins sometimes gave to this book. This name assumes that the book of Deuteronomy is a repetition of the Mosaic legislation. This, however, is hardly true; it is rather a renewing of the covenant, a sort of summary on the part of Moses, of his previous messages along with many new counsels and exhortations adapted to their immediate situation, about to enter the land of promise. This later view of the book is suggested by another title, sometimes given to it by the Rabbins, namely: "The Book of Admonitions." It is rather a book of exhortations than of historical narratives or ceremonial ordinances, and it resembles closely the later prophets, especially Jeremiah, to whom, indeed, it has often been attributed by the critics who question the Mosaic authorship of the Pentateuch.

# CHAPTER 1

## MOSES' FIRST ADDRESS ON THE PLAINS OF MOAB

### Deuteronomy 1–4:43

### RETROSPECTIVE

This address is introduced in the five opening verses of the book by a simple historical reference to the circumstances in which it was given. It was spoken on the plain of Moab "in the fortieth year, on the first day of the eleventh month" (Deuteronomy 1:3), after their victory over Sihon, king of the Amorites, and over the king of Bashan. It contains a striking little parenthesis which is more emphatic than the whole chapter (verse 2): "It takes eleven days to go from Horeb to Kadesh Barnea by the Mount Seir road." This little sentence stands in contrast with the 40 years of their wandering, and is a hint of what might have been had they promptly believed and obeyed God. Alas! many a journey in our Christian pilgrimage is made a thousandfold more sad and long by our refusing to obey the Lord.

The address proper consists of two portions; first, a recapitulation of their history up to the present time (1:6 to 3:29); and secondly, an exhortation to obedience (4:1–43).

### SECTION I—*Recapitulation*
### Deuteronomy 1–3

#### DEPARTURE FROM HOREB

1. Moses goes back to their departure from Horeb (1:6–8), and their setting out for the land of promise. "You have stayed long enough at this mountain" (1:6) is the Lord's message.

Break camp and advance into the hill country of the Amorites;

go to all the neighboring peoples in the Arabah, in the mountains, in the western foothills, in the Negev and along the coast, to the land of the Canaanites and to Lebanon, as far as the great river, the Euphrates. See, I have given you this land. Go in and take possession of the land that the LORD swore he would give to your fathers—to Abraham, Isaac and Jacob—and to their descendants after them. (1:7–8)

Here there is no long interval, no weary wilderness march even suggested; the land is right before them as God's immediate purpose for them to inherit; and back of the command stands the oath of God to their fathers. It was well that it was so, for had it not been for their sakes the promise would have been of no effect; but when they forfeited their claim, the covenant with Abraham still stood fast, and by virtue of it their children entered in. It is well for us that the covenant is not with us and the mercy of God is not for our sakes, but wholly on account of the Lord Jesus Christ, our covenant Head. "For God's gifts and his call are irrevocable" (Romans 11:29).

## ORGANIZATION OF THE CAMP

2. Moses next refers to his plan for the organization and government of the host.

The multitude had grown so vast that it was necessary that there should be a system of administration in detail. This was rendered the more necessary by what Moses pathetically refers to as their burden and their strife. Alas! it was this element of human self-will, discontent and murmuring, which caused most of his burdens and their sorrows. This, alas! is still true. It is not our troubles that burden the Master, but our strife. To meet the innumerable cases of complaint and litigation that would arise, Moses appointed judges and commanders "of thousands, of hundreds, of fifties and of tens" (Deuteronomy 1:15) and laid upon them the most solemn charges with regard to the patient and righteous administration of justice in all the minor difficulties that might arise. He reserved to himself for personal decision the cases that might prove too complicated for them. We have here a wise example of the importance of a careful, thorough organization in the work of the Church of Christ.

George Whitefield once said: "The Lord gave me as great a work as John Wesley, but he organized and I did not; the result was his became an enduring system, and mine, so far as visible and organic results were concerned, a rope of sand."

## THROUGH THE WILDERNESS

3. He next recalls their journey through the wilderness from Horeb to

Kadesh Barnea. "Then, as the LORD our God commanded us, we set out from Horeb and went toward the hill country of the Amorites through all that vast and dreadful desert that you have seen, and so we reached Kadesh Barnea" (1:19).

The remembrance still seems to cause a shudder of horror as he speaks of the great and terrible wilderness. Like them we too must pass into our inheritance through a waste and desolate region of separation from the world and crucifixion with Christ. But it need not be long. It was only 11 days' journey, and it was utterly unnecessary that they should return to it again and again and wander in it for the remaining 40 years. And so we too must pass through the earlier conflicts which meet us into a deeper rest; yet the ordeal need not be long, and certainly need not be renewed and prolonged through all the weary pilgrimage of life. He that is brave enough to pass quickly through the border land and utterly to follow the Lord will find that this is the secret of a peaceful and happy life, free from the struggles and conflicts which should be settled at the beginning. But he who is afraid utterly to die and wholly to obey will find his whole life a long and ineffectual struggle of useless misery.

## THE CRISIS

4. The crisis of their history has now come.

> Then I said to you, "You have reached the hill country of the Amorites, which the LORD our God is giving us. See, the LORD your God has given you the land. Go up and take possession of it as the LORD, the God of your fathers, told you. Do not be afraid; do not be discouraged." (1:20–21)

This represents the crisis hour in our Christian life when the soul comes face to face with the question of entire consecration and entering into the fullness of Christ's blessing. It is a moment that never will come again, and on which the issues of a lifetime hang. Happy are they who stop not to reason and compromise, but literally go up at once and possess it.

## THEIR FIRST COMPROMISE

5. They began to reason about the promise of the Lord.

> Then all of you came to me and said, "Let us send men ahead to spy out the land for us and bring back a report about the route we are to take and the towns we will come to."
> The idea seemed good to me; so I selected twelve of you, one man from each tribe. They left and went up into the hill

> country, and came to the Valley of Eshcol and explored it.
> Taking with them some of the fruit of the land, they brought it
> down to us and reported, "It is a good land that the LORD our
> God is giving us." (1:22–25)

Alas! they now made the fatal mistake of beginning to reason about that which the Lord had distinctly promised and commanded. They came to Moses and proposed that the spies should be sent up to reconnoiter the land, and bring word again concerning the country and the way by which they should go. While, on the superficial view, this looks plausible enough as a human proposition, yet as a people supernaturally led by the very hand of God, such a resort to mere human wisdom was inconsistent and dangerous. If the Lord was to lead them what need had they of man's counsels? And if the Lord had told them what the land was, how dared they question it even sufficiently to try to find it out by human wisdom? And yet, even Moses was caught in the snare, and admits in his address, "The idea seemed good to me" (1:23). He even went to God and obtained the divine permission for this arrangement. God Himself allowed it to test their faith and show the folly of leaning on human understanding and the mistake which even the best of men are sure to make when they fail to act upon the simple prin ciples of obedience and faith.

The spies were able to successfully accomplish their inspection and even to bring back with them a sample of the wonderful products of the land. And surely this ought to have been at least a pledge that the dangers were not insurmountable, if 12 men could go safely through this foreign territory.

## REBELLION

6. Their compromise was followed speedily by a bolder step of disobedience and rebellion.

> But you were unwilling to go up; you rebelled against the command of the LORD your God. You grumbled in your tents and said, "The LORD hates us; so he brought us out of Egypt to deliver us into the hands of the Amorites to destroy us. Where can we go? Our brothers have made us lose heart. They say, 'The people are stronger and taller than we are; the cities are large, with walls up to the sky. We even saw the Anakites there.' "
> (1:26–28)

They did not question the merits of the land but their cowardly hearts were afraid of the perils of the way. "Our brothers have made us lose heart. They say, 'The people are stronger and taller than we are; the cities are large, with walls up to the sky. We even saw the Anakites there' " (1:28). Discouragement soon led to darker thoughts of God, and they dared to say, "The LORD hates us; so he brought us out of Egypt to deliver us into the hands of the Amorites to destroy us" (1:27).

So, still, the unbelief of God's people does not question the excellency of His promises or the reality of divine things and of the higher possibilities of Christian life, but it questions their own ability to live such a life, and faints before the dangers and temptations of the way and the helplessness of their own weakness and sinfulness; leaving God Himself quite out of view and forgetting that He is greater than all difficulties and mightier than all our weakness.

## MOSES' APPEAL

7. Moses appeals to them with this very thought.

"Then I said to you, 'Do not be terrified; do not be afraid of them. The LORD your God, who is going before you, will fight for you' " (1:29–30), and then he reminds them of their own previous experience of His victorious power "as he did for you in Egypt, . . . and in the desert. There you saw how the LORD your God carried you, as a father carries his son, all the way you went" (1:30–31).

This is the ground of our confidence for all our spiritual victories; this is the answer to all our difficulties and all our fears; we are not sufficient for anything, but Christ is all-sufficient, and we "can do everything through him who gives [us] strength" (Philippians 4:13). When the soul sees the living Christ and His infinite resources, it has the pledge of perfect victory. They could not see God because their eyes were full of their enemies and their own insignificance.

## THEIR UNBELIEF

8. And so the crisis ends in utter unbelief and disobedience.

"In spite of this, you did not trust in the LORD your God" (1:32). This is the root of all disobedience and sin. The fall of man at first sprang from doubting God. Salvation begins with the recovery of our lost faith, as apostasy always originates in some form of faithlessness. Let us "see to it, brothers, that none of you has a sinful, unbelieving heart that turns away from the living God" (Hebrews 3:12).

## GOD'S REJECTION

9 Their unbelief is immediately followed by the divine rejection (Deuteronomy 1:34–40).

When the LORD heard what you said, he was angry and

> solemnly swore: "Not a man of this evil generation shall see the
> good land I swore to give your forefathers, except Caleb son of
> Jephunneh. He will see it, and I will give him and his descen-
> dants the land he set his feet on, because he followed the LORD
> wholeheartedly." (1:34–36)

That whole generation is refused by an angry God and consigned to an ignominious grave in the wilderness, and their little children, for whom they
pretended to be afraid, are chosen to inherit the land which they refused.
The only exceptions to this sweeping sentence of exclusion are Joshua and
Caleb, the two faithful spies, who stood alone in the dark and awful hour of
their people's revolt and pleaded with them at the risk of their lives to trust
and obey Jehovah and go up at once and possess the land. Even Moses himself intimates that his own exclusion was in some measure due to the
people's sin: "Because of you the LORD became angry with me also" (1:37).

It was their perverse spirit which provoked the meek and gentle lawgiver
and for once in his life seemed to infect even him with the spirit of their unbelief. And, as the law could show no mercy even to its author he must become a monument of its inexorable severity.

## THEIR REMORSE AND RECKLESSNESS

10. The reaction from their desperate act soon comes and leads them into
an attitude of presumption as wicked as their cowardice had been before.

> Then you replied, "We have sinned against the LORD. We will
> go up and fight, as the LORD our God commanded us." So
> every one of you put on his weapons, thinking it easy to go up
> into the hill country.
> But the LORD said to me, "Tell them, 'Do not go up and
> fight, because I will not be with you. You will be defeated by
> your enemies.' "
> So I told you, but you would not listen. You rebelled against
> the LORD's command and in your arrogance you marched up
> into the hill country. The Amorites who lived in those hills came
> out against you; they chased you like a swarm of bees and beat
> you down from Seir all the way to Hormah. You came back and
> wept before the LORD, but he paid no attention to your weeping
> and turned a deaf ear to you. (1:41–45)

As soon as they find that they have lost the inheritance through their wickedness, they go to the opposite extreme of remorse and regret, acknowledge
their sin and offer immediately to go forward. But this is only the passionate

impulse of the sorrow that works death; and even had God met them in this position they would signally have failed, and soon after proved that they did not possess any permanent element of true repentance or faith. And so He righteously refuses to allow them to go forward; they have chosen the issue and they must meet it. They soon show that their spirit is not truly chastened or penitent, by refusing to obey the warning of Moses, and rushing presumptuously forward against the enemy. They are terribly defeated and smitten by the Amorites and driven back in confusion and despair. So the willful and unbelieving heart swings from the extreme of doubt to that of daring presumption; attempts to do in its own strength what it had refused to do in the Lord's, and is met with desperate failure and disaster.

> There is a time, we know not when,
> A place, we know not where,
> That marks the destiny of men
> For glory and despair.

Let none of us trifle with God's nows; but today, while it is called today, if we will hear His voice, let us harden not our hearts (Hebrews 3:13, 15). There is a sorrow that has no healing in it; a remorse that has no repentance in it, a weeping that has no softening, sanctifying power; a grief that even God has no compassion for, because it is the cry of a willful, proud and sinful heart; as self-willed in its weeping as it was in its defiance. What infinite pathos and despair there is in the closing words: "You came back and wept before the LORD, but he paid no attention to your weeping and turned a deaf ear to you" (Deuteronomy 1:45).

## WASTED YEARS
11. The Interval spent in Kadesh became wasted years.

"And so you stayed in Kadesh many days—all the time you spent there" (1:46).

How long they remained in Kadesh after this melancholy occurrence we do not know, and the narrative reads as if it did not matter much. There are chapters in life's history that are as blank and cold as the face of an iceberg. They count for nothing in the annals of God and eternity; they are simply, bitterly and utterly vague—barren and empty as the desert wind. What a suggestive meaning there is in this sentence, "And so you stayed in Kadesh many days—all the time you spent there" (1:46). That is to say that there were just so many days and they were counted simply by the number of days, and not by any event of the slightest interest or importance. They were just passed by and that was all. They were not according to the will of God, or according to the plan of His love and ordering, or according to the useful service with which they were filled, but they were just according to the number of the days. They had 38 years to throw away, to finish the tramp of their vain and lost existence, and it seemed to be little matter where they spent them.

Oh! it is pitiful to be living a life with God above us, immortality within us and eternity before us with such an awful record of vanity; and yet, such is the life of all who live not for God. They are just filling up the time until the next chapter, the long, the sad eternity.

## THE WILDERNESS AGAIN

12. The wandering in the wilderness is even sadder.

This is, if possible, still more sad. "Then we turned back and set out toward the desert along the route to the Red Sea, as the LORD had directed me. For a long time we made our way around the hill country of Seir" (2:1).

A single verse completes the history of 3 million people for 38 years. "Then we turned back and set out toward the desert along the route to the Red Sea, as the LORD had directed me. For a long time we made our way around the hill country of Seir" (2:1). What a mournful picture; still more desolate as the speaker draws it out into days rather than years. Oh! how long and dreary they must have seemed to him in retrospect. Nearly 14,000 days of useless ineffectual wandering, and that when he himself was nearly 80 years old, and was wasting the last 38 years of his already almost finished life in this dreary land. In the 90th Psalm he has given us some conception of those scenes: "All our days pass away under your wrath;/ we finish our years with a moan" (90:9). Day by day and year by year he saw them fading before his eyes. Fathers and mothers wandered in the burning sands with their thirsty little ones, and saw one and another of their neighbors faint and sink amid the sands, gasp out their lives, and leave their bones to whiten in the desert, and they knew that soon their turn would come; for them there was no prospect but death.

Oh! how vivid a picture it is of the emptiness and failure of the Christian life which hesitates wholly to follow the Lord and to enter into the fullness of our inheritance. There will be very little history for many lives. One single verse in the book of Numbers (33:37) tells the story of most of the 40 years as we have already seen in that book. This very verse is the sole memorial, in the address of Moses, of that melancholy time from which his thoughts would gladly turn away. It is a chapter from the annals of eternity, and such awful blanks will meet many of us, it is to be feared, when we come face to face with the issues of life and the books of the judgment.

## THE NEW DEPARTURE

"Then the LORD said to me, 'You have made your way around this hill country long enough; now turn north' " (2:2–3).

13. The 38 years of wandering have about passed; and now the command comes to turn northward from the territory of Edom toward the land of promise. The last days of the wilderness are spent in passing through, for the last time, the territory of the Edomites. Their first aggressive work is now to begin. Through many adversaries they are to fight their way into their inheritance.

## THE EDOMITES

14. The Edomites are not to be attacked.

> Give the people these orders: "You are about to pass through the territory of your brothers the descendants of Esau, who live in Seir. They will be afraid of you, but be very careful. Do not provoke them to war, for I will not give you any of their land, not even enough to put your foot on. I have given Esau the hill country of Seir as his own." (Deuteronomy 2:4–5)

They are their own brethren, the race of Esau, and their territory is not to be disturbed because of the covenant with Esau. They are to deal honestly by them and pay for all which they shall require, both food and drink; even their inhospitality is not to be avenged, but they are to be treated with forbearance and justice, even as the children of God today should act in all their dealings with the world and even with those that are most unkind and selfish.

## THE MOABITES

15. The Moabites also are spared because they are the descendants of Lot, and thus distantly related to the Hebrew race.

> So we went on past our brothers the descendants of Esau, who live in Seir. We turned from the Arabah road, which comes up from Elath and Ezion Geber, and traveled along the desert road of Moab.
> Then the LORD said to me, "Do not harass the Moabites or provoke them to war, for I will not give you any part of their land. I have given Ar to the descendants of Lot as a possession." (2:8–9)

## THE YEARS OF WANDERING

16. Here the narrative pauses a moment to mark the close of the 38 years of wandering.

> Thirty-eight years passed from the time we left Kadesh Barnea until we crossed the Zered Valley. By then, that entire generation of fighting men had perished from the camp, as the LORD had sworn to them. The LORD's hand was against them until he had completely eliminated them from the camp. (2:14–15)

As they cross the brook Zered, on the borders of Moab, the last of the unbelieving generation has passed away, and Moses sets up a memorial stone, as it were, in the record, to mark the beginning of the new departure and to recognize the hand of God in the solemn and awful dissolution of a whole generation. He adds, "The LORD's hand was against them until he had completely eliminated them from the camp" (2:15). "That entire generation of fighting men had perished from the camp, as the Lord had sworn to them" (2:14). How very dreadful it is to have the hand of the Lord against us; not one of all those millions escaped. Patiently His judgment waited until the work was thoroughly finished, and every soul was sifted from among the whole population. God's purposes, both of blessing and of judgment, are as immutable as eternity. Happy is he who has that mighty Hand upon his side.

## THE AMMONITES

17.  They next pass the territory of the Ammonites.

> The LORD said to me, "Today you are to pass by the region of Moab at Ar. When you come to the Ammonites, do not harass them or provoke them to war, for I will not give you possession of any land belonging to the Ammonites. I have given it as a possession to the descendants of Lot." (2:17–19)

And they, too, share the same immunity which their brethren, the Moabites, received on account of their relationship with Israel. Some important incidents of the earlier history both of the Moabites, Ammonites and Edomites, are here interspersed, giving us an account of how these tribes had dispossessed the former inhabitants, which were of the race of the giants, and had occupied their territory.

## THEIR FIRST CAMPAIGN

18.  The first aggressive movement follows immediately after this.

> Set out now and cross the Arnon Gorge. See, I have given into your hand Sihon the Amorite, king of Heshbon, and his country. Begin to take possession of it and engage him in battle. This very

day I will begin to put the terror and fear of you on all the nations under heaven. They will hear reports of you and will
tremble and be in anguish because of you. (2:24–25)

God would not let them fight until the old generation had all passed away.
Now with a new race they enter upon their career of victory. It is not until
the old generation in our heart has died that we can fight the battles of the
Lord or claim the victories of faith. And so, immediately after the 38 years
are ended, they commence the irrepressible conflict which is to be consummated on the other side of the Jordan.

Their first antagonist is Sihon, the king of the Amorites; and he is permitted to bring upon himself the conflict which ends in his destruction. A
courteous message is sent to him asking permission to pass through the territory, and promising to respect the rights of person and property, and to
buy honorably all supplies that may be needed. Sihon met the request with a
hostile army and disputed the passage at Jahaz, but was utterly defeated, his
whole race exterminated, the spoil of his rich land confiscated, and all his
fortified cities captured and held. This was Israel's first aggressive victory,
and it must have been an unspeakable inspiration to the long discouraged
and passive tribes, as well as an acquisition of invaluable territory and exten-
sive and costly possessions.

This, as well as the subsequent victory, represents the conflicts and triumphs into which the Lord leads His people, even before they cross the Jordan in the full experience of death and resurrection life. The death of the old
generation and the advent of the new perhaps represents the new life and
birth in Christian experience, while the passage of the Jordan symbolizes the
deeper experience of death and resurrection into which the converted soul
passes afterwards, before its full inheritance of the land of promise. Israel had
many glorious experiences even on the wilderness side of the Jordan; and so
the children of God may pass through much victory and blessing even
before they enter into the full meaning of death and resurrection with
Christ. Most of their victories occur just as this conflict with Sihon occurred,
out of the obstacles met with in the ordinary course of life. It was the refusal
of Sihon to grant them a polite request which led to the possession of his entire territory. And so, the things that we call hindrances, difficulties and even
injuries are the very occasions out of which God desires to bring, if we
would only let Him, the most glorious triumphs of our experience.

## THE SECOND CAMPAIGN

19. The conflict with Og and Bashan next follows.

Next we turned and went up along the road toward Bashan,

and Og king of Bashan with his whole army marched out to meet us in battle at Edrei. The LORD said to me, "Do not be afraid of him, for I have handed him over to you with his whole army and his land. Do to him what you did to Sihon king of the Amorites, who reigned in Heshbon."

So the LORD our God also gave into our hands Og king of Bashan and all his army. We struck them down, leaving no survivors. (3:1–3)

His was a still more valuable territory than that of the Amorites, including Bashan and Gilead. He was the last of the primitive race of giants and his tremendous stature may well suggest some of the formidable adversaries which confront us in our earlier experiences. Every one of them may become a trophy as valuable and yield us an inheritance as precious, as their position was threatening.

## DIVISION OF THE NEW TERRITORY

20. Next comes the distribution of Gilead and Bashan among the two and a half tribes.

Of the land that we took over at that time, I gave the Reubenites and the Gadites the territory north of Aroer by the Arnon Gorge, including half the hill country of Gilead, together with its towns. The rest of Gilead and also all of Bashan, the kingdom of Og, I gave to the half tribe of Manasseh. (The whole region of Argob in Bashan used to be known as a land of the Rephaites. Jair, a descendant of Manasseh, took the whole region of Argob as far as the border of the Geshurites and the Maacathites; it was named after him, so that to this day Bashan is called Havvoth Jair.) And I gave Gilead to Makir. But to the Reubenites and the Gadites I gave the territory extending from Gilead down to the Arnon Gorge (the middle of the gorge being the border) and out to the Jabbok River, which is the border of the Ammonites. Its western border was the Jordan in the Arabah, from Kinnereth to the Sea of the Arabah (the Salt Sea), below the slopes of Pisgah.

I commanded you at that time: "The LORD your God has given you this land to take possession of it. But all your able-bodied men, armed for battle, must cross over ahead of your brother Israelites. However, your wives, your children and your livestock (I know you have much livestock) may stay in the towns I have given you, until the LORD gives rest to your

brothers as he has to you, and they too have taken over the land
that the LORD your God is giving them, across the Jordan. After
that, each of you may go back to the possession I have given
you." (3:12–20)

This territory was divided between Manasseh, Gad and Reuben, whose
families were to remain in the cities while their men of war crossed the Jordan and completed the conquest of Canaan with the other tribes. All this
Moses rehearsed to them just on the eve of the last great movement across
the Jordan itself.

## MOSES' DISAPPOINTMENT

21. Now comes the most tender part of all his retrospect, his own sad disappointment.

> At that time, I commanded Joshua: "You have seen with your
> own eyes all that the LORD your God has done to these two
> kings. The LORD will do the same to all the kingdoms over
> there where you are going. Do not be afraid of them; the LORD
> your God himself will fight for you."
> At that time I pleaded with the LORD: "O Sovereign LORD,
> you have begun to show to your servant your greatness and your
> strong hand. For what god is there in heaven or on earth who
> can do the deeds and mighty works you do? Let me go over and
> see the good land beyond the Jordan—that fine hill country and
> Lebanon."
> But because of you the LORD was angry with me and would
> not listen to me. "That is enough," the LORD said. "Do not
> speak to me anymore about this matter. Go up to the top of Pis-
> gah and look west and north and south and east. Look at the
> land with your own eyes, since you are not going to cross this
> Jordan. But commission Joshua, and encourage and strengthen
> him, for he will lead this people across and will cause them to in-
> herit the land that you will see." So we stayed in the valley near
> Beth Peor. (3:21–29)

His heart has been so stirred up by seeing these mighty victories of the
power of God over the enemies of Israel, that he longs to cross over with the
people, even into the land of promise itself. And he ventures to ask the Lord
once more, even if it be but to set his foot upon it and to see it; but his request is refused, as he pathetically tells them, for their sakes. His own offense

would seem to have been provoked by their sin. All that the Lord would permit him to have was the view of the land from Pisgah's top. With this he is content, and cheerfully obeys the command to prepare Joshua, his successor, for the great work which is so soon to devolve upon him and encourages him by the assurance that the same divine presence will accompany him which God has just begun to manifest through Moses. And so he pauses in the recapitulation and turns next to:

## SECTION II—*The Exhortation*
### Deuteronomy 4:1–40

### *GOD'S LAW*

1. He charges them to remember the sacredness and integrity of the divine law: "Do not add to what I command you and do not subtract from it" (4:2).

> Hear now, O Israel, the decrees and laws I am about to teach you. Follow them so that you may live and may go in and take possession of the land that the LORD, the God of your fathers, is giving you. Do not add to what I command you and do not subtract from it, but keep the commands of the LORD your God that I give you. (4:1–2)

### *GOD'S JUDGMENTS*

2. He reminds them how their own eyes have seen the judgments that have come in the past to all that have transgressed divine commandments, and how their obedience has brought them divine protection and blessing to this day. "You saw with your own eyes what the LORD did at Baal Peor. The LORD your God destroyed from among you everyone who followed the Baal of Peor, but all of you who held fast to the LORD your God are still alive today" (4:3–4).

### *THEIR HIGH CALLING*

3. He charges them as a nation to remember the distinguished honor that is put upon them in being trusted with the divine law and the direct revelation of His will, and reminds them that this is to be the glory and strength of their wisdom and their understanding in the sight of the nations.

> See, I have taught you decrees and laws as the LORD my God commanded me, so that you may follow them in the land you are entering to take possession of it. Observe them carefully, for

this will show your wisdom and understanding to the nations, who will hear about all these decrees and say, "Surely this great nation is a wise and understanding people." What other nation is so great as to have their gods near them the way the LORD our God is near us whenever we pray to him? And what other nation is so great as to have such righteous decrees and laws as this body of laws I am setting before you today? (4:5–8)

## SACRED MEMORIES

4. He specially impresses upon their hearts the remembrance of the majestic and solemn scenes amid which the law was given to them at Horeb with His living voice, and graven with His fingers on tables of stone, that they might be forever impressed upon their memory and hearts with lasting solemnity.

Remember the day you stood before the LORD your God at Horeb, when he said to me, "Assemble the people before me to hear my words so that they may learn to revere me as long as they live in the land and may teach them to their children." You came near and stood at the foot of the mountain while it blazed with fire to the very heavens, with black clouds and deep darkness. Then the LORD spoke to you out of the fire. You heard the sound of the words but saw no form; there was only a voice. He declared to you his covenant, the Ten Commandments, which he commanded you to follow and then wrote them on two stone tablets. And the LORD directed me at that time to teach you decrees and laws you are to follow in the land that you are crossing the Jordan to possess. (4:10–14)

## WARNINGS AGAINST IDOLATRY

5. Especially he warns them against the sin of idolatry, which he foresaw was to be their future national snare, and which involved a direct apostasy from their covenant, as a people, with Jehovah.

You saw no form of any kind the day the LORD spoke to you at Horeb out of the fire. Therefore watch yourselves very carefully, so that you do not become corrupt and make for yourselves an idol, an image of any shape, whether formed like a man or a woman, or like any animal on earth or any bird that flies in the air, or like any creature that moves along the ground or any fish in the waters below. And when you look up to the sky and see the sun, the moon and the stars—all the heavenly array—do not be enticed into bowing down to them and worshiping things the LORD your God has apportioned to all the nations under heaven. (4:15–19)

He reminds them in this connection that amid all the majestic manifestations of the divine presence at Sinai there was no similitude of God, on any ground whatever, to authorize them in forming unto themselves any image or likeness of His spiritual and invisible person.

## THE NATIONAL HISTORY

6. He reminds them of their previous national history, their glorious redemption from Egypt and their separation unto God as His chosen inheritance, and calls upon them by all the sacredness of their high calling to be true to their covenant with Jehovah. "But as for you, the LORD took you and brought you out of the iron-smelting furnace, out of Egypt, to be the people of his inheritance, as you now are" (4:20).

## HIS OWN EXAMPLE

7. He further impresses upon them the danger of disobedience, from his own personal example, and the judgment which has fallen even upon him because of a single offence, in excluding him from the land of promise; and he warns them that the God who has dealt thus with him will prove to them an inexorable Avenger if they presume to trifle with His sacred words, and warnings.

The LORD was angry with me because of you, and he solemnly swore that I would not cross the Jordan and enter the good land the LORD your God is giving you as your inheritance. I will die in this land; I will not cross the Jordan; but you are about to cross over and take possession of that good land. (4:21–22)

## GOD'S JUDGMENTS ON ISRAEL

8. He next warns them in the most solemn manner of the judgment which shall come upon them and their posterity if they disobey and apostatize from Jehovah.

Be careful not to forget the covenant of the LORD your God that he made with you; do not make for yourselves an idol in the form of anything the LORD your God has forbidden. For the LORD your God is a consuming fire, a jealous God.
After you have had children and grandchildren and have lived in the land a long time—if you then become corrupt and make

> any kind of idol, doing evil in the eyes of the LORD your God
> and provoking him to anger, I call heaven and earth as witnesses
> against you this day that you will quickly perish from the land
> that you are crossing the Jordan to possess. You will not live
> there long but will certainly be destroyed. The LORD will scatter
> you among the peoples, and only a few of you will survive
> among the nations to which the LORD will drive you. (4:23–27)

The words are almost a literal prophecy of the trials that have actually
come to these people.

## FUTURE RESTORATION

9. At the same time he lights up even this dark future with the gracious
promise that if, even in the lands of the enemy they shall repent and turn to
God, He will mercifully forgive and even yet restore.

> But if from there you seek the LORD your God, you will find
> him if you look for him with all your heart and with all your
> soul. When you are in distress and all these things have happened
> to you, then in later days you will return to the LORD your God
> and obey him. For the LORD your God is a merciful God; he
> will not abandon or destroy you or forget the covenant with your
> forefathers, which he confirmed to them by oath. (4:29–31)

## THE APPEAL OF LOVE

10. By the tender sanctions of love does Moses finally seek to bind them
to obedience and faithfulness, as he lingers with peculiar tenderness upon
the blessings and privileges which have been poured out upon them, the love
which has been displayed to them and the purposes of mercy which God has
in store for them if they will not hinder His gracious plan by their own
transactions and rebellion.

> Ask now about the former days, long before your time, from
> the day God created man on the earth; ask from one end of the
> heavens to the other. Has anything so great as this ever hap-
> pened, or has anything like it ever been heard of? Has any other
> people heard the voice of God speaking out of fire, as you have,
> and lived? Has any god ever tried to take for himself one nation
> out of another nation, by testings, by miraculous signs and
> wonders, by war, by a mighty hand and an outstretched arm, or
> by great and awesome deeds, like all the things the LORD your
> God did for you in Egypt before your very eyes?

You were shown these things so that you might know that the LORD is God; besides him there is no other. From heaven he made you hear his voice to discipline you. On earth he showed you his great fire, and you heard his words from out of the fire. Because he loved your forefathers and chose their descendants after them, he brought you out of Egypt by his Presence and his great strength. (4:32–37)

# CHAPTER 2

## MOSES' SECOND ADDRESS ON THE
## PLAINS OF MOAB

### Deuteronomy 4:44–26:19

## DIDACTIC AND HORTATORY

This long address consists of two principal parts: First, a solemn recapitulation of the covenant in general, which God had made with Israel, and a series of appeals and exhortations to faithfulness (chapters 5 to 11); and secondly, a series of particular statutes and judgments with reference to the details of their personal, social and national life (chapters 12 to 26).

### SECTION I—*The Covenant in General*

The decalogue is the basis of the covenant (chapter 5).

### *INTRODUCTION*
This begins at the close of the fourth chapter after a brief reference to the cities of refuge appointed on the east side of the Jordan (4:41). There is an introductory paragraph respecting the nature of the address which is to follow, which is called the law, or Torah, which Moses set before the children of Israel. And then he speaks of the testimonies, statutes and judgments which he also spoke to them: the word testimony referring to the divine attestation of the law by signs and wonders; statutes and judgments, the first referring to special commandments and the second to individual precepts. The paragraph closes with a reference to the time and place of the address in the land of Sihon, after their victory over him and Og, the king of Bashan.

## THE PARTIES OF THE COVENANT

Moses summoned all Israel and said: "Hear, O Israel, the decrees and laws I declare in your hearing today. Learn them and be sure to follow them. The LORD our God made a covenant with us at Horeb. It was not with our fathers that the LORD made this covenant, but with us, with all of us who are alive here today. The LORD spoke to you face to face out of the fire on the mountain. (At that time I stood between the LORD and you to declare to you the word of the LORD, because you were afraid of the fire and did not go up the mountain.)" (5:1–5)

Moses specially reminds them that they themselves, as individuals, are parties to this covenant. It was made not with the fathers who are buried in the wilderness, merely, but with them who were present as little children, who have been kept alive all these years and who still remember the awful scenes of Horeb and Sinai. The other party was the Lord Jehovah, whose covenant name is repeated five time in these four verses. Face to face He talked with them on the mount out of the midst of the fire, and they knew Him to be the personal and present God. Moses, too, was a party in this covenant and a witness to it, the mediator through which it was administered and who is a witness to their obligations and the divine commandments. "At that time I stood between the LORD and you to declare to you the word of the LORD, because you were afraid of the fire and did not go up the mountain" (5:5).

## THE PREFACE OF THE COVENANT

"I am the LORD your God, who brought you out of Egypt, out of the land of slavery" (5:6).

The sacred law was introduced by Jehovah with a reference to their redemption, implying very tenderly both for them and for us that the supreme ground of our obligation to God and others is His redeeming love. "I am the LORD your God, who brought you out of Egypt, out of the land of slavery" (5:6).

## THE WORDS OF THE COVENANT

This is substantially a repetition of the 10 great words of the Decalogue as previously given in the book of Exodus. There are some slight variations, chiefly in the fourth, fifth and 10th commandments. In the fourth commandment the word *keep* is substituted for *remember* in the previous record. The manservant and the maidservant are included among those that are to be protected from toil, and the obligation to rest is based not on the law of creation but on their redemption out of Egypt.

In the fifth commandment there are two additional phrases, "As the LORD your God has commanded you," and "that it may go well with you" (5:16). And in the 10th commandment the word desire is used instead of covet in reference to "your neighbor's house" (5:21), and is added to the things which are not to be coveted.

## THE TWO TABLES

The law contains two tables. The first, usually called "The precepts of piety," and the second, "The precepts of probity." The Ten Commandments have been thus admirably summed up by thoughtful minds.

(1) The object of worship. God alone revealed in His unity and supremacy.
(2) The method of worship. The avoidance of idolatry and every outward resemblance of God and the most simple and profound spirituality.
(3) The spirit of worship. Reverence toward the divine name and all by which God makes Himself known.
(4) The time of worship.

Under the second table we have

(1) The religion of the home. Fifth commandment.
(2) The religion of the temper. Sixth commandment, substantially requiring love.
(3) The religion of the body. Seventh commandment, requiring purity.
(4) The religion of the hand. Eighth commandment, requiring diligence and honesty.
(5) The religion of the tongue. Ninth commandment.
(6) The religion of the heart. Tenth commandment, requiring holy desires and motives as well as acts and words.

## THE SOLEMN CIRCUMSTANCES OF THE COVENANT

These are the commandments the LORD proclaimed in a loud voice to your whole assembly there on the mountain from out of the fire, the cloud and the deep darkness; and he added nothing more. Then he wrote them on two stone tablets and gave them to me.

When you heard the voice out of the darkness, while the mountain was ablaze with fire, all the leading men of your tribes and your elders came to me. And you said, "The LORD our God has shown us his glory and his majesty, and we have heard his voice from the fire. Today we have seen that a man can live even if God speaks with him. But now, why should we die? This great fire will consume us, and we will die if we hear the voice of the LORD our God any longer. For what mortal man has ever heard the voice of the living God speaking out of fire, as we have, and survived? Go near and listen to all that the LORD our God says. Then tell us whatever the LORD our God tells you. We will listen and obey."

The LORD heard you when you spoke to me and the LORD said to me, "I have heard what this people said to you. Everything they said was good. Oh, that their hearts would be inclined to fear me and keep all my commands always, so that it might go well with them and their children forever!

"Go, tell them to return to their tents. But you stay here with me so that I may give you all the commands, decrees and laws you are to teach them to follow in the land I am giving them to possess." (5:22–31)

The consuming fire, the overshadowing cloud, the thick darkness, the living voice of God, the graven words in the tables of stone, all these so overwhelmed the trembling multitude that they entreated Moses to stand between them and God. God was pleased with their veneration, and said, "Oh, that their hearts would be inclined to fear me and keep all my commands always, so that it may go well with them and their children forever" (5:29). All this Moses reminds them of, and then adds his own exhortation.

## MOSES' EXHORTATION

"So be careful to do what the LORD your God has commanded you; do not turn aside to the right or to the left. Walk in all the way that the LORD your God has commanded you, so that you may live and prosper and prolong your days in the land that you will possess" (Deuteronomy 5:33).

They are not only to do, but to be careful to do it; they are not only to walk, but they are not to turn aside to the right nor to the left, but to walk in all the ways of the Lord.

## THE SPIRIT OF TRUE OBEDIENCE
### Deuteronomy 6:1–25

This is described in the present chapter by two apparently opposite terms, whose happy blending constitutes the very essence of true Christian motive. The one is the fear, the other is the love of God. "That you . . . may fear the LORD your God" (6:2), and "Love the LORD your God with all your heart and with all your soul and with all your strength" (6:5). "Fear the LORD your God, serve him only and take your oaths in his name" (6:13). And the Lord commanded us to fear the Lord our God, "so that we might always prosper" (6:24).

Thus, these two opposite threads mingle all through the texture of this address. And yet they are not opposite, but one, and together they constitute the true spirit of Christian obedience.

True, however, to the spirit of the dispensation of law, there is more to fear than of love; and yet it is a fear whose foundation is love, and a love which is rooted in filial fear.

This chapter is an anticipation of the New Testament law of love and it is the basis of our Lord's own teaching in Mark 12:29. It is the first of all the commandments: "Hear, O Israel, the Lord our God, the Lord is one. Love the Lord your God with all your heart and with all your soul and with all your mind and with all your strength" (Mark 12:29–30). This is the first commandment.

Without this spirit there can be no hearty obedience. It takes the bondage out of duty and enables us to see, as is so beautifully expressed in the 24th verse of the sixth chapter, that the Lord commands us to do all these statutes "that we might always prosper" (Deuteronomy 6:24).

This beautiful sentence (6:5), expresses the very essence of the ancient law. The Jews begin their daily liturgy with it, and the fifth verse is written in the manuscripts with the first letter of the first word, and the last letter of the last word in larger characters, to emphasize this golden sentence; and to mark, as they say, in an emphatic manner for a witness, the claims of Jehovah to our life and obedience.

It is not for His own selfish pleasure, or to gratify a despotic will on His own part, that He has given us His sovereign law, but it is as the expression of that which is itself eternally right and beautiful, and it is as necessary to our welfare as it is to His glory. His object is that we ourselves may be right; so it is added in the 25th verse, "And if we are careful to obey all this law before the LORD our God, as he has commanded us, that will be our righteousness" (6:25). We ourselves shall be right, and what higher good can any being claim than to be right with God?

Of course, there is also in these words the judicial idea, so prominent in the Old Testament, of righteousness, in the sense of meeting the claims of God, and standing justified in His sight through perfect obedience. This was one design of the ancient law, to give to man the opportunity of proving whether he could and would thus meet the claim of righteousness. And Christ Himself expressed this in His answer to the young ruler, "If you want to enter life, obey the commandments" (Matthew 19:17). Of course, God knew that man in his own strength could not thus achieve righteousness, but the kindest thing that He could do was to let him find it out. Thus the law became their schoolmaster and led them to Christ.

The love side of the law must not be lost sight of amid all the severity of the ancient dispensation. In the bosom of the darkest cloud there was always a rainbow of covenant promise. While dealing with men on the principles of justice and righteousness, God was ever anticipating the tenderer revelation of His Fatherhood and grace, which was to be manifested through Jesus Christ in the gospel. And so this book of Deuteronomy especially presents the tenderest appeals of the divine heart for the love and obedience of His children. At the same time the element of fear must be added, and is still added in perfect harmony, even in spirit, with the gospel, to give additional strength to the solemn sanctions of God's holy law. This is the spirit which fears, not so much His wrath, as the loss of His favor; it has its real root in love, and so values His smile that it fears to lose it by the slightest form of disobedience.

Moses wisely foresaw the danger, that when they should have entered into their inheritance and become surrounded with prosperity and every earthly blessing, they might forget the Lord (Deuteronomy 6:10–12). Therefore, they are solemnly reminded that the Lord their God is a jealous God, and they must not slightly tempt Him or provoke His anger (6:15–16), but diligently keep His commandments (6:17), cherish them in their hearts (6:6), teach them to their children (6:7, 20), talk to them when they sit in the house, when they walk by the way, when they lie down and when they rise up; bind them for a sign upon their hand, and as frontlets between their eyes, write them upon the posts of their houses and upon their gates (6:7–8).

The original is very expressive in some of these verses. The seventh verse, which requires them to teach the law to their children, implies that they are to impress them as the incisive mark of a sharp instrument. They were to be bound upon the hand to impress the righteousness of their actions; between their eyes, signifying the direction of their thoughts and purposes; and upon their doorposts and gates as expressing the consecration of their business and their home life.

Literally following this command the Jews at a later period established the custom of carrying about their person slips of parchment with sentences of the law written upon them. These are the phylacteries referred to by Christ in the New Testament, and they retained the outward form long after they had lost the true spirit of love and obedience.

There is a beautiful sentence in the closing of this chapter which strikingly expresses the full purpose of redemption, "He brought us out from there to bring us in" (6:23). This is the story of grace both in the Old Testament and the New. God must take us out before He can bring us in; but He never takes us out without intending to give us a better incoming, and a far more blessed inheritance than anything we can lose.

## SEPARATION

The necessity of separation from the heathen nations was in order to maintain the faithful keeping of God's covenant.

> When the LORD your God brings you into the land you are entering to possess and drives out before you many nations—the Hittites, Girgashites, Amorites, Canaanites, Perizzites, Hivites, and Jebusites, seven nations larger and stronger than you—and when the LORD your God has delivered them over to you and you have defeated them, then you must destroy them totally. Make no treaty with them, and show them no mercy. Do not intermarry with them. Do not give your daughters to their sons or take their daughters for your sons, for they will turn your sons away from following me to serve other gods, and the LORD's anger will burn against you and will quickly destroy you. This is what you are to do to them: Break down their altars, smash their sacred stones, cut down their Asherah poles and burn their idols in the fire. (7:1–5)

He here proceeds to show them the indispensable necessity of their being wholly separated from the world if they are to walk in faithfulness with God. This indeed is the very purpose that He has had in "bringing them out that He might bring them in." He knew it was not possible for them to be a holy people unto Him while surrounded with all the example and influence of the idolatrous Egyptians, and so He warns them with solemnity against the danger of association with the Canaanitish nations among whom they are soon to enter. They must not think of any association with them, by covenant or intermarriage, but must utterly destroy and exterminate them, and must not fear their power but trust in the strength of the Lord, and persevere until they are utterly cast out (7:1–5, 16–26).

This is for us extremely instructive. Many Christians try to obey God without being upon the ground of obedience, which is separation from the world, and, therefore, they ignominiously fail.

God's ancient people could not stand a moment in partnership with the heathen. Their assistance was much more to be deprecated than their resistance; and so still the most formidable enemy of the Church of God is a smiling and fawning world. We must, therefore, be separated wholly from it in spirit and confession, and go outside the camp with our blessed Master, bearing His reproach. Then shall we be filled with the divine power and enabled to stand in victory and draw others to our side. The child of God can never overcome the world until he stands apart from it in protest. On its own level he will utterly fail ever to lift it to his standpoint, but from the level of the cross of Calvary he can draw all men unto his Lord, but not until he has said, "May I never boast except in the cross of our Lord Jesus Christ, through which the world has been crucified to me, and I to the world" (Galatians 6:14).

## MOTIVES TO OBEDIENCE AND FAITHFULNESS

1. God's personal love to Israel and His gracious choice of them as His people and inheritance is shown.

> For you are a people holy to the LORD your God. The LORD your God has chosen you out of all the peoples on the face of the earth to be his people, his treasured possession.
>
> The LORD did not set his affection on you and choose you because you were more numerous than other peoples, for you were the fewest of all peoples. But it was because the LORD loved you and kept the oath he swore to your forefathers that he brought you out with a mighty hand and redeemed you from the land of slavery, from the power of Pharaoh king of Egypt. Know therefore that the LORD your God is God; he is the faithful God, keeping his covenant of love to a thousand generations of those who love him and keep his commands. But
>
> > those who hate him he will repay to their face by destruction;
> > he will not be slow to repay to their face those who hate him.
>
> Therefore, take care to follow the commands, decrees and laws I give you today. (Deuteronomy 7:6–11)

The words used in verse 6 mean, literally, a people of property, that is, His own peculiar property. This is the very essence and foundation of consecration, even in the New Testament sense, as expressed in First Corinthians and First Peter: "You are not your own; you were bought at a price. Therefore honor God with your body" (1 Corinthians 6:19–20). "But you are a chosen people, a royal priesthood, a holy nation, a people belonging to God, that you may declare the praises of him who called you out of darkness into his wonderful light" (1 Peter 2:9).

The ground of God's gracious choice is declared to be His sovereign love to Israel, and also the covenant which He had made with their fathers. So He loves us not for our own sakes but for His sake and for the love of the Lord Jesus Christ in whom we are chosen and made accepted in the

Beloved. His love is not a mere caprice, but is faithful and eternal even to a thousand generations (Deuteronomy 7:9), to those that keep His commandments; and yet back of it there is a jealous and consuming displeasure which will meet unfaithfulness with judgment and recompense (7:10).

## SPECIAL BLESSINGS

2. The second motive is the promise of special blessing if they obey the Lord and keep His covenant.

The blessings are then specified.

> If you pay attention to these laws and are careful to follow them, then the LORD your God will keep his covenant of love with you, as he swore to your forefathers. He will love you and bless you and increase your numbers. He will bless the fruit of your womb, the crops of your land—your grain, new wine and oil—the calves of your herds and the lambs of your flocks in the land that he swore to your forefathers to give you. You will be blessed more than any other people; none of your young men or women will be childless, nor any of your livestock without young. The LORD will keep you free from every disease. He will not inflict on you the horrible diseases you knew in Egypt, but he will inflict them on all who hate you. (7:12–15)

## PROSPERITY

The first is temporal prosperity, including their children, their flocks, the fruit of the land, the corn, the wine, and the oil and every other blessing of a generous, national prosperity.

The word wine here properly means the ripe grapes, and is so used in various places.

## HEALTH AND HEALING

The next special blessing is health: "The LORD will keep you free from every disease. He will not inflict on you the horrible diseases you knew in Egypt, but he will inflict them on all who hate you" (7:15). This is simply a renewal of the covenant which had been made at Marah 40 years before. Lest it should be said that the covenant was only for their experience in the wilderness, the same promise is here renewed in even stronger terms for their future national life, and so, undoubtedly, intended to be permanent, and to teach, both them and us, that God is the true Source of His people's life for body as well as for soul and spirit. To apply these words, as some have done, to the plagues of Egypt, and intimate that they simply contain a promise that they should be spared those special judgments, seems extremely frivolous when it is considered that Israel never had suffered from these plagues and certainly needed no such exemption. This is the renewal of God's ancient covenant of healing, and it is still continued in the provisions of the New Testament and the gospel of our Lord Jesus Christ. But, as in ancient Israel, it is still connected with a life of separation and obedience unto God; and it is distinctly recognized here as a special chastening upon the enemies of God and His people even as still later in this book (chapter 28) it is distinctly referred to as the curse of disobedience.

## VICTORY

3. The third special blessing promised as a motive to this covenant is victory over their enemies (7:16-26).

> You must destroy all the peoples the LORD your God gives over to you. (7:16)

> The LORD your God will drive out those nations before you, little by little. You will not be allowed to eliminate them all at once, or the wild animals will multiply around you. But the LORD your God will deliver them over to you, throwing them into great confusion until they are destroyed. (7:22–23)

Not all at once should this deliverance be realized, for the Lord shall "drive out those before you little by little" (7:22), but none the less complete shall the deliverance be if they will be but faithful unto the Lord and not fear their adversaries but trust in His almighty presence and victorious power.

## PAST MERCIES

4. The next motive by which Moses encourages Israel to obedience is the recollection of God's past mercies and especially His sustaining love and power during their wanderings in the wilderness (8:1–6).

"Remember how the LORD your God led you all the way in the desert these forty years" (8:2).

Especially are they to remember the great purpose of God in all His dealings with them, namely, their moral and spiritual discipline "to test [them] in order to know what was in [their hearts], whether or not [they] would keep his commands" (8:2). Moreover, He also designed to show them the all-sufficiency of His protecting care and how fully He was able to provide for all their needs in the most trying circumstance.

"He humbled you, causing you to hunger and then feeding you with manna, which neither you nor your fathers had known, to teach you that man does not live on bread alone but on every word that comes from the mouth of the LORD" (8:3).

The fact of God's almighty care in the face of the perils and trials of the wilderness was fitted to encourage them to trust and obey Him in the most difficult situation, and to know that if they were faithful they had nothing to fear. Our Lord quotes this passage in His answer to the tempter. He applies it not only to Himself, but to man in general, teaching us thus that God is able to sustain our physical life by His word and Spirit as directly as our spiritual life, and that there are times and circumstances in which we must rise above the natural to the supernatural provisions of His grace, and live, not by our own strength, or even the original means of sustaining it, but directly by His own life. This was really what He was teaching Israel in the wilderness, and what all His children need to learn, even in their physical life, and when we learn it, it becomes a blessed incentive and inspiration to holiness, and the physical blessing is only a steppingstone to the far higher spiritual blessing.

Not only did God's care extend to their health, but even to their very raiment. "Your clothes did not wear out and your feet did not swell," (that is, through the wearing out of your sandals), "during these forty years" (8:4).

So, still, the blessing of God, while we need not expect it miraculously to clothe us, will provide for the wants of His trusting children in many gracious and providential ways, and the answers to prayer in the annals of Christian life, in supplying daily bread and clothing dependent children, are as wonderful as the story of the wilderness.

Further, they are to remember not only this blessing in the wilderness, but also the chastenings of the Lord, as an incentive to faithfulness. "That as a man disciplines his son, so the LORD your God disciplines you" (8:5). It is a good thing to remember God's chastenings. He means that we shall remember them, therefore He sometimes makes them very sharp, but He also means that we shall remember them without bitterness or sting. Therefore, He adds, "Know then in your heart that as a man disciplines his son, so the LORD your God disciplines you" (8:5).

The memory of our trials is salutary, and linked with the deepest spiritual blessings of our lives. Thus he recalls to their minds the blessings and the trials of the 40 years which they had passed together and encourages them, by the review, to faithfulness in the oft-repeated sentence: "Observe the commands of the LORD your God, walking in his ways and revering him" (8:6).

## FUTURE PROSPECTS

5. He next incites them to obedience by looking forward to the future, and reminds them of the good land into which the Lord is about to bring them in blessing (8:7–20).

The fertility and abundance of the land is described. "A land with streams and pools of water, with springs flowing in the valleys and hills; a land with wheat and barley, vines and fig trees, pomegranates, olive oil and honey; a land where bread will not be scarce and you will lack nothing; a land where the rocks are iron and you can dig copper out of the hills" (8:7–9).

All these material blessings are but types of the richer spiritual inheritance into which God brings His children now, where they still may find the fountains of grace and the depths that come both from the valleys and the hills; not only the staple blessings of our spiritual life, but also the pomegranates and the honey, and even the stern rocks yield us the iron and brass of spiritual strength.

Then they are next reminded that in the fullness of their blessings they are not to forget the bounty of the Giver and imagine that they have achieved these triumphs and blessings by their own power, but are still to recognize their dependence upon Him and "remember the LORD your God, for it is he who gives you the ability to produce wealth, and so confirms his covenant, which he swore to your forefathers" (8:18).

So, too, in our spiritual inheritance, even our highest blessings will become a curse if they ever encourage us to self-sufficiency or independence of God, or lead us to forget that "in him we live and move and have our being" (Acts 17:28), and must ever cling to Him as helplessly in our fullest blessing as in the time of our deepest depression.

## THEIR OWN UNWORTHINESS

6. The next consideration by which he urges them to a spirit of humble obedience and faithfulness is the review of their own past unworthiness and the signal mercy of God in forgiving their repeated sins, and sparing them through his own intercession for them (Deuteronomy 9:4–10:20). The special object for this review is to anticipate any thought of self-righteousness on their part.

> After the LORD your God has driven them out before you, do not say to yourself, "The LORD has brought me here to take possession of this land because of my righteousness." No it is on account of the wickedness of these nations that the LORD is going to drive them out before you. It is not because of your righteousness or your integrity that you are going in to take possession of their land; but on account of the wickedness of these nations, the LORD your God will drive them out before you, to accomplish what he swore to your fathers, to Abraham, Isaac and Jacob. Understand, then, that it is not because of your righteousness that the LORD your God is giving you this good land to

possess, for you are a stiff-necked people. (9:4–6)

And then, in order to thoroughly humble all their pride, he takes them back to the humiliating story of their provocations in the wilderness.

> Remember this and never forget how you provoked the LORD your God to anger in the desert. From the day you left Egypt until you arrived here, you have been rebellious against the LORD. At Horeb you aroused the LORD's wrath so that he was angry enough to destroy you. (9:7–8)

Then, after the account of his own separation with God on the mount, Moses reminds them of the sin which he witnessed on his return.

> Then the LORD told me, "Go down from here at once, because your people whom you brought out of Egypt have become corrupt. They have turned away quickly from what I commanded them and have made a cast idol for themselves."
>
> And the LORD said to me, "I have seen this people, and they are a stiff-necked people indeed! Let me alone, so that I may destroy them and blot out their name from under heaven. And I will make you into a nation stronger and more numerous than they."
>
> So I turned and went down from the mountain while it was ablaze with fire. And the two tablets of the covenant were in my hands. When I looked, I saw that you had sinned against the LORD your God; you had made for yourselves an idol cast in the shape of a calf. You had turned aside quickly from the way that the LORD had commanded you. So I took the two tablets and threw them out of my hands, breaking them to pieces before your eyes.
>
> Then once again I fell prostrate before the LORD for forty days and forty nights; I ate no bread and drank no water, because of all the sin you had committed, doing what was evil in the LORD's sight and so provoking him to anger. I feared the anger and wrath of the LORD, for he was angry enough with you to destroy you. But again the LORD listened to me. And the LORD was angry enough with Aaron to destroy him, but at that time I prayed for Aaron too. Also I took that sinful thing of yours, the calf you had made, and burned it in the fire. Then I crushed it and ground it to powder as fine as dust and threw the dust into a stream that flowed down the mountain. (9:12–21)

Then comes the brief glance at the scenes of their murmurings and chastisement at Taberah, Massah, Kibroth Hattaavah and finally the culminating rebellion which shut their fathers out of the land forever.

"And when the LORD sent you out from Kadesh Barnea, he said, 'Go up and take possession of the land I have given you.' But you rebelled against the command of the LORD your God. You did not trust him or obey him. You have been rebellious against the LORD ever since I have known you" (9:23–24).

Then, more fully he recalls to them his own intercession for them for 40 days and 40 nights at Sinai, and shows them that it was not their worthiness, or for their sake that they were preserved and blessed, but through the mercy and grace of God.

In the opening verse of the following chapter Moses continues the account of his intercession the second time in Horeb; referring more especially to the results of this intercession (10:1–5), namely, the giving of the tables of the law a second time, written with the finger of God, and preserved in the ark of the covenant. It would seem as though Moses thus reminded them that God had forgiven them on account of that of which the ark was a type, His new covenant with us in Christ.

For the same reason, probably, also he refers next (10:8–11) to the separation of the tribe of Levi for the service of the priesthood as a type of the intercession of the Lord Jesus, our Great High Priest. Thus from their own unworthiness, even, their thoughts were led up to the mercy of God in the new covenant of grace, which all His dealings with them are meant to teach us more fully.

## A SIGNIFICANT CHANGE

In connection with this there may be a typical meaning in the brief accounts of their journeyings introduced at this point.

"The Israelites traveled from the wells of the Jaakanites to Moserah. There Aaron died and was buried, and Eleazar his son succeeded him as priest. From there they traveled to Gudgodah and on to Jotbathah, a land with streams of waters" (10:6–7).

Some have supposed that the transition from Beeroth of the children of Jaakan, which signifies "the wells of trouble," to Jotbathah, the land of rivers of waters, which means "pleasantness," was intended to symbolize the gracious dealings of God with them. All this long review of the saddest story of all their past, namely, their wickedness and rebellion, was designed to humble them and to guard them against all thought of self-righteousness.

And so, sometimes it is well for us to remember our faults and errors and to be deeply humbled by the forbearance and mercy of God toward our unworthiness. Even sin itself is sometimes overruled, like David's and Simon Peter's, to lead to a deeper self-crucifixion and a humbler and holier walk with God.

The verses that follow are simply the application of this style of exhortation common to this class of writings. But, although so oft repeated, it is never a vain repetition, but full of tender pleading and holy sweetness. How full of the spirit of the gospel were such appeals as these:

> What does the LORD your God ask of you but to fear the LORD your God, to walk in all his ways, to love him, to serve the LORD your God with all your heart and with all your soul, and to observe the LORD's commands and decrees that I am giving you today for your own good?
>
> To the LORD your God belong the heavens, even the highest heavens, the earth and everything in it. Yet the LORD set his affection on your forefathers and loved them, and he chose you, their descendants, above all the nations, as it is today. Circumcise your hearts, therefore, and do not be stiff-necked any longer. (10:12–16)

## THE GREATNESS OF THEIR GOD

7. The next motive to which Moses appeals is the majesty and greatness of the God to whom they are bound in covenant obligation, as shown in all His glorious dealings and mighty works in their past history (10:17–11:8).

> For the LORD your God is God of gods and Lord of lords, the great God, mighty and awesome, who shows no partiality and accepts no bribes. He defends the cause of the fatherless and the widow, and loves the alien, giving him food and clothing. And you are to love those who are aliens, for you yourselves were aliens in Egypt. Fear the LORD your God and serve him. Hold fast to him and take your oaths in his name. He is your praise; he is your God, who performed for you those great and awesome wonders you saw with your own eyes. Your forefathers who went down into Egypt were seventy in all, and now the LORD your God has made you as numerous as the stars in the sky.
>
> Love the LORD your God and keep his requirements, his decrees, his laws and his commands always. Remember today that your children were not the ones who saw and experienced the discipline of the LORD your God: his majesty, his mighty hand, his outstretched arm; the signs he performed and the things he did in the heart of Egypt, both to Pharaoh king of Egypt and to his whole country; what he did to the Egyptian army, to its horses and chariots, how he overwhelmed them with the waters of the Red Sea as they were pursuing you, and how the LORD brought lasting ruin

on them. It was not your children who saw what he did for you in the desert until you arrived at this place, and what he did to Dathan and Abiram, sons of Eliab the Reubenite, when the earth opened its mouth right in the middle of all Israel and swallowed them up with their households, their tents and every living thing that belonged to them. But it was your own eyes that saw all these great things the LORD has done.

Observe therefore all the commands I am giving you today, so that you may have strength to go in and take over the land that you are crossing the Jordan to possess. (10:17–11:8)

It is well for us also to realize the majesty of our King, and to transfer all this glory to the head of Jesus of Nazareth, our beloved Lord. It is well for us at times to ascend the transfiguration mount with Him, and behold His majesty, or lie prostrate, with John, at His feet, and hear Him say, "I am the First and the Last" (Revelation 1:17), or amid all the majesty and splendor of His throne to listen to the gentle whisper which assures us, "It is I. Don't be afraid" (Matthew 14:27).

## THE BALANCE OF HOPE AND FEAR

8. The final motive presented for their obedience is the mingled light and shadow of promise and warning, hope and fear, the blessing and curse (Deuteronomy 11:26–29). It is summed up in the closing words of this chapter.

See, I am setting before you today a blessing and a curse—the blessing if you obey the commands of the LORD your God that I am giving you today; the curse if you disobey the commands of the LORD your God and turn from the way that I command you today by following other gods, which you have not known. When the LORD your God has brought you into the land you are entering to possess, you are to proclaim on Mount Gerizim the blessings, and on Mount Ebal the curses. (11:26–29)

## SECTION II—*Particular Statutes and Judgments with Reference to Details of Religious, Civil, and Social Life*
### Deuteronomy 2̶4̶–26
### 12

### A. Religious

## IDOLATRY DESTROYED

1. The shrines of heathen idolatry were to be destroyed.

"Destroy completely all the places on the high mountains and on the hills and under every spreading tree where the nations you are dispossessing worship their gods. Break down their altars, smash their sacred stones and burn their Asherah poles in the fire; cut down the idols of their gods and wipe out their names from those places" (12:2–3).

These would be incitements to them to follow the customs of the heathen, and every link of association must be removed.

## THE PLACE OF WORSHIP

2. They were to worship Jehovah in the place which He Himself should choose.

> But you are to seek the place the LORD your God will choose from among all your tribes to put his Name there for his dwelling. To that place you must go; there bring your burnt offerings and sacrifices, your tithes and special gifts, what you have vowed to give and your freewill offerings, and the firstborn of your herds and flocks. There, in the presence of the LORD your God, you and your families shall eat and shall rejoice in everything you have put your hand to, because the LORD your God has blessed you. (12:5–7)

Not in every place were they, at their own capricious will, to worship after their own pleasure, but in the one place which God would choose, thus preparing their minds for the New Testament revelation of Jesus Christ, as the only way of access to the Father, and the limitations of prayer, according to Jesus' revealed will and way of approach.

Still, we too must be led of the Lord to the place that He should choose for the consecration and service of our life.

## BLOOD PROHIBITED

3. They were at liberty to eat freely of the flesh of all clean animals, but they must sacredly remember the law prohibiting the use of blood.

> Nevertheless, you may slaughter your animals in any of your towns and eat as much of the meat as you want, as if it were gazelle or deer, according to the blessing the LORD your God gives you. Both the ceremonially unclean and clean may eat it. But you must not eat the blood; pour it out on the ground like water. (12.15–16)

## THE TITHES

4. There is a beautiful provision for their eating their own tithes—corn,

wine, oil and the firstlings of their flocks—before the Lord in the place that He should choose; thus transforming their very sacrifices into feasts of joy and holy gladness.

> You must not eat in your own towns the tithe of your grain and new wine and oil, or the firstborn of your herds and flocks, or whatever you have vowed to give, or your freewill offerings or special gifts. Instead, you are to eat them in the presence of the LORD your God at the place the LORD your God will choose— you, your sons and daughters, your menservants and maidservants, and the Levites from your towns—and you are to rejoice before the LORD your God in everything you put your hand to. (12:17–18)

This sheds a lovely light on the principle of sacrifice and consecration, teaching us that it is meant to be to us a joy as well as service for God and others. At the same time they were by no means to forget the Levite in the sacrifices, and the principle of love was to be thus the handmaid of joy.

## HEATHEN CUSTOMS

5. They were carefully to avoid all the customs of the heathen.

> And after they have been destroyed before you, be careful not to be ensnared by inquiring about their gods. . . . You must not worship the LORD your God in their way, because in worshiping their gods, they do all kinds of detestable things the LORD hates. (12:30–31)

It is possible that even after we have protested against the sin of another we may ourselves imitate it.

## FALSE PROPHETS

6. Still more stringently to guard against these dangers, all false prophets and enticers to idolatry were to be put to death (13). Three such cases are supposed. The first is that of a worker of signs and wonders, or a false prophet, who should entice them to idolatry and appeal, perhaps, to his signs and wonders (13:1–5). He was to be put to death.

The second is the case of a near relative; a brother, a son, a daughter, a wife, a friend, who should entice them to idolatry. The command was: "Do not yield to him or listen to him. Show him no pity. Do not spare him or shield him. You must certainly put him to death. Your hand must be the first in putting him to death, and then the hands of all the people. Stone him to death, because he tried to turn you away from the LORD your God" (13:8–10).

What a solemn spiritual lesson this is, for us to resist, at any cost, the enticements of those that we love the best to lead us from God. While we may not now literally put the tempter to death, we are to slay without mercy the affections that would lead us astray, and cut off the tie that would thus ensnare us.

The third case is the case of a city among them that should be led into idolatry.

In this case they were to destroy the inhabitants with the sword, and burn with fire every particle of the spoil, and thus solemnly and utterly exterminate the very roots of idolatry from among them (13:12–18).

## PERSONAL DEFILEMENT

7. They were to avoid all personal defilement.

First, in regard to their bodies, by imitating the customs of mourning in heathen nations, the mutilating of their flesh, the shaving of their eyebrows.

> You are the children of the LORD your God. Do not cut your-selves or shave the front of your heads for the dead, for you are a holy people to the LORD your God. Out of all the peoples on the face of the earth, the LORD has chosen you to be his treasured possession. (14:1–2)

Compare Leviticus 19:28; Jeremiah 16:6; 18:36; Ezekiel 7:18; 27:31.

Secondly, this is to apply to their food.

They are not to eat any unclean animals. The same distinctions already given in Leviticus are here repeated. This, as already shown, was intended as an object lesson to lead up to the higher conception of moral and spiritual right and wrong.

There is a very striking prohibition at the close of these injunctions. "Do not cook a young goat in its mother's milk" (Deuteronomy 14:21).

There seems to be something here suggesting the utmost delicacy of feeling, teaching us that there are certain things that are unnatural, and which are to be avoided from a fine instinct of spiritual sensitiveness. It could not harm either the kid or the mother, but it seemed a little hard, and apparently suggests the cruel and painful separation between the little victim and its dam.

## THEIR OFFERINGS

8. The system of tithes was to be faithfully observed.

They were to be presented either in kind, or by commutation to be paid for in money. The principle of the tithes was that God was to be recognized as the owner of all their possessions, and the offering was given as a pledge of the whole. But, even the presenting of this to God was to be accompanied with rejoicings. It was not to be a task, but a feast, and the givers themselves partakers of the feast when their offering was presented. The first two years' tithes were given for the support of the ordinances of the Lord. Every third year the tithe was devoted to the poor, the stranger and the Levite. The New Testament law of giving is not lower, but higher. We are to count all as the Lord's and give abundantly, as He has prospered us, and to give systematically for the support of His cause, and the relief of His suffering children.

## THE YEAR OF RELEASE
**Deuteronomy 15:1–11**
"At the end of every seven years you must cancel debts" (15:1).

9. Every seventh year was to be sabbatic. The land was to rest from cultivation; debts were to be suspended for a whole year in the case of their own brethren, but in the case of aliens, they might exact payment. They were to be especially ready to lend unto their poor brethren, and must not allow the approach of the year of release to limit their generosity in this respect, or tempt them to say, "The year for canceling debts is near" (15:9). They were especially to remember the poor and have them in their midst, and open their hands wide unto them, nor be grieved when they had thus helped them, "because of this the LORD your God will bless you in all your work and in everything you put your hand to" (15:10).

## THE RELEASE OF SLAVES
**Deuteronomy 15:12–18**
10. Every slave was to be set free at the end of seven years without respect to the ordinary year of release; no matter at what time his service began, the seventh year brought his freedom; and he was to be dismissed and started in his new life with liberal supplies for all his needs.

"And when you release him, do not send him away empty-handed. Supply him liberally from your flock, your threshing floor and your winepress. Give to him as the LORD your God has blessed you" (15:13–14).

One exception was made to this rule if the servant did not want to be released, namely, to thrust an awl through his ear into the door, and master and dedicate himself to perpetual servitude. Then the beautiful custom formerly referred to in Exodus 21:1–6, was to be performed as the ceremony that sealed this voluntary contract: "Then take an awl and push it through his ear lobe into the door, and he will become your servant for life. Do the same for your maidservant" (15:17).

## THE FIRSTLINGS OF THEIR FLOCKS
**Deuteronomy 15:19–23**

11. All the firstborn of animals, they are reminded again, are to be the Lord's. "Do not put the firstborn of your oxen to work, and do not shear the firstborn of your sheep" (15:19). It was to be sacredly the Lord's, sacrificed unto Jehovah, and eaten in the sacrificial meal in token of the mutual fellowship of God and the worship in the blessed service of consecration. If there should be any blemish in it, it must not be sacrificed to the Lord, but might be eaten in their own homes. The first fruits, in this case, were intended to recognize all the rest of their flocks as the property of the Lord.

## THE YEARLY FEASTS

12. The three great feasts which required the presence of the whole people at the sanctuary are here re-enacted, namely, the Passover, Pentecost and Tabernacles. The Feast of Trumpets and the Day of Atonement were not referred to here, because they did not require the assembling of all the people. There is no special difference between the requirements here given and the previous enactments for these festivals. We have already seen that these three feasts specially symbolized the three great events of the Christian Dispensation, namely, the sacrificial death of Christ, the descent of the Holy Spirit and the Second Coming of our Lord, introducing the age of glory and blessedness. It is fitting that this beautiful picture of the gospel age should close this section with respect to the religious laws and institutions of the Mosaic age.

## B. Civil and Social Statutes

## THE APPOINTMENT OF JUDGES AND OFFICERS

1. Judges were to be appointed from each tribe. "Appoint judges and officials for each of your tribes in every town the LORD your God is giving you, and they shall judge the people fairly" (16:18).

Two classes of officers are here provided, judges and officers, or secretaries, who would be the lawyers and clerks of the courts. God is author of civil government and requires the most impartial righteousness and uprightness on the part of all who administer justice. Some of the highest examples of Christian character, even in modern times, have been found among this class, and when this great office is perverted the fountains of public righteousness are defiled, and the foundations of civil society in danger.

## TO GUARD THE CLAIMS OF GOD

2. The highest exercise of public justice is to guard the claims of religion,

and to punish disloyalty to the Supreme Judge, God Himself.

Therefore, the very first statute in their civil code had reference to idolatry. It was never intended that human government should be detached from religion, but distinctly recognize it as its first concern; not in the sense of controlling the religious life of the people, but of requiring fidelity to the religious laws already established by the Lord Himself, and punishing treason against Jehovah in the form of idolatry. Therefore, in verses 21 and 22, in connection with the appointment of judges, it is required that no asherah, or idol, nor any pillar, such as that associated with idolatry, should be set up near the altar of the Lord.

In connection also with the judicial office, it was required that they should guard against any perversion of the divine worship by the offering of a blemished sacrifice. "Do not sacrifice to the LORD your God an ox or a sheep that has any defect or flaw in it, for that would be detestable to him" (17:1).

## TO PUNISH IDOLATRY
**Deuteronomy 17:2–7**

3. The punishment of idolatry was to be faithfully executed.

The trial was to be justly administered, and not less than two or three witnesses required, and the hands of these witnesses were to be the first that should be laid upon him to inflict the punishment of death.

## A COURT OF APPEAL

4. A supreme court seems to be provided for.

> If cases come before your courts that are too difficult for you to judge—whether bloodshed, lawsuits or assaults—take them to the place the LORD your God will choose. Go to the priests, who are Levites, and to the judge who is in office at that time. Inquire of them and they will give you the verdict. You must act according to the decisions they give you at the place the LORD will choose. Be careful to do everything they direct you to do. (17:8–10)

In cases where the local judge was not able to decide, the matter was to be referred, in this case, to the court at the sanctuary, consisting of the priests and the judge presiding there. The sentence of this court was to be final, anyone replying against it being regarded as acting in defiance of the authority of God Himself.

## PROVISION FOR THE KINGLY OFFICE
**Deuteronomy 17:14–20**

5. There is here an anticipation of what actually occurred in the time of

Samuel. While the choice of the king is recognized even here as their will, rather than the Lord's, yet it is provided for on condition that they shall choose one whom the Lord shall choose, and that he shall be one of their brethren, and in no case a foreigner.

Then several important rules are laid down for the government of the king, which it would have been well for Israel if their rulers had always obeyed. He must not multiply horses or wives, or treasures of silver and gold, and he must keep a copy of the law of the Lord, and faithfully keep its commandments as the condition of personal blessing and national prosperity.

The spirit of a true king is beautifully expressed by the closing verse, requiring, on his part, that humility which is always the accompaniment of true greatness, and that righteousness on the part of himself and his children which ever afterwards brought blessing to Israel, as in the reigns of David, Jehoshaphat and Josiah, while the absence of humility ever involved them in disaster and national judgment.

## CARE FOR THE PRIESTHOOD

6. In connection with the judicial office, the protection of the Levite, the granting of their rights and their support by the people is provided for. They had no inheritance in Israel, but they were to receive the sacrifices of the people and the tithes, and they were to be always welcome whenever they should come among the people from any quarter of the land, the object of a common hospitality, and the Lord's own charge upon the bounty and beneficence of His people.

## FALSE AND TRUE PROPHETS

Deuteronomy 18:9–22

7. The most stringent laws were to be executed against false prophets and all forms of superstition.

The worship of Moloch is first forbidden (18:10). (Editor's Note: The terms from Deuteronomy 18:10–12 discussed in the following are a combination of KJV words and those of Simpson's. Most of the definitions Simpson gives are clarified by the NIV.) Divination, which is more fully described in Ezekiel 21:21, was the observing of times, referring to augury or sorcery, and was common among the Romans and other nations. Enchantments referred to the arts of magic and witchcraft which were practiced through nostrums and unlawful arts. A dreamer seems to refer to the custom of opening certain knots of different colors of threads connected with certain incantations. A consulter with familiar spirits is identical with modern clairvoyance and the ancient oracles of Apollo. A wizard literally means a wise one, one that pretended to occult science and arts not commonly known. A necromancer means, literally, one dealing with the dead, those who profess to call up the dead, and is thus identical with modern spiritualism. All these things were an abomination to the Lord, as well as forms of devil worship. In contrast with all these, Moses utters the solemn prediction of the coming of the true Prophet, and the purity and authority of His divine teachings.

> The LORD your God will raise up for you a prophet like me from among your own brothers. You must listen to him. For this is what you asked of the LORD your God at Horeb on the day of the assembly when you said, "Let us not hear the voice of the LORD our God nor see this great fire anymore, or we will die."
>
> The LORD said to me: "What they say is good. I will raise up for them a prophet like you from among their brothers; I will put my words in his mouth, and he will tell them everything I command him. If anyone does not listen to my words that the prophet speaks in my name, I myself will call him to account." (Deuteronomy 18:15–19)

Any false prophet who should presume to speak that which the Lord had not spoken should be punished with death; and a sufficient test was given by which they might distinguish the false from the true.

There never was an age when these solemn touchstones of truth and warning against error were more practical and timely than our own.

## CITIES OF REFUGE
### Deuteronomy 19:1–13

> This is why I command you to set aside for yourselves three cities.
>
> If the LORD your God enlarges your territory, as he promised on oath to your forefathers, and gives you the whole land he promised them, because you carefully follow all these laws I command you today—to love the LORD your God and to walk always in his ways—then you are to set aside three more cities. Do this so that innocent blood will not be shed in your land, which the LORD your God is giving you as your inheritance, and so that you will not be guilty of bloodshed. (19:7–10)

8. This section provides for the three cities of refuge which were to be set apart on the west side of the Jordan. The law for those on the east of the Jordan had been enunciated (4:41). These were to be in the midst of the land. Provision is here specially made for the roads leading to these cities.

Provision was also made for three additional cities of refuge, when the land should be further enlarged to the utmost limits of the ancient covenant promise.

The purpose of these cities was not to protect a willful murderer, but to prevent the shedding of innocent blood. In the case of the willful murderer, just retribution was to be inflicted. While this was the foreshadowing of the gospel, it was also a wise and humane judicial provision, preventing private revenge and yet guarding, by the most careful sanctions, the sacredness of human life.

## PROTECTION OF LANDMARKS AND THE
## RIGHTS OF PROPERTY

"Do not move your neighbor's boundary stone set up by your predecessors in the inheritance you receive in the land the LORD your God is giving you to possess" (19:14).

9. Much is said in other portions of the Scriptures about the sacred regard that should be paid to ancient landmarks (Job 34:2; Proverbs 22:28; 23:10; Hosea 5:10).

The object of this was not only to protect individual rights, but to emphasize the immutable and inalienable title by which the inheritance of every Israelite was secured to him, according to the original apportionment of the land.

Even so God has guarded our spiritual inheritance, and it would be well if Christians as firmly held to all their redemption rights, and clung to the landmarks of primitive Christianity.

## RULES OF EVIDENCE AGAINST ACCUSED PERSONS

10. It was required that no person should be convicted of any crime on the testimony of a single witness, and the punishment of bearing false witness was that the false accuser should be punished with the same punishment that he had sought to have inflicted upon his neighbor. Thus all malice and slander were guarded against and the utmost candor required in all matters of litigation.

## RULES OF WAR

11. Many humane and merciful statutes were appointed for the government of military affairs. Every war was to be regarded as the Lord's battle, and the Lord as their Commander. Therefore, they were to march forth without doubt or fear, but to be assured of victory through His presence and power. Certain exemptions were to be made from military service: a man who had built a new house and not dedicated it, a man who had planted a vineyard, and not eaten its fruit, a man that had betrothed a wife, and had

not taken her, and whosoever was afraid and fainthearted, lest he should discourage his comrades by his timidity.

Rules were also laid down for dealing with their enemies. The city which submitted to them was to be spared and to become tributary; and that which resisted was to be captured, the men smitten and the women and children and spoil retained by the conquerors. An exception was to be made always in the case of the nations of Canaan, who were to be wholly exterminated (Deuteronomy 18:16–18).

Provision was also made for sparing the fruit trees around the cities that they might besiege, and keeping the track of war as far as possible from the desolation which usually follows the march of human armies.

## PROVISION FOR VINDICATION

12. The case supposed is that of a murder committed by some unknown person. The law provided for certain ceremonies by which the elders of the city where the victim was found might publicly protest against the crime, and be exonerated, by saying, "Our hands did not shed this blood, nor did our eyes see it done. Accept this atonement for your people Israel, whom you have redeemed, O LORD, and do not hold your people guilty of the blood of an innocent man" (21:7–8). Thus God provided against even all suspicion of guilt, and showed the sacredness with which He regarded human life.

This was accompanied by a beautiful ceremony, in which the elders of the city were to slay a heifer in the open valley, and wash their hands over her. It must have been in allusion to this that Pilate washed his hands over the Savior's false condemnation and vainly sought to vindicate himself of the crime, and the Israelites, unlike the elders in this picture, assumed the awful guilt.

## PROTECTION OF FEMALE HONOR

**Deuteronomy 21:10–14**

13. The Mosaic law had a most beautiful provision for guarding the sanctity of woman's honor. This is so charming that we quote the entire passage:

> When you go to war against your enemies and the LORD your God delivers them into your hands and you take captives, if you notice among the captives a beautiful woman and are attracted to her, you may take her as your wife. Bring her into your home and have her shave her head, trim her nails and put aside the clothes she was wearing when captured. After she has lived in your house and mourned her father and mother for a full month,

then you may go to her and be her husband and she shall be your wife. If you are not pleased with her, let her go wherever she wishes. You must not sell her or treat her as a slave, since you have dishonored her. (21:10–14)

The observance of this law by other nations would have spared the world the most cruel and revolting horrors of the history of war.

In this case a beautiful captive has fallen into the hands of a soldier. His heart is smitten with her fair face, but he is not allowed to take the slightest advantage of her helplessness, but is obliged to treat her with the utmost respect and tenderness. He may bring her to his home, but for a whole month he must leave her at liberty to fulfill the days of mourning, and then, after his kindness and respect have won her confidence, he may take her for his wife, but in honorable marriage.

Some spiritual expositors have seen in this picture Christ's love in dealing with His own chosen bride, the Church. She is a conquered captive, like this foreign maiden, but He gently deals with her and wins her confidence by His tenderness and love. The shaving of her hair and the cutting of her nails is a symbol of the putting off of the natural life, and the carnal robes of self and sin, and then she is received into the deeper intimacy and fellowship of His love.

## MITIGATIONS OF THE EVILS OF POLYGAMY

14. Even under the imperfect system of plural marriages the law made the best possible provision against the wrongs that might result from the partiality on the part of a husband to a favored wife. If the firstborn son is the child of the less favored woman he must, by all means, inherit the firstborn's right, notwithstanding the prejudices or preferences of the father.

## PUNISHMENT OF FILIAL DISOBEDIENCE

15. A stern and terrible retribution was provided for a son who presumptuously dared to disobey a parent's voice, and gave up his life to wickedness and sensuality. In this case, the rebellious child was to be stoned to death in the presence of all the men of the city as an awful example. "You must purge the evil from among you. All Israel will hear of it and be afraid" (21:21). Thus solemnly did the Old Testament emphasize the necessity of parental discipline and filial obedience as the very groundwork of human society.

## THE ACCURSED TREE

If a man guilty of a capital offense is put to death and his body

is hung on a tree, you must not leave his body on the tree overnight. Be sure to bury him that same day because anyone who is
hung on a tree is under God's curse. You must not desecrate the
land the LORD your God is giving you as an inheritance.
(21:22–23)

16. This subordinate provision of the Hebrew code for the taking down
of the body of a criminal after he had been publicly hanged, contains the
touching and far-reaching foretokening of the cross of Calvary. It was in reference to this that Peter said of the Lord Jesus, "whom you had killed by
hanging him on a tree" (Acts 5:30). It was on this that the same apostle
wrote, "He himself bore our sins in his body on the tree" (1 Peter 2:24). And
it was of this that Paul said, "Christ redeemed us from the curse of the law
by becoming a curse for us, for it is written: 'Cursed is everyone who is hung
on a tree' " (Galatians 3:13–14). So that, even in this little wayside line, we
see the whole gospel reflected.

## LAWS CONCERNING LOST PROPERTY

17. The finder of lost property was to deal honestly by his neighbor, restoring it to the owner, if known, and if not, keeping it carefully until he
came to seek it, and showing a kind and neighborly spirit in relieving even
the suffering brute which belonged to his neighbor, or rather, his brother.
The term used throughout this passage, even regarding one whom they
know not, is a tender one, which implies the beautiful principle of the
brotherhood of men, especially of Christians.

## RULES FOR THE SEXES

"A woman must not wear men's clothing, nor a man wear women's clothing, for the LORD your God detests anyone who does this" (Deuteronomy
22:5).

18. The interchange of dress, on the part of men and women, and anything which could confound the natural difference between the sexes, was
sacredly prohibited because of its unnaturalness, and its certain tendency
towards vice.

## THE BIRD'S NEST

"If you come across a bird's nest beside the road, either in a tree or on the
ground, and the mother is sitting on the young or on the eggs, do not take
the mother with the young" (22:6).

19. This is but a little incident, but it tells the story of the heart of God.
How gentle is the love of that Creator who will not allow the little birdlings
to be left without their dam in their wayside nest, to gratify the selfishness or

cruelty of man.

## RESPONSIBILITY FOR THE PROTECTION OF LIFE

"When you build a new house, make a parapet around your roof so that you may not bring the guilt of bloodshed on your house if someone falls from the roof" (22:8).

20. Even in the building of a house they were to take proper care lest human life should be endangered by the absence of a battlement, on that flat roof, where they often slept at night. We see here the first trace of building laws which have since become so necessary in our crowded cities.

## LAWS AGAINST UNNATURAL THINGS

21. They were not to confound their husbandry with several kinds of seeds; to plow with an ox and an ass together; to wear a hybrid garment, or even a slovenly tunic without proper fringe and tassels. Thus, God provided for even neatness and taste in the dress of His ancient people, and also, at the same time, combined it with simplicity.

## THE TREATMENT OF WOMEN

22. This section provides against all injustice, unworthy suspicion or violence against the honor and person of women.

First, in reference to a wife unjustly or justly suspected of unfaithfulness (22:13–21). Secondly, in reference to violence against a married woman (22:22). Thirdly, against a betrothed maiden. Fourthly, against a maiden not betrothed. In the latter case, if she has been wronged, he must make her his wife and pay a heavy fine for his crime. In the case of a similar transaction against the betrothed woman, or a wife, he is to be put to death. And, if she has been willfully guilty, her punishment is to be equally severe. Finally, the most revolting crime of incest is provided against (22:30), in the form which created such scandal, and occasioned such severe rebuke in First Corinthians 5:1–13.

## LAWS REGARDING SEPARATION

23. Six classes of person were excluded from the congregation of the Lord; namely, persons mutilated in such a way as to degrade their physical manhood, persons born under the ban of shame, Ammonites, Moabites, Edomites and Egyptians. The latter might not enter the congregation themselves, but in the third generation their children might be admitted.

## LAWS RESPECTING PERSONAL CLEANLINESS

24. They were required to respect their own bodies, and act with highest regard to their manhood and personal purity, because the Lord was witness

of every private and secret act, and personal uncleanness would defile them and bring defeat upon their armies for the sake of their transgression.

### LAWS FOR THE PROTECTION OF RUNAWAY SLAVES

"If a slave has taken refuge with you, do not hand him over to his master. Let him live among you wherever he likes and in whatever town he chooses. Do not oppress him" (Deuteronomy 23:15–16).

25. The poor fugitive slave was not to be given back to his master, or returned to the land, probably a heathen and foreign nation from which he had fled for refuge to the territory of Israel; but he was to be welcomed and treated with kindness, and not enslaved by the one whose protection he claimed.

### LAWS RESPECTING PROSTITUTION

"No Israelite man or woman is to become a shrine prostitute. You must not bring the earnings of a female prostitute or of a male prostitute into the house of the LORD your God to pay any vow, because the LORD your God detests them both" (23:17–18).

26. The most stringent legislation was proclaimed against that crying sin which was the shame of heathen nations, and is, today, the canker of modern society; especially against the infamy so common in idolatrous nations of consecrating this hideous vice to the very worship of their temples, and making it a part of their unholy religion. No sum of money which had ever come from such a life was permitted to be received in the service of the Lord. The more shameful vice, even on the part of men in a more unnatural form, is also forbidden in this verse, where the guilty person is called a dog, as such persons are in Revelation 22:15.

### LAWS RESPECTING USURY

27. Stringent prohibition was placed upon all usury, by which was meant not unlawful interest, but any interest whatever. They must freely lend not only money, but victuals, to their brethren as their need required, without further compensation than the return of the article loaned, when the borrower was done with it. This, however, was permitted in the case of foreigners, from whom the Jews were permitted to take usury, and they have certainly well profited by the permission, as they have become the money lenders of the world, and have given to the word usury the extreme meaning which the term has come to bear.

### LAWS RESPECTING VOWS

"If you make a vow to the LORD your God, do not be slow to pay it, for the LORD your God will certainly demand it of you and you will be guilty of sin" (Deuteronomy 23:21).

28. The utmost fidelity was required in fulfilling their vows unto the Lord. These were perfectly voluntary, and not to be rashly made, but when made they were to be promptly and faithfully fulfilled, as the Lord would not excuse remissness and folly on their part in anything which they had dedicated unto Him.

## LAWS RESPECTING HUMANITY

"If you enter your neighbor's vineyard, you may eat all the grapes you want, but do not put any in your basket. If you enter your neighbor's grain-field, you may pick kernels with your hands, but you must not put a sickle to his standing grain" (23:24–25).

29. A hungry traveler might eat all he could in his neighbor's vineyard or corn field, but he must not carry any away. This is still the custom among the Arabs of the East, and is founded upon a beautiful principle of simple humanity, which rendered poverty and want an impossibility, and recognized all men as having certain common rights up to the measure of their actual wants.

## LAWS RESPECTING DIVORCE

**Deuteronomy 24:1–4**

30. The emphasis in this passage is on the fourth verse, which forbids the first husband to live with his divorced wife if she has been wedded to another. Our Lord, however, declares that these laws with regard to divorce were not wholly pleasing to the Lord, but were simply given on the principle of tolerance, because of their hardness of heart, and were not in harmony with the original purpose and law of marriage, which was intended to be lasting. The spirit of the New Testament is opposed to divorce, except for the most flagrant cause.

## GOD'S TENDER REGARD FOR MARRIAGE

"If a man has recently married, he must not be sent to war or have any other duty laid on him. For one year he is to be free to stay at home and bring happiness to the wife he has married" (24:5).

31. This beautiful law provides for a whole year of exemption on the part of the newly married from military service, and any pressing business engagements which could separate the groom from his wife.

This was intended to be in contrast with the previous paragraph respecting divorce, and to afford a picture of the sweetness and sanctity of the marriage bond as God regarded it and desired to maintain it.

## FORBEARANCE AND MERCY IN COLLECTING DEBTS

Do not take a pair of millstones—not even the upper one—as

security for a debt, because that would be taking a man's livelihood as security. . . .

When you make a loan of any kind to your neighbor, do not go into his house to get what he is offering as a pledge. Stay outside and let the man to whom you are making the loan bring the pledge out to you. If the man is poor, do not go to sleep with his pledge in your possession. Return his cloak to him by sunset so that he may sleep in it. Then he will thank you, and it will be regarded as a righteous act in the sight of the LORD your God. (24:6, 10–13)

32. In enforcing the payment of debts no pledge should be taken which could seriously injure the debtor in his vital interests, or expose him to hardship and poverty. The nether or upper millstone must not be taken. The pledge must not be kept overnight. No man could enter into another's house, and with violent hands seize and carry away any article of clothing or furniture, but he was required to stand outside the door and let the debtor bring to him the pledge. Thus, even the most severe execution of the law was tempered with a mercy little known in what are called civilized times.

## LAWS AGAINST MAN-STEALING

"If a man is caught kidnapping one of his brother Israelites and treats him as a slave or sells him, the kidnapper must die. You must purge the evil from among you" (24:7).

33. No Hebrew could sell a brother into slavery. The penalty for such an act was death, and thus the root of human slavery was struck and the sacredness of human liberty solemnly sanctioned.

## THE RIGHTS OF LABOR

**Deuteronomy 24:14–15**

34. The hired servant must be treated with justice, and his humblest need and sorrow is regarded by the kind and thoughtful Father in heaven, and in pathetic language his cry is recognized as going up to heaven against the oppressive or negligent master, and bringing judgment upon his head. "Pay him his wages each day before sunset, because he is poor and is counting on it. Otherwise he may cry to the LORD against you, and you will be guilty of sin" (24:15).

## IMPARTIAL JUSTICE

"Fathers shall not be put to death for their children, nor children put to death for their fathers; each is to die for his own sin" (24:16).

35. The father was not to be punished for the sin of the child, or the child

for the parent's wrong.

The cruel custom among heathen nations of sacrificing a whole family, if one member offended a capricious king, was to be repudiated, and every soul dealt with according to its own deserts.

## THE RIGHTS OF THE STRANGER

"Do not deprive the alien or the fatherless of justice, or take the cloak of the widow as a pledge. Remember that you were slaves in Egypt and the LORD your God redeemed you from there. That is why I command you to do this" (24:17–18).

36. Not only were the children of Israel to be thus guarded by sanctions of righteous and civil law, but the stranger was to be fully protected; and especially the fatherless and the widow. No pledge could be taken from the latter for the payment of a debt, but the spirit of humanity and mercy must ever be shown.

## THE RIGHTS OF THE POOR

> When you are harvesting in your field and you overlook a sheaf, do not go back to get it. Leave it for the alien, the fatherless and the widow, so that the LORD your God may bless you in all the work of your hands. When you beat the olives from your trees, do not go over the branches a second time. Leave what remains for the alien, the fatherless and the widow. When you harvest the grapes in your vineyard, do not go over the vines again. Leave what remains for the alien, the fatherless and the widow. Remember that you were slaves in Egypt. That is why I command you to do this. (24:19–22)

37. This beautiful provision is a model of beneficence. The gleanings of the harvest field, the olives that remained upon the tree after it was shaken, the forgotten sheaf in the field, and the clusters that were overlooked upon the vines were to be for the stranger, the fatherless and the widow, in remembrance of their bondage in Egypt, and as an example to later ages of the magnanimity which always brings its recompense even in kind.

## THE RIGHTS OF THE CRIMINAL

**Deuteronomy 25:1–3**

38. Even the condemned criminal must be protected from undue severity in his punishment. Forty stripes, and no more, must be given as the extreme punishment, and less, if the offence required it. The feelings even of the criminal must be respected, and they must be careful lest "your brother will

be degraded in your eyes" (25:3). They were never to forget that the most unworthy of Israel's race was still a man and a brother, and must not be lashed like a slave.

## THE RIGHTS OF THE CATTLE

"Do not muzzle an ox while it is treading out the grain" (25:4).

39. This little verse covers the whole animal creation with the light of the divine beneficence and care, and in the New Testament has been applied, most strikingly, by Paul, to the rights of the Christian ministry to be cared and provided for by the people of their charge.

> For it is written in the Law of Moses: "Do not muzzle an ox while it is treading out the grain." Is it about oxen that God is concerned? Surely he says this for us, doesn't he? Yes, this was written for us, because when the plowman plows and the thresher threshes, they ought to do so in the hope of sharing in the harvest. If we have sown spiritual seed among you, is it too much if we reap a material harvest from you? If others have this right of support from you, shouldn't we have it all the more?
>
> But we did not use this right. On the contrary, we put up with anything rather than hinder the gospel of Christ. Don't you know those who work in the temple get their food from the temple, and those who serve at the altar share in what is offered at the altar? In the same way, the Lord has commanded that those who preach the gospel should receive their living from the gospel. (1 Corinthians 9:9–14)

## LEVIRATE MARRIAGES

**Deuteronomy 25:5–10**

40. The object of this peculiar law, respecting marriage, was to preserve the inheritance of any of the families of Israel in the family. It was provided by this law that a widow, who was without a child or heir, should be taken by her husband's brother, and that the firstborn of such a union should succeed in the name of the brother that had died, to preserve his name in Israel. This, however, was not compulsory, but voluntary, and where the brother was not willing to fulfill this obligation of affection to his brother's memory, he could escape it by a ceremony that left upon him a lasting reproach; the widow coming to him in the presence of the elders, loosing his shoe from his foot, as a symbol of degradation, perhaps a hint that he had the spirit in him not of a Hebrew, but of a slave, and then spitting in his face, in further insult, and thus committing him to lasting dishonor as the price by which he

had saved his own inheritance and name. It would seem that when a brother failed, then the nearest of kin was to perform this duty, as Boaz did in the case of Ruth.

This beautiful type has suggested a type of our Redeemer's love, in becoming for us the nearest of kin, and by the sacrifice of His own name, the identifying of His life with ours, buying back for us our lost inheritance. In all this, as we shall see when we come to the book of Ruth, the story of Boaz is the exquisite picture of Christ Himself.

## FEMALE INDELICACY
### Deuteronomy 25:11–12

41. This law was intended to provide for the punishment of any woman who should act with indecency; the punishment being the loss of her offending hand. And the design was to guard the respect which woman should ever show to man, as well as man to woman.

## COMMERCIAL INTEGRITY
### Deuteronomy 25:13–16

42. This law provided against all false weights and measures, and dishonesty in most all trade. It would not hurt our boasted modern business legislation to admit the old and simple code, and enforce it.

> "Do not have two differing weights in your bag—one heavy, one light. . . . You must have accurate and honest weights and measures, so that you may live long in the land the LORD your God is giving you" (25:13–16).

## LAWS AGAINST THEIR ENEMIES

43. This had special reference to Amalek, a neighboring tribe who had met them in a most unneighborly spirit in their helplessness as they came forth out of Egypt. It was not in retaliation, but as the divine expression of eternal hatred to that of which Amalek was but the type.

The Lord had sworn at that time to have war with Amalek from generation to generation. It was because Amalek was the type of the flesh in our spiritual life, the nature of Esau and earthliness, that there could be no compromise, and it was because Saul afterwards failed to fulfill this to the letter that he lost his kingdom and his life.

## PROVISIONS FOR THE PUBLIC OFFERINGS OF THE PEOPLE
### Deuteronomy 26:1–15

44. It is assumed in this passage that the Israelites have kept the commandments now given, and have been rewarded by Jehovah by receiving the

land of their inheritance (26:1).

Having thus come into their possession they are to take of the firstfruits of the land and present them to the Lord as a special thank offering, with a form of liturgy exceedingly beautiful and expressive of gratitude for the divine bounty and beneficence which indeed is a model for the public services and freewill offerings of God's people.

> Then you shall declare before the LORD your God: "My father was a wandering Aramean, and he went down into Egypt with a few people and lived there and became a great nation, powerful and numerous. But the Egyptians mistreated us and made us suffer, putting us to hard labor. Then we cried out to the LORD, the God of our fathers, and the LORD heard our voice and saw our misery, toil and oppression. So the LORD brought us out of Egypt with a mighty hand and an outstretched arm, with great terror and with miraculous signs and wonders. He brought us to this place and gave us this land, a land flowing with milk and honey; and now I bring the firstfruits of the soil that you, O LORD, have given me." Place the basket before the LORD your God and bow down before him. (26:5–10)

Having presented their offering with this solemn appeal on the part of the worshiper, they are to enter into the enjoyment of the Lord's blessings with the assurance of His acceptance and favor, and rejoice before Him in every good thing which the Lord has given them.

In addition to this special offering of firstfruits the law respecting the special tithe of the third year was also repeated, and a similar form of public acknowledgment was added, referring especially to the obedience of the offerer to all the commandments which Moses had just given.

> Then say to the LORD your God: "I have removed from my house the sacred portion and have given it to the Levite, the alien, the fatherless and the widow, according to all you commanded. I have not turned aside from your commands nor have I forgotten any of them. I have not eaten any of the sacred portion while I was in mourning, nor have I removed any of it while I was unclean, nor have I offered any of it to the dead. I have obeyed the LORD my God; I have done everything you commanded me. Look down from heaven, your holy dwelling place, and bless your people Israel and the land you have given us as you promised on oath to our forefathers, a land flowing with milk and honey." (26:13–15)

It was, probably, in reference to this beautiful requirement that the prophet Malachi charged the people so solemnly in the closing days of the old dispensation, "Yet you rob me [God]" (Malachi 3:8), and said to them, as the condition of blessing still,

> "Bring the whole tithe into the storehouse, that there may be food in my house. Test me in this," says the LORD Almighty, "and see if I will not throw open the floodgates of heaven and pour out so much blessing that you will not have room enough for it. I will prevent pests from devouring your crops, and the vines in your fields will not cast their fruit," says the LORD Almighty. "Then all nations will call you blessed, for yours will be a delightful land," says the LORD Almighty. (3:10–12)

## CONCLUSION OF THE ADDRESS

45. Moses now sums up his long and comprehensive address by solemnly appealing to the covenant which has just been consummated and declaring its sacred meaning and obligations.

> The LORD your God commands you this day to follow these decrees and laws; carefully observe them with all your heart and with all your soul. You have declared this day that the LORD is your God and that you will walk in his ways, that you will keep his decrees, commands and laws, and that you will obey him. And the LORD has declared this day that you are his people, his treasured possession as he promised, and that you are to keep all his commands. He has declared that he will set you in praise, fame and honor high above all the nations he has made and that you will be a people holy to the LORD your God, as he promised. (Deuteronomy 26:16–19)

This word *declared* means the public acknowledgment and profession which both God and the people have made, which has constituted a covenant bond of eternal separation and consecration.

# CHAPTER 3

## MOSES' THIRD ADDRESS ON THE PLAINS OF MOAB

### Deuteronomy 27–30

### PROSPECTIVE

In this shorter address Moses seeks to bind them to their sacred obligations, by pointing them forward to the blessing and the curse which are to be dependent upon their obedience or disobedience, and which are here solemnly added as the sanctions of the divine law.

### MONUMENTAL RECORDS

1. He provides for the writing of the law on monuments of stone after they enter the land of promise.

> Moses and the elders of Israel commanded the people: "Keep all these commands that I give you today. When you have crossed the Jordan into the land the LORD your God is giving you, set up some large stones and coat them with plaster. Write on them all the words of this law when you have crossed over to enter the land the LORD your God is giving you, a land flowing with milk and honey, just as the LORD, the God of your fathers, promised you. And when you have crossed the Jordan, set up these stones on Mount Ebal, as I command you today, and coat them with plaster. . . . And you shall write very clearly all the words of this law on these stones you have set up." (Deuteronomy 27:1–4, 8)

This was to be done in the valley of Samaria, that lies between Mounts Ebal and Gerizim. The former was to be the mount of cursing; the latter, of blessing.

It was very significant that the law was to be written upon the mount of cursing. This suggests that the predominant idea in the ancient covenant was judgment and condemnation. Therefore it is called by the apostle, "The ministry that condemns" (2 Corinthians 3:9). It was to be recorded on the face of great stones, plastered over so as to bring out the characters in bolder outlines, and to afford a smooth surface on which to make the inscription. Such monuments and inscriptions are still to be found in ancient ruins.

The law written on these stones may have been the entire Mosaic code. Undoubtedly it was the principal portion of it, moral and civil.

All the words of this law are distinctly specified, and it is added, "You shall write very clearly" (Deuteronomy 27:8).

God has made His will most explicit, and He expects His witnesses to proclaim it unmistakably.

## MERCY AMID JUDGMENT

2. In the midst of this paragraph there is a beautiful provision, right on the mount of cursing, for the setting up of an altar of sacrifice.

"Build there an altar to the LORD your God, an altar of stones. Do not use any iron tool upon them. Build the altar of the LORD your God with fieldstones and offer burnt offerings on it to the LORD your God. Sacrifice fellowship offerings there, eating them and rejoicing in the presence of the LORD your God" (27:5–7).

This passage shines with all the light and glory of the cross, and corresponds, most signally, to the beautiful provision for the altar of sacrifice at the close of the 20th chapter of Exodus, just after the terrors of the giving of the law on Mt. Sinai had been recorded (Exodus 20:24–26).

There, we have already seen, the meaning was typical of God's gracious provision in the gospel for the transgression of His law.

Here also it is assumed that the law would be broken and the curse incurred; yet, notwithstanding, under the shadow of Ebal, there was an altar of sacrifice where the sin could be expiated, and they could still enter into the fellowship of a reconciled God, and "sacrifice fellowship offerings there, eating them and rejoicing in the presence of the LORD your God" (Deuteronomy 27:7).

## RESPONSIVE SERVICE

3. A still more impressive ceremony was then provided for (27:11–26).

The whole camp of Israel was to be assembled in the valley, and divided into two sections, one-half consisting of the tribes descended from Rachel and Leah, representing the firstborn rights, who were to stand on Mount Gerizim, the mount of blessing. The other half, representing the tribes descended from the bondwomen whom Rachel and Leah gave to Jacob, with the addition of Reuben, the cursed son of Leah, and Zebulun, representing the youngest born, were to stand on Mount Ebal, the mount of cursing, and respond alternately, in chorus, the blessing and the curse, and the mighty host on the mountain, in a voice of thunder to say, "Amen!"

It is very remarkable that the words of the curse only are recorded here, the formula of the blessing being omitted. This, too, is significant of the Old Testament spirit of condemnation under the law.

The curses are arranged in a series of 12, corresponding with the 12 tribes. The first 11 represent special acts of sin, standing for the other sins of the same class. Verse 15 represents the first table of the law; verses 16–25 the second table of the law; verse 16 representing the fifth commandment; verses 17–19, the sixth commandment, all offenses against the civil rights of others; verses 20–23, the seventh commandment; verse 24, the eighth commandment; verse 25, the ninth commandment; and verse 26 covers the whole law by pronouncing a curse upon everyone that does not carry out all the words of the law.

## THE BLESSING AND THE CURSE

4. Moses' exhortation to obedience was founded upon this announcement of blessing and cursing (28:1–68).

This is divided into two parts: verses 1–14, the blessing; 15–68, the curse. Here again the blessing occupies 14 verses only, and the curse 54, nearly four times as many. The blessing is repeated six times, the curse as often. The blessing is personified in the strong figurative language as a pursuer, and as following close behind and overtaking them.

## THE BLESSING

"All these blessings will come upon you and accompany you if you obey the LORD your God" (28:2).

It covers all the relationships of their life as individuals, families and the covenant people. Of course this was, primarily, a temporal blessing, and in this respect it differs from the terms of the gospel, but their earthly blessings were types of our higher spiritual welfare.

The promise was to cover all possible blessings both in the city and the field. It was to include all fruitfulness in their body, their grounds and their flocks. It was to be in their basket, or wallet, and in their kneading trough. It was to be with them in coming in and going out. It was to give them victory over their enemies and prosperity in all to which they should set their hands. It was especially to separate them unto God as a holy and peculiar people in the sight of all the nations, to be crowned with all the fullness of His good pleasure, the bounty of His Providence, abundance of wealth and pre-eminence above all other peoples.

## THE CURSE

The curse, however, is amplified still more fully until it becomes an awful and literal prediction of the calamities that have actually come upon Israel.

There seem to be five panoramic pictures of the curse, in as many distinct paragraphs, corresponding to the stages of judgment threatened in Leviticus 26.

*a.* The curse is to rest upon all they do, to bring upon them the pestilence, disease in every form known to us, including consumption, fever, inflammation. It is to fall upon their land, by the sword of their enemies and the elements of nature in the form of blasting, mildew, skies of brass, rain of dust and sand, defeat before their enemies and dispersion among all peoples.

*b.* The next series is pictured from verses 27 to 37.

The curse falls with the plague, the scourges of Egypt, revolting disease, madness, blindness and astonishment of heart, disappointment in their tenderest affections, disaster in all their business and property, the captivity of their children, the oppression of their enemies, madness because of their grief and sorrow and such horrors and calamities as shall make them an astonishment and proverb above all nations (verse 37).

*c.* The next series extends from verses 38 to 48, and portrays the failure of all their work, their harvests through locust, their vineyards through the worm, their olive trees through casting their fruit, their very children through their shameful captivity, their subordination to the alien and the stranger in their midst, until they shall become the tail and not the head, and shall suffer hunger, thirst, nakedness, and want of all things, and a yoke of iron upon their necks.

*d.* The next picture is a vivid description of the horrors of foreign invasion, and their subjugation and captivity under the Chaldeans.

They are described as a nation of fiercest countenance and without mercy to young or old. They shall sweep away the fruit of their land and their cattle shall perish in their cities until parents shall eat their very children for hunger, and the ties of human affection shall be changed into unnatural hatred until they strive for a morsel of each other's flesh. And even the tender and delicate mother shall be glad to eat her newborn babe and her very own flesh in the horrors of famine.

*e.* The last picture gives the climax of the curse, and seems to be a literal prediction of the later calamities of Israel since the last destruction of Jerusalem and their dispersion among the Gentiles. How solemn are some of the awful words!

The closing picture of their slavery in Egypt was literally fulfilled in the Middle Ages, in the case of the multitudes of Hebrews driven from Spain to northern Africa and sold as slaves by their oppressors.

## THE COVENANT RENEWED

5. The solemn renewal of the covenant was done in view of these threatenings and promises (Deuteronomy 29–30).

*a.* Brief recital of their past mercies.

He reminds them of all that God has done for them, and yet stops to bewail their blindness and stupidity to understand all His teachings and blessings.

*b.* Solemn renewal of the covenant.

All degrees and classes of the people are solemnly united in this great covenant—the captains, the elders, the officers and all the men of Israel, their wives, their little ones, the stranger in their midst and the very bondmen that waited on them.

The covenant was expressed in the most imperative language, not only a covenant, but an oath of the most solemn and binding obligation, but no less sacred than the pledge which He Himself had sworn unto their fathers. The question of how far we should enter into such personal covenants with God is a very important one. If we rightly understand the nature of God's covenant relation with us as individuals, and the divine ground on which the covenant rests, namely, the mediatorial work of the Lord Jesus Christ, we cannot too impressively seal our engagements with Him.

It is delightful to know that to each of us in Christ, God has sworn His oath of eternal faithfulness, and that in the strength of Christ we may enter into the covenant with equal definiteness and sacredness; and that He will accept our plighted vow and become in us the power to keep it, if we enter into it with intelligent faith, not as the covenant of the law, but as the covenant of grace, of which Christ is the sponsor and the pledge. "See, I have made him a witness to the peoples" (Isaiah 55:4).

If our covenant is thus in Him, it will be eternal and unbroken, and our part will be kept through Him as well as His unchangeable promises to us.

*c.* Warnings against unfaithfulness to the covenant, or omission on their part, with respect to these obligations, and terrible intimations of the retribution which will follow unfaithfulness.

Especially are the warnings directed against all whose heart is even already turning away from the Lord, and beginning presumptuously to say, " 'I will be safe, even though I persist in going my own way.' This will bring disaster on the watered land as well as the dry" (Deuteronomy 29:19), that is, perhaps, not only desiring evil, but satiating himself with evil.

This he calls a root that bears bitter poison. This is the passage which the apostle quotes in Hebrews 12:15, "See to it that no one misses the grace of God and that no bitter root grows up to cause trouble and defile many."

The threatenings denounced against the soul that dares thus deliberately to calculate upon the pleasures of sin, quiver like the fiery lightnings in their consuming blaze. "The LORD will never be willing to forgive him; his wrath and zeal will burn against that man. . . . The LORD will single him out . . . for disaster" (Deuteronomy 29:20–21).

The same judgments are denounced against the land if it shall become apostate, until it shall be made a frightful monument before the eyes of all nations of the Lord's displeasure.

*d.* Exhortation to faithfulness.

"The secret things belong to the LORD our God; but the things revealed belong to us and to our children forever, that we may follow all the words of this law" (29:29).

The meaning of this verse seems to be that the reason why Moses is so plainly and practically speaking to them the word of the law instead of merely entertaining them with curious revelations is because the very purpose of God's Word is not to minister to our speculative curiosity, but to guide our feet into the path of obedience, and to preserve us from the snares of sin and death.

Therefore we are not vainly to inquire into the secret things with which we have no concern, or use our Bibles for the mere gratification of the love of novelty, but to treat God's Word as a plain and faithful message from a loving Father of "the things revealed [which] belong to us and to our children forever, that we may follow all the words of this law" (29:29).

*e.* Promises of restoration even to those who should depart from the law, on condition of their sincere repentance.

Moses here assumes that they shall apostatize from God, and be scattered among the nations, and that the words that he is speaking to them now shall come into their hearts in the days of their captivity. He tells them that even then, if they shall return unto the Lord with all their heart, and with all their soul,

> Then the LORD your God will restore your fortunes and have compassion on you and gather you again from all the nations where he scattered you. Even if you have been banished to the most distant land under the heavens, from there the LORD your God will gather you and bring you back. He will bring you into the land that belonged to your fathers, and you will take possession of it. He will make you more prosperous and numerous than your fathers. (30:3–5)

Not only so, but still better, "The LORD your God will circumcise your hearts and the hearts of your descendants, so that you may love him with all your heart and with all your soul, and live" (30:6).

And this spiritual restoration will bring the fullness of temporal prosperity and national blessing. "Then the LORD your God will make you most prosperous in all the work of your hands and in the fruit of your womb, the young of your livestock and the crops of your land. The LORD will again delight in you and make you prosperous, just as he delighted in your fathers" (30:9).

This blessed promise still awaits repentant Israel, and shall be literally fulfilled in the spiritual revival and national restoration of God's ancient people.

*f.* Concluding appeal in which Moses applies God's message solemnly to their hearts and consciences, and sets before them for personal decision, the blessing and the curse, the evil and the good, the way of death and the way of life.

First, he meets the possible excuse that the word he has spoken is too hard, too mysterious, too far off, or too high up. It is not in heaven, nor is it beyond the sea, but it is very near them, even in their mouth and in their heart.

> Now what I am commanding you today is not too difficult for you or beyond your reach. It is not up in heaven, so that you have to ask, "Who will ascend into heaven to get it and proclaim it to us so we may obey it?" Nor is it beyond the sea, so that you have to ask, "Who will cross the sea to get it and proclaim it to us so we may obey it?" No, the word is very near you; it is in your mouth and in your heart so you may obey it. (30:11–14)

This is the foundation of the Holy Spirit's appeal to us even in the gospel (see Romans 10:6, etc.)

For us the meaning is that God's message is not impracticable, or His demands impossible, requiring some long preparation, some lofty height of experience, some profound depth of feeling or meaning. It meets us just where we are and as we are, and may be accepted and acted upon by every one of us the very instant we hear it.

And so, secondly, Moses demands of each of them an immediate decision: "I have set before you life and death, blessings and curses" (Deuteronomy 30:19).

It is a personal matter, not with the nation now, but with each man, woman and child. It is not something to be put off, but to be decided this day. And according to the spirit in which we are willing to meet the decision promptly and fully, shall be the issue of our future life.

The soul that hesitates in making this choice will be very apt to hesitate in executing it, and in each emergency demanding promptness in the future, will be almost sure to falter and parley until even the act of obedience is frustrated by indecision.

Very solemnly does he call to witness both heaven and earth in this momentous covenant, and very really does the universe thus witness every man's decision. Eyes innumerable are looking down at every crisis of our lives; tablets, more enduring than stone, are receiving the record of our conduct, and even as some of us read these lines it may be that the years of eternity are being determined for us.

"This day I call heaven and earth as witnesses against you that I have set before you life and death, blessings and curses. Now choose life, so that you and your children may live and that you may love the LORD your God, listen to his voice, and hold fast to him. For the LORD is your life, and he will give you many years in the land he swore to give your fathers, Abraham, Isaac and Jacob" (30:19–20).

Let the voice of the lawgiver, long silent in Nebo's grave, speak to us with the added witness of the gospel, these ancient words in their New Testament light: "I have set before you life and death, blessings and curses. Now choose life, so that you and your children may live and that you may love the LORD your God, listen to his voice, and hold fast to him. For the LORD is your life, and he will give you many years" (30:19–20).

> "Do not say in your heart, 'Who will ascend into heaven?' " (that is, to bring Christ down) "or 'Who will descend into the deep?' " (that is, to bring Christ up from the dead). But what does it say? "The word is near you; it is in your mouth and in your heart," that is, the word of faith we are proclaiming: That if you confess with your mouth, "Jesus is Lord," and believe in your heart that God raised him from the dead, you will be saved. For it is with your heart that you believe and are justified, and it is with your mouth that you confess and are saved. (Romans 10:6–10)

More deeply than we sometimes think, the heart of Moses understood the spiritual meaning of God's covenant. There is nothing more profound in the New Testament than the words, "the LORD is your life, and he will give you many years" (Deuteronomy 30:20). It is the very heart of Christianity, nay, rather, the very heart of Christ.

# CHAPTER 4

## CONCLUSION OF THE BOOK OF DEUTERONOMY

### SECTION I—*Concluding History*

#### Deuteronomy 31–36

Moses gathers Israel around him after his three long addresses, and announces to them the approaching end of his life. Verses 1 and 2 reiterate to them the promise of their victorious entrance into the land of Canaan, under Joshua, his successor; verse 3 assures them of the subjugation and destruction of all their enemies; verse 4, 5 and 6 solemnly charge them to be strong and of good courage, to fear not, nor be dismayed, for the Lord would go before them and not fail them nor forsake them.

Then he calls Joshua unto him in the sight of all Israel and commits to him his sacred charge, promising him the divine protection and presence in all his ways (verses 7, 8).

*a.* He writes the law and delivers it to the priests and Levites, and solemnly charges them, every seven years, "the year for canceling debts" (15;9), as Israel shall gather before the Lord, that it is to be publicly read to them in the Feast of Tabernacles, that they may hear and learn and fear the Lord their God, and observe to do all the words of this law; and that their children, which have not known anything, may hear and learn to fear the Lord their God, as long as they live in the land they go to possess.

*b.* He takes Joshua and presents him before the Lord in the tabernacle of the congregation, and solemnly inducts him into his ministry. Then the glory of the Lord appears above the door of the tabernacle, Jehovah Himself recognizing the new leader of His people.

Then the Lord reveals to Moses that after his death the people are going to backslide into unfaithfulness and idolatry, and to be visited with many judgments and sorrows; and He therefore commands Moses to write a song and rehearse it in the ears of all Israel, that it may be a witness in the day of their declension, of the faithful warnings of their covenant God.

> And the LORD said to Moses: "You are going to rest with your
> fathers, and these people will soon prostitute themselves to the
> foreign gods of the land they are entering. They will forsake me
> and break the covenant I made with them. On that day I will be-
> come angry with them and forsake them; I will hide my face
> from them, and they will be destroyed. Many disasters and dif-
> ficulties will come upon them, and on that day they will ask,
> 'Have not these disasters come upon us because our God is not
> with us?' And I will certainly hide my face on that day because of
> all their wickedness in turning to other gods.
>
> "Now write down for yourselves this song and teach it to the
> Israelites and have them sing it, so that it may be a witness for
> me against them." (31:16–19)

*c.* He commits the law to the hands of the Levites and priests to be kept
in the ark of the covenant, as a further witness for Jehovah.

Finally he gathers the elders and officers of Israel around him and publicly
utters in their hearing, the song itself.

## SECTION II—*Moses' Song*
### Deuteronomy 32:1–47

It consists of seven parts.

(1) Introduction.

"Listen, O heavens, and I will speak;/ hear, O earth, the words of my
mouth./ Let my teaching fall like rain/ and my words descend like dew,/ like
showers on new grass,/ like abundant rain on tender plants" (32:1–2).

In the most solemn manner he appeals to the heavens and the earth to witness to the gracious words which he is about to speak, and which he com-
pares to the gentle rain and the soft dew of night as it falls upon the heated
earth and withered grass and herb.

(2) The theme of his song.

"I will proclaim the name of the LORD./ Oh, praise the greatness of our
God!/ He is the Rock, his works are perfect,/ and all his ways are just./ A
faithful God who does no wrong,/ upright and just is he" (32:3–4).

It is the name of the Lord and the greatness of our God, the Rock, "his
works are perfect" (32:4).

(3) The contrasted picture of God's people.

"They have acted corruptly toward him;/ to their shame they are no longer his children,/ but a warped and crooked generation./ Is this the way you repay the LORD,/ O foolish and unwise people?/ Is he not your Father, your Creator,/ who made you and formed you?" (32:5–6).

Very different are they from Him. "They have acted corruptly toward him;/ to their shame they are no longer his children,/ but a warped and crooked generation" (32:5). They are a foolish people and unwise, thus to requite so great and good a God for all His kindness.

(4) The recital of His goodness and faithfulness to them (32:7–14).

"Remember the days of old;/ consider the generations long past./ Ask your father and he will tell you,/ your elders, and they will explain to you" (32:7).

Far back in the past His love began, and many generations have magnified it. Even in the commencement of earth's nations, when the Most High divided to them their inheritance, and separated the sons of Adam, He formed His great providential plans with reference to Israel's honor and blessing. "He set up boundaries for the peoples/ according to the number of the sons of Israel" (32:8), for He had set His heart on them, choosing them for His portion and His inheritance. His providential care and love had been in all their past: He had found them in the desert waste and had led them and kept them as the apple of His eye; as sensitive to their slightest want as the tender pupil of our eye is to the slightest particle of dust. As the mother eagle trains her young to fly by breaking up her nest and then compelling her fluttering brood to strike out their little wings and learn to bear themselves upon their native air, and, when weary and sinking, puts her own strong pinions under their sinking strength and bears them on her wings, so God had led them and trained them to trust and obedience. And then the days of trial had been exchanged for the fullness of blessing; the wilderness had given place to the fruitful land of Gilead and Bashan, and He had made him to "ride on the heights of the land/ and fed him with the fruit of the fields./ He nourished him with honey from the rock,/ and with oil from flinty crag,/ with curds and milk from herd and flock/ and with fattened lambs and goats,/ with choice rams of Bashan/ and the finest kernels of wheat./ You drank the foaming blood of the grape" (32:13–14). So had He loved and led them all their days.

And so does He still love and lead His unworthy children. A picture more beautiful of His fatherly and motherly care has never been written by the inspired pen of prophet or apostle, than the poetic imagery of these solemn words.

(5) Israel's ingratitude in spite of all God's goodness (32:15–18).

Very characteristic is the name with which the lawgiver introduced the picture of Israel's sins. Jeshurun, he calls them, meaning the righteous one, as if solemnly asking the question, How true has Israel been to their high name? "Jeshurun grew fat and kicked" (32:15). Like the ox that has become unruly through his very abundance, "he abandoned the God who made him/ and rejected the Rock his Savior" (32:15). The Hebrew here for "rejecting," means to treat as a fool, and it implies the indignation with which God had felt their insulting conduct towards one so great.

Then he describes their cursed wickedness. "They made him jealous with their foreign gods/ and angered him with their detestable idols./ They sacrificed to demons, which are not God—/ gods they had not known,/ gods that recently appeared,/ gods your fathers did not fear./ You deserted the Rock, who fathered you;/ you forgot the God who gave you birth" (32:16–18).

The word *jealousy* implies very tenderly the marriage bond which God had established with His people, and in connection with this, their worship of demons implies that the great adversary has been received by them instead of Jehovah Himself.

(6) At length the notes of judgment fall, and the sorrow of God's anger is dealt out in terrible eloquence and majesty. And yet, it is more like a wail of love than a thunder of vengeance. Pathetically, He pauses in the midst of His purpose of judgment, and cries: "But I dreaded the taunt of the enemy,/ lest the adversary misunderstand/ and say, 'Our hand has triumphed;/ the LORD has not done all this' " (32:27); and then bursts out into upbraiding complaint: "they are a nation without sense,/ there is no discernment in them./ If only they were wise and would understand this/ and discern what their end will be!/ How could one man chase a thousand,/ or two put ten thousand to flight,/ unless their Rock had sold them,/ unless the LORD had given them up?" (32:28–30).

Reluctantly returning again to the inevitable sentence of judgment. He says, "It is mine to avenge; I will repay./ In due time, their foot will slip;/ their day of disaster is near/ and their doom rushes upon them" (32:35). And yet it is rather as the sentence of a judge who stops to weep over the criminal that he is about to commit to the bonds of shame, or the doom of death; but even when the sentence is uttered it is immediately arrested by the closing message (32:36–40).

Already He sees them sinking beneath His stroke; their power is gone and there is none shut up or left. Their idols have failed them, their enemies are gloating over their helplessness and misery. Then He waves the sword of His vengeance against their persecutors and lifting up His hand to heaven, he swears:

> See now that I myself am He!
>   There is no God besides me.
> I put to death and I bring to life,
>   I have wounded and I will heal,

and no one can deliver out of my hand.
I lift my hand to heaven and declare:
    As surely as I live forever,
when I sharpen my flashing sword
    and my hand grasps it in judgement,
I will take vengeance on my adversaries
    and repay those who hate me.
I will make my arrows drunk with blood,
    while my sword devours flesh:
the blood of the slain and the captives,
    the heads of the enemy leaders. (32:39–42)

This is not the picture of Israel's judgment, but of God's judgment on Israel's foes, as He awakes for their defense in the hour of their captivity and sorrow.

And then the song closes as it began, with an appeal to the nations to witness His vengeance upon His foes, and His mercy to His people and His land.

"Rejoice, O nations, with his people,/ for he will avenge the blood of his servants;/ he will take vengeance on his enemies/ and make atonement for his land and people" (32:43).

And so the solemn song is ended, and Moses thus adds his own conclusion: "He said to them, 'Take to heart all the words I have solemnly declared to you this day, so that you may command your children to obey carefully all the words of this law. They are not just idle words for you— they are your life. By them you will live long in the land you are crossing the Jordan to possess' " (32:46–47).

Like the dying swan, which sings itself to death, Moses closes his song by receiving the intimation of his immediate death on Mount Nebo.

On that same day the LORD told Moses, "Go up into the Abarim Range to Mount Nebo in Moab, across from Jericho, and view Canaan, the land I am giving the Israelites as their own possession. There on the mountain that you have climbed you will die and be gathered to your people, just as your brother Aaron died on Mount Hor and was gathered to his people. This is because both of you broke faith with me in the presence of the Israelites at the waters of Meribah Kadesh in the Desert of Zin and because you did not uphold my holiness among the Israelites. Therefore, you will see the land only from a distance; you will not enter the land I am giving to the people of Israel." (32:48–52)

It would seem as though it was intended to be God's very seal in the eyes of the people, of the words that Moses had so often spoken, that they might know and see in the death of their lawgiver how inviolable were the threatenings of the law that he himself had given them, and came with ten thousands of saints. They saw how inexorable God's sentence was, from which even Moses could not escape and that in his death they might have a still more memorable and never-to-be-forgotten pledge, that the word of God must stand and that they could not with impunity disobey its statutes or despise its judgments.

### SECTION III—*Moses' Blessing*
#### Deuteronomy 33:1–29

Under the formal announcement of his death Moses pronounces his blessing upon the tribes of Israel. Was this a foreshadowing of the greater spiritual truth, that the blessing of the gospel would come with the passing away of the law?

(1) The introduction.

> This is the blessing that Moses the man of God pronounced on the Israelites before his death. He said:

> "The LORD came from Sinai
>   and dawned over them from Seir;
>   he shone forth from Mount Paran.
> He came with myriads of holy ones
>   from the south, from his mountain slopes.
> Surely it is you who love the people,
>   all the holy ones are in your hand.
> At your feet they all bow down,
>   and from you receive instruction,
> the law that Moses gave us,
>   the possession of the assembly of Jacob.
> He was king over Jeshurun
>   when the leaders of the people assembled,
>   along with the tribes of Israel." (33:1–5)

It commences with the majestic description of the appearing of Jehovah at Mt. Sinai as He came, literally, from the midst of ten thousand of His holy ones to give His fiery law, and yet, to gather His people as a loving Father at His feet and to reveal Himself as the true King in Jeshurun, His righteous nation. Moses was but the mediator of the law, which he left to Israel as their precious inheritance from their heavenly King.

(2) The blessing of Reuben.

"Let Reuben live and not die,/ nor his men be few" (33:6).

On account of Reuben's shameful crime Jacob had left an hereditary cloud upon the tribe and therefore we find that even in the brief history of the wilderness the numbers of the tribe have greatly diminished, so that it may have seemed to many of them that there was a serious danger of their extinction. The blessing of Moses seems to suggest this danger and to answer this fear. "Let Reuben live and not die, nor his men be few" (33:6). And the blessing was fulfilled in their succeeding history by their continuance, although they never became a leading tribe of Israel. Compare Numbers 1:21 with Numbers 26:7.

(3) The blessing of Judah.

"And this he said about Judah:/ 'Hear, O LORD, the cry of Judah;/ bring him to his people./ With his own hands he defends his cause./ Oh, be his help against his foes!" (Deuteronomy 33:7).

The expression here, "The cry of Judah," implies that Judah is to call upon Jehovah and to recognize God as the source of his prosperity and blessing. "Bring him to his people" means, bring him back in triumph as he goes forth in war. "With his own hands he defends his cause" has been translated, "with his hands he contendeth with the people," as describing his warlike enterprise. "Be his helper against his foes," pledges divine assistance in all his conflicts. The blessing was fulfilled in Judah's pre-eminence among the tribes of Israel, and the victorious wars of David, Uzziah, and others of Judah's kings.

The same picture had been given in Jacob's blessing, in even more vivid colors.

(4) The blessing of Levi.

This is a far higher blessing. Judah was to be helped of God, but Levi was to be wholly the Lord's and absolutely carried and sustained by Him.

> About Levi he said:
> "Your Thummim and Urim belong
>    to the man you favored.
> You tested him at Massah;
>    you contended with him at the waters of Meribah.
> He said of his father and mother,
>    'I have no regard for them,'
> He did not recognize his brothers
>    or acknowledge his own children,
> but he watched over your word

> and guarded your covenant.
> He teaches your precepts to Jacob
>   and your law to Israel.
> He offers incense before you
>   and whole burnt offerings on your altar.
> Bless all his skills, O LORD,
>   and be pleased with the work of his hands.
> Smite the loins of those who rise up against him;
>   strike his foes till they rise no more." (33:8–11)

Levi is here called "your holy one," the tribe separated and consecrated wholly unto the Lord; and his fidelity had been tried not only in Moses and Aaron themselves, as they stood firm amid the murmurings of the people at Massah and Meribah, but also in the loyal stand of the Levites themselves in the frightful hour of Israel's apostasy (Exodus 32:25–28), when they stood up even against their dearest friends and were faithful to God, to the sacrifice of their fathers and mothers, their brethren and their children (Deuteronomy 33:9). But their righteousness was not their own.

Let your Thummim and your Urim be with Levi is Moses' prayer. God is their Urim and their Thummim, their Light and their Might. Their highest honor is that they are to "teach [God's] precepts to Jacob/ and [God's] law to Israel./ Offer incense before [God]/ and whole burnt offerings on [God's] altar" (33:10).

Levi represents the spiritual priesthood, that live where we are wholly the Lord's and have no portion of our own, not even of strength, or righteousness, but the Lord is our inheritance, both for holiness and happiness, both for strength and all-sufficiency.

(5) The blessing of Benjamin.

"About Benjamin he said:/ 'Let the beloved of the LORD rest secure in him,/ for he shields him all day long,/ and the one the LORD loves rests between his shoulders" (33:12).

This is nearer and dearer still; to be the beloved of the Lord, to dwell secretly in His presence, or more literally, on Him, as one that lies upon His breast, to be covered by the Lord all the day long, and hidden under the robes of His righteousness, the wings of His unfolding love, and to dwell between His shoulders. That may be in His bosom, or on His back, where the father carries his children, representing the supporting and upholding strength of God. This is the place of John, on Jesus' breast.

Some have found in this beautiful blessing an allusion to Benjamin's future location, as a tribe, with Jerusalem and Zion and the abiding presence of Jehovah in the temple, within the borders of their tribe.

An added beauty is given when we remember that the original of Benjamin is Benoni, "the son of my sorrow," and it afterwards became Benjamin, "the son of my right hand."

(6) The blessing of Joseph.

> About Joseph he said:
> "May the LORD bless his land
>     with the precious dew from heaven above
>     and with the deep waters that lie below;
> with the best the sun brings forth
>     and the finest the moon can yield;
> with the choicest gifts of the ancient mountains
>     and the fruitfulness of the everlasting hills;
> with the best gifts of the earth and its fullness
>     and the favor of him who dwelt in the burning bush.
> Let all these rest on the head of Joseph,
>     on the brow of the prince among his brothers.
> In majesty he is like a firstborn bull;
>     his horns are the horns of a wild ox.
> With them he will gore the nations,
>     even those at the ends of the earth.
> Such are the ten thousands of Ephraim;
>     such are the thousands of Manasseh." (33:13–17)

It begins with the rich bounty of nature and providence. The precious things of the heavens, with their fertilizing rains, the dew, with its gentle refreshing, the deep that coucheth beneath, with its subterranean fountains, the sunshine of heaven, the mild and quickening radiance of the gentle moon, the treasures of the mountains and the hills and the fruitfulness of the earth, all these are upon the land of Joseph, and the tribes of Ephraim and Manasseh. Better still is the good will of Him that dwelt in the bush, that is, the covenant blessing pronounced in Midian on Moses, when God first revealed His glorious name *Jehovah* as the title of His covenant relation with Israel. It may also mean the good will of the God who comes to us in our fiery trials as well as in our earthly prosperity, and in whose presence no flame can consume or sorrow harm.

Three reasons are given for Joseph's blessing. The first is that he was separated from his brethren. This may mean his early trials and separation. For us, it most surely does mean that complete separation unto God and from the world in which the fullness of blessing must ever begin.

The second and higher reason was "In majesty he is like a firstborn bull" (33:17). This figure, we need not say, expressed the idea of sacrifice and entire consecration.

The firstling of the Hebrew flock was the Lord's, and was wholly laid upon the altar. And so Joseph thus stands as the type of our complete surrender as a living sacrifice unto Jehovah. Then shall we know the fullness of His love.

The third reason is, "His horns are the horns of a wild ox [unicorns, KJV]" (33:17). One peculiarity is that the unicorn has but one horn, and so Joseph is to have only one source of strength, God, and God alone. They of whom this is true, like Joseph, "will gore the nations,/ even those at the ends of the earth./ Such are the ten thousands of Ephraim;/ such are the thousands of Manasseh" (33:17).

This is a beautiful picture of the secret of blessing; separated unto God, covenanted with Him, as He that dwelt in the bush, baptized with His holy presence and His consuming fire, consecrated on His altar and armed with His strength alone, we must have Joseph's blessing and Joseph's victory.

(7)  The blessing of Zebulun and Issachar.

"About Zebulun he said:/ 'Rejoice, Zebulun, in your going out,/ and you, Issachar, in your tents./ They will summon peoples to the mountain/ and there offer sacrifices of righteousness;/ they will feast on the abundance of the seas,/ on the treasures hidden in the sand' " (33:18–19).

Bold enterprise and peaceful rest are the promises given to these two tribes.

The territory of Zebulun reached to the shores of the sea of Galilee; and from the sand of the coast the most costly glass work of ancient times was made. This may explain the reference to "the abundance of the seas,/ on the treasures hidden in the sand" (33:19).

The other promises seem to refer to their bold aggressive spirit, and their faithfulness to God's covenant, in the conflicts with Jabin and Sisera (Judges 4:15–18).

Perhaps this prophecy was also more distinctly fulfilled in the parts which these two tribes sustained, as the counselors and helpers of David, when he assumed the kingdom of Israel (1 Chronicles 12:32–33).

(8)  The blessing of Gad.

"About Gad he said:/ 'Blessed is he who enlarges Gad's domain!/ Gad lives like a lion,/ tearing at arm or head./ He chose the best land for himself;/ the leader's portion was kept for him./ When the heads of the people assembled,/ he carried out the LORD's righteous will,/ and his judgments concerning Israel' " (Deuteronomy 33:20–21).

His spacious territory is first referred to, covering as it did the fertile plains of Gilead; next, his bold, swift, martial movements, sweeping as the lion, upon his enemies; next his claiming for himself the first inheritance in the conquered regions east of the Jordan.

This is the correct translation of the 21st verse because there the leader's portion was reserved. Gad was the leader in the wars of Joshua, going before their brethren armed, until the rest of Canaan was subdued, and then returning to gain their inheritance in Gilead, and faithfully keeping the covenant, as they had promised Moses. Thus, Moses here assumes in his blessing, "he carried out the LORD's righteous will,/ and his judgements concerning Israel" (33:21).

(9) The blessing of Dan.

"About Dan he said:/ 'Dan is a lion's cub,/ springing out of Bashan' " (33:22).

The figure is that of a wild and swift attack upon his foes. Perhaps this is an allusion to the bold and even cruel attack of Dan upon the defenseless tribes of the north (Joshua 19:47; Judges 18:27).

(10) The blessing of Naphtali.

"About Naphtali he said:/ 'Naphtali is abounding with the favor of the LORD/ and is full of his blessing;/ he will inherit southward to the lake' " (Deuteronomy 33:23).

This is a picture of earthly prosperity. Their inheritance lay on the west coast of Galilee, which was "the garden of Palestine," extending up to the head water of the Jordan, and including the most beautiful scenery and the most productive land in the whole country. But they were also to have the blessing of the Lord.

(11) The blessing of Asher.

"About Asher he said:/ 'Most blessed of sons is Asher;/ let him be favored by his brothers,/ and let him bathe his feet in oil./ The bolts of your gates will be iron and bronze,/ and your strength will equal your days' " (33:24–25).

Asher's inheritance was in the extreme northwest of Palestine, reaching up from Mount Carmel to the coast of Tyre and Sidon, and the base of Lebanon and Hermon.

If we take the "bolts of your gates" to mean fortress, and strength to mean rest, the significance of the promise will be that Asher should be strongly defended from his enemies, and that the inheritance should be stable and quiet as long as his days should last.

However, the words have become too precious to change their meaning without very high authority, and the received translation is reasonably sustained by the best authorities. It makes the promise a heritage of spiritual blessing to the Christian heart, pledging to us the anointing of the Holy Spirit, the keeping power and love of God in all our steps, and strength according to our daily need, whether for soul or body.

(12) The blessing of Jehovah. Above all Israel's tribes, Moses blesses God Himself. Moses ascribes to God Himself his closing benediction.

There is no one like the God of Jeshurun,

who rides on the heavens to help you
and on the clouds in his majesty.
The eternal God is your refuge,
and underneath are the everlasting arms.
He will drive out your enemy before you,
saying, "Destroy him!"
So Israel will live in safety alone;
Jacob's spring is secure
in a land of grain and new wine,
where the heavens drop dew.
Blessed are you, O Israel!
Who is like you,
a people saved by the LORD?
He is your shield and helper
and your glorious sword.
Your enemies will cower before you,
and you will trample down their high places.
(33:26–29)

He gives Him the tender name of the God of Jeshurun, that is, "the Righteous One," lovingly assuming, as ever, to allure his brethren to fidelity, that Israel will keep their covenant with God, and prove indeed His Jeshurun.

How sublime the picture of God's protection, reaching to heaven in His help, and riding upon the sky for our deliverance, and then stooping to the profoundest depths, as He places under our lowest need His everlasting arms. It is before Him and not them that the enemy should be thrust out. He is the shield of their help, and the sword of their excellency, and through Him shall they tread upon the high places of their foes.

But the secret of Israel's blessing must ever be to dwell alone. They cannot mingle with the nations, but they must be wholly separated unto the Lord their God. Then shall it indeed be true, "Blessed are you, O Israel!/ Who is like you,/ a people saved by the LORD?" (33:29).

What if they failed to claim the fullness of their blessing? It remains for us through Jesus Christ, our true Jeshurun, who leads us into their "land of uprightness" (Psalm 143:10, KJV) and becomes for us a surety of all the promises.

Simeon is absent from this catalogue of blessings, and afterwards seems to have performed an insignificant part in the national history of Israel.

Was there a lost tribe among the Israelites as there was a Judas among the twelve?

## SECTION IV—*The Death of Moses*
### Deuteronomy 34:1–12

This, of course, was added by a later hand.

(1) We have the dying vision.

> Then Moses climbed Mount Nebo from the plains of Moab to
> the top of Pisgah, across from Jericho. There the LORD showed
> him the whole land—from Gilead to Dan, all of Naphtali, the
> territory of Ephraim and Manasseh, all the land of Judah as far as
> the western sea, the Negev and the whole region from the Valley
> of Jericho, the City of Palms, as far as Zoar. Then the LORD said
> to him, "This is the land I promised on oath to Abraham, Isaac
> and Jacob when I said, 'I will give it to your descendants.' I have
> let you see it with your eyes, but you will not cross over into it."
> (34:1–4)

How oft the closing hour is an hour of vision to the saints of God. Moses
saw not only the beautiful land of promise, but also its spiritual meaning;
and, in the distant future, no doubt, the form of the Son of man who should
traverse it, and perhaps the hour when he should stand with Him in the
transfiguration glory and talk of the decease which He should accomplish at
Jerusalem, and in which all the fullness of the Mosaic ritual should at last be
fulfilled.

We, too, may have such a vision, but before beholding it we must come to
the place of death, the death of self. Standing beside our own grave we can
see farther than Moses saw, and then come down, as he could not, and
literally enter in.

(2) The death of Moses.

"And Moses the servant of the LORD died there in Moab, as the LORD
had said. He buried him in Moab, in the valley opposite Beth Peor, but to
this day no one knows where his grave is" (34:5–6).

Even Moses must die. The giver of the law must be the most pre-eminent
monument of its truth and sanctions; and his death must have in it the dark
shadow of judicial execution. While it was glorious indeed, it was also sad. It
had the remembrance of sin, and was the divine mark of a single act of disobedience and unbelief.

So, even to the saint of God, death is the decree of justice and the fruit of
sin; and yet for us, as for him, it becomes an hour of transfiguration and the
gate of heaven.

The actual nature of Moses' death we know not. Perhaps God sweetly kissed his spirit away. Perhaps, like Enoch and Elijah, his body was transformed in anticipation of the resurrection to the heavenly glory. More probably, however, he really died, and was literally buried, and raised from the tomb afterwards, to stand on the mount of transfiguration with Christ, and enter the land of promise through Jesus Christ, as he could not through the law.

The contention of the devil about his body may have been on account of God's preserving it from corruption and guarding it for his future resurrection. Satan may have claimed his right to every human body after death, on account of the penalty of sin.

(3) Moses' supernatural strength.

"Moses was a hundred and twenty years old when he died, yet his eyes were not weak nor his strength gone" (34:7).

This remarkable strength is mentioned, no doubt, with the intention of suggesting its supernatural cause in the sustaining grace and power of God.

The same strength was given to Caleb, and the same quickened life is promised to us through Jesus Christ, and the abiding of the Holy Spirit, for "if the Spirit of him who raised Jesus from the dead is living in you, he who raised Christ from the dead will also give life to your mortal bodies through his Spirit, who lives in you" (Romans 8:11).

(4) The character and influence of Moses.

> The Israelites grieved for Moses in the plains of Moab thirty days, until the time of weeping and mourning was over. . . .
>
> Since then, no prophet has risen in Israel like Moses, whom the LORD knew face to face, who did all those miraculous signs and wonders the LORD sent him to do in Egypt—to Pharaoh and to all his officials and to his whole land. For no one has ever shown the mighty power or performed the awesome deeds that Moses did in the sight of all Israel. (Deuteronomy 34:8, 10–12)

His influence among his own people is shown in the sincere mourning of Israel for him for 30 days, and in the almost supernatural respect paid to him in later times. God Himself bears witness here to his place of honor and service. No other prophet stood so near to the Lord, "whom the LORD knew face to face" (34:10).

However, we must remember that this high eulogy was paid to Moses before the days of Elijah, Isaiah and John the Baptist, and we must read it in the light of the time when it was given. Our Lord tells us that "among those born of women there is no one greater than John; yet the one who is least in the kingdom of God is greater than he" (Luke 7:28).

So high is the new dispensation above the old, that in the bosom of Jesus, and leaning upon His breast, we shall find that God has "planned something better for us" (Hebrews 11:40), and that "(for the law made nothing perfect), and a better hope is introduced, by which we draw near to God" (7:19).

(5) The succession of Joshua and the testimony paid to his wisdom.

"Now Joshua son of Nun was filled with the spirit of wisdom because Moses had laid his hands on him. So the Israelites listened to him and did what the LORD had commanded Moses" (Deuteronomy 34:9).

This perhaps is not the least testimony to Moses himself, for the wisdom of Joshua is connected with the fact that Moses had laid his hands upon his successor and, with a spirit as beautiful and humble as it was effectual, committed to him not only his work, but the same divine efficiency which had been given to him.

The highest spiritual lessons of the book of Deuteronomy will be perceived by us if we remember that it was a temporary message, and represented the transfer, or transition, from the law to that period under Joshua which was to be especially the type of the gospel. We must not, therefore, be surprised at Israel's failure, or even Moses' death, for all this was intended to prepare us for the insufficiency of the law to bring in the fullness of the blessing.

These were great educational dispensations, and the law was but the schoolmaster to bring us unto Christ, that we might be justified by faith.

Hence, before entering the land of promise, we find a complete reorganization and new departure.

There is a new generation of Israel, a new numbering of the people, a new edition, as it were, of the very law itself, at least a renewal of the covenant based upon the law, and a new leader; preparing our minds for the great spiritual truth that before we can enter into our full inheritance in Christ "the old has gone," the world, the flesh, the law, the life of self, "the new has come" (2 Corinthians 5:17).

Then we are prepared for the next great message with which the book of Joshua begins: "Moses my servant is dead. Now then, you and all these people, get ready to cross the Jordan River into the land I am about to give them—to the Israelites" (Joshua 1:2).